route to elsewhere

ROUTE TO ELSEWHERE.

Published by Principia Media, LLC, 2025
www.principiamedia.com

An Ode to the People and Places That Undergirded This Adventure
by Dirk Wierenga © 2025

Cover art by Sean Sterzer
Designed by Frank Gutbrod

Library of Congress Control Number: 2025940540
ISBN 978-1-61485-010-6

First Edition 2025
10 9 8 7 6 5 4 3 2 1

Printed in the United States of America

route to elsewhere

A PERSONAL JOURNEY

DIRK WIERENGA

PRINCIPIA
MEDIA

An Ode to the People and Places That Undergirded This Adventure

They were and still are there for me.
It could not have otherwise happened.
Countless people,
Some here, others elsewhere.

Here is where I was born and still remain.
There is where the others are,
Well over a hundred,
Here and elsewhere.

A path I laid out here,
There where I followed it,
Towns and roads and places,
All of them elsewhere.

Here a place of sand and water,
There a combination of geographies,
Mountains, plains, forests, lakes,
Spread out elsewhere.

A call I heard in my youth,
Now I'm older, it is time.
Experiences were and are many,
Here and elsewhere.

Here are those I am thankful for.
They stood up and helped and know who they are.
Whatever I needed, they provided,
Standing with me while I am here and elsewhere.

A series of projects over a long period of time,
We stood together then,
I know we always will,
For we and they are close by and elsewhere.

Here, where the fires are burning bright,
The warm feelings remain.
There is a permanence.
It is something I carry elsewhere,

A feeling of thankfulness
Here and there and elsewhere.

1

"We were and are a peaceful people. We even welcomed the wasiclll ['white man']. Only when we saw them building roads, forts, killing off the game, committing buffalo genocide, when we saw them ripping off our land for gold, only then did we realize that what they wanted was our land. They took away our pride, our customs, our MEDICINE. Then we began to fight. For our earth, for our children. That started what the whites call the Great Indian Wars of the West. I call it the Great Indian Holocaust."

—Leonard Crow Dog (Medicine Man)

It was the fall of 1998, and I was in over my head. A major church denomination, the Presbyterians, had given me an assignment to write a book about faith in America as experienced in the Presbyterian Church (USA)—an assignment I had initially approached them about.

Sitting in a motel room in Wolf Point, Montana, I contemplated meeting a minister later that morning thirty miles away in Brockton. Like a metronome, Reverend Enright Bighorn, Sr., always picked up his mail each day at the post office there. It would be our second meeting. The previous day, we'd met at the Fort Peck Assiniboine and Sioux Tribes' Reservation tribal offices in nearby Poplar. There, he'd introduced me to several tribal leaders. Like an appendage, I'd shadowed him as he went about his daily tasks. Observation—as a photographer, a writer, and a documentary filmmaker—was part of my method of learning about people.

This day felt different. Enright was taking me to Fort Kipp to the Lloyd Red-Eagle Memorial Presbyterian Church, one of the churches he served and where he'd been baptized. From our conversations the previous day, I knew that church was special to him. Yet, I also knew we would discuss some pressing issues facing the people who lived on the reservation: alcohol and drug abuse, youth suicides brought on by hopelessness, and Dakota Sioux history, which had helped shape his own beliefs. Subjects difficult yet important to discuss.

That day, during a stop for lunch, I learned how Enright himself dealt with daily struggles faced by his people. We drove up to his favorite restaurant, which sold food and alcohol. When we exited his car, he directed me to enter through the door under a sign that read "Food," which was beside a second door with a sign reading "Bar." Both doors actually opened to the same room.

Enright said, "If people are to respect me as a minister, I cannot be seen entering a bar, so the optics of walking through a door that says 'Bar' give the wrong message. Because if I ever drink or use drugs, I will have to leave the ministry. I need to lead by example." He went on to talk about joblessness and hopelessness being the primary causes of substance abuse on the reservation. "If a person doesn't have a job, they lose hope, and people without hope are more likely to seek it with a needle or in a bottle."

Those words stuck with me. Here, an area where six thousand people lived in a place almost as large as the state of Connecticut, life was difficult. Weather could be wicked; the dry prairie land, unforgiving; and, with fewer than four people per square mile, it could be lonely. Getting to a large, full-service hospital required driving more than three hundred miles. Full-time jobs with benefits were hard to find. Yet, Enright remained optimistic. It showed in the way he greeted people. Ever hopeful and encouraging, he had a soft, gentle voice with an infectious laugh. He was always looking for the best in people.

At one point, Enright told me about the day he'd officiated at a funeral for five people who had died in a car crash. One of the attendees said that after the minster left, they'd hold their own service. "He didn't want a religious service because he didn't want to hear praying." Months later, that same man lay dying in a hospital and asked Enright to pray for him, saying, "I don't want to die." As Enright surmised, "He wanted to make things right with God." And when the man died, Enright was asked to officiate at his funeral. It was an example of the complicated relationship between the church and native people.

"The church did many things that hurt our people, like banning the use of our Dakota language. Back then, they were punished if they spoke in the native tongue. As a result, parents discouraged the use of the language because they didn't want their children to get in trouble." Enright added, "This warning was passed down from generation to generation."

Enright told me that treaties had been made, but, once signed, the government broke them. "Our people were starving. We needed to take a stand to insist the treaties were obeyed." It led to the Minnesota Uprising of 1862, after four young Dakota warriors returned from yet another unsuccessful hunt and stole some eggs from a white settlement. Then things escalated to a full battle between the white settlers and the Dakota warriors, in which several hundred people on both sides were killed.

After the uprising, many of the warriors fled—some to Canada, some to the Dakotas, others to Montana. Eventually, two thousand Dakota people were rounded up, tried in court, and found guilty, after which three hundred warriors were sentenced to death. President Abraham Lincoln pardoned many of those held hostage, except for thirty-eight whose sentences were carried out. All were hung in Mankoto, Minnesota, making it the largest public execution in U.S. history.

"The men who were hung were not a part of the Minnesota Uprising," Enright said. "They were in the wrong place at the wrong time." As the sentence was carried out, several of the men sang the Dakota death song, which was now Hymn 141 in the Dakota hymn book. "When I heard that story," Enright said, "I was thinking of those men. When the men sang that hymn, they stood side by side in a circle, holding one another's hands. And as they were hung, many continued to hold hands."

After our days together, Enright and I tried staying in touch. Yet, over the years with moving and life's complications, we lost track of each other. Finally, we reconnected several years later, through an acquaintance of his son, Enright Bighorn, Jr., who now lived on the Fort Peck Reservation.

At the time, we discussed getting together once again, but . . . life happened. During the intervening years, I had closed my successful communications and graphic design firm, gotten into publishing, released a couple of documentaries, and established myself as a commercial photographer, developing my skills in landscape photography.

Yet again, more time passed, and on June 18, 2022, I was sitting in my car at a small cemetery in Fort Kipp, Montana, looking at Enright's grave—my tire flattened by a hole in its sidewall caused by a shard of glass. Enright had died months earlier, and I had returned to the reservation from my home in Michigan to attend his memorial service. It would be held the next morning: Father's Day. Fitting for a man who had worked tirelessly his entire life to care for his family, along with those in his tribe. He and I had last spoken the previous year. This man, who had sacrificed so much during his entire life, needed to borrow his son's phone in order to take my call.

With a sad heart, an unfortunate hole in my tire, and no working spare onboard, I awaited a tow to Williston, North Dakota, sixty miles away. I would be forced to miss Enright's memorial service the next morning.

I stared down the hill past the cemetery toward the Montana badlands in the distance. A mist rose from the nearby Missouri River, in that peaceful place where Enright and I had once stood. It was getting late. The tow truck operator had just called to say he was still a good hour away.

As with so many of my trips during the last forty years, I had packed my schedule way too tight. A plan to photograph the dancers at the Red Bottom Celebration that night in Frazer an hour to the west was impossible. Attending Enright's memorial in Fort Kipp, now out of the question. My car would be disabled until the following day.

It was dark when my tow finally arrived. While I waited, as if by providence, Enright's family arrived. They had been at the nearby community center preparing for the next day's memorial and had decided to stop by his gravesite. That chance meeting allowed me to express my sympathy and explain why I couldn't attend Enright's service.

My friendship with Enright Bighorn, Sr., was one of the most impactful of my life and had become the basis of the travel I'd done ever since our first time together in 1998.

2

An idyllic life, it's not always as it seems . . .

I was born, was raised, and have lived much of my life in Grand Haven, Michigan—a beachfront town on Lake Michigan, protected by sand dunes. When I was growing up, my dad owned a TV and appliance store. He had followed in his father's footsteps. My grandfather had founded the store after being kicked out of the ministry and discovering he had a gift for selling wringer washers—the high-tech appliance of that day. There were photos of me arranging lightbulbs on a display while still in kindergarten. That's how much our store meant to our family.

If you held your hand up as if it were a mitten, as many Michiganders did, our town was located opposite the thumb. We were a bedroom community of Grand Rapids, forty miles inland with a population of two hundred thousand. Grand Haven was in West (or Western) Michigan, a dynamic, growing region of more than a million people with a population density that was more suburban than rural.

When my brothers and I were growing up, we didn't know any of this. All we knew was that in the summer we went to the beach, and in the winter we shoveled snow. To us boys, our town meant our neighborhood on Woodlawn, a desirable hilly street with nice homes, winding past Duncan Woods. This old-growth forest in the middle of town was where we played. In the warmer seasons we made tree forts, and in colder weather we rode our Champion Flyer sleds down snow-covered hills.

Yet, early on, I had wanderlust in me. It started whenever my parents returned from a vacation and gave me roadmaps of the places they'd visited. I'm fairly certain those trips helped them keep their sanity by leaving four rather rambunctious, independent boys at home.

I would spread the maps out on the floor and study them. I got so excited looking at all of the details—the towns, the roads, the lakes—and dreaming of going to those places. That led to my life-long infatuation with geography, globes, roadmaps, and atlases. Though the locations were only dots on the maps, they represented the freedom I dreamed about and the knowledge I could receive from the people who lived there.

Our parents were not at all wealthy. My dad's store struggled for as long as I could remember. Still, my parents wanted their four boys to experience life outside our small, tree-lined beach town.

Each summer during my childhood, we took a family vacation. To save money, we traveled east to Metuchen, New Jersey, where my mother's parents lived. My dad, a history buff, insisted we see historic Civil War battlefields, tour the Capital building in Washington, D.C., and visit Flushing, Queens, to see the New York World's Fair. My mother, though, was an advocate for social justice. She made sure we visited the gravesite of President John F. Kennedy the summer after he was assassinated. I still remember the white picket fence surrounding his temporary grave at Arlington National Cemetery. She also insisted we witness the silent vigil on the Capital steps just before the passage of the Civil Rights Act of 1964.

In order to test my independence, when I was fourteen my parents took me to Chicago's Union Station where I boarded the *Santa Fe El Capitan* passenger train with members of my Boy Scout troop. We endured a two-week backcountry adventure at the 140,000-plus-acre Philmont Scout Camp near Cimarron, New Mexico. There, we learned the basics of survival as we hiked from campground to campground while carrying our food, sleeping bags, and other provisions. While on the train to and from New Mexico, I spent hours gazing out the window as we rode through vast landscapes. I watched in awe as the land changed from region to region, just as the roadmaps and the geography books had shown me years ago.

As a young adult, for several years I made an annual winter drive west to ski in the mountains of Colorado and Utah. Each time I made the trip, I found new adventures. One time, during a winter storm, I drove my Honda Civic off Happy Jack Road west of Cheyenne, Wyoming, into the Vedauwoo climbing area. I ended up stuck in a couple feet of snow several miles from the nearest plowed road. Luckily, a group of guys in off-road four-wheelers happened upon me and towed me out. These fortuitous rescues have repeated themselves to this day as I attempted to go where small, two-wheel-drive vehicles should never travel.

It was back then that I began to take special notice of people who lived where few others did—the 10 percent of the U.S. population who lived on roughly 95 percent of the land.

I wondered how people "out there" could make a good living, get adequate healthcare, and receive a decent education. I studied the latest annual reports from the USDA about the challenges of living in rural areas.

That didn't mean all rural areas were isolated. They weren't. Rural places came in many types and sizes. Some were within a fairly easy drive of a midsize city. However, many were hours away from a town that offered the services people required, especially emergency healthcare services and well-rounded schools. Yet, there were still counties that had no dentists, no eye doctors, no surgeons—and forget about specialized services. They simply didn't exist for anyone who lived where few people did.

Some rural towns were tiny, with fewer than a hundred people. I wondered how a town so small could even function. Where did the kids go to school? Were there enough well-paying, full-time jobs with benefits in those places? And as for restaurants, stores, or even gas stations, some small towns didn't have any of those conveniences within a close drive. For folks living in towns with dwindling populations, it begged the question: Would they last into the next generation or become yet more ghost towns?

Deepening my love of rural places, for more than ten years I had a place in a small rural town in Michigan's Upper Peninsula along the shores of Lake Superior. There, I learned the dynamics of rural living in a close-knit community filled with caring people.

I also acquired a dislike of urban centers. Not to visiting them, but to living anywhere nearby. I guess that made me a small town kinda guy, one who preferred four seasons to warm environments. I'd been to Phoenix in the summer; I would have none of that.

With much of my work in the last few decades taking place along the many less-traveled roads crisscrossing our country, I was fortunate to experience rural America's more intimate side. In short, I'd met a lot of people, many through interviews or in passing conversations while on the road. In the process, I learned much. Lumping rural people together as if they were a single entity was a huge mistake. They possessed so much diversity of thought, perspective, and life experience. The phrase *the rural-urban divide* described the urbanization in much of the country, which encouraged migration from rural to urban areas as America grew after World War II. Yet, certain beliefs of rural people blamed the cause of the divide on how they were treated when they went to the big cities.

I wanted to learn more about those who lived where few others did before I was too old to travel. Over time, I painstakingly laid out a rural route from Maine to Washington State and back to Maine by a different way. My journey would follow America's northern border from coast to coast in search of our country's last unspoiled frontiers. In this vast area, sparsely inhabited by people who had been largely ignored, I hoped to learn from those I'd meet.

The word *Elsewhere* in the title is a reminder of the Aesop's fable "The Town Mouse and the Country Mouse." This story from my youth describes two mice: one lives in the city, the other in the country. The two mice, who are cousins, each visit the other in his own environment. Both want to convince the other that they live in a better place. In today's world, people who live in less populated areas don't like going to the city; they talk about all the hustle and bustle and want none of it. Similarly, people who live in big cities don't need to go to the country anymore. Interstate highways allow them to travel without ever having to go through small towns, while those who fly see the country only as a patchwork quilt of tiny squares below as they fly over at forty thousand feet.

So, with that, I left my hometown to discover the "elsewhere" that existed along the route I'd so carefully laid out in my home studio over a period of months. There, I hoped to meet people who could help this traveler learn more about life.

3

Getting to where the journey began was always an adventure. For me, it meant sprinting to my initial destination in Fort Kent, Maine, in two days on major highways. I used interstates in Michigan and crossed into Canada over the Blue Water Bridge, which took me from Port Huron, Michigan, to Sarnia, Ontario. So far, so good. Traffic wasn't too busy and was light in spots. I saw cool, calm drivers enjoying the open road.

Once in Ontario, I took ON-402 for nearly an hour until it merged onto Canadian 401 (Kings Highway). There, the busy traffic from Detroit widened the highway from two double lanes to triple lanes in both directions. And as the traffic grew, so did the number of mean, fast, busy drivers.

That got me thinking about how my method of driving differed from others'. I thought every person taking a journey would experience it differently. I was a spontaneous wanderer and tried not to do much preparation. I didn't carry too little or too much because there was no reason to over-complicate travel. For me, that meant a duffle bag of clothes and a backpack filled with cameras, a laptop, and other essentials. Also, a favorite pillow and a sleeping bag in case I got stranded when I was unable to find a room.

For transportation, I needed something economical. On this trip, I drove what I called a "mixed-breed car": part EV and part gasoline fueled, known in the auto world as a PHEV. In my case, it was a 2018 car I'd purchased used in 2021. She—in my mind, cars were she's and trucks were he's—was my lifeline of sorts. Whenever I couldn't find a room or had somehow managed to get stuck, the battery in my plug-in hybrid would keep me warm in the winter and cool in the summer, while also providing electricity.

My first stop, the ON-Route Travel Plaza near Toronto.

Like most rest stops along superhighways, it felt homogenized, sanitized, hypnotizing. Whether in the United States, Canada, or any other developed country, roads like this were much the same. Miles and miles of highway with exits and plazas and similar businesses. It was enough to make one scream.

This plaza had two coffee shops, a fried chicken restaurant, burger and pizza joints, and even a booth selling sushi. It was pre-fab, pre-built, pre-programmed so you could park your car, walk in, use the restroom, get some food, and head back to the car. Trucks in the back, cars in the front. Gas station conveniently next to the on-ramp.

The lobby had a food court with flies circling over tables, sofas, and a big-screen TV showing the weather. Sedate music, not too fast or too slow with a touch of Eminem—if such a style of music is possible. A large wall-mounted map with an indicator showing "You are here." Soda and ice cream machines along the wall. A gift shop with T-shirts, mugs, and cheaply made, overpriced sunglasses.

Travelers were eating fast-food burgers and chatting on their cell phones.

Discarded straw wrappers, paper napkins, and scrunched-up Styrofoam cups littered the floor.

It got me to remembering when I'd traveled with my parents. We'd drive to the East Coast on toll roads for two days through boring terrain. We couldn't wait to go through the tunnels along the Pennsylvania Turnpike because we knew the end of the trip was near. The rest stops back then had chain restaurants of a different era, mainly Howard Johnson's. As a family, we would order a sit-down meal from waitstaff who wore matching, baby blue–checked uniforms and creased aprons, blending in with the Naugahyde chairs and glass-covered table tops. In that era, people were in less of a hurry and enjoyed the adventure of travel.

I found a room that night in Ganonoque, Ontario, halfway between home and Fort Kent. I checked in just as a tour bus pulled up, and the entire place devolved into mayhem.

Ganonoque—or Gan, as locals called it—had a population just over five thousand and sat along the Saint Lawrence River. The gateway to the Thousand Island region, it was home to the Leaping Muskie Fish Statue, which paid homage to the world's record muskie (sixty-nine pounds) caught there by H. A. "Dooley" McCarney.

The next morning, I started on the final leg of my drive to Fort Kent, Maine—five hundred miles away. With a fresh attitude and plenty of coffee, I knew it was time to gut it out.

At some point that day, I began to think deeply about my own life up until then. Here I was on the road again at an age when most people had already retired. I wondered, *How many more trips are left in me?* I knew I was at a point in my life when I had more time already lived and had less time to go. Mindless travel along super highways could divert one's attention from the business of driving.

I asked, *What is the purpose of my current journey?*

Then it hit me. I was living out in real time the message of Dr Seuss's book *Oh, the Places You'll Go.*

But how could I justify that message when I'd already lived much of my life?

I realized that if I was still able to learn, then learn I should. After all, I'd carefully laid out my journey by highlighting it on a map back in my studio. There would be folks I'd meet, stories to hear, people who could teach and inform me. There would also be time to reflect on my own life up until then.

Just then, I crossed the border from Ontario into Quebec Province. The traffic was even busier on Autoroute 20, which would take me through the spaghetti of congested highways of Montreal and across the St. Lawrence River and let me avoid Quebec City.

The day wore on, and I still had a ways to go. Then, finally, I reached the TransCanada Highway section of Autoroute 20 and exited at Rivière-du-Loup, a small city. There, I picked up Autoroute 85, which took me to Dégelis, Quebec, where I encountered my first stop sign in five hundred miles.

Once I arrived near the beginning of my journey, I would find a place to sit a while and write.

After heading south on Route du Lac-Baker, I continued on Route-120 for fifteen miles. Then I saw an opportunity. I drove into the parking lot of Goodies Cafe, across the St. Johns River from Fort Kent, Maine, where my journey would begin and where I would finally be able to breathe.

It had been a two-day trip of more than a thousand hard-fought miles, and now, finally, I could take the time to reflect deeply on my life.

I asked, *What would make me a better person?* I knew the answers would be out there where few people lived and I had more time to think. Like so many, I had brought along some baggage, partly physical and the rest in memories.

4

While sitting in the parking lot of Goodies Cafe, a small bakery and coffeehouse, I pulled out my notepad. I decided to start with a memory from forty years earlier. In poor penmanship that even I could hardly read, I wrote out the story of the younger me—a time when my life went off the rails. Though I have referred to it as running away from home, it was actually when I ran away from my life.

In my twenties, I was in a hurry to get on with my life. My goal was to be married and have a successful business. Yet, those two accomplishments were not for me. I'd spent three years in a marriage that was not working out, while employed at my father's store, which had lost so much money it was about to go out of business. I felt it was time to move on. With a final paycheck and a divorce decree in hand, I left my hometown for the East Coast where I hoped to find a good-paying job.

As I was about to back out of my parents' driveway, I heard a tap on the driver's side window. It was my dad. He wanted a hug. I said I needed to go. He said he knew that and had one thing to say: "I'm proud of you, son."

It broke me up. I still remembered that more than forty years later.

So, off I went, a small town guy, to the large East Coast cities to seek my fortune. After driving all night on various interstates and turnpikes, I was on the Schuykill Expressway cutting through the heart of Philadelphia. Then I spotted a billboard that I hoped would be my goose that laid the golden eggs. It said, "Salespeople needed, apply inside," with an arrow pointing at large building. At that moment, I was about to run out of money and needed a job, pronto. So, I spoke to the person at the front desk and said something to the effect of "I'm your person."

"For what?" she asked.

"The job on the billboard."

"Oh, that," she said with a slight laugh and a "we gotta sucker here" expression.

"That's not about an actual job," she said, "it's what we call the lure of a job that doesn't yet exist." Perhaps that wasn't exactly what she said, but it was nonetheless what she meant. After we exchanged looks for a few seconds that felt like an hour, she handed me an application, saying, "You might as well fill this out. Just in case."

So I did fill out the application, and within minutes I was on my way to the address in New Jersey that I'd written on the application. The place where someone could get hold of me. All the while, I thought, *This was a waste of time.*

A while later I got to the home of a relative in a small New Jersey town, across the Delaware River from Philly. A couple hours later, the unlikely happened: the V.P. of some department or another called from the headquarters of Wall-to-Wall Sound, where I'd applied for a job. He said words to the effect of, "Do you still want that job?"

With that golden egg from the fable still on my mind, I replied with a resounding, "Yes!"

Then he said, "I do need to tell you something that might change your mind." And just as quickly as the golden egg had appeared, it turned into a cracked egg. The V.P. told me that a person with a gun had just shot up their Wilmington, Delaware, store, leaving one employee dead and two others wounded.

With a calm, measured voice, I asked two questions. Did they capture the killer, and had anything like that ever happened before in that location? He said they had the killer in custody, and the store had never had been robbed in the past. With that, I said, "I'll take the job."

After a restless night, I got up early to make the hour or so drive to work. When I arrived, I had to climb over police tape to get in the door. And once inside, I watched as workers patched bullet holes in the walls and cleaned blood stains off the carpet.

It was the beginning of the Christmas shopping season, and everything was "Hurry up!" Within a couple hours, the doors opened, and customers flocked in. The store sold high-end audio and video equipment back when it was all the rage. For the next few weeks, it was balls-to-the-wall busy. I barely had a chance to speak with my fellow store employees. People would walk in and ask whether we had this or that, and if we did, they'd say, "Wrap it up." It was a very small store located within a few feet of the Pennsylvania state line. Its popularity was due to Delaware having no sales tax and Pennsylvania having a high sales tax. Customers figured, "Why pay tax when it wasn't charged in the state just up the road?"

As quickly as products arrived at the store in unopened boxes through the loading dock, they went out the front door in customers' hands. Within a week or so, I was the most successful salesperson in the twenty-store chain. I was elated and thought, *The golden goose had landed.*

Once the Christmas season was over, the store was still busy but not quite as much as before the holidays. At that point, I started to notice something. Well-dressed young women in heels were regularly stopping by and being whisked into the backroom office, which was always locked. Within minutes, they'd leave carrying small paper bags. I thought, *Something is happening in the backroom office.*

Then one day a few months later, while walking past the office, I noticed the door was left ajar. I peered inside and saw a triple-beam scale with a pile of white powder that looked suspicious.

I do believe someone saw me look through the door because it wasn't long before I was invited to a private party in an upscale mansion in a upper-class neighborhood on the other side of the city. I was assured it would be worth my time to attend, so I decided to go. When I arrived, people were milling around and drinking cocktails in expensive stemmed glassware as if waiting for something to happen. A while later, an unshaven, poorly dressed guy arrived with a super large bag. Without saying a word, he grabbed a giant piece of framed art from the wall and placed it on the dining room table. He poured out a pile of white powder and immediately arranged the powder in long, skinny lines across the painting. He then handed out tightly rolled hundred dollar bills to the guests. Soon, people were snuffing up the powder into their noses and acting happy and wired.

At that time, a fellow store employee took me aside and asked whether I wanted a part-time job that paid royally. I did not say yes or no, only that I would think about it. He said, "Let me know tomorrow morning, first thing sharp."

My apartment was across the Delaware Memorial Bridge near Cowtown Rodeo, just off Route 40. The minute I got back to my place, I put a plan into action. My suspicion that I was working at a mob-owned operation had been confirmed, and I needed to disappear. So, I loaded up my car and left behind a partly furnished apartment and what remained of a year-long lease. And just as I had done when I'd first arrived, I drove through the night back to my hometown. Although I needed to take a couple of temporary jobs, I landed on my feet a year or so later when I formed a business partnership that provided graphic design and marketing communications services to corporate clients. This business was successful for more than fifteen years.

Thinking back to Dr. Seuss, I wondered, *Have I embraced the journey, not just the destination?*

I walked into Goodies café, where everyone was talking in French, a language that I did not speak or understand. I pointed at the photo of what appeared to be a large mocha and said the word *hot*, which they seemed to understand. And soon I was back in my car.

With my notes written and stuffed in the glovebox, it was time to cross the Clair–Fort Kent Bridge over the St. Johns River to Maine. As a solo voyager, I would begin my journey back and forth across the continent with the roadmap and the route highlighted in yellow.

5

When I landed back in America, I thought about the last time I'd visited Maine. It had probably been thirty years ago. But those trips, back then, were to places along the southern Maine coast, nearer to Portland than Aroostook County. A place Mainers called The County. This area of the state was known for its pine forests, moose, and scarcity of people. It crowned the northern portion of the state, which was where the nickname Pine Tree State had originated.

But, as I learned, Aroostook didn't come easily. Just as fences made good neighbors, so too could fenceless borders, but only if they were measured accurately. It was somewhat similar to the way those of us who lived in Michigan thought about our own borders. And the Mainers' reference to Aroostook as The County reminded me of how we referred to the northern peninsula of our state as the UP.

As Michiganders, we were taught a history lesson early on about the Michigan–Ohio War (officially known as the Toledo War), which determined the boundaries of the Great Lakes State. In that case, the war was over a small strip of land along the mouth of the Maumee River on the southern border of Michigan. Whichever state won would control the shipment of farm crops from the fertile land that Michigan claimed as its southern border when it applied for statehood in 1835. After both states called up their militias, resulting in one person being wounded, the conflict was solved by a compromise signed in 1836. During a signing ceremony called the Frostbitten Convention, Michigan gave up the disputed southern border in exchange for the remaining three-quarters of what became the Upper Peninsula of Michigan.

In the case of Maine, its border war was about determining the United States' northern border, which required several agreements with the British during sixty-three years before both sides finally settled on the location of the border. Though the Treaty of Paris, signed on September 3, 1783, had ended the Revolutionary War, it had relied on outdated maps that were improperly drawn, ambiguous, and not well defined.

At that time, the Commonwealth of Massachusetts owned much of Maine. That ownership dated back to the 1650s when timber from Maine's interior forests was used to construct homes for Bostonians, and profits from the shipping ports of coastal Maine lined the pockets of wealthy Massachusetts merchants. To complicate matters further, in 1819 the people of Maine formally petitioned Massachusetts for statehood. Yet, once that proposal went before the federal government, the issue of slavery reared its ugly head. Discussions about the balance of power were split between the Southern slave states and the Northern free or anti-slavery states.

For Congress to admit Maine to the union, the pro-slave state Missouri also had to be admitted. The Compromise of 1820, also known as the Missouri Compromise, allowed both states to simultaneously be admitted to the union. Though Maine was feverishly against slavery, the only way to free itself from Massachusetts was to support the bill, which its legislature did after much discussion.

On March 6th, 1820, the bill was signed by President James Monroe, making Maine an independent state.

Even with Maine's statehood, the location of its northern border was still in dispute. It took more than twenty years for that issue to be settled by what was called the Aroostook War (or the Bloodless War).

6

I began my journey in Allagash in Aroostook County, where the Allagash River met the St. John River. As a photographer, I often saw things differently than others did. So it was when I pulled over onto the shoulder, got out, and grabbed my camera. I pushed in on the zoom and captured the squiggly road ahead. And just then this guy pulled up and rolled down his window.

"Having problems?"

"No," I said, "just capturing."

"What?"

"The road ahead."

"Here?"

"No, up ahead."

"Where?"

I pointed. "There."

"Why there?"

"I'm a photographer; you?"

"I'm a logger."

"Care to talk about what you do?"

"Who's asking?"

"Me."

"Who are you?"

"A photographer and a writer."

"What you writing about?"

"Places and the people who occupy them. People willing to take a little time to talk. Got the time?"

"Sure, I got a few minutes."

"What's your name, and what's your business?"

"Jim Kelly, and you can see by the stuff I'm carrying that I'm a logger."

He gestured toward the bed of his pickup, full of small pieces of equipment, and said, "For much of my work, I use my own cable skidder to pull the logs out of the woods. The company I work for hauls it around for me. They tell me how much they're going to pay me to cut certain trees. Everything is all set before I get there. What I like about it is the independence. They put me on a log, they drop me off, and I cut the wood, bring it out. Nobody's around, nobody to bother me."

I asked, "What kind of logger?"

"An old school, independent logger. Meaning, I don't work for one of those big logging companies. The company I work with owns all their own land. They market the logs so I don't have to bother with that. I selectively cut without clear cutting. That's what the large operations with heavy equipment do."

"So, if you don't do your logging around here, where do you cut your logs?"

"A hundred and fifty miles away. Towards Bangor. I stay there all week and come home on the weekend."

Jim said there were probably only a half-dozen loggers like him left. "There's no young people doing this kind of logging anymore. Once those of us doing it are retired, there won't be anyone left. It's a shame because it's our heritage. But that's the way the world is going."

I asked about young people locally, what did younger workers do?

"My son left here and went to Vermont and got a computer engineering degree. Now he works with bank equipment. He likes to turn a wrench. So, he fixes ATMs and money recyclers, the whole gamut of bank equipment. But it's too bad he couldn't stay here. There's just nothing for young people here."

I asked Jim what kept him here.

"It's a beautiful place to live, and I wouldn't want to live anywhere else. My wife actually moved here from Connecticut to go to college in Fort Kent. She loves it here, and so do a lot of people. She's lucky she found a good job at the university. But if she hadn't, she couldn't have stayed."

Jim Kelly, old school logger near Allagash, Maine

That got me to wondering what made Jim tick. Obviously, it wasn't money. Otherwise, he'd be working for one of the large logging operations. Jim was a lifer, having been born and raised here and still living near Allagash in his mid-sixties. He didn't see that changing. I'd heard this for years from people who lived in rural places. For them, love of the outdoors was more important than the everyday conveniences that people in urban and suburban areas demanded.

"How long have you been doing this?"

"All my life since graduating high school at seventeen, so it's been forty-six years."

Jim had to go but said, "You need to talk to Darlene over at Two Rivers Lunch. It's just a few miles farther. She knows everything that goes on here. You'll drive over the Allagash River, near where it meets the St. John's River. . . . Her place is on the right, Two Rivers Lunch. The two of you will get along. Everyone likes Darlene."

We talked a little about how Jim felt when he drove past the confluence of the St Johns and Allagash rivers on a small, nearly unnoticeable bridge along the road leading into Allagash. He appreciated the beauty of where the two rivers met and stated, "I just like it there."

And with that, he jumped into his pickup and drove away.

Next, per Jim's advice, I drove to Two Rivers Lunch. Around a half-dozen snowmobiles, known as sleds to those of us who lived in the north, were parked in front. The front porch had stacks of logs for burning and bundles for sale. Colorful painted flowers were mounted on the wooded siding next to the entrance. A nice touch. Something an artist would do. The restaurant was located a quarter mile or so up the road from the Allagash Pentecost Church and just past a small stand of birch trees. I had arrived between breakfast and lunch. Walking in, I asked the man on the grill if I could speak with Darlene.

Over the sound of bacon frying, he said, "She's off today. If you can, stop back tomorrow, anytime in the morning. She'll be here. Earlier the better. It gets busy here."

With a rasher of bacon in hand, I headed back to my car and drove farther west. I stopped by the historical society building; it was closed. There were no fresh footprints in the newly fallen snow. The road from there looked impossible for me to navigate, so I returned to Fort Kent.

It being between seasons, not many guests were staying at the Northern Door Inn. So, I decided to stay another night.

While driving through the downtown business district of Fort Kent, I noticed that the bookstore Bogan Books was open. The small, rather plain-looking brick building had a sign portraying an outline of a crane leafing through an open book. Stopping in, I met a young woman with long brown hair and an engaging smile named Jamie Pelletier who worked there. After properly introducing myself and telling her what I was up to, I asked whether she was from "around here."

"I grew up here and lived in St. Francis with my dad," she said.

"Ever live anywhere else?"

"Yes, in 2016 my fiancé and I moved downstate to Newport. But in 2019, when my dad got sick, we moved back up here."

"Did he get better?"

"Unfortunately, no. He passed away in 2021."

"Yet, you decided to stay."

"Yes, we stayed because of my kids liked going to school here."

Jamie and I talked a bit about the years she'd lived downstate near Bangor, a few hours away. "Compared to here," she said, "Bangor has a good number of stores. Here the closest mall is about an hour and a half away. When we lived in Bangor, their mall was ten minutes away."

I asked her about winter in the Maine North Woods.

"We don't get as much snow as we used to. When I was younger, there were snowmobiles galore, with snowbanks up to the wires on the telephone poles. . . . My dad's family is from Allagash; my grandfather and a lot of my relatives live in the Allagash and St. Francis area."

"How about your kids?"

"My middle child hated school, but when we came up here, he actually loved it. Our youngest will be eleven this year. And our oldest child is more into working. He'd work seven days a week if you'd let him. He's twenty this year. Going to graduate from college this year, the two-year community college in Presque Isle for diesel hydraulics. He wants to be a diesel mechanic."

Jamie talked about how the shortage of diesel mechanics affected logging operations and the importance of keeping equipment used in the North Woods properly maintained. "That's where a lot of the jobs come from up here, running equipment and stuff. But with equipment comes problems, so that's why my son wanted to go into fixing diesel engines. It's hard to find people who want to turn wrenches."

"Will you stay here?" I asked.

And after a pause and a sigh, she said, "Well . . . we're pretty much set on staying here. 'Cause I find a lot of people who move away, they still end up coming back as they get older."

"How about people who are not from here?" I asked.

"A lot of out-of-staters buy camps in the Allagashes, and then they come up in the winter. Snowmobiling up here is huge. My fiancé builds race sleds, so he's into snowmobiling, and the kids are, too. That's what they do all winter. My guys are very much into the outdoors."

Back at the Northern Door Inn, there sat Debra behind the front desk. "You're from Michigan, right?"

"Yes."

"Been to Maine before?" Before I could answer, she said, "Betcha you've never been to Aroostook County."

Not waiting for me to answer, she jumped right in and began to rattle off facts. "We are the second-largest county east of the Mississippi. We grow a lot of potatoes here, also broccoli and buckwheat, which we use in ployes, our local delicacy. When you come through here in the summer, it looks like colored blankets with the white potato flowers, yellow canola, and red buckwheat. This valley here, the Saint John, has an Acadian heritage. Many of the residents are bilingual Francophones and are proud of their French Acadian heritage. That name dates back to the mid-1500s, when French explorer Giovanni da Verrazano described the northeast coast of North America as *Arcadia*, an ancient Greek word meaning 'earthly paradise.' Over time, Nova Scotia became known as 'Acadia' after the 'r' was dropped. In 1604, the first settlers from France arrived in the Maritimes and established a peaceful coexistence with the native Mi'kmaq people. On both sides of the river, there are families that are related. Before 9/11, people traveled across the border without having to say much at all. Now you need an act of Congress to get into Canada. A lot of Canadian women married American men; they wanted dual citizenship. Lots of French up here. French speakers, French names."

"You seem to know a lot about things around here, but you don't sound like you're from here."

"Yeah," she said, "I moved here from Connecticut. This is my retirement job."

"Got a piece of paper? I want to write some of this down."

Continuing, Debra said, "On the east, the north, and the west, our border is inside of Canada, with the St. John River separating Maine from Canada. Betcha didn't know forests cover 87 percent of the state—mostly white pine. That's why Aroostock County has a totally different kind of lifestyle than southern Maine, which is more like Massachusetts than up here in the St. John River Valley."

"Does that mean the area here is more like Canada?" I asked.

"It does," she said, "but don't tell any Mainers that."

Just then, someone from a town near Bar Harbor came in to register for a room.

"You got a fishing pole," she said. "Whatcha fishing for?"

"Muskie."

"No muskie up here."

"I know, I'll be on a lake south of here," he said, as he grabbed the key and headed for his room.

I asked Debra, "What's your last name?"

"Deprey, but it was Depres before it was Americanized."

"Where did you go to school?"

"The Catholic school near where we lived. The nuns, who were very French, punished pupils for speaking French in school. I still speak French, French Acadian, which is different from regular French."

"How so?"

"It's a seventeenth-century dialect of the language. You might have noticed the flags around here, French flags with a gold star in the upper left corner of the blue section. It represents Our Lady of the Assumption, the patron saint of the Acadians."

Later, when I got back to my room, I got to thinking about my own last name, which I'd been told had been Americanized. The native language had it as Wieringa, but once the Dutch moved to America, they changed it to Wierenga by making the second "i" an "e." That wasn't much of a change. It was still hard for most people to say.

The next morning I stopped by a local breakfast joint to get a coffee to go. Just then, logging trucks rumbled by, as if to remind me I needed to head back to Allagash to see whether Darlene Dumond was working at Two Rivers Lunch. It was still early, 6 a.m. or so. A forty-five-minute drive got me there. On entering, I saw Darlene standing at the grill. She wore tortoiseshell glasses and a colorful bandana and was simultaneously flipping over-easy eggs and a grill full of hash browns that were crisping nicely. I asked whether she could spare a little time to talk.

"Give me a couple minutes to put this order up," she said. "Then I should have a little bit of time."

I showed her my copy of *Blue Highways* by William Least Heat-Moon and unfolded a large Rand McNally map of my route highlighted with a yellow marker. I said I intended to write a similar book that followed the path I had highlighted.

After a little talk about this 'n' that, all the while I was noticing the antique cameras up on a shelf next to photos of areas in and around Allagash. I assumed she had captured them. I asked, "Have you lived here all your life?"

"I grew up here," Darlene said. "Went to school in the small building over there." She pointed in its direction. "I went in as a kindergartener and walked out twelve years later with a high school diploma. Then I went on to college, here and there."

"Then you left?" I asked.

"Yes, I was married briefly in the 1980s and have a son and a daughter. My daughter, Sarah, was born with multiple disabilities. She needed more medical care than what was available here. So, we moved to southern Maine to be nearer to the hospital. I stayed there for over twenty years. Had another child, Robert, there."

Thinking about what Darlene had said, I asked, "Did you ever travel?"

"Yes, back then my idea of living was to get out and see things. I crisscrossed the country and Canada. When you're raised in the wilderness, you've got to see what's out there. I purchased an old Airstream and planned on leaving southern Maine with just enough gas to get to another state. I had a business partnership that had gotten a little yucky and wanted to move away from that. I wanted a chance to try my hand at photography. I figured wherever I ran out of gas, I would have to work there. Having grown up in Allagash, I could do anything. Pump gas, flip burgers, jobs like that. I wasn't afraid of finding work. All I needed was to keep going. While I was in that period, I figured I'd meet people, interview them, and take their photo. It would be the people and my journey. But life has a way of interrupting. That was in 2001. I still have the Airstream, and now I Airbnb it."

"So you came back," I said.

"Yes, but after twenty-two years had passed. In 2011, I decided to come home. Took over the family restaurant so my mom and dad could retire."

In turn, I said something about how I could relate, having also come back to my own hometown to help out in our family business.

I looked around. Old family photos were scattered about that showed the restaurant in all stages of construction. I said, "Tell me how your restaurant started. Its history."

Darlene, pointing at specific photos lining the walls, said, "It has been our family restaurant for more than forty-five years." She explained that her dad had built it as a to-go stand with hot dogs and hamburgers. As the business grew, however, her dad had added two tables where people could eat. Yet, because they lacked the savings to really build, it stayed small. Then, in 1991, an event that she described as the "ice jam of the century" happened. "The entire community of Allagash flooded. All the bridges were washed out, and several homes were destroyed. One of the bridges had been for loggers to cross the St. John River. The piers of the logging bridge had been constructed of large timbers. After the ice jam washed out the bridge, the timbers were floating in the river." Darlene said her dad and her two brothers went out, "lassoed them," and brought them down the river. At the time, "a mountain of ice lay on both sides of the river, so they tied the timbers to sturdy trees along the river bank until the ice melted."

"What happened next?" I asked.

"They dragged them up the bank and milled them," Darlene said. "With that lumber, they expanded the restaurant, adding the dining room and a bunkhouse out back."

Then Darlene headed back to the kitchen to fill a few orders. While enjoying scrambled eggs, bacon, hash browns, and toast on the side, chased by hot black coffee, I took notice of items that made the restaurant so personal. There were taxidermied bucks on the walls, one that purposely had an antler rack replaced by another ill-fitting one; a bearskin rug; a collection of framed family photos; an old candy scale; felt hangings of sunflowers in various colors; mounted canoe paddles; ceiling fans with wooden, leaf-shaped blades; Chinese lamps hanging by twine; and many other objects that showed how much the restaurant meant to the family.

When Darlene returned, she told me how special Allagash had become to visitors and its many part-time residents. "People come here to get away. Something pulls them into the quiet of the wilderness. They come here and fall in love with this place. There's a different mindset out here, and they can feel it." She gestured out the window. "The Allagash River is right over there and has been canoed by thousands. Adults may have canoed it as Boy Scouts and now come back with their children. The St. John River, right here, is a whitewater river that many paddle in the spring after the snow has melted."

I asked about the off season and what happened then.

"Two Rivers is the only restaurant here. Our community has only two hundred year-round residents. The restaurant makes a little more during the busy season, and we have to spend our money wisely to carry us over to the next busy season. We have committed to staying open year round because we're the only place people who live here can gather. Locals have been coming here for years for coffee and conversation, and we can't take that away from them."

By now, the restaurant was packed. Mostly locals, with few vacationers this time of year. Some ordered lunch, and others wanted breakfast. Since we'd begun talking, Darlene had been working alone; then one of her coworkers showed up. While Darlene headed for the grill, the coworker began taking orders. People at nearby tables noticed I wasn't from there and immediately included me in their conversations, laughing, greeting, and needling. They made me feel welcome. It was special.

After an hour of watching the line grow as more and more people wanted to get a table, I caught Darlene's attention and thanked her for taking time to speak with me.

From behind the grill, where she had now switched from making eggs to cooking burgers, Darlene said, "You come back."

"I will," I told her.

As I pulled away from the restaurant and headed back toward Fort Kent, I thought about how my own life story had mimicked Darlene's. Each time I'd left my own hometown to head across the country, I'd wondered whether I'd ever

Darlene Dumond, owner, Two Rivers Lunch in Allagash, Maine

return. And, just like Darlene, something had pulled me back. When Darlene talked about coming back home to take ownership of her family's restaurant, that remark cut to my core because I had also returned to my dad's store to save it. In my case, though I'd worked my tail off, it was a business that could not be saved.

I had been in northern Aroostook County for three days and had barely scratched the surface. Much of the North Maine Woods was on privately owned land. Due to the conflict over the border in the 1800s, when Maine was still owned by Massachusetts, the challenge had been to get the lumber out of the North Woods without it flowing to Canada. Unfortunately for Mainers, the rivers ran north and not south. But that didn't stop the loggers, who built locks and dams to reverse the course of the rivers. This allowed the logs to float toward Bangor where many mills were located. Eventually, companies solved the problem by constructing small-gauge railroads to haul the logs out.

In 1966, the Maine Legislature created the Allagash Wilderness Waterway to "preserve, protect and enhance the wilderness character of the unique area" with a 92-mile-long series of lakes, ponds, rivers, and creeks that wound through vast commercial forests. People accessed the wilderness by taking backroads. Even though the northern entrance was only seventy miles away, it took upward of three or four hours to drive there when using a four-wheel-drive vehicle.

With me driving a 2018 Prius Prime that had pretty much no ground clearance and could seemingly get stuck on a piece of wax paper, it would have been an impossible journey.

It was said that Henry David Thoreau visited the Allagash in 1857, accompanied by the guide Joe Polis, a member of the Penobscot tribe. Thoreau affectionately called Polis "wild man," in part because he had asked for a man with "a bone in his back; one that you cannot put your hand through" as his guide. The trip was an inspiration for his book *The Maine Woods,* when, during a period of three years, Thoreau made three trips to the then mostly unexplored North Woods of Maine.

7

From Fort Kent I drove to Caribou, an hour to the south. Earlier, I'd learned the word *Aroostook* came from the Native American Mi'kmaq (Micmac) language, meaning "clear or beautiful water." Though originally the home of the Micmac and Maliseet tribes, its more recent history blended Acadian, Native American, Scandinavian, and Amish traditions.

Caribou was famous for the first successful solo transatlantic crossing by a helium balloon. There, retired USAF Colonel Joe Kittinger lifted off in a balloon named *Rosie O'Grady* on September 14, 1984, and landed eighty-six hours afterward in Montenotte, Italy. During a later visit, Kittinger recalled, "We had a Catholic priest, a Protestant minister, and a Jewish rabbi come here to give a prayer before the launch. I figured you might as well use every advantage you could ever get."

I decided to overnight in Caribou, in part because I saw a motel that had a homey look and certainly was not fancy. What I liked about staying in motels was that you could generally park next to your room. The owner or the manager usually lived on the premises, and I often felt a certain kind of friendliness toward me when I met them. It was evening when I stopped by the office, and there I met Sheena Hinxman, the motel's manager. We got to talking about life and things. Sheena said she was a lifetime Mainer and had moved to Caribou in 2021 with her husband. It was after they'd managed a motel farther south in Maine.

At some point in our conversation, I asked Sheena what she liked about living in Caribou.

"People here are honest and true and genuinely still care about other people. If a car breaks down around here, people stop and lend a hand. In my experience, this just doesn't happen in most towns."

I asked what she did before moving to Caribou.

"In my previous jobs I had direct contact with people. I had a slew of them. Worked in a Dunkin' Donuts several times over multiple years. Worked in a gas station. Sold Kirby vacuums, did cold calling for a company once. That was rough."

I asked Sheena what she'd found difficult about cold calling, adding that I'd done the same thing early on. I had quit shortly after being hired when someone slammed the door in my face and told me never to come back.

Sheena said she could top my story. "The company I worked for ripped pages out of a telephone directory and said to call everyone with a listing." When she called one of the listings, a woman answered. Sheena asked for the man whose name was listed and was told that he had just passed away. "I quit that job right on the spot. It was traumatic for me."

For her next job, Sheena said she provided personal care assistance for shut-ins—something she didn't enjoy. After that, Sheena enrolled in cosmetology school but got pregnant and had to drop out. She then had an opportunity to go to the University of Maine for nursing but decided not to take it, saying, "That was a young and dumb mistake. After that, I ended up working at Subway."

"How did you meet your husband?" I asked.

"We met at work. He was managing a different Subway, and I called his store because we were out of pickles. He dropped them off himself. We started as friends, but the deal sealer was the day he stopped by with a dachshund. Seeing how he treated that puppy made me fall in love with him." She added, "We got married last year after living with each other for seven years."

What Sheena said about her marriage made me remember one of mine. Just after my first marriage had ended, I met someone special while on a vacation. Thinking about it now, I realize it was way too soon. I had not yet recovered from my first marriage. That mistake on my part had ruined my second marriage. I've met people who said they never made a mistake or had regrets. I'm not too proud to admit that I've made a ton of mistakes during my life, a lot of them I still regret.

Rather than let my mind go further down that rabbit hole, I asked Sheena, "How did you begin managing motels?"

"My husband started doing maintenance for a family-owned motel. I was hired to manage the front desk. Then he left that job and started doing maintenance for another member of the same family who owned a couple of apartment buildings. Those buildings were sold to the owner's uncle, who purchased them with the understanding that my husband would continue to maintain them. While working that job, he met a man who owned several motels and eventually hired him. I came along to manage one of the motels."

"So, by managing a property you get a place to live?"

Sheena Hinxman, manager, Russell's Motel, Caribou, Maine

"Yes, but it's a love-hate thing. It's nice until you have to go to work, and all you do is stumble outside, and there's work. It's hard to get away from work because you don't feel as if you're going home. We're always on call. Whenever the phone rings, we've got to answer. But it's not just the phone. It's the doorbell, e-mail that comes in constantly, social media messages, multiple online booking services. It can be daunting at times. No matter where I go, I need to carry my phone because a guest might need me."

"Yet you stay."

"Yes. Make no mistake, I love my job. We both do. Best job we've had. We are treated well by the owners; they've always got our backs. We get along so well, one of the owners was the best man at our wedding. They are great people and good to work for. We also meet a lot of interesting people."

I asked, "Is this the first motel you've managed?"

"No, this is our second motel. The first was in downstate Maine, which was hopping in the summer months. Here it's the opposite. It is busiest here in the winter. When the snow thaws here, it slows down, and we get to grab a pole and go fishing. We like to get in the car and check out streams and lakes, some as far away as a couple hours. Frankly, I don't like to eat fish. I just like to go fishing. I also like kayaking. Once I took a reservation while fighting the current of a river."

After my time with Sheena, I retired to my room and thought about an experience I'd had when we first began our marketing and graphic design firm. Being new, we needed all the work we could muster up. One day I received a call from a young entrepreneur who had come up with a new product. He had designed it to protect elderly people who feared they would be robbed. He wanted me to come up with an ad idea for a national tabloid that specialized in celebrity gossip. At the time, tabloids were the place for small businesses to get their new ideas promoted. The cost for a small, one-column by two-inch ad in black type was around a hundred or so dollars, cheap for getting an advertisement seen by millions of people—a lot of them elderly. With an idea in mind, I asked for a meeting. The young entrepreneur asked me to stop by his office. We arranged a time, and I drove to the address he gave me.

But instead of an office building, it was a one-stall carwash with an apartment office in the backroom. When I walked in, he invited me to sit at his kitchen table, which was littered with scraps of food, dirty dishes, open cereal boxes, and much more. I had to push enough of that stuff to the side to place a sheet of paper on the table. I asked to see his "big idea," and out came a cassette audio tape that he pushed into a tape deck and turned on. It happened that his way to protect the elderly was a tape with the sound of a dog barking.

I looked to the side, and there sat a German shepherd, listening to himself barking. I thought, *Whatever*, and went on with my pitch. I'd written the ad with no idea about what I would be trying to sell. It said, "You are awakened by a burglar. Here's what will save you." In smaller print, it described the scenario of an elderly person being surprised by a criminal. I made the sale. He sold zero tapes. I got paid, and I never heard from him again. If memory serves, that was the first ever client for our brand new and untested marketing and communications agency. After Sheena had told me about all her previous jobs, I thought she would get a kick out of the story.

The next morning, with that memory in my head, I stopped by the motel office, but it was closed. A sign said they'd be back later. I wished I could have shared my story with Sheena. At some point, I will.

8

After leaving the motel, I stopped at the Tim Horton's on US-1 for a mocha and maple-topped donut on my way to Houlton, Maine, while thinking, *I should have opted for an English muffin with egg and cheese and a hot black coffee.*

Along the road to Houlton, I could see potato farms on both sides of the road. The spuds smelled earthy, slightly musty. But by the time I reached Houlton where US-1 and US-2 merged together, all I could smell were fries from the local McDonald's.

Historically, potatoes have been Maine's most valuable crop, worth almost $200 million per year with 90 percent of them grown in Aroostook County. Just standing in the spot where US-1 and US-2 joined up for a mile, I could see that a lot of activity converged in Houlton. From that spot, US-2 began its journey west, I-95 started south, and, at the border, New Brunswick Route 95 ran east.

There were also "used-to's." They used to build furniture components there. They used to have a four-year college. There used to be a Woolworth's five-and-dime downtown, and Houlton itself, in the early 1900s, used to be one of the top ten wealthiest communities in the United States. You could tell by the number of Victorian-age houses that still dotted its landscape.

Houlton was also near the location depicted in a bestselling mid-1960s Country and Western song about truckers who hauled potatoes. That hit record helped put Aroostook County on the map. The performer sang about the danger of hauling potatoes in semis and included the lyrics:

> If they'd buried all them truckers lost in them woods,
> There'd be a tombstone every mile.

To find out more, I sat down with local historian Leigh E. Cummings, Jr., at the County Co-op and Farm Store, where he was manning a booth. Member owned and controlled, the store had several hundred members with vendors selling local food and homemade crafts.

Leigh, the retired postmaster and a formidable source of information, had been known to spin stories as if they were skeins of yarn. Once I got Leigh's attention, I asked, "What are your earliest memories?"

"That's a toughie. One of my earliest memories is coming down off the subway in Boston. Climbing the stairs and seeing how different it was. It was not a trip we made often, which is why it stood out."

"But you grew up here."

"Yes, I grew up on the poor end of the highway. My father was a clerk in a hardware store that was right around the corner from here. But with three children and then another, six years later—a surprise child—on a hardware clerk's salary, we didn't have much."

Leigh said their backyard neighbor was a doctor, and one day Leigh stopped by their house to visit. He said, "I remember quite vividly. He made a bologna sandwich with two pieces of bologna. I thought at the time, *I'll really have it made if I can ever put two slices of bologna into one sandwich.*"

"Did things improve?"

"Yes, my father took a second job working evenings in a laundromat. Back then, people worked second jobs so they could build a camp. It was a big thing in the late fifties through the sixties. Having a camp [a cottage] on one of the nearby lakes."

"Did it have plumbing?"

"Yes, plumbing was common on lake camps. A lot of the woods camps and whatnot have a back house, but the ones built on the lake had either a leach field or a holding tank. In his case, the holding tank was built of logs. I think it's only been pumped twice since 1964 when it was built."

"It's still in the family?"

"My youngest brother has it. Dad paid $450 for three 50-foot lots. People told him he was crazy paying $3 a foot. Now Bostonians will pay a $1,000 a foot. Yeah, Dad paid $450 for the land and a total of $3,800, including the construction of the camp. A friend of his was lead carpenter and did it on the side."

Remembering that Maine was once the property of Massachusetts before its statehood in 1820, I asked Leigh whether Bostonians were trying to buy Maine back, one lot at a time.

"Yeah. And not just Bostonians, people from other places. Even Texans like this place. So, yeah, we weren't poor, but poor is relative. The people you're around . . . if everybody's poor, you don't know anything else. You know, the doctor behind us had one of the very first Ski Doos before snowmobiles were popular."

Changing the topic, I asked, "So, you graduated here from high school and then went on to school?"

"All the way through high school I was sure I was heading to Vietnam. I graduated in '71, but in that last year before I graduated, they instituted the first draft lottery, and I got number 362. I went from 1A to 1H. I was very fortunate that I got a federal work study job at the post office to go to college here in town at Ricker College. I graduated in '75, and the college closed in '78. I had some really good teachers. So, I was very, very fortunate. I was a history major, political science minor."

"How soon after that did you go to work for the post office?"

"I went into the post office six weeks before I graduated from high school. May 1st of '71 under the federal work study program. So, I went in and planned on being a secondary school history teacher. Which, when I graduated from college in '75, paid $6,000 a year. As a part-time flexible postal clerk, I was making $8,000 a year."

"Easy choice."

"Yeah, you don't have to be real good at math to figure that out. So, I stayed on with the post office thirty-eight years. Until 2008."

"How did you become postmaster?"

"That was quite a story. Back in the day, we had what we called the 'Triple P Alliance' that ran Houlton for many years. The Putnams, the Pierces, and the Peabodys. I felt that as someone who was brought up at the poor end of the Highland Avenue bridge, I was at a disadvantage and would have an extremely tough time ever succeeding in Houlton. Well, the Putnams, the Pierces, and the Peabodys proved me wrong. The postmaster at the time—whose mother was a Peabody—stayed on an extra year so that I would be eligible to apply for his job. I needed to have a job in a supervisory position in order to apply. The postmaster had already maxed out his retirement, but he stayed on that extra year so I could apply. I got the position in 1986, and, as a result, my family was economically stable. My kids grew up not worrying about whether or not we could afford a pair of hockey skates. So, yeah, you have different impressions when you grow up without a lot, which can become a limiting factor. In the end analysis, how successful you are depends on you. Ability and effort. You've got to have both."

"How many generations of Cummings families have lived in Houlton?" I asked.

"I can stand at the grave of our firstborn son, who died at birth. From there, I can go back seven generations. By jumping from the Catholic side to the

Leigh E. Cummings, retired postmaster and local historian, Houlton, Maine

Protestant side, I can see seven generations if I'm standing in one spot. The first ones that I know of came here in 1825."

When Leigh mentioned the grave of his firstborn son, it stopped me dead in my tracks. I felt for him and his wife, Sandy. Such good people, now friends. I may have muttered something like, "I'm sorry to hear that." There was a pause in our conversation, but the pause was short. Just as I was about to speak, Leigh motioned over a volunteer, saying, "Hey, Paula, I've got someone you need to meet." And with that, Paula made her way to where Leigh and I were sitting.

Watching Paula as she walked toward us, I could tell she was a person whom people felt comfortable to approach.

Someone in produce asked, "What's the price on the small jar of honey? It isn't marked."

A coworker waylaid her and asked, "Can you work for me Friday? I need to go to Bangor for a doctor's appointment and can't be here to work that day."

Someone else stopped her to make an introduction. "I'd like you to meet my friend from Boston."

Once she was seated and able to give me her full attention, I asked Paula how she'd gotten involved in the co-op.

"I moved back here from North Carolina after I retired. I had broken my arm during the first winter back. Every time I went to physical therapy, I stopped

Paula Woodworth, volunteer, The County Co-op & Farm Store, Houlton, Maine

at the co-op afterward to get coffee and a cookie—as my reward for getting through a PT session. So, that's sorta how I got involved."

Paula said during that first winter, she noticed the co-op was having a special night when visitors could come in and sample prepared foods that were regularly available. That got her attention, so she decided to attend. She found the food to be fabulous. When she inquired about the cost of membership in the co-op, they told her it was $200 for a lifetime membership. Being a member supported the community and the people who made things—from food to the works of local craftspeople and artists. She joined the co-op and since then had been an active member.

Paula said, "The co-op draws a certain group of people who are interested in what we offer. We have a huge influx in the summertime when people come to the lake. People who were originally from here, who still own or inherited a lake house. We call them our summer people, and we love it when they are here. They tend to spend more money than people who live here. They buy a lot of food. Summer people are a great asset because they dine at local restaurants and shop in local stores. They help keep our local businesses open."

I asked whether the co-op attracted regulars.

"Yes, we have a very faithful following." Pointing at a group of two-top tables along the side wall, she said, "Every morning at ten, people will be at that table over there, drinking coffee and discussing the goings-on in town. It's just a good way to connect. Especially in the wintertime when you feel so isolated. People don't care how cold it is, even if it's five below, they still come in."

"What did you do in North Carolina?" I asked.

"Several things. I started out working in an orthodontist's office. I was there for ten years. Then I worked for a marriage counselor. Then I moved to a different part of the state and managed a dental office. I worked there for twenty-five years."

"Why did you move back?"

"I grew up here. My mom was still here, but she was getting older and needed help. My sister, who also lived in North Carolina, called me one day and said they were tired of the rat race there, so they were moving back home. I didn't want to stay there by myself. I celebrated holidays with them. So, she said, 'You just need to move back with us.' And that was it."

As Paula spoke, I thought about my brother Mark, who was a realtor. He told me much the same thing, that people who were born and raised in my hometown, Grand Haven, Michigan, oftentimes moved away to have a career, and once they retired, they moved back.

I asked Paula about her accent. "Do people here think you have a bit of a Southern drawl?"

"They say I don't sound Bostonian like coastal Mainers or Canadian like many up here. Just different. Friends I still have in North Carolina think I've changed since moving back. But they just assume because I'm in Maine, I live along the coast."

"Yes," I said, "people I know in Michigan think everyone in Maine works for L.L. Bean and feeds on various crustaceans. But since I came here, the only food from Maine I get are whoopie pies here and ployes farther north."

Paula's moving back home to help a parent was very common. If she had moved back to a large city instead of a rural town, she might not have met new friends because people who lived in busy cities were less likely to seek out new residents. That was one advantage about moving back to Houlton.

Someone asked Paula about a piece of jewelry, so she said she had to go and went over to help a person looking at a ring.

I motioned to Leigh, who was now talking to another customer.

"Oh," he said, looking at me, "that's right, you needed some directions."

"Yeah, it's getting a little late," I said, "and there was a storm brewing from the coast, so it would be good to get directions to the location mentioned in the song 'A Tombstone Every Mile.'"

Leigh told me about the route I would take, US-2A, also called Military Road. "It's fairly flat for a few miles until it passes an abandoned motel in an area called Cary's Mills. The road goes down a long hill at what appears to be the beginning of a forest. At the bottom of the hill it crosses two small creeks before curving its way up another long hill. At the top of that hill the road continues to curve as it passes several potato farms. It then enters the town of Linneus, which is the portion of the road where the song 'A Tombstone Every Mile' begins."

I decided to make the drive, and sure enough, just as Leigh said, from Linneus to Haynesville the road was a challenge. As I entered Linneus, population 947, I noticed an older woman using a walker who was loading her roadside wagon to sell freshly picked vegetables.

"Sorry to disturb you."

"Nothin' else for me to do, so no disturbance talking to you."

"Lived here long?"

"All my life."

"I hear this is where the song 'A Tombstone Every Mile' began."

"Yep."

"Do you remember a lot of semi crashes growing up?"

"A few, hard to remember how many."

"Was the road always paved?"

"Yep, hard surface all my life."

"How do you remember the road back in the early days?"

"I remember miles of snow fences at least five feet high lining the road. Wind blew hard, and snow drifted across the road. Lots of crashes and cars in ditches. Farther south where the hills are steeper, the road crews placed barrels filled with sand so drivers could get up the hills."

"Do you remember semis hauling potatoes?"

"I do, though some farmers shipped their potatoes by rail."

"So, the story in that song, in your memory, is fairly accurate."

"Yep."

I headed farther through the woods toward Haynesville, as the road kept twisting, turning, and going up and down hills, some with hairpin curves. So much so, it was hard to navigate at faster speeds. At a roadside picnic area, I happened on a couple with an older model Ford sedan, standing next to the car and having a smoke.

"I'm visiting here from Michigan. Where are you from?"

"Up the road a ways, Mars Hill."

I asked whether they had heard the story about a tombstone every mile. They had, and, in fact, the woman said that to this day, she would not drive that route after the sun went down. "Too many creepy stories about people getting lost, trucks going off the road, unreported deaths, and other mayhem occurring along that stretch of highway. No, thank you. I will not allow myself to drive this route after dark."

Then the man said, "It's getting near sunset. We need to leave real soon."

Before they left, I asked, "If there were tombstones every mile, where are those tombstones now?"

"The drivers were mostly from Maine," she said, "so their families buried them near the towns where they lived."

Satisfied that I'd learned whatever I could, I headed farther along US-2A through the town of Haynesville until it joined up with US-2 just past Macwahoc.

While driving through Macwahoc, I spotted a man standing next to the road. I stopped to speak with him. It turned out he was a potato farmer. I asked him about his farm and his crop.

"Up here, our cash crop is all potatoes," he said. His grandparents bought the land way back when. Over the years, he'd learned that potato farming was all about acquiring land to grow more and more potatoes. However, he said, "We borrow money to buy the land. The more land we buy, the more potatoes we need to store until the market is right to sell them. But to store more potatoes requires us to borrow more money to build sheds to store them."

I'd heard this during all of my travels whenever I talked to a farmer. Some said farmers these days were land rich and cash poor.

When I first arrived in Aroostook County, I learned a little about the history of potatoes in this area of the state. To really make potatoes pay off required a railroad. Once the rail lines were completed in the early 1860s, starch factories were built. Initially, starch factories used potatoes to "size" and stiffen textiles. Potatoes were also used to produce a powdery substance to be a thickener for soups, sauces, and pie fillings. This made potatoes an essential crop as the factories and the cities of the Northeast grew. As more and more fields were carved out of the white pine forests, farmers discovered fertile soil that, combined with the cool northern climate, made it the perfect environment for growing potatoes. With Maine's proximity to burgeoning East Coast cities, there was a ready market for potatoes.

9

The route from Macwahoc to Canaan was where US-2 paralleled I-95. At certain spots, it was possible to see and hear the traffic on the Interstate as cars whizzed by. By taking the slower route, I was able to stop at a local museum in Bangor, which was how I learned about Reverend Seth Noble, a Congregation pastor. He had moved into the area in 1790 by way of Nova Scotia, where he found settlers in need of religion. Not only was he one of the founders of Bangor, he also unwittingly provided its name as well. It happened in February of 1791 when Noble was in Boston on orders from local officials to name the town Sunbury. Because at the time Maine was still the property of Massachusetts, Noble had to travel to Boston to register the name of the town. While waiting to see the court to incorporate the settlement, he was singing a favorite hymn named "Bangor." Just then, he was summoned to request the name for the new town. But instead he thought he was being asked the name of the hymn, which was how Bangor got its name.

As I continued my drive to Canaan, I was just outside Newport, where solar farms sat next to cropland, creating a contrast between old times and new tech. Fifteen miles later, I arrived in Canaan, where I decided to car-camp at a local campground—very convenient whenever regular camping took too much time to set up the tent. With my plug-in hybrid, I was able to get electricity for power.

After my car was plugged in, the family in the campsite next to mine invited me to join them and their friends around their fire.

Sitting near the fire was a good-size man, who, with his brother, owned a body shop south of Canaan. He said, "My shop is so busy, I rent my campsite year-round. It's like having a cabin in the woods without all the bother. No time spent fixing this or that or cutting the lawn. Too busy for all that."

"Just like me," I said. "That's why I own a condo because I'm away for months at a stretch."

We bonded.

Next to him was a lady. She said, "I'm a home healthcare worker. I used to be a prison guard."

"How'd the job pay?"

"Paid well, wasn't worth it. Way too much drama there. I make a lot less money now, but I'm so much happier. The people I'm caring for are thankful for what I do."

Her daughter, sitting next to her, was listening in. She said, "I can't even begin to tell you how proud I am of my mother. . . . Seeing my mom happy got me to take a job at the VA caring for vets who have Alzheimer's."

Across from me sat a used car salesman from Augusta. He said, "The dealer I work for took me under his wing. He taught me that volunteering my time for something worthwhile would make me a better person."

"Did it?" I asked.

"Not sure."

I thought, *Wish I'd done a lot more volunteering when I was young.*

The conversation went into the night. As the sparks from the campfire drifted into the dark sky and the campground grew quieter, I said goodnight. I crawled back into my car and slept almost till dawn.

Knowing the folks I'd met the night before had little ones, I left without saying goodbye. But had I stayed, I would have told them all how impressed I was with each of their stories. With every one, I'd thought, *I wish I'd done that.* But I hadn't. Growing up, I wished I'd heard affirmation more often, but there was too much going on within our family. A lot of depression. Talk of suicide. An actual suicide. Time spent away in psychological institutions. A bank that foreclosed on our father's business and family home. Friends' and family's change of heart from steady Republicans to staunch Democrats, due to the heartless being in control. We went through a lot. It all passed through my head as I took leave.

I had ramped up my head with negative, troubling thoughts and had not gotten nearly enough sleep. I needed to get to Lancaster, New Hampshire. To make it there in one piece, I decided to look for a few diversions. My first stop was in downtown Skowhegan, where I shopped a block-long farmers' market that had a myriad of fresh vegetables, cookies, petting zoo sheep, a fundraiser for a local charity, fresh-brewed coffee, and scones. I bought a cup of coffee and a blueberry muffin and headed on my way. Then came Norridgewock, where the local museum was having a sale. I bought a couple of books and found someone who knew where I could find the gravesite of Father Rasle, the French Jesuit missionary who had learned the language of the Abenaki, only to be executed in 1724 by the British for sticking up for the tribe.

I drove through Franklin and Oxford counties, admiring the farms. A lot of dairy cows, hay, and potatoes. Lingering for a while in the university town of Farmington, I stopped at a coffeehouse in its historic downtown. Back on US-2, heading west, I was deep in thought. My life had been full of so much stuff. Opportunities lost. New adventures. Counting miles. Seeing things. It hit me once again why I enjoyed driving the local highways—because you saw things you might otherwise miss while on the interstates.

Had I not stopped in Rumford and looked around a bit, I would have missed seeing the Strathglass Park neighborhood, which was listed on the National Register of Historic Places. While walking through the downtown, I entered a store where the merchant told me that Rumford was once a company town for the Oxford Paper Company. The unofficial town motto was that the stench from the local paper mill was the smell of money being made. He also told me the well-designed duplex homes in Strathglass Park that I had just walked past, built by the benevolent original owner of the paper mill, were now in poor shape.

I asked, "Doesn't the listing on the National Register of Historic Places protect the integrity of the houses within the park?"

"Nope, it doesn't," he said. "You need to get grants for that." He explained that small towns like Rumford could not afford grant writers who were essential in getting funding from nonprofits and governmental agencies. One more reminder of the challenges of living in a rural area: the lack funding for projects that large urban areas received.

From Rumford, I attempted to make a mad dash to Lancaster, New Hampshire. When I stopped along the Maine-New Hampshire border at the Evans Notch Overlook, however, a group of bikers had American flags with large letter Q's emblazoned on the red-and-white stripes. I asked what that meant and was met with expletives. Not wanting to hear any more of that, I got the heck out of there.

I upped my speed to ten above and made the two-hour trip to Lancaster in about an hour and a half. There, I unwound for the night at a motel with a view of nearby Mount Cabot.

10

The land separating the towns of Lancaster, New Hampshire, and Lunenburg, Vermont, was a fertile agricultural valley with farm after farm that appeared to grow mainly corn. The farms ended as the road climbed a long hill to the town of Lunenburg.

Lunenburg distinguished itself by its block-square, tree-lined commons with lush green grass. Bronze plaques featured inscriptions of its fallen soldiers from several wars. The commons was surrounded by a historic white-sided church, a city hall, a school, and a museum. I saw a family having a picnic lunch, with the kids laughing and the parents enjoying the sun under the shadow of a Union soldier statue. I would have stayed a while longer had I not had an appointment with a former governor on my schedule.

While driving out of Lunenburg, I felt as if I were jumping off a gentle cliff because the town sat on a shelf of land overlooking hills, valleys, and forests. I stopped for a minute to take a photo of the landscape below the town.

This portion of Vermont, called the Northeast Kingdom, had some of the best timberland in the state. Comprised of the counties of Essex, Orleans, and Caledonia, it was one of the least populous areas of New England. The road to St. Johnsbury followed the Moose River from North Concord to Concord, two small neighboring towns that were the epitome of New England with white clapboard churches and flag-draped houses. The Northeast Kingdom was like that: picturesque, proud, independent, and the heart of Vermont's maple syrup country. Its name was first coined by former Senator George Aiken who, in 1947, said, "You know, this is such beautiful country up here. It ought to be called the Northeast Kingdom of Vermont." The name stuck.

About thirty miles west of St. Johnsbury, I passed by the granite mine in Graniteville, within the town of Barre. I briefly stopped at the overlook to see the mine in action. That was where I met Mary, whom I dubbed "the can lady" because she had volunteered to pick up cans littering the side of the road.

I asked about the granite slag in the yards of people living along Graniteville Road. There, houses' back yards abutted the open granite pit and piles of granite so high they dwarfed the houses. She said the neighbors along that road lived with the dangers of accidental collapse and granite dust that was so fine, it could seep inside houses. When blasts occurred in the quarry, nearby houses could shake. Oftentimes, the mine avoided blasting on days with full sun because the cloud of dust could appear like a dust storm. People living there feared for their health because the dust could get into their lungs. Yet, since the mine offered good jobs with benefits, a rarity in the area, there were few, if any, complaints.

From there, I headed to Montpelier and stopped at its gold-domed capital building. I watched white-shirted legislators playing volleyball on the capital grounds with grade school–age kids in T-shirts and shorts.

At the edge of Montpelier was Green Mount Cemetery, where the statue of a crying lady wrapped in a stole was located. I got the attention of the groundskeeper, who told me the statue was nicknamed Black Angus after the ghost that watched over the grave of John Erastus Hubbard. He said legend had it that people who sat in the statue's lap were cursed and would die, especially if it was done at midnight during a full moon.

As I left the cemetery, I picked up a brochure that told the story of John Hubbard. Later on, I read that it all had started quite innocently. Born into a well-to-do Montpelier family in 1847, Hubbard grew up to become a prominent businessman. When his wealthy aunt Fanny Maria Hubbard Kellogg of New York City died in 1890, she intended for her money to go to her birth home of Montpelier. John Hubbard, however, redirected the money to himself and gave only a tiny amount to the city to fund the building of its public library. As word got out about what he'd done, his reputation was rightfully tarnished. Nevertheless, when he died in 1899, he did give a portion of his money to the City of Montpelier. Part of that money funded the cemetery's gate and chapel, along with the Black Angus statue designed by the Austrian artist Karl Bitter. Called *Thanatos* after the Greek god of death, the statue had this inscription:

Approach thy grave
Like one who wraps
The Drapery of his couch
About him and lies down
To pleasant dream

It took me an hour and a half to drive the winding county roads from Montpelier to Middlebury, which looked and felt like a quaint midsize New England town. Its name came from its location midway between the towns of Salisbury and New Haven. Overlooking the main quad of Middlebury College in Monroe Hall was where I found a former four-term governor of Vermont. I initially addressed him as Governor Douglas, but he immediately said, "Call me Jim."

He had entered the scholarly world of Middlebury College on January 6, 2011, just after his final term as governor ended. He became an executive in residence and taught a 24-student course titled "Vermont Government and Politics." Jim was a busy guy. Besides his duties at the college, he also served on the Governors' Council of the Bipartisan Policy Center in Washington, D.C. and concurrently as the interim director of the Vermont Historical Society. I found him to be an "aw-shucks," wholesome, straight-talking gentleman with a disarming smile and humor to match. Not your average politician. He was unassuming and assured. Basically, he acted like an adult, rather than one of those crazies who had come along of late.

I asked Jim how the rhetoric in politics had changed during his career.

"I'm worried about the tone of public discourse. When I went to the legislature in the 1970s, I literally didn't know what party everyone belonged to.

You didn't have party-line votes like you do today. There were urban versus rural coalitions. Folks along the eastern side of the state had strong views about tax policy. We had farmers and different professional blocs, but it wasn't partisan."

I babbled on for a minute about certain members of both parties and how they seemed to be all about themselves over the interests of the people.

He agreed. "Legislators now vote strictly along party lines. I regret that because it's no longer as collegial. I sometimes half-jokingly suggest we shouldn't have built the interstate highways because we had far fewer commuters in our legislature in those days. Now you can drive from Montpellier, the capital, to Saint Albans, a city in the Northwest Kingdom, in less than an hour. As a result, there's no reason to stay here overnight. In my day we had dinner, we socialized and attended various events so we could get to know one another. Now there's not as much of that. Regarding civility, I used to tell some of my fellow legislators, 'You'll be less shrill or vitriolic toward a colleague if you know you're going to be with him for dinner tonight.'"

I asked, "How's the temperature of the rhetoric in Congress these days?"

"It's high there as well. I had lunch a few years ago with our congressman, and he took me to the House dining room. My first question was, 'Where is everybody?' He said, 'Nobody comes here anymore. They're all home or at the party headquarters, fundraising. I don't even know all my fellow Democrats. We've really drifted away from that human interaction.'"

Jim Douglas's office was smaller than I would have expected for a former governor, yet tastefully decorated with several awards, photographs, and shelves of books. Rather than sitting behind a desk during our conversation, he sat next to me. He was casual yet nicely dressed. From his office window, the Middlebury College campus looked like an Ivy League school with its classic, majestic buildings—as you'd expect for one of the nation's top liberal arts colleges.

Continuing, former governor Douglas said, "I was at our state capital the other week talking with a senate committee about the open meetings law and access to governmental bodies by the public. There's a lot of interest in remote access. My thoughts were that you really lose something when you're not sitting down with someone and reasoning with that person—going over your differences and finding common ground. I understand the value of the technology when someone can't attend due to health issues and Zooms in, but it shouldn't be the norm. I'm afraid a lot of people are increasingly treating it as such. I think we have to be careful about that."

I said, "I see some advantages to communicating that way in remote areas for certain medical consultations or even some specialized classes. But I'm concerned about people's ability to be anonymous while on the Internet. For example, by creating a fake name and writing a letter to the editor."

Laughing, Jim said, "The other day I got a message from Hotdog 13."

"Yes," I said, "we're apt to say things that are not civil if we don't have to identify ourselves."

Jim added, "We learned about the advantages of face-to-face meetings where you actually got to know people and show your value. The trend in younger Internet generation people is that everything can be done via Zoom, email, or social media. I'm on the board of a bank. They sometimes lose a bank loan officer who's working remotely to a larger bank. We try to explain to them that when business softens, remote workers tend to be the first to go. I used to tell some of my fellow legislators to be less shrill or vitriolic toward colleagues. It's important to make eye contact and shake one another's hands."

We talked about the Depression-era CCC and WPA government programs. "We've decided that government is always bad," I said. "Yet we created the national parks and made them better with government programs."

Jim told me, "We didn't have a national park here in Vermont until a generation ago, but we had a lot of CCC workers back during the Depression years in the state parks and ski areas. Today we do have Vermont Youth Conservation Corps, which is a little like the CCC, where young people work outdoors on public service projects. It's a way for them to earn money for college."

"So many rural people have part-time jobs without benefits," I said. "Sometimes they work four or five part-time jobs."

"I know, it's a shame. However, during the last couple decades we actually have more visitors in the summer than in winter, so we are creating a few more year-round jobs. For example, our college has a ski resort and a golf course, so those workers have year-round jobs. People piece together a living. There's an old line that a fellow says, 'I read the other day that the government just created more jobs. I have four of them.' A neighbor down the road is a farmer who just got through a sugar season that did well for him. He raises row crops, goats, and lambs and puts together a fairly good living. There are others not in agriculture who do the same thing, piecing together a living. People find a way to get by."

Our conversation shifted to the topic of Vermont and its heritage.

Jim said, "We were the first state to ban slavery—in 1777. Yet, during the Civil War, we still fought, we had passion. We were the first state to allow people to vote no matter their race. The Civil War was a big deal for Vermonters. A lot of kids left the farm, enlisted, and paid a heavy price for it. But on a town-by-town basis, some local governments appropriated funds to pay their soldiers at least a little compensation."

I asked whether Vermont had found ways to increase its population, noting that the booming era from the 1970s to the year 2000 had waned during the last couple decades.

Jim said, "I now teach a course titled 'Vermont Government and Politics' and another class on 'Presidential Autobiographies.' Of course, Calvin Coolidge was born here, you probably know that. Most of the students are from out of state. My pitch is to get them to stay. I tell them, 'You're here for four years; why not enjoy a lifetime here?'"

"You must have thoughts about government service," I said, noting he had been a member of the Middlebury College Republicans in the early 1970s. He had been elected to various governmental posts, beginning with the Vermont House of Representatives when he was twenty-one. He served as House Majority leader at age twenty-five. After working in government for forty years, he decided not to seek reelection as governor of Vermont in 2009. He figured it was time to give back to the next generation by teaching classes at Middlebury College.

Jim said, "I wish elected officials would go into public service with an open mind and a willingness to listen, learn, and interact in search of that elusive common ground. Former Maine senator Olympia Snow wrote a memoir where she said, 'We need to get back to a time when compromise is not only accepted but valued.' I sense more and more newly elected officials come with an agenda and are unwilling to compromise. I remember, during my tenure in the House, a colleague who felt so passionately about an issue at the time. An issue that escapes me now. When she didn't prevail, she got physically ill. I remember thinking, *I want to be passionate but not that passionate.* I learned from that experience that I'm not going to prevail every time. Move on to the next issue and maybe come back to that in a different way. But not to be devastated if I don't succeed. I tell students, 'Do not get your news from a single source. Instead, force yourself to watch other networks and read other periodicals, online sites, and newspapers. One source can be an echo chamber. You need to know what other sources are saying. You need multiple perspectives.'"

For the next few minutes, we talked about local news coverage and that most TV and radio stations were part of national conglomerates, that more and more people had cut their cable TV in favor of streaming, and that online algorithms served up only what consumers wanted to see in terms of politics and even what they might want to purchase. Jim told me the local newspaper in Middlebury and the local CBS affiliate no longer covered town council meetings. We agreed it was a sad time for independent news coverage and that neither of us had a good solution. That prompted me to ask, "What about the need for money in politics and the idea to limit the amount of money people can give?"

Jim said, "There are congressional models where candidates have a quota they need to come up with every year. Party headquarters is very close to the congressional offices. I'm just thankful we have it a little easier than most other states, due to our size. But there have been Supreme Court cases on that very topic. The PACS can raise nearly unlimited funds. There are some limits by state, but the PACS are not subjected to those limits."

Looking for hope and a way out of all the hoopla of politics, I asked, "Do you see yourself as optimistic about the future?"

"I wish I could see the path forward to get back to a time when we were more collegial. I'm okay with partisanship. Part of the strength of our democracy is a combination of ideas, and one party holds more or less a set of values, and the other, the same. That's the process. But now it's so polarized. Studies show that the American people are not as polarized as elected officials. Yet, we keep electing them. I often say maybe it's time for term limits for Congress. We historically haven't supported them, but it couldn't be any worse, could it? I was speaking with a former congressman from another state, and he said it's not about those who have been here for a long time. It's the newcomers. For myself, I'm warming to the idea of term limits as an option, just to push the reset button. People complain about the choices they've had. I agree, we need better people who are willing to run."

When I asked about rural voters, Jim didn't respond right away. He paused, then said, "I think they feel left behind. That the political elite are running the show."

Former Vermont Governor Jim Douglas, at Middlebury College in Middlebury, Vermont

We walked outside. It was a bright, sunny day. Students were outdoors studying, walking about, and enjoying the weather. From the middle of the campus, I could see the Green Mountains in the distance. We discussed that for a campus of under three thousand, it attracted students from every state and many countries yearly.

Jim wondered whether I wanted to ask anything else.

"One question. Is the population of the state growing or shrinking? Are there opportunities here?"

"The three northern New England states are the three oldest by median age," he said, "and our workforce is shrinking and has been for decades. We have fewer and fewer kids in our schools, which puts pressure on closing and consolidating. In 2020, there were fewer live births in Vermont than deaths. So, it's a real problem. People here are wondering if they want to bring a kid into the world." After a pause, he said, "I'm very concerned about free expression. We're not listening to other voices. Problem is, this is the time in a student's life that they should hear multiple points of view so they can form their own opinions. Even voices that make them feel uncomfortable or are offensive. The world beyond this campus is out of safe spaces. Now is a time when they have a support system. I always told my staff that I was okay with saying I don't know or I would have done that differently. Now politicians double down, instead of looking for the truth or admitting they were wrong."

While speaking with former governor Douglas, who was a Republican, my mind wandered, as it often does, back to when my father switched from being a dedicated Republican to a staunch Democrat.

Once back to my car, I got out my note pad to write down the story.

It happened during the early 1980s, around the time I'd decided to leave the family business and move east to find a better job. In the weeks before I left, I remember my father sitting at the kitchen table with a small portable black-and-white TV turned on. He was not actually watching a program. Instead, he was staring blankly at the screen, worried because he had lost all hope of saving our family's store. What I didn't know until much later was the cause of his angst. He had received a registered letter from an attorney representing his bank, demanding he pay what he owed the bank.

As a small-town merchant, my father, like too many local businesspeople, had a long relationship with his bank. The bank financed the store inventory through a banknote that my father backed with his good credit. My dad's bank held all of his business debt, and my father had trouble paying the monthly payment. It was a time of high inflation when interest rates had increased to record levels. The bank had upped my dad's interest rate from 12 percent to nearly 20 percent.

The burden of trying to pay his bills, combined with fear of losing his store, buildings, and home from foreclosure, had made my dad give up all hope. In the end, the bank did take all of my parents' assets, along with their home. If not for a friend who had a second home that was vacant, my parents would have been homeless.

My dad, from that point on, voted Democratic. He felt that Ronald Reagan's trickle-down economy had made him a victim of Republican economic policies.

From Middlebury I drove to Burlington, an hour or so north on US-7. The traffic was heavy. Though it was getting late, I wanted to visit Intervale Center on the north end of the city before it turned dark. I had read so much about this unique cooperative farm, sitting on 350 acres of flood plain between the Winooski River and Lake Champlain. Intervale was a sanctuary in the city where people interested in working on a small community farm could raise crops and, to a certain extent, make a living while learning about farming responsibly. The brainchild of a man named Will Raap, it was located in an area that the native Abenaki people had farmed for centuries.

Once there, I headed to the center's office where I met a young lady working at the front desk. I began by asking questions about the farm, explaining I had just met with the former governor of the state who was likewise enthusiastic about what was happening there. I told her I lived in Michigan and was passing through town. She was not impressed and said that if I wanted to know about the farm, I would need to submit a request form on their website. I would not get permission to speak with anyone until their board or management or whomever weighed in. I asked if she could answer just a couple questions. She gave me one of those "whatever" looks, saying she was way too busy. Then she walked over to a group of young people and hugged one of the men, possibly her main squeeze. She ignored me for what seemed like an hour but was probably closer to ten minutes. On returning to her desk, she still looked totally uninterested.

I asked once again if she could spare a minute. With a scowl indicating she'd had enough of me, she finally said, "You can't talk to anyone here, but if you want to walk down along the road to the small independent farms, you might be able to speak to someone."

Here I was in the midst of that old battle where policy outweighed practicality. I felt like Henny Penny, a.k.a. Chicken Little, trying to alert this Gen-Z'er that the sky was falling. I walked out of there and down the road all the way to the end, where the independent farmers were tending their small fields. I ran into a guy who was cleaning out picking bins after a long day of working his field. I wasn't sure whether I got his name right—it could have been Dylan or Ryan or something similar. He said he was part of a multi-person collective farm of similarly minded urban farmers. He'd been raised in Philadelphia by caring parents who baked and sold knishes in their home and made a living doing that for many years. He first discovered his love for farming while working on his grandmother's Christmas tree farm in rural Pennsylvania. When he'd heard about Burlington's Intervale Center, he felt it was his chance to begin to make a difference. That was more than thirty years ago, and he was still there.

Knowing it wasn't proper to ask a farmer the size of his farm, ever so gently I asked anyway.

"Fifteen acres," he said, "used responsibly."

I asked what that meant.

"Twenty-five varieties of vegetables sold at farmers' markets and independent grocery stores, to be served in local restaurants."

I asked what their operation was named.

"Diggers Mirth, which came from a movement in England in the mid-1600s. It emphasized collective land ownership and creating a connection between people and their natural environment. Now I gotta get back to work."

I overnighted in a small local motel, one where I pulled my car up to the door. It was one of those places where contractors in white trucks stayed and hung out at the picnic table, smoking cigarettes and drinking beer. The next morning I awoke to the sound of traffic, and once I got through it, I drove a half-hour south to meet with former *Burlington Free Press* investigative reporter and columnist Sam Hemingway.

His place was out of the way and difficult to find, on land near a series of public access natural areas.

When I arrived, Sam showed me around a bit. His land was one of the beneficiaries of Vermont's Act 250, a land use and development law enacted in 1970 as a way to stop runaway developments in the state. He said, "At the time, there were a lot of ski areas being developed in the southern part of the state. People worried that we would turn into another Massachusetts, which Vermonters wanted no part of. When I joined the paper in 1977, it was the first story of consequence I worked on at the paper."

I commented on how incredible the land was around his home.

"Yes," Sam said, "it's beautiful land. A lot of towns in Vermont are holding onto farmland and other land that they don't want to see get developed. Within the village of Hinesburg, a lot of houses are being built. As a result, its population is growing. There's a belief that concentrating growth within the village keeps everything, stores and restaurants, within walking distance. And that's a good thing."

"And that's because of Act 250?" I asked.

"Yes, a Syracuse company that constructs commercial developments wanted to build a 500,000-square-foot mall in Williston right off the Interstate at exit 12 just outside Burlington. People here thought if that happened, Burlington would be like every other town that had been destroyed by suburban malls. Fortunately, the motion was defeated by the commission. After the vote, I went up to the lead developer, asking for a comment. He said, 'I feel like I just lost three years of my life.' That's Vermont. That is why all the land around me is like it is, with all the protected land and nature preserves."

"Tell me about yourself," I said.

"I was born in New Haven, Connecticut, in 1948, and I grew up in a small town just north of there named Mount Carmel near the Sleeping Giant State Park. I lived in a house my grandparents had bought near the time of the Great Depression. They gave the house to my father when he came back from World War ll. I have two brothers, one older, one younger. After growing up in Connecticut, Vermont was like the great frozen north to me. It was a sorta mystical place with hardly any people and lots of trees, farm fields, and ski areas. But I never really thought a lot about Vermont until after college. I went to college during the 1960s and was very much involved in the peace movement. Because I had a low draft number and did not want to go to Vietnam, I applied for and received a 1Y classification."

Sam told me that a 1Y classification, which was discontinued in 1971, meant a registrant was qualified for military service only in time of war or national emergency. Since 1941, Congress had declared war only six times, all during World War II. Congress authorized troop deployment in Vietnam, but, because it did not issue a declaration of war against North Vietnam or the Vietcong, the Vietnam War was not considered a war. It meant someone classified as 1Y could not be drafted.

"What did you do next?" I asked.

"I called a friend in northern Vermont and kind of landed here. I've been here since '71. I lived close to the bone for a while, working on a community newspaper that we printed on a small press. It was a difficult time, but anyhow I ended up here. Got married, had a child, started doing freelance for the *Villager Free Press.* Taught a journalism class at St. Johnsbury College. Then I was finally offered a job at the *Burlington Free Press* and moved to Burlington in 1977. Got divorced. Met my wife, Lee, in 1979. She had two children, and I had one. Kids still live nearby. I've lived in Hinesburg since 1999. Retired in 2014. Initially was a business reporter, then an investigative reporter, then editor, then columnist for the last thirteen years."

I asked, "How did the paper do once people began using the Internet for the news?"

"I call it the Walmart-ization of local media. The *New York Times* is a wonderful newspaper, but they don't cover anything in Vermont when it comes to local news. Our paper is the largest newspaper in the state, but as circulation declined, so did the coverage. I left just before another round of cuts but will always stand with the local papers even if they aren't what they once were. I hope that they someday figure it out because they bring a community together and are a watchdog. That was entirely what my writing was about. Without a free and independent press, all kinds of terrible things can go on, and nobody will even know about it. It's part of what a free democratic country is all about. Right now, we don't really have that on a local level. And that bothers me. Here in New England, most news is through Boston. States like New Hampshire get their news from Massachusetts because many people commute to large metropolitan areas like Boston. Vermont is different; it has a more remote population."

"In my area," I said, "we're starting to see some nonprofit presses pop up."

"Here we have public radio, which covers statewide stories but not local news. But there needs to be local news available and ways to make it accessible to everyone for free or a nominal fee. As for sophisticated journalism, I'm not sure how to fund it. Years ago, I was a hippie, and part of me still is. People looked at Burlington like it was another world. Much different from the rest of Vermont, the Northeast Kingdom being an example. But that's changing as more people work in Burlington and commute in from rural areas. Our county is where the money and votes are and where the people are."

"So," I said, "Burlington is where people go to shop, dine, see a show, visit a doctor, see a dentist, and pick up groceries, and where many people go to work."

"You mentioned earlier you'd been to Intervale," Sam said. "Land conservation is very strong in this state. Look at the land here, in this area. Everything around here is in land conservation mode. That's because in the 1950s a woman came here, bought a lot of land, built a restaurant, and then, when she got old, sold us and other people land. A lot of the other land got put into a land trust. The farmer who used to be there agreed to put his property in the trust. He wanted to keep it from being developed. Dave Zuckerman, the former lieutenant governor, runs a farm over there. He owns his buildings, but the land is in a trust. He leases his land in order to grow vegetables. A lot of towns are holding onto farmland and other land that they don't want to get developed. As you saw when you drove through there, it's beautiful land."

I asked Sam how the land originally developed.

"A lot of towns up here were created by wealthy people who lived throughout New York and New England. They would send somebody up to lay claim to a place. Give it a name because there wasn't anybody there. Eventually, somebody would move there. A lot of towns here were formed that way. Yet, that was when the United States was in its formative years during the early 1800s. But now we are what we are. So much that's affecting us comes from way beyond our borders, climate change, population explosion, food shortages, global conflicts. If you could poll everyone in the world and ask them what they want, everybody has their own agenda. Mother

Earth would say, 'If you're going to fuck it up, fuck it up. The world will survive if people don't. The human race is just a parasite on the world.' However, I like to think we're going to figure this out as a species, even though at times it's demoralizing."

"How about the government," I asked, "what is its role?"

"The government is always the target for things that are not going right in people's lives. It's partly because Americans have a deep independent streak. But as citizens we also want certain things. We want a highway system, we want safe food, water and air quality. We want rules for safe places to work. We want Social Security; we want Medicare. The list goes on and on. We want it all to work perfectly. It *is* true that there's a swamp in Washington. It's easy to see that our system isn't working very well. Yet, although there are inefficiencies, a lot of government workers are doing the best they can and doing a lot of good. We need to have a country that keeps in mind what is best for everybody and not just what's best for the wealthy. It always mystifies me that people who are of not much means will support policies that are to their detriment in terms of taxes. For example, tax cuts that benefit the wealthy without helping those without very much. It makes no sense to me. There's such a distrust of the press. It always has been demonized but not to this extent, with politicians who need to control the press."

We talked about the upcoming national election and what would happen if a certain individual were elected. Both of us agreed if that occurred, the wealthy would get even richer and the poor, poorer. I told Sam about all the people living in poverty I'd witnessed along the route I followed. I feared the plight of those who already suffered now if the wrong candidate won.

Moving on, I asked, "So, what do you see in your own future?"

"We grapple with how long we can stay here as we get older. That's a big question for us. I don't think we'll ever move away from Vermont because our children are here. We're still in denial about needing to be closer to medical care. We think about it, but it's not something either of us wants to worry about. We also think about things we have in storage. We need to get rid of that stuff. You hate to leave behind a pile of stuff that other people will have to deal with. But it's hard to get rid of stuff. So, there's that. "

"Are you still writing?"

"Not professionally. That was the biggest thing that changed. When I retired, I thought I might continue writing. I loved being a reporter, an investigative reporter. But I also decided that was a chapter in my life—a very long chapter. It was my career. Do I really need to perpetuate this career into my very old age? I don't think so. I kinda feel I've turned inward, and I'm starting to look at myself in terms of sorting out some of the other things that are in my self-conscious or my own personal history. The draft being one thing. I'm trying to make some sense of other things that happened in my life and learning how to be really present and grounded in my thinking and my acting and my emotions. That's something when you're a reporter. I felt like every day I was putting on my armor and having to be a certain kind of person. I couldn't display how I felt about things because that's not being objective. My job was to get other people to give me their stuff, and sometimes they would be in great pain or discomfort doing it."

I told Sam it was the same for me, emotionally, when I made a documentary or conducted interviews for my own writing. I couldn't show how I felt about things and still keep my objectivity, either. It was part of what I considered my job and why I used a voice recorder when I conducted my interviews. The exact words of people I spoke with mattered. I thought, *Sam must have a lot more to say about his days as a reporter.*

"Tell me about the stories you covered," I said.

"I covered everything from opioid addiction to Afghanistan, murders, priest sex abuse, and arms smuggling. A lot of stuff was painful, and I lived through it as a reporter. I loved breaking stories. I loved all of that. But it also takes an emotional and intellectual toll. I'm not complaining, but I didn't want to continue it anymore. It's been a sort of slow evolution away from the kind of person I needed to be then to the person I am now. I feel like one of the more significant moments of the last few years was when a friend of mine died. We were in a men's group together. Watching him deal with that with such grace, in such a beautiful way, laughing as he was leaving. Not in a superficial way. Full of love, full of grace. I thought, *I would like that.* I learned a lot from him. So, I want to figure out how to be at peace with myself at the end of my life."

"They talk about stages of life as attributes of aging," I said. "Some might call it theology, others philosophy. It's looking inside and looking back and a little bit forward. Kind of centering, not really reliving the past but reflecting on it."

"I'm definitely reflecting on it. I don't want to live in the past. I have people in my life who spend a lot of time reliving their high school years. I don't feel like I'm seventy-four. I feel like I'm still younger than that. And I'm glad I feel that way. A lot of people my age don't feel that way. At some point this vessel of my body won't be able to do it anymore. The more I can work through that stuff, think through it, feel through it, the better I'll be. I've had a very blessed life. It didn't happen because I'm so smart and brilliant, it happened because of my place. That I was born in this country, I'm white, and I'm male. I may not have thought that way when I was twenty, but I'm more and more aware of that now. At certain points in my life when I first got to Vermont, I was homeless. So, I know what the other side feels like. Not that I lived that way for a long time, but I understand it. That's part of what drove me into journalism. I take that all into account."

Sam paused and reflected more before continuing. "Some of the stories I've worked on keep coming back. Some of the most significant ones were about

Sam Hemingway, retired investigative journalist, Hinesburg, Vermont

an orphanage here where children were abused. Stories started coming out in the 1990s. After I finished those stories from various sources, I once thought of writing a book about it. Later, someone else came along and updated the stories and put them on *BuzzFeed*, and now it's a big deal. So, now this orphanage story that got buried in the '90s is out there. It wasn't ready to come out yet when I initially wrote it."

We talked about a few insignificant things before Sam admitted he might someday write a book about his life so his kids would understand what he went through—though he didn't think he'd publish it. But if he did, he could describe what his childhood was like growing up.

Remembering back, Sam said, "My mother, who died fairly early at age sixty-six, grew up in Chicago in sorta semi high society. Her father was in real estate and had a house on Mackinac Island. I put on my journalistic hat and discovered my father's side went way back to the Revolutionary War, and one of the first people to go to Yale was a Hemingway. Then I found out my great-grandfather was in real estate and built a section of a development in the north side of Chicago but later, in the 1920s, fell or jumped out of a window to his death. Turned out, my grandfather, who was also in real estate, never shared that story. I had no idea about any of this."

I found my way back to US-2 and drove through the congestion of Burlington, then island-hopped the northerly route across Lake Champlain through Grand Isle, South Hero, North Hero, and the Albert Peninsula into New York State.

During that time, I thought about Sam and his great-grandfather falling or jumping out of a window. It made me remember my dad's mother, my paternal grandmother, who committed suicide. In her case, she took an overdose of pills and passed away. My grandmother's story was a sad one. Born into a very religious family, she was told by her parents she would make a great minister's wife. They pushed her into that role, and she married my grandfather, in part because he was about to become a minister. It was her dream come true. But when he lost his ministry, she went into a deep depression that would not end. My grandparents lived a block away from my family. My father would stop to see my grandmother every night. My mother realized his visits were not helping, so one night he decided not to drop by. The next morning my grandmother's body was discovered in a closet, after she'd overdosed on pills. I remember my father's shout that morning when he heard the news. It was one of the few times I'd heard him swear. He bolted down the stairs and past my room. Hitting the gas, he drove our family wagon down the hilly street to my grandparents' house. My grandfather was inconsolable, and at my grandmother's funeral I heard him weep.

While driving north over the Alburgh Tongue, I took the road to Isle La Motte to visit Saint Anne's Shrine and the statue of Samual de Champlain, the discoverer of Lake Champlain. He first landed on Isle la Motte in 1608, making way for the first European settlement in Vermont during 1666.

Yet, it was the Shrine of Saint Anne, an open-air church, that got my attention. I sat on one of the pews for a few minutes. I felt consoled while sitting there. I'd had a day of emotional thoughts. Soon it was time to drive over the bridge to New York State.

11

The town of Champlain comprised the villages of Rouses Point and Champlain. It was raining when I crossed the bridge into Rouses Point. Once in the village, I made my way to the Rouses Point Village Hall where I paid a visit to local historian and retired auto mechanic Brandon Racine. His office was on the second floor of the building housing the village museum.

After I told him about my cross-country journey, we discussed how I could find a rural route from the nearby Canadian border to the Upper Peninsula of

Michigan. The problem was how to avoid Montreal and Ottawa, two cities that had grown exponentially since the early days of motoring. They made it nearly impossible to take a rural trip west through Canada from Rouses Point without relying on a myriad of side roads.

Though Brandon had lived there most of his life, he did not have a definitive answer to my question. The conversation then shifted to the subject of the Rouses Point Bridge along US-2, which I had just crossed—a topic Brandon knew well.

"During the Great Depression," he said, "when the first Rouses Point Bridge was built, to save money it was decided to use the concrete walls of nearby Fort Montgomery for construction. That was the greatest mistake the forefathers of Rouses Point ever made. When they tried blowing up the walls, it was so well built that they couldn't. They ended up needing to drag rocks out of the quarries in Vermont to build the bridge."

I asked Brandon whether the building of US-2 was seen as a plus for the community.

"I think our forefathers saw the beginning of US-2 as an asset to Rouses Point, which it was in a way since it allowed semis to use the highway. Before that, they had to be ferried across Lake Champlain. The village leaders thought the added traffic would bring in more business, but instead the traffic coming through didn't have any reason to stop."

Brandon liked to split his time between his home in Rouses Point and what he called his "woodlot," which was the size of a small forest and was located twelve miles out of town. He said he liked to live off the grid. As he was talking, I did a double-take, asking, "Did I hear you say you make your own gas?"

"Yes, I make ethanol using a still. Everyone I know out there is into making moonshine and what not."

"You might as well make rocket fuel," I quipped. "But seriously, how do you get your car to run on it?"

"I converted the engine. It runs on ethanol now."

I gave him a "side eye" look and moved to another question. "So, tell me more about your place out there."

"It's kinda like an escape. I've hunted on it for thirty years and harvest my own game. I raise bees, I've got apple trees, a well with a hand-pump system and also a solar pump. I almost bought an Amish shed that I was gonna put up. I wanted a place where I could stay in the winter. Right now, I've got a forty-foot trailer. I've got a wood stove, but I've gotta properly mill the lumber so it can burn jet fuel, gasoline, wood, whatever you want to burn. I've got propane heat, but the price of fossil fuel has gone up. I like to live off the land and not use any pocket money. With the windmill and solar panels, I'm getting toward the point where I can pretty much get everything I need."

"What type of game do you hunt there?" I asked.

"I've got rabbits and partridge, deer, bobcat, bear, porcupine, opossum."

Joking, I said, "Porcupines must be hard to skin."

"Actually pretty easy, if you do it from the belly. There's no quills on the belly. I've done it before. They taste kind of evergreen-ish because they eat a lot of pine."

Using the well-worn phrase, I said, "So, you're telling me they don't taste like chicken."

"No, but groundhogs pretty much taste like chicken, though they're fatty. And the venison we get in the mountains near Lake Placid, when we have our hunting camps up there, it's really gamy tasting because the deer are really scrounging to find what to eat. On my woodlot, we're right on the Canadian border where we've got apple orchards. We've got all the corn and farmland. So, basically the deer that come off my woodlot taste more like veal. I prefer it over beef. It's organically grown with what's in it. When you buy beef in the store, it's like a crapshoot. You don't know where it came from. I've seen farmers send animals that were sick to the auction for slaughter. You want to eat sick animals? I don't."

By then, I was chiding myself, *Why in the world did I ask about the game he kills when, as someone who is close to being a vegetarian, I would never consider eating wild game.* So, I diverted the conversation.

"What crops do you grow out there?" I asked.

"There are black walnuts that taste like walnuts but are harder to crack. It's one of the hardest nuts in the world. It's an acquired taste."

"So, what do you use, a vise?"

"There's a special nutcracker. You can use vise grips, too. Or you can use a hammer. I've also got acorns, not as many oaks as I'd like. I've got a lot of maple trees."

"Are any of them sugar maple?" I asked.

"No, but my brother-in-law down the street has them. It's a lot of work, though."

"That's what I hear," I said. "Plus, the reduction is around fifty gallons to get a gallon."

"Yeah, you also have to be there 24/7 to keep the fire stoked. You can't just start a fire and walk away. I've seen people tap trees and use a Cool Whip container to collect it. They make small batches for themselves. When we were kids, we drank the sap, but it does go through you pretty quick. It's like sugar water. Before they had manmade sugar, the original sweetener was honey. People have gotten away from the taste of honey. For myself, I use honey in place of sugar."

"Do you live in town most of the time?"

"Yes, but I like to spend my summers in the woods. My wife says my woodlot is more like an animal preserve."

"So, you were born in Rouses Point?"

"Nope, nearby in Plattsburgh, but I was raised here—just down the street. My father was born in Champlain on a farm, and my mother, like me, was born in Plattsburgh and raised in Rouses Point. Where I live now is family property once owned by my great grandfather, W. J. Laundrie, who at one point owned ninety-eight percent of the town. Unfortunately, his offspring didn't have enough foresight to hold onto the property."

"Do you have a copy of the Acadian flag?" I asked.

"No, but I do have an original version of the American flag. You can see by the stitching that it is hand sewn."

As I looked at the flag and touched the stitching, Branden said, "I used to travel back and forth to Plattsburgh for work and liked to listen to loud rock music in my car. I was once clocked at 183 mph. That got the attention of the cops, but they couldn't catch me, so I pulled over to let them catch up. Then, when I was twenty-two, I had a car accident. I was coming home from work, and I passed a car on a corner with a double solid line. I hit the car because I was six inches into his lane. They said it was second-degree manslaughter because I used my signal light. The judge said it was an attempt to commit murder, so they classified my car as a weapon. The judge hated me because they offered me a plea bargain before I went to court and gave me a sentence of one to four."

"You said the other driver died. I'm very sorry to hear that. Were you injured?"

"I was pronounced dead at the scene and was given my last rights. The only reason I'm here today was that a friend of mine was on the rescue squad and later told me they could hear me gurgling and were able to bring me back to life. From the accident site to the hospital in Plattsburgh, they gave me four pints of plasma because I'd lost so much blood. My heart was beating so fast when they brought me into the ER that I was shutting off the EKG machine. I was in a coma for twenty-two days. When I finally woke up, I had to learn how to walk again. I was found guilty by a jury of my peers. I won my first New York State appeal within a year. I had a unanimous decision on a crime cut. They gave me the max, five to fifteen years, which is illegal for a first crime offense. I got a reduction to two to seven. I got the judge disbarred. I could have had the state police force punished because they forged the medical records by saying I had a blood test that was positive. They forged the records because they needed the judge's permission to take the test and never got it. Then I caught the Bureau of Criminal Investigation officer lying on the stand because he said they had a picture of a torque converter lying in the road, the part that holds the motor and the transmission together. He said that to literally come apart to that degree, the car would have to be blown apart, due to excessive speed. But they didn't realize I still had the car, and the torque converter was in my car. It was a spare one I kept for parts in my trunk. Crap like that. It was like going to the railroad station, it was a ride. My attorneys were great. They couldn't believe I'd been convicted. They took my appeal for free. I ended up doing a year and a half in Attica. That was in the late 1980s. I actually completed college while in prison."

"How long did you serve?" I asked.

"Two years and four months. My job was waiting for me when I got out of prison. Same job as I had before the accident, as an auto mechanic at the Chevy dealer here."

"Are you still there?"

"No, I got hurt in 2010 and worked until 2017 with a spinal injury. So, they operated on me, and I had to retire. All in all, I turned wrenches for thirty-three years."

"How do you get by now?"

"My wife is originally from Ticonderoga and moved here when she was young. We decided early on that she would be a stay-at-home mom. We live on very little, which is how we can afford our home here in Rouses Point, along with my wood-lot. We met through my mother's school. My wife was the mother of one of the kids from there and a friend of my mother and my sisters. When I got out of prison, I just wanted to settle down, have a family, have a wife, and keep a low profile. She had a son who I adopted. He was five when I met her, and we had my daughter. There's ten years between my son and daughter. My daughter was working at the Shelburne House in South Burlington, Vermont. A home for abused boys who are taken away from their parents. Now she's a social worker for the state of Vermont. My son has an IT job in South Carolina."

"Does your wife enjoy spending time in the wood-lot?" I asked.

"No. She doesn't like going there. She's more of a city girl and isn't into the outdoors. You see, I used to dump fish out there that we used for baiting and tagging bear in conjunction with Cornell University. My wife didn't like the smell of rotting fish."

"Let's talk about living off the grid," I said. "How can anyone ever fully live off the grid if they've got to pay taxes?"

"Where my camp is, a lot of people live in campers. But once you build a porch, it gets taxed as a dwelling. If you don't want it taxed, you have to move the trailer a few feet every six months."

"You did your time," I said. "How are you treated now?"

"I'll always be considered a felon. It will always be on my back. When I get pulled over, they come up to the car with their guns drawn. But here in Rouses

Brandon Racine, Village Historian, Rouses Point, New York

Point, I'm known as Santa Claus. My wife is Mrs. Claus, and my daughter is one of the elves. I did the Christmas tree lighting. I'm the town's Santa Claus. Have been for years."

When I left Brandon's office, I jumped into my car and headed south on US-11. While following the shoreline of Lake Champlain, I thought more about what Brandon had told me. I was like a dog that tilted its head sideways, as if trying to understand what had just happened. I had no doubt Brandon was the most interesting person I had met up until then. On one hand, he did not seem to have much empathy for the person who had died as a result of the crash he had been convicted of committing. Yet, during all the years after he was released from prison, he had been the village's Santa Claus. Though Brandon and I did not agree on most anything, especially politics, I enjoyed our conversation and thought of him as a friend. I doubted whether I'd enjoy a feast at his woodlot because the critters he ate were not to my liking. Yet, I would have been interested in seeing how he'd managed to become energy efficient. Maybe someday. As I kept driving toward Pittsburgh, where I planned to stay that night, thoughts of Brandon swirled in my head. I laughed out loud when I thought of him trying to catch a porcupine. I wondered whether there was such a thing as a porcupine glove, one that kept quills from cutting up one's hand. I was still laughing when I arrived at my motel.

Then, while registering, I laughed a lot more when I overheard a conversation between a French Canadian gentleman and the woman at the front desk. The gentleman who had just checked in said, "I found a cat in my room."

At that, I did a double-take. I might have even exclaimed, "Huh?"

The woman behind the desk, not quite understanding, said, "But, sir, you paid extra to room your cat for the night."

I think I was giggling when I heard that. And then I overheard the man say in broken English, "I'm not talking about my cat. It was in the room already. The cat was under the bed."

The desk attendant repeated what she had already said, that he had in fact paid extra to house his cat in the room.

At that, the man said in a firmer voice, "I'm telling you it is not my cat. My cat is in a carrier."

The attendant then took another tact. "Sir, are you sure you didn't bring a spare cat that you are trying to rid yourself of?"

To which the man said, "Come to my room. I will show you."

Begrudgingly, the desk attendant followed the man toward his room, and, not wanting a cat myself, I decided to wait at the counter, thinking, *In over thirty years of travel I thought I had seen it all . . .*

Apparently not.

I laughed my way back to my room.

And I laughed again the next morning while checking out, when I overheard a very loud discussion/argument between the motel manager and a housekeeper.

"Did you get that cat yet?"

"No, that cat is wily. It runs out of one room, then finds another room when we're doing our cleaning. Doors are open, it knows that."

"Well, keep the doors shut."

"Can't, need to pull the vacuum from room to room."

"Close the doors behind you."

"Can't, need to go from room to room. Can't do as many rooms if we do that."

"Catch it!"

"Can't, that cat's wily."

"Bait it with food, then catch it!"

"Can't, that cat don't like me. Figured out I don't like cats!"

"Then, what you gonna do?"

"Not my job, you're the manager. You figure it out."

I was laughing so hard when I grabbed an English muffin from the breakfast counter that I almost spilled the terrible coffee they were offering. As I got into my car, I was still laughing, all the while thinking, *In all my years of travel, I've never experienced anything like that.*

I needed to get back to US-11 to continue my way west to the Cornwall, Ontario, border crossing. But first I diverted to the Village of Champlain, a historic town named after the French explorer Samual de Champlain. While driving through, I noticed parts of the city had fallen into disrepair, and several storefronts were vacant.

Then I saw what appeared to be a new business in the historic downtown and decided to stop. There I met a woman who had recently moved to town from Vermont and was using her imagination to fill her store with small gifts, kitchen wares, and artistic crafts. On one wall was a fully stocked snack bar with coffee, soda, and other treats. She had painted the interior in fun colors, all geared to test the waters to see which items locals and visitors would enjoy. She asked whether I'd like a cup of coffee, and we sat at the counter for a chat. I asked about the museum next door because just before entering her store, I had knocked on the museum's door, and nobody answered.

The woman said, "Here's her phone number. Why don't you give her a call?" And that's how I met Celine Racine Paquette, who popped into the museum to meet with me, without much warning.

With a warm smile, Celine greeted me. "Come on in, I'd like to show you around."

After I had followed her through the museum for a while, I asked Celine where she was from originally.

"I live here in Champlain and grew up here. Left for college for a twenty-seven-year career. When I returned, I married a man from here who had an insurance agency. I joined him in that. That's my full circle."

"Where did you go to school?"

"I went to SUNY Plattsburgh, graduated with a degree in nursing, and worked in a school district south of Albany. While there, I earned a master's and a doctorate and eventually became a school principal in Ticonderoga."

"If you started in Albany, worked your way north to Ticonderoga, and ended up farther north in Champlain, it must have been quite a journey."

"It was. And you're right, I ended up here."

"So, how did you get interested in the museum?"

"It's a long story. Larry, my husband, had a heart condition, and five years after we were married, he died. I decided to take over the insurance agency and ran it for the next sixteen years. During that time, I became very active in the community. I was a county legislator for twelve years. Then I was appointed by the governor to be on the board of trustees of the State University of New York. During that time, I served on a lot of boards. I would say, I could build a house with all the boards I served on. In fact, I continue to be on boards even today. I'm just about to head for a board of trustees meeting at Saint Michael's College in Colchester, Vermont."

"Where does the museum come in?"

"Ever since I was young, when I walked by this building on my way home from school, I dreamed of owning it. When I returned to Champlain, however, it was a bank. Yet, because it had been built in 1880 and no improvements had been made, it was in bad shape. After the bank closed, a Canadian purchased it and was trying to turn it into office space. But try as he might, the kids kept vandalizing it."

After a sigh and a long pause, she said, "I don't know what I was thinking, but I decided to purchase it. And once I did, I started restoring it."

The building was gorgeous. Though other buildings in the downtown were in need of remodeling, I couldn't believe her building had ever been in disrepair. It had a stained-glass window of the French explorer Samuel de Champlain above the entry door and a collection of antique skis depicting the era when a company in Champlain made downhill skis. There were photos and scale models of boats once built locally. Meeting rooms had wooden furniture and flat art files, which I assumed were filled with photos and other artwork. I just could not imagine the cost and the effort Celine had put into the museum.

"Was that when you decided to turn it into a museum, when you were finally able to acquire the building?" I asked.

"Yes, I loved the look of the building, but I do have a story to tell. When I was growing up, this room that we're in was the town library. And when I attended school at St. Mary's Academy, the Catholic school in Champlain, I always walked by here on my way home. I was probably five years old at the time, and I could smell the books in that old library back then. So, even at five, I knew it was a library and that I loved books."

At that point, Celine picked up a book that looked to be written in French, carefully ran her fingers over the cover's raised type, and said, "Growing up, I didn't speak English because I was raised in a family that only spoke French. Interestingly, the librarian only spoke English, yet we got along just fine. In fact, the summer that I graduated from high school, I worked downstairs in the bank."

Celine said her husband had still been alive when they purchased the building and that they had no idea what they'd do with it.

"What made you want to turn it into a museum?" I asked.

"Well," she said, "I figured it would be a good place to move my books, along with some of the artifacts I had. So, that's how it all started—and I've been at it ever since."

I wondered how in the world Celine had been able to start a museum. In my hometown, we needed taxes to pay for ours. I asked, "When did all this happen?"

"I bought the building in 2002 when I was still at the insurance agency, and I hired a contractor right away to work on it. At the time, there was no heat in the building. We even had to do the sheet rock. Windows were broken, there were no stairs, and the floors had deteriorated. The building was in bad shape. It was slow going. The contractor worked at this whenever he could. But later, when I sold the insurance agency, I realized I needed an office. After that, the job was completed in record time."

In addition to Celine's own collection of books and artifacts, she also purchased items online. "I have the largest collection of Franco American books in the state. Downstairs in one of the bank vaults, we were able to archive the papers and other materials. There is quite a lot of reference material about the workings of the village, all now catalogued and stored in acid-free boxes."

As we talked, Celine showed me school attendance records from as far back as 1906 and old yearbooks from the local school. She told me she wasn't Acadian, and her ancestors were from Quebec.

"What do you think of Champlain?" she asked.

Trying to be both accurate and complimentary, I said, "My first impression is that Champlain has beautiful buildings, but they could use a little work."

"I agree."

Celine's grandfather had come to the United States in 1928 and bought a farm. At one time, while she was growing up, there were a lot of small farms in the area. Her father had a dairy farm, as did many of his friends.

Celine Racine Paquette, President, Samuel de Champlain History Center, Champlain, New York

"It was a lovely little village. In fact, people can't believe what it looks like now. But we have tremendous pictures of Main Street from way back, filled with hotels and restaurants and a lot of stores owned by people who lived here and kept nice homes. Lots of possibilities here," she added, looking at me with confidence

"The Canadian border is just across the river. We have a great relationship with Canada. It's where we go to get our hair done, to buy groceries, and for other goods and services. We are starting to see a few Canadian businesses interested in relocating here. In addition, our beautiful health center was built recently and has around a dozen doctors on staff. Many of the physicians live in Montreal and commute in, but we hope they will relocate here."

As a rural community in upstate New York, Champlain once relied on the Chazy River to drive its economy, with boat building its main industry. But as manufacturing jobs diminished, so did the population of Champlain. Celine loved her hometown, and though the town was still a little rough around the edges, things were gradually improving. It was the mark of a good citizen to help move things forward—and Celine was doing just that.

I thought of my own hometown and my involvement in its development. During that time, the area was shifting from manufacturing to tourism. Just as in Champlain, our downtown buildings were in various states of disrepair. But as more people like Celine got involved in our central business district, buildings were sold, fixed up, and rented to businesses with a better chance of survival. Gradually, as more buildings were improved, people wanted to live in our downtown area. That led to an explosion of growth as former factories were turned into condo developments, and the second and third stories of buildings transformed from being low-end rental units into upscale condos. Now the place to live for those looking for great housing is in our central business district. And it all started with local people, like Celine, who loved their town and wanted it not only to survive but to thrive.

As I drove out of Champlain, I kept thinking about what a gift to her town Celine had become. In my mind, with my experience in watching towns emerge from the past to become places where people with newly created jobs wanted to live, I predicted that at some point, Champlain would be a very desirable place to live. With people like Celine driving the economy forward, they would make that happen.

12

On my way to the border crossing at Cornwall, I passed by good-size farms with well-cared-for homes and barns on hilly land with spectacular views. I took a few side trips to head north to see places that overlooked the St. Lawrence

River. And before I knew it, I was in Rooseveltown, about to cross the Seaway International Bridge and enter Cornwall, Ontario.

Cornwall. That was where my border crossing didn't go so well.

I had some history here. Earlier in my career, I had a marketing and communications company that did a lot of work in the contract furniture industry. My largest client had a wood furniture manufacturing division in Toronto. My client told me it was never a good idea to tell Canadian border agents that I was entering the country on business but instead to say I was there for pleasure. The reason was that the Canadian government would want to know exactly what that business was, whom I was seeing, and whether there was any potential for Canadian secrets to seep out to other countries.

I wasn't sure whether what my clients told me was true, but their advice always worked. At least, until this crossing.

At the Cornwall, Ontario, crossing station, after I'd spent several days in New England, I was grilled by a kind, nice, agreeable border agent who asked my reason for wanting to enter Canada. I said I was there for pleasure. When she asked how many days I'd be in Canada, I said I wasn't entirely sure, possibly a week or more. The kind, nice, agreeable agent then asked where I would be staying. I said in various places, and I wasn't sure where. Now the kind, nice, agreeable agent was suspicious. At that point, she looked at the amount of stuff I had in my car.

"You are carrying a lot of items, eh?"

"Yes, I don't exactly travel light."

With that, she signaled me to drive over to a numbered parking space next to the border-crossing office. Once parked, I was instructed to go inside the building. There I was greeted by not one, two, or three agents but four. The officer in charge asked for my license and keys, then told me to sit in a glass-enclosed area.

"Can I be of any help?" I asked, wondering whether I should follow him to my car to help them inspect my possessions.

His stern response: "Sir, just sit over there."

I believe when he left the room, I heard the sound of a door latch, sorta like a door in a prison, as if he had locked me into the glass-enclosed space.

Many minutes went by, and I thought about all the stuff in the car, from granola bar wrappers to paper coffee cups to things lying on the passenger seat, camera bags, luggage—and, damn, what about all the dirty laundry in bags in the back seat? There were maps from at least twenty states. A sleeping bag, a sleeping pad, and two pillows. All of these thoughts jumbled together in my head as I waited. Ten minutes. Twenty minutes. A half-hour. Now I was wondering whether they'd even let me into the country.

Forty minutes, then one, two, three, four. All the officers came back in. All four huddled. Five more minutes passed. Then the agent in charge summoned me to the counter.

"Sir, tell me what you are really up to."

With that statement, I began nervously shivering from the top of my head to my toes. I was so scared I would have admitted to a crime I'd never committed, gotten on my knees and begged for leniency, and sworn allegiance to the king. I would have pretty much admitted to anything.

Then, with all the strength I could muster up, I said, "Officer, I'm writing a book. It's about travel. I'm going to be gone a couple months. That's why all the stuff."

"Sir, why didn't you say that when you first came to the gate?"

I told him what one of my clients had advised me to say decades earlier when I did business in Canada.

Then the agent cracked a smile. A big smile. "Sir, you are living my dream. Here are your keys and license. Enjoy your time in Canada." He shook my hand. "Next time tell the agent you are a writer. We like it when people come to visit here and want to write about our country."

Relieved, I climbed into my car and headed to a little motel just north of Cornwall. At the front desk, I asked for a first-floor room because it had been a hell of a long day, I had a lot of gear to unload, and I was tired.

That brought a smile to the man at the counter. "No problem, sir, we only have one floor." Ugh!

The next morning I began my drive from Cornwall to Sault Ste Marie, Ontario. To help me get there, I first stopped at a Tim Horton's and picked up a bagel with a schmear and a large latte to go.

Here I was, following the 10,000-mile rural route I had laid out in my studio back home. So many challenges to solve. One, finding an alternative route through Canada that did not go through the cities and the suburbs of Montreal and Ottawa. Frankly, the same issues I had in finding that rural route still haunt me as I write about it. The problem was less about the route and more about me, my feelings of insecurity, because in grade school, I did everything I could to avoid learning any foreign languages. I took a year of German—that was it. And I doubt whether I paid attention in class.

Today I was traveling in an area of our two countries, known as Francophone communities, where having a working knowledge of French would have come in handy. In truth, I was now paying for my lack of learning while I was the age when education actually would have sunk in. I remembered why I'd had a problem learning in school, something I'd never told my guidance counselors about. It was during the time when I was the victim of bullying and had lost much of my self-confidence. So, instead of paying much attention in class, I spent most of my time in the band room where the band director had me do various chores. Now, thinking about it, I wonder if he realized I had some issues at home, had taken pity on me, and allowed me hang out with him instead of insisting I go back to class.

As I continued to think about my lack of self-confidence in school, the farmland north of Cornwall kept rolling by. The farms were a mirror image of those across the St. Lawrence in upstate New York. Even though many towns in and around Cornwall were French settlements, Cornwall—named after the English Duchy of Cornwall—though an English settlement, had a fairly high percentage of Francophones.

And although the Canadians were known to be peaceful and courteous people, the English of Ontario and the French of Quebec didn't necessarily get along.

I wanted to find rural roads to the small community of Arnprior because that was where Canada 417 became the two-lane Route 17, heading west. Though it was known to many travelers as the Trans-Canada Highway, people who lived along this two-lane highway still called it Route 17.

The terrain was relatively flat and consisted of farmland with stands of mixed hardwoods. There was very little traffic along the road, aside from farm tractors, combines, and an occasional semi. The area economy along this stretch was Ag-based and made up part of Canada's farm basket. In the few small towns scattered about, I saw farm equipment stores and service dealers, feed sellers, and businesses providing basic necessities, such as gas stations and convenience stores. This route pretty much threaded the needle, avoiding the busy superhighway 401 to the south and the metropolitan area of Ottawa to the north.

I continued past the eastern border of the United Counties of Leeds and Grenville for another seven miles to reach Kemptville. This community of roughly four thousand had shopping, restaurants, medical services, and a historic downtown.

While in Kemptville, I stopped by an outdoor food truck and met the owner, a former farmer. He had sold his multi-generational family farm and moved to Ontario from Quebec because of what he called "the French thing." Not knowing what he meant, I asked him to explain.

"For over a century my family owned a farm in Quebec," he said, "and with each passing year, more and more French was being spoken, and I was unable to break that language barrier." When he hit retirement age, with no members of his family wanting to go into farming, he sold the farm and moved to Kemptville. There, he purchased a well-equipped food truck as his retirement job.

I continued toward Arnprior, and just before crossing Ontario Route 7, I noticed a sign for an organic farm that raised free-range cattle, sheep, and goats. I turned down the road toward the farm but found the gate closed. A sign instructed people to be sure to close it after passing through. A couple hundred yards down the gravel road I discovered the farm, humming with activity.

Worked by Robert Oechsli and Petra Stevenson, Alpenblick Farm was known for their cattle, lamb, and goats; homemade cheese and cheese curds; honey; eggs and farm store; plus hand-cut meat delivered daily to customers.

Robert grew up on a farm in Switzerland; Petra was born and raised in Germany.

Their farm animals were all free range, grass- and hay-fed. All organic. None of their animals were restrained in any way and roamed freely throughout their 200-acre farm.

While I talked with Petra, who was amused by the animals, she'd interrupt to give a rundown on things that were happening.

"Here come the goats," she said. And sure enough, there they came, one after another, all heading to the barn.

Then, a few minutes later, Petra said, "Here come the cows," and just like the goats, they followed one another into a different barn. Next, "Here come the sheep," and, like clockwork, there they were. The sequence repeated itself, over and over. The goats to the barn, followed by the cows and the sheep. Then, the order reversed itself with the sheep heading back out to the field, the cows following, and the goats after that. Each time the parade began again, Petra was just as amused as she had been previously. Her facial expressions revealed how much she absolutely loved what she did.

Robert, who was in bed recovering from a surgical procedure, wanted to talk. He explained that he went to culinary school and worked in restaurants before becoming a trainer of narcotic- and drug-sniffing dogs for the Royal Air Force. Once he moved to Canada, he decided to farm, and Petra joined him in that adventure.

They spoke candidly about an emerging housing project a short distance away. A busy highway had been constructed nearby, along with two other housing developments and a golf course. Many small rural farms were being encroached upon by burgeoning suburbs that not only raised property values, but the new residents also demanded additional services, from better roads to more schools. This made it difficult for small farms to earn any money. People everywhere loved the idyllic look of farms and barns, as if they were on a postcard. Yet, if we lose small family farms, we'd also lose the individualists like Robert and Petra, who add so much to the social fabric of an area.

Over and over, as towns outgrew their boundaries, farms were impacted—especially small family farms that struggled to begin with. The additional zoning laws, government regulations, and higher taxes made the going hard. What Robert and Petra told me during my visit was exactly what had happened elsewhere in the United States where cities occupied the best farmland and were growing outward.

As more suburbs were built, less of the best farmland was available in America. This decreased the amount of crops grown on the most fertile farmland, leaving crop growing to areas with poorer soil and more need for irrigation. On land with no available irrigation where rainfall was less prevalent, people needed to resort to "dry land farming."

As I left Alpenblick Farm, I couldn't stop thinking about the challenges farmers like Robert and Petra would face with an influx of more people.

That night I took a room at a mom-and-pop motel in Renfrew, and when morning came, I stopped at the motel breakfast bar. It offered three kinds of cereal, a Belgian waffle maker that looked too difficult to operate, and a dispenser filled with bread, muffins, and bagels, along with jam, honey, and cream cheese. I filled a Styrofoam bowl with dry cereal and grabbed a bagel with a packet of cream cheese. Then I hit the road, heading for Sturgeon Falls. I planned to car-camp there that night.

I was on a mission because I had reserved a spot at a campground near Sturgeon Falls that had no electricity.

On my way there, I decided to see whether I could get a charge for my plug-in hybrid to get power for lights, heat, and air conditioning. All I needed was a charging station with the right configuration to charge my battery. Entering North Bay, a town with several EV charging stations, I figured I could get a charge to last the night.

I stopped at a downtown car dealer listed online as a free charging station. It took me a while to find it because it was mounted outside on the back wall of the dealer's indoor service garage, which had already closed for the day. I was just about to plug in when I noticed a hand-scribbled note on the wall: "This is out of order, and it has been for six months. Please take it off the listing of local EV charging stations." The sign was right; it didn't work.

Undeterred, I headed to the next charging station on my list, on the other end of town next to a big box department store. Half the stations were occupied so I figured it worked. Yet, when I pulled up to a charger, it didn't have the proper hookup to fit my car. Because there was another charging station at a fast food restaurant a couple miles away, I thought I'd give that one a try. But once again, the configuration of the plug-in differed from the one on my car.

A few miles farther away was another charging station—this one owned by a local First Nation tribe. When I pulled up, however, I realized even though the charging station had several adaptors, not a single one fit my car.

While I was there, a man named Don drove up in his fairly new, gas-powered, luxury car. He said, "I couldn't help but notice you seem to be having problems with the charger."

"Yes, the hookup doesn't fit my car."

Don said he had looked into purchasing an EV but was hesitating because he was afraid there were too few charging stations. I explained my plight that day but said that I felt there would soon be more and that any incompatibilities would eventually be fixed.

In the course of our conversation, Don said he had recently lost his wife after she'd battled a long illness.

"How are you coping with your loss?" I asked.

"By working. It's the only way I know how to cope."

He said he'd grown up working on his family's farm, which he inherited after his parents died. Being an unemployed engineer at the time, he said that when he evaluated whether the farm could make enough money to feed his family, he figured that at five hundred acres it couldn't.

"The cost of land has gotten expensive. I knew there was no way to get the money to buy or rent additional acreage. So, instead I leveraged the property to finance the building of a small factory where I could use my expertise to start an injection-molding company."

Impressed with his ingenuity, I asked whether his gamble had paid off. It had. He now had customers in several Canadian provinces, along with many in the States. That intrigued me, as we talked for several minutes in the cold parking lot with a raw wind swirling, Don had studied his options and figured out a way to make a good living and create several jobs. It was the kind of resourcefulness and initiative that could be a boon to rural towns where few full-time jobs with benefits existed.

When I finally arrived at the campground, a hand-painted sign caught my attention. It announced an annual pig roast and dance that was happening that night. At my campsite, I noticed most of the campers were regulars, some who rented by the season. I wasn't going to attend, but then the person in the campsite next to mine invited me, saying it was a regular event held at the end of each camping season.

"You'll feel welcome," he said. "They are good people." So, I decided to check it out.

There was a pavilion with a stage and a dance floor, and a few people outside tended to a pig on a tow-behind roaster. Others stood by a fire and a band setting up their equipment. Surrounding the entire scene were drive-in camping spaces packed with all manner of Airstreams, conversion vans, class A and C motorhomes, travel trailers, fifth wheels, toy haulers, camping trailers, and destination trailers.

In all the mayhem, I talked to a fairly large guy whose name escapes me, who spoke only in broken English. He motioned for me to grab a plate and get into the food line. Another man—I can't remember his name either—invited me to join him at his table. We had a nice conversation about camping and how much his family enjoyed the outdoors as others got up for second and third helpings.

"What do you think of the pork?" one asked, burping.

Another said, "Better hurry before they run out of stuff."

A guy across from me had the nasty habit of picking his teeth with the long blade in his Leatherman.

A group of kids trying to be funny played music with arm farts. I was not interested in joining them.

Before long, I'd had enough. I pretended to walk toward the food line before diverting back to my car. There, I leaned back in my seat and tried to ignore the noise. Though I was tempted to open my window and yell something like, "Enough!" I didn't.

To make matters worse, the Country and Western band soon began its first set. People sang and laughed while I was trying to get some sleep. The later it got, the louder it got. By the time the band started its third set, the musicians were singing out of key. The awful music went on past midnight. I was about to scream or send a volley of bear spray their way. Finally, the racket ended past 2:00 a.m., and my mood was even worse.

I got up at dawn and was still groggy. Even though I still felt a little ticked, I slowly drove out of the campground with my lights off. I did not blow my horn as I left, even though I thought about it. There were remains from the previous night everywhere: campfires smoldering, people wrapped in blankets sleeping in folding chaise lounges, the bandstand filled with instruments. Some guitar amplifiers were still turned on.

I made a left turn on Route 17 and headed toward Sudbury, a 55-mile stretch. Yet, only 10 miles had passed before I was once again distracted. I stopped in Verner at the No Frills Mobil, in front of the No Frills Grocery, to fill my tank. A guy in the station was speaking French. I said, "English," and he said, "Yes." I said, jokingly, "I'm not in Quebec, so what the heck. French?"

I said, now a little more seriously, "I thought fewer than five percent of those living in Ontario speak English." He replied, "But not here. You're in Verner. It's our history here."

He then told me the story of a priest named Charles Alfred Marie Paradis who settled the area back in 1890 when he brought a contingent of French-speaking people from Michigan. His reason for bringing people to Canada was fear. The fear of losing their French language and customs because he could see the future of the United States, and it did not include the French-speaking people who would undoubtedly be Americanized. He told me that to this day, more than 70 percent of the population in and around Verner still spoke French in their homes, and a good number also spoke English, though mostly at work. I then made a quip that only Michiganders could appreciate. "Do you have any Verners in your cooler?"

Having overstayed my welcome, I paid for my gas and headed farther west.

Forty-five miles later, while entering Sudbury, I noticed there were nickel mines everywhere. The tourist trap Big Nickel was proof of that. A gigantic, thirty-one-foot-tall statue of a 1952 Canadian nickel sat atop a hill overlooking the city. Nickel super stacks and chimneys lorded over the area. No doubt, nickel mining had been essential to the growth of the municipality. I spotted large rocky cliffs that were chiseled to clear the way for roads. Within the city of Sudbury's large footprint were two preserves, a provincial park, a bird sanctuary, and multiple city parks. Acres upon acres of toxic tailings from the extraction of nickel were stored in ponds underwater to prevent oxygen from reaching them.

Within the municipality of Sudbury were nine nickel mines, two mills, two smelters, and a nickel refinery. This was undoubtedly why EV battery manufacturers needing nickel were major investors in mines in and around Sudbury.

From Sudbury, I drove along the Spanish River through Espanola, Webbwood, Massey, Walford, and Spanish, where the river emptied into the Georgian Bay. Ten miles later, seeing a sign for Elliot Lake, I wondered, *Isn't that where the Canadian government used to mine uranium?* To find out, I headed north on Ontario Route 108. A couple miles north of the city of Elliot Lake, I located the Stanleigh Mine, one of the many closed uranium mines in the area. It operated from 1957 to 1996 and was owned and operated by Rio Algol, Ltd. A "no trespassing sign" on the road leading to the former mine read: "Uranium mine tailings management area operated under radioactive waste facility operating license by the Canadian Nuclear Safety Commission."

I spoke with a woman who was walking her dog. She said she was the owner of a nearby house. I asked what that sign meant. She said a few years back, the Canadian Nuclear Safety Commission found that Rio Algom was operating the mine "below expectations," due to radium releases from the effluent treatment plant. And the tailings that were held under water had a half-life of thousands of years. When she tried to sell her home, there were no buyers. So, she remained in the area with the hope that her health wouldn't be negatively affected.

After the mines closed, the population of Elliot Lake plummeted from a high of 26,000 to around 6,000. It had since leveled out at around 11,000, after major investments in affordable homes combined with low taxes, an influx of immigrants, and the redevelopment of older buildings, which, as a result, attracted healthcare workers for Elliot Lake retirees.

While driving through Elliot Lake, I stopped by Miners' Memorial Park along the shores of Horne Lake. There, I found several monuments dedicated to those who had once mined uranium. In the park, I noticed a guy in blue jeans and a matching jacket, toking on a cigarette while leaning against an old pickup. He stared straight ahead as if he were looking at past ghosts.

"Were you a miner here?" I asked.

He glanced at me, then looked away. "Yeah, I mined here."

And that was all he'd say.

He used the smoked cigarette to light another, then flung the old one away and ground it into the dirt with his muddy boots. Minutes passed, and, without saying anything else, he jumped into his pickup and drove away.

On returning to Route 17, I noticed a noise coming from one of my tires. It was probably the result of my driving over something while cruising around Elliot Lake. By the time I entered Blind River, the tire was going flat.

I'd forgotten that it was Victoria Day, and no repair shops were open, but I found the name of a 24-hour towing service. Responding to the call was the towing services owner, a man by the name of Jesse.

After a tow to his garage, we got to talking as he jacked up my car, removed the tire, and began to patch it. Jesse was in a grumbling mood, perhaps because I had disturbed his holiday. As he applied the patch and got ready to reinstall my tire, he complained about the shortage of young people willing to work the trades. Now in his sixties and not in the best of health, Jesse said he needed help. But nobody was willing to take the job. At one point, he said, "Young people just don't want to work!" And right before I drove off with my car, he said, "Nobody wants to get dirty anymore."

An hour later, I was passing through the Garden River First Nation. While there, I stopped at the Garden River railroad bridge along Route 17B to check out the spray-painted notice on the side of the bridge: THIS IS INDIAN LAND. This statement of pride and protest had been posted by the Garden River First River Band of Ojibway People.

I thought, *I get it.* Every time native people signed a treaty with my white European forefathers, before the ink from the quill pen dried, the treaties were broken. It happened in 1850 when Chief Shingwaukonce ("Little Pine") signed a treaty with the Canadian government on behalf of his people, for the permanent establishment of a First Nation settlement on land near Sault Ste Marie, Ontario, where the Garden River emptied into the St. Marys River. The traditional land had been the home of the Garden River First Nation people for thousands of years. But as people who didn't record their history through the written word, the tribe always relied on telling their story through legends passed down through their oral tradition.

Many years later, when the Route 17 bypass skirted the reservation, the First Nation people objected to naming the road Highway 638. They erected their own signs naming the route Highway 17B, which the Canadian government eventually agreed to enforce.

Yet, another story also began in the Garden River First Nation. Nolan—a mother of twelve and the widow of Stan, who had died a decade earlier of heart failure—was killed by a drunk driver. She was only thirty-nine. One of her sons, Ted, went on to a storied hockey career and later became an NHL head coach. Ted, who himself was not averse to drinking, watched as several of his siblings became addicted to alcohol. With the help of others, Ted kicked the habit and started a foundation to empower young indigenous women to see the greatness in themselves. Later, joined by his two sons, Brandon and Jordan, who were well known in the hockey world, they decided to start a hockey school named 3 NOLANS. It influenced more than 2,500 indigenous youths from First Nation communities to live healthy, active lives and to become role models while learning hockey skills. One of Ted Nolan's brothers, Rick, had painted THIS IS INDIAN LAND on the Garden River railroad bridge years ago.

The Nolan family had lived in poverty in a small house without running water or electricity on the Garden River reserve and had lost everything with the death of their father and later their mother, yet they went on to greatness, proving that people should never give up. Good could happen if people were properly motivated.

At this point, I was only around fifteen miles from the American border in Sault Ste Marie, Michigan—home of the Soo Locks that made it possible for ships to pass from Lake Superior to the lower Great Lakes. An engineering marvel, the locks contributed greatly to the winning of World War II.

While crossing the expanse of the Saint Marys River via the International Bridge, I imagined earlier times when the Ojibway paddled their canoes laden with beaver pelts and had to portal along the river to avoid certain death from the rapids. One of the oldest cities in America, Sault Ste Marie was settled by French missionaries in 1668, but before that, in the 1620s, French fur traders were trading with the Ojibway in this strategic location.

13

It was evening when I arrived in Sault Ste Marie, Michigan, on the U.S. side of the St. Marys River. I stopped along the waterfront near the Soo Locks observation tower and museum. There, visitors, many from other countries, could view up close the ships passing through the locks. On that cold, damp evening, bone-chilling winds howled off Lake Superior. Just then, a giant lake freighter began passing through the locks.

By chance, I met a man from Italy named Alberto who was on a two-month tour of the United States. He said it was a very different kind of journey because he was intentionally taking back roads and minor highways in an attempt to see the "real" America—something the two of us had in common. As we talked, Alberto lamented the struggles that family farms faced in Italy from European Union regulations. A farmer himself, during his trip he toured both a Caterpillar plant in Peoria and a John Deere plant in Moline.

I asked what he enjoyed most about America. Without hesitation, he said the rural areas, places where he could relax and think.

Alberto mentioned touring George Washington's home at Mount Vernon. They were displaying the actual handwritten copy of the 27th Amendment to the Constitution, which took more than two hundred years to pass. The document had three signatures on it: George Washington, James Madison, and Bill Clinton. That impressed him because it showed the consistency and continuity of our government.

"You know," he said, "more people need to see that document because it shows the strength of your country."

All the while, as we talked, a cold north wind was blowing in from Lake Superior. Yet, during our time together, his warm, friendly smile remained.

I felt good to be back in the Upper Peninsula of Michigan—a land so vast, it had taken me years of living there to even begin to understand its rural ways. Although the U.P. made up nearly a third of the state's landmass, only 3 percent of Michigan's population lived there. And with me being born into the other 97 percent, there was no way I would ever be a true Yooper.

While heading west, I decided to take the northernmost roads, a route that followed the shoreline of Lake Superior.

As I passed through the Bay Mills Indian Community, I stopped at the Dancing Crane coffeehouse. There, I met up with Jim Lablanc, who owned it, along with his wife, Cathy. Its logo depicted a crane dancing in the middle of a Native American medicine wheel. Jim was fond of saying, "I went into semi-retirement as a therapist by building a coffeehouse."

Jim offered me a cup of coffee while we talked. That was when I discovered that dark-roasted Ethiopian coffee was so strong, it sent me into the jitters. I told Jim the next time I'd order one of his milder beans. He laughed.

A descendent of the Ojibwa (Chippewa) people who had lived in the Upper Peninsula of Michigan for the last 1,500 years, Jim saw his life as not one but multiple lives, each a different season, much like the colors in the medicine wheel.

I asked Jim whether he'd always lived on the Bay Mills reservation.

"No, I was born near Detroit in Highland Park." I nearly spit out my coffee, thinking, *He's from Highland Park? The city where Henry Ford built the Model-T.*

Then he added, "I had polio when I was young. I was a sickly kid after that and wasn't expected to live."

Jim told me when he was thirteen, his family moved to Detroit, which, he said, "wasn't any fun for me. They put me into remedial classes, so I skipped a lot of school and then dropped out in the eleventh grade. When I was sixteen, I was managing a gas station where I got held up five times. I got seriously injured when I was eighteen with a wound on the hand. I got drafted and went back to high school, which got me out of that round of the draft. I graduated when I was nineteen and got drafted again."

I asked Jim what year that was.

"1969."

"Did you go in?"

"Not exactly. This time, to avoid the draft, I joined the Marine Corps. I was number 34 in the lottery, so I figured the army would draft me. I mentioned to the Marine recruiter that I had crushed my left hand, and it wasn't fully operational. At the time my hand had been in a cast for a year, so I figured the Marines would reject me. My doctor told me that within three weeks, they would either reject me or I'd be in. They accepted me, so I became a Marine and served for three years. Being in the Marines got me into better shape, so I don't have any regrets about it. They put me into aviation school, which was a good experience."

"What did you do after your release?"

"I became a sheet metal trade worker. Then the oil embargo hit in 1973, which knocked the hell out of that industry. I came up here to Bay Mills in 1975 to wait it out. I did a little commercial fishing, some logging, made wood stoves. I didn't go to college until I was twenty-eight. By that time, I had been married and divorced. Had a little girl."

Remembering my own broken marriages, I asked, "How did that affect you?"

"I needed a reset after all that, the Marine Corps and the divorce. To sit down and rethink everything. That's when we came to the U.P. During the reset period, I took all the boundaries away. That's what led me to school. I'm still not sure how that happened because when I tried to enroll, they laughed at me due to my high school grades. The next semester I reenrolled, and once again they asked for my transcripts and laughed at me again."

"So, how did you get into college?"

"Some professors stuck up for me, so they put me in on probation. I ended up getting two degrees, three associates, in psychology, human services, substance abuse, and law enforcement. Lake Superior State College for the undergrad and Northern Illinois University in DeKalb, Illinois, for graduate school. I hold a master's degree in marriage and family therapy. I practiced for twenty-two and a half years, first in Illinois, then with Families First in the Tribal Counsel

Jim Leblanc, Owner, Dancing Crane Coffeehouse, Brimley, Michigan

in Michigan, next in the Bay Mills Heath System as a contractor, and finally in Marinette, Wisconsin, where I did the same thing. I retired in 2006."

I asked Jim how they'd decided to open the coffeehouse.

"When we looked at what we wanted to do in our retirement, we came up with the idea of a café. But soon after that, we attended a coffee trade show, and our interest turned to coffee. It was an eye-opening experience because you begin to look at coffee in a different way. We learned that coffee originated in Ethiopia."

"Ethiopia?" I asked. "No way!'

"Yes, herders were having a hard time locating land to raise their goats. To find vegetation, they drove their herds up into the mountains. Because it was a long journey, they got tired and took a nap. And when they woke up, they saw their goats dancing after eating certain plants. That's how they discovered coffee. In my mind, I said, *Cranes also dance,* so, for our logo, we put a dancing crane in the circle of life, the medicine wheel, as an invitation for the world to come and have a cup of coffee. We decided to call it the Dancing Crane so it would become a gathering place for the community. We combine traditional Ojibwa culture, the culture of coffee, and music, along with the tradition of storytelling. We used the medicine wheel in our logo because it's a good place to start when learning about Native American thought and culture."

Jim told me the logo was based on the four principle medicines: sweetgrass, tobacco, cedar, and sage. Each applied to the circle of life. "When we're walking our path, then we're learning more about medicine that people use and our other relations from the plant world. And from the animal world, we learn more medicines. The more we learn, we become better at medicine. By the time we reach our elder stage, we turn back and try to help the community walk their path. That's the nature of medicine.

"The medicine wheel is not a religion. It's more of a map. I think our ancient elders knew we would get lost. The medicine wheel is always carved in stone so we will know the way back. It's a great way to view the world, a good way to learn what questions to ask."

As I was getting ready to leave, Jim said they planned to retire, but "whoever takes over the business will need to have a passion for it."

I agreed.

We walked out into the parking lot together, and as I jumped into my car, Jim asked where I was heading next.

"To Copper City, by way of Whitefish Point. I've got a friend in the Keweenaw."

"We have friends there, too," Jim said. "We're just too busy to get up there much."

14

On a bluff atop Whitefish Bay stood Point Iroquois Lighthouse, which I passed along the way to Whitefish Point. In an area called "the shipwreck coast," I could hear the waves of Lake Superior calling out to the twenty-nine passengers who went down with the *SS Edmund Fitzgerald.* It sank on November 10, 1975, and the nearby Great Lakes Shipwreck Museum told their stories.

I hiked down the sandy coast a bit, then up a sand dune, where I met a couple of birders looking through spotting scopes. One of the guys said he lived inland and worked for the county, plowing snow and working on roads, depending on the season.

Paradise, a small town south of Whitefish Point, touted itself as the "wild blueberry capital of Michigan." This designation was made possible, I heard, by a wildfire in 1922 that destroyed the land's natural foliage, leaving the area with sandy soil perfect for wild blueberries to take root.

I cut inland from Paradise along M-123 to Newberry, passing Upper Tahquamenon Falls and Lower Tahquamenon Falls. The upper falls had a 48-

foot drop with a torrent of rushing water, while the lower falls was a series of five smaller falls cascading around an island.

Newberry, population roughly 1,500. Today was the first day of firearm deer hunting season, and the buck pole in front of the American Legion was loaded with deer. According to the news, sixteen deer were hanging there.

West of Newberry was a series of tall hills that flattened out at Kings Creek, five miles from Seney. Once a lumber camp with more bars than people, many of the bar brawlers were buried in Boot Hill along the Old Seney Road. Seney was known as the toughest, meanest town in the Upper Peninsula during the late 1800s. One of its infamous residents was Leon Czolgosz, the anarchist who assassinated President McKinley in 1901.

Logs were moved by sleds and big-wheeled carts pulled by oxen, mules, and horses, then floated down the Fox River. Ernest Hemingway made it famous in the short story "The Big Two Hearted River," but he didn't mention the river by name because he didn't want anyone to know his favorite fishing spot. Later, it was said he had fished the Fox River, which ran just north of Seney.

I decided to head north from Seney along M-77 to Grand Marais. Though it had also been a logging town until the late 1800s, its sleepy location along the often wicked Lake Superior now made it an ideal tourist town. Being near the east entrance of Pictured Rocks Nationals Lakeshore, the town drew many visitors.

I'd had a place in Grand Marais for more than ten years and can attest to both its beauty and the lake's fury. People often said, "It's not the end of the world, but you can see it from here."

As a small, isolated town with about two hundred year-round residents, it was a place where everyone knew everyone else's business. I still miss my time in Grand Marais, which ended with my third divorce around a dozen years ago. But with the divorce and no longer having a place in town, I always found it difficult whenever I visited friends who lived there.

Grand Marais had a long history of being a harbor of refuge for ships caught in the storms of Lake Superior, one of only a few sanctuaries for boaters on the Great Lakes.

Stretching for nearly fifty miles west of Grand Marais has been the domain of Pictured Rocks National Lakeshore since October 15, 1966, when it was designated the first national lakeshore in the United States. As President Lyndon B. Johnson signed the bill creating the park, he said, "When our forefathers came here, they found nature's masterpiece."

The area first came to the attention of the country at large in 1855 with the publication of Henry Wadsworth Longfellow's poem "The Song of Hiawatha," based on Henry Rowe Schoolcraft's writings about the Ojibway people. Since then, Pictured Rocks has been a destination for visitors drawn to its sandy Lake

Superior beaches and towering, multicolored sandstone cliffs bordering its western gateway in Munising.

When I first had a place in Grand Marais, the route through the park was a two-lane, dusty dirt road that was nearly impossible to navigate. By the time my place was sold, however, more than a decade later, the road had been turned into a silky smooth, paved road that drove like a dream. It was such a delight that I regularly rode my bike all the way to Munising to enjoy a locally caught whitefish dinner.

During my time in the Upper Peninsula, I laid out a 200-mile bike route that began and ended in Grand Marais. Included on the route were the towns of Newberry, Manistique, Marquette, and Munising. I rode the entire route several times, and friends of mine also rode the route after I left the U.P.

From Munising, the road west snaked along the shoreline of Lake Superior to Marquette, the Upper Peninsula's largest city, passing through Christmas and Au Train along the way. Marquette, population roughly 20,000, had Native American roots going back centuries. While standing near the massive concrete-and-steel ore dock on the lower harbor waterfront, I met a young couple who looked to be in their twenties. Both were wearing dark-green-and-gold Green Bay Packer gear. The young man, looking bewildered, asked me, "What is that?" as he pointed to the ore dock. I explained the historical function and use of the structure, and how the lake freighters would move into position on either side of the dock. They both gave me that open-mouthed "Duh" look, and eventually one said, "Cool," as they walked away.

Though iron ore was still an important industry, it no longer dominated the local economy. Marquette, during the last decades, had diversified, driven by education, healthcare, and a vigorous hospitality industry.

One of the most notable features of Marquette was Presque Isle Park. In 1891, Fredrick Law Olmstead, who designed New York City's Central Park, made a visit to Marquette. When city leaders asked his opinion of the park, Olmstead replied, "Don't touch it." Enough said.

People could access Presque Isle's trails by following the two-mile-long, scenic Peter White Drive. This road winnowed its way around the perimeter of the 323-acre park. Trails took hikers and casual walkers to areas of spectacular beauty, such as the sandstone cliffs overlooking Lake Superior, an inland forest with too many species of plants and trees for me to remember, and the black rocks along its west shore, beckoning visitors to take a cold dive in the chilly waters.

I headed west past the mining towns of Negaunee and Ishpeming, vast forests, and Lake Michigamme.

To reach Craig Lake, near the town of Michigamme, I took a five-mile drive along a rocky, nearly impassable road. I rode along with a good friend who had a vehicle with high ground clearance. Had I not gotten a ride, the trip would have been impossible to make. Once at Craig Lake, the most remote state park in Michigan, I hiked along a trail that had some incredible foliage.

From the Craig Lake turnoff, I continued on to Michigan's Keweenaw Peninsula—a finger that looked as if it were stirring Lake Superior. Copper was first discovered there in 1841 when state geologist Douglass Houghton reported its existence. People by the hundreds headed to the Keweenaw Peninsula to stake claims. Soon more copper came from this area than from anywhere else in the country. The life of a copper miner was difficult due to the long, snowy winters and isolation from his loved ones. Salvation came with the release of the Model T when Henry Ford recruited many of his workers from the Keweenaw to work in his Detroit area factories. As for copper mining in the Keweenaw, by the late 1960s demand for copper had decreased, resulting in the last area mine closing in the late 1990s.

I decided to meet up with an old friend who had recently moved to Copper City in the Keweenaw. I had met Carol Rose the first time on my last day in Grand Marais. At that time, we both had places in Grand Marais. Even though we met on the day I was about to leave the area, we immediately formed a bond of friendship, based on us both being writers and artists. When Carol moved to the Keweenaw, it was to be nearer to her son, Tom Fouts, and daughter-in-law, Sue.

Soon after Carol moved there, Tom and Sue purchased a former bank building that they turned into a restaurant. To show appreciation to their local community, they provided part-time employment to locals, which was sorely needed in most rural places.

While visiting the restaurant, I met one of their employees, a young lady who worked the front counter. At the time, she was an eleventh-grade daughter of an electrical worker employed nearby and a mother who lived in the Carolinas. I asked what she planned to do after high school. I expected that she had some sort of plan but learned she had no idea at all.

With my inquisitive mind in flummoxed mode, I decided to drill down deeper and asked her what she loved doing. At that point, she opened up more, saying, "I'm not sure. My dad asked if I'd like to join the military, but I don't want to."

I continued to press further. "Do you love learning in school?" By her expression, she wasn't into that either. So, I asked, "What classes do you enjoy in school?"

"I'm taking a class in welding in a local training school."

I asked, "Do you love it?"

"Not really."

"How about people? Do you love working with people?"

She said she liked it but didn't love it.

Not giving up, I asked, "Do you like big cities?"

"No," she said, she liked her space. It was a common response by people raised in rural areas who liked where they lived but felt they needed to leave in order to make a good living with benefits.

Tom arrived soon afterward. He had been picking up restaurant supplies. I asked about his growing-up years and how he ended up in the Keweenaw.

"I was born in Muskegon Heights, Michigan, in the lower peninsula," he said, "and grew up north of there in Traverse City. I left after high school and wandered around a bit. I met my wife, Sue, in Wisconsin and moved here in the spring of 1989."

I asked him what kind of work he did in his early years.

"In my youth I worked in grocery stores. I was an apprentice meat cutter as a teenager and as a young man became a professional meat cutter. But the wages didn't match the effort. At the time I had a young family I needed to support, so I started driving an over-the-road truck."

"Long distance or local?" I asked.

"Sorta long distance, but I was home every weekend. I wasn't out months at a time. I've always insisted on being home on weekends."

"What launched the idea of starting restaurants?" I asked "Was it Sue?"

"Yeah, when Sue worked at the school she had summers off, so she took summer jobs like a lot of teachers have done over the years. One day I read in the local newspaper that concessions were open for bid at McLean State Park. I said, kinda half-jokingly, 'Sue, here's your summer job.' Well, we won the bid. And then fast-forward about five years, Copper Harbor concessions came up for bid, and we got a call from the state because nobody was bidding on it. Lo and behold, we won that bid. And then a couple years later when our local bank was closing the branch here, Sue mentioned that the bank had a drive-through that could work for a restaurant. I said, 'Oh, you're a genius.' So, we approached the bank about buying it. We eventually agreed to terms and bought the building. Ever since we've been busy, and that's a good thing 'cause it could have gone the other way. Could be worse. It could be slow."

"Your mother told me one of your goals is to employ local young people," I said.

"We employ roughly twenty-five young people in the summer tourist season. They are all locals, 100 percent from Keweenaw County or nearby Houghton County."

"What comes next once they are finished with high school?" I asked.

"That's a big issue here. So, you grow up in a rural area, and there are only so many jobs. You can go into logging, become a log truck driver, you can work for the college, you can work for a hospital. Those are the good-paying jobs. Other than those, you can work for grocery stores or fast-food restaurants and make only minimum wage. There are not many trades. A couple places have opened up recently right here in Keweenaw County—an electronics manufacturer and a metal fabrication shop—that are paying pretty decent wages. But that's about it."

I asked if he knew the move-out rate, the so-called brain drain, for the Keweenaw. Tom didn't but figured it was high, adding, "Most people leave, but eventually they come back later in life after they retire. The military is an attractive choice. It allows them to see the world, and they have benefits and can learn a trade. If you're going into the infantry, you're not going to learn so much as a trade. But if you're going into carpentry—like, say, you're a vertical engineer—you're learning a trade. Heavy equipment, and you're learning a trade. Truck driving, and you're learning a trade."

I asked whether the price of housing had gone up.

"The prices around here are insane. What concerns me are working-class youths who do stay in the area. They can't afford to purchase homes now because people from the big cities are able to work from home, and they're moving to rural America. People who are used to paying half a million dollars for a house in the city come up here and buy a fixer-upper for around a hundred thousand.

Carol Rose and her son Tom Fouts, Sundae in the Park Restaurant and Ice Cream Shop, Mohawk, Michigan

They think they're getting a deal. In the meantime a local kid who's only making 35 grand a year, how can he save up a down payment for a $150,000 house? So, it's all turning into Airbnbs, and that's hurting rural America."

Still, thinking about it, Tom said, "You can't blame the people selling their houses and getting the best price. A lot of them are elderly, looking to move into something smaller or into assisted living. They're selling their houses and getting the most that they can. That's fair."

I told Tom that the Keweenaw was no different than other places I'd visited. And that the topic of Airbnbs came up everywhere.

That night I car-camped on Carol's side lawn. We talked into the night. She had recently had cochlear implants. Prior to having them fitted, she had learned how to read lips. As someone approaching eighty, an age when so many refused to make any changes in their lives, Carol had learned how to hear again. Cochlear implants could be difficult to master because of the technology individuals were required to know to use them properly.

The next morning I drove west to Ontonagon, a town with a rich past. It had once been a copper boom town and later home of a large paperboard container manufacturer. Those days, however, were long gone. Its location along the shores of Lake Superior hadn't helped the town much. With residents having a median age of nearly seventy, its population had dwindled from 2,500 to around 1,200 since the 1970s. Even with an influx of summertime residents, its local economy had little to offer those in their working years. The local hospital was purchased by an out-of-town hospital that closed it. Then the nearby nursing home closed, resulting in more local full-time jobs being lost. The closest town of any size was more than an hour away, which put commuting out of reach. I stopped by the gas station and bought a box of Boston baked beans. While checking out, I heard a rumor that a nearby copper mine that had closed decades ago might be opening back up. Though the mine might provide good-paying jobs for ten years of mineral extraction, it could be a long haul before the area would bring in longer-term employment.

15

West of Ontonagon, just past the Porcupine Mountains—"the Porkies," for short—was the east end of the Gogebic Iron Ore Range, which ran west for eighty miles. This belt of distinctive Precambrian bedrock had a narrow sliver of iron ore deposits in northeastern Wisconsin and the western portion of the Upper Peninsula of Michigan. The mountain range began near the end of Route M-28, along the Sunday Lake dock in Wakefield, and ended in areas near Ashland, Wisconsin.

I stopped in Wakefield, Michigan, to check out a statue titled *Nee-Gaw-Nee-Gaw-Bow* ("Leading Man") by Peter Wolf Toth. Carved out of a single pine tree, the twenty-foot-tall statue was one of the Whispering Giants created to honor Native Americans. Toth had carved seventy-four similar statues with at least one in every state, plus in several Canadian provinces. Toth was twenty-four years old in February 1972 when he completed his first sculpture, a stone Indian head, carved from the cliff at Wind and Sea Beach in La Jolla, California. Later that year, Toth switched to wood as his medium of choice when he selected a dead elm stump in Sand Run Park in Akron, Ohio. He said at the time, "I will make a sculpture of an Indian, to honor them, in each of the fifty states." When he finished the statue in Wakefield, it was his fifty-ninth.

At the statue I met an old friend, one I had last encountered in Rouses Point, New York. From the statue, I could see a stoplight where M-28 ended and my old friend, US-2, began. A friend that would accompany me once again and take me all the way to the Pacific. It would be with me when I skirted Glacier National Park and would be my constant companion along the plains of North Dakota. It would lead me when I once again visited the Fort Peck Tribes' Reservation and would take me near the place where my friend Enright Bighorn, Sr., was buried. It would carry me through the Cascades and get me close to the Grand Coulee Dam.

So I turned right at the stoplight and drove onward through the Gogebic Range, which itself came on with a bang and petered out with a whimper.

On September 16, 1886, the *Chicago Tribune* trumpeted the beginning of the initial iron ore boom along the Gogebic Iron Ore Range in a story that began with the following: "Hundreds of people are arriving daily from all parts of the country and millionaires are being made by the dozens."

And over the next eighty years, the high-grade iron ore produced in the Gogebic Range led to a series of booms and busts in the cities and the counties that made up the 80-mile-long area of iron ore deposits. Iron ore production peaked in the 1920s, had a brief rebound during World War II, then steadily declined until 1967 when the last mine on the Gogebic Range closed.

Starting in the 1920s, each of the counties and the towns along the Gogebic Range lost population, with some still losing population even now.

The four counties that made up the crescent-shaped area of land that comprised the Gogebic Range are the Gogebic and Ontonagon counties in the Western Upper Peninsula of Michigan and the Iron and Ashland counties in northeast Wisconsin.

County	1920 Population	2020 Population
Gogebic	33,225	14,320
Ontonagon	12,428	5816
Iron	10,261	6137
Ashland	24,538	16,027
Total	**80,452**	**42,300**

During this same time, from 1920 to 2020, the population of the United States grew from 106 million to 331 million. Had the counties of the Gogebic Range grown at the same rate as the United States, the population in the four counties would have grown to a stunning 245,000 as opposed to 80,000.

In this area of the country, immigrants from Finland, Ireland, Scandinavia, Sweden, Germany, Croatia, and Italy, along with French Canadians, came to work the mines.

Ironwood, Michigan, was the city where the population dropped the most. In the 1920s, the population peaked at 15,739, and a hundred years later, it had dropped to 5,545 in the 2020 census. And though the population decreased, there were now signs of recovery as more people were attracted to living there and put the city back on the map. Tourism also revived the area. Many city officials, businesspeople, and members of the general population had done their part, as had Michael Meyer, who served as executive director of the local Chamber of Commerce.

Michael Meyer had spent the entirety of his life heading north after being born in Red Bud, in southern Illinois. After a year, his family moved farther north to Mendon; he attended college in Madison, Wisconsin; and then he headed north once again to Appleton. After that, he accepted the position in Ironwood.

When I met Michael Meyer, he was wearing his trademark bib overalls, To better understand Michael, his education was in historical geography because of his interest in twentieth-century urban population patterns. Once educated, though, he turned to other endeavors, initially by becoming an apprentice for a Norwegian house painter who specialized in detailed work on historical buildings. As Michael said about the house painter, "He was looking for someone who liked to get up at six o'clock in the morning and show up promptly at seven. I learned all sorts of things about residential and commercial woodwork painting because he had been taught by people from the 1920s. And all the buildings we worked on were historic projects. I found that to be a fascinating process. In fact, I wish I were still doing it because it's great fun restoring old stuff."

Michael eventually settled down and moved to Appleton, where he stayed for about thirty years and had a variety of jobs. He principally continued his painting business and took a position teaching middle school classes at a small rural Catholic school for ten years. "It would have been nice if I had been a little younger than my fifties before starting out with young people who acted like four-year-olds."

After raising two families during two marriages in two different Wisconsin towns, Madison and Appleton, Michael found himself needing a change. That was when he moved to Ironwood. According to him, "My introduction to Ironwood came when my wife at the time asked me to accompany her to where she had been born. Her father had been a miner from the 1930s to the '50s before the mines closed. So, even though my wife at the time had been born in Ironwood, she did not grow up here because as the mines died, the miners had to find employment elsewhere. Her father ended up in Denver, Colorado, working for the Gardner Denver company, making mining equipment. That was my introduction to Ironwood in 1985, when I first saw this community."

I asked Michael what shape the town was in when he first laid eyes on it.

"It was a very sad-looking community at that time. Many streets were unpaved, and it was full of empty buildings. The depot, where I sit now, was boarded up and in danger of immediately being torn down by the city. After my former wife's parents moved back, however, during the course of driving back and forth from Appleton for several years, I began to notice that here within the Gogebic Range, things were beginning to change. Younger people got into local government, the existing businesses went through a transitional period as they passed on to younger family members, and people started to fix some of the infrastructure. They paved streets, put up lights on the streets, and tore down some of the derelict buildings. By the early 2000s, people had begun to discover the town."

"So, when did you decide to move to Ironwood?"

"In 2014. I wanted to move so I purchased a small former miner's house for $14,000 and began fixing it up."

"How did you end up running the Chamber of Commerce?"

"Indirectly, through people I had met here, I found out the Chamber of Commerce was dead, and they were looking for somebody to try to restart it. I said, 'I don't know anybody here,' and they said, 'That's why we want you because everybody around here remembers what everybody's brother did to everybody else since the 1950s after the mines closed, and having a local be a chamber person has not worked out well.' So, I took on this little position, and over the course of years, I've managed to get the chamber built up to about 250 members. Now we have all of the services that usually go with a Chamber of Commerce and are able to contribute back to the community, sponsor events, host educational sessions, have visitor brochures, and talk to people who stop in. That was my transition from Wisconsin to this place. Though I'm still a Yooper in training, I am working

Michael Meyer, Director, Ironwood Chamber of Commerce, Ironwood, Michigan

on that Yooper accent, and it's getting there. Plus, they never made me give up my bib overalls."

As Michael said that, I thought, *I'm glad there is no dress code,* because I was wearing an old black T-shirt, trail shoes covered in dirt, and a pair of pants that looked like they'd been through the Civil War. It was how I had dressed since closing my marketing and graphic design business, where I was required to wear a different pressed shirt, tie, and suit each day.

During our conversation, when Michael talked about his passion for detail during his house-painting days, I thought about my own passion for music. I was sure Michael could appreciate it because he had become the organist at the local Methodist church. In my case, while in college I was on a track to become a music teacher. But when I saw that my father's store needed a lot of help, I left school to help him out. My regret was that I gave up on my own passion. And though I did eventually go into the arts, it was as a photographer, a documentary filmmaker, and a writer. I still wish I had done more with my music training.

To unwind, I headed to Black River Road, which took me to where the Black River emptied into Lake Superior. Then I took out my camera and focused on the lighthouse. It was a happy place for me, being near water and having a lighthouse to boot. I stayed there until well past dark when I packed up my gear and headed to the Classic Motor Inn. I stopped by the motel office to spend a little time with owners Bob and Annette Burchell. After a chat about this and that, I headed to my room.

The next morning I met with local historian Ivan Hellen, who hung out in Erwin Township, just outside Ironwood. Ivan was a guy whose family tree was burnished with iron ore and copper, the two forms of mining that had been in the Upper Peninsula.

Getting to know Ivan required me to do a lot of hiking and snowshoeing. Ivan was what I would call a "worker bee who liked working outside." He also liked getting things done and often started on new community projects before he'd gained the buy-in from community leaders. He was a local and remembered when his boyhood school buddies suddenly began to disappear. He grew up during the gradual, deliberate shutting down of the iron ore mines. "I'd go back to school after a summer off," Ivan said, "and many of my friends had moved away. Later I found out that their fathers had either been transferred or been laid off and left town."

During the 1960s, when Ivan was in school, mines along the Gogebic Range were shut down, one by one, never to open again.

When I first met Ivan, he was digging out heavy brush to uncover the entrance to one of Ironwood's former iron mines. The project, for the City of Ironwood, had become Miners' Memorial Park. Ivan told me, "I always wanted to place signs at the entrances of the former mines and establish a trail to walk from mine to mine. One day in the library I was shown a map that identified all the mine sites. To me, it was important to mark them to honor the miners who worked there."

Ivan came from a mining family. "My grandfather worked in two different iron ore mines, forty-three years underground, the most dangerous type of job. Tough as nails, he was in charge of shoring up the timbers that kept the mine from caving in. He worked at the Newport Mine, which had a maximum depth of 3,260 feet. Later he worked the Geneva Mine, east of the Newport Mine. So, after forty-three years, he had two separate pensions. One was for $50 a month, and the other was for $43 a month. After all those years, he got a $93 pension."

Like Ivan's grandfather, his father also worked the mines—in his case, the copper mine in White Pine, an hour away. Both his parents and grandparents had dairy farms to supplement the family income. "The milk man would come with the truck and pick up their milk twice a day. When my grandfather worked, my grandmother did the milking. That's probably why she was such a good milker compared to him. Twice as fast."

"Milking the old-fashioned way?" I asked.

"Yes. There were thirty-five dairy farms right here in Erwin Township, where we lived. Everything was done by hand. But when they went to pasteurization of milk, they put the small farmers out of business because they couldn't afford to buy bulk stainless steel milk tanks and milking machines. You couldn't milk by hand. Everything had to be sterile. I don't know why it became such an issue when, for a couple hundred years, people milked by hand."

As Ivan said that, I thought, *Pasteurization saved lives because before it was put into practice, milk was a common source of the bacteria that caused tuberculosis, Q fever, diphtheria, severe streptococcal infections, typhoid fever, and other foodborne illnesses.* Instead, I said, "Tell me about your schooling here in the township."

"The school here closed when I was in the eighth grade. We were transferred to the city school in Ironwood. We learned that city kids weren't as disciplined as us country kids. If we messed up, we knew what would greet us when we got home."

Ivan said that during his growing-up years, "We worked on our farm—actually, two of them when I also count my grandparents' farm. They were smaller farms but still a lot of work because we didn't have modern equipment."

Ivan learned the importance of manual labor early in life. "When I was around seven years old, we moved out to an old farm, and my father decided to build a new driveway to make it easier to get through the snow. Our job as kids was to pick rocks from a rock pile and throw them into a dump truck, then dump them where we wanted the driveway to be. It was a very large job and took a lot of time. That was my first experience with real work, and I've been working hard ever since." Ivan explained it as the Finish tradition *Sisu*, a hard-to-define word that meant "strength, perseverance in a task that to some people might seem crazy to undertake, almost hopeless."

"My grandparents were a big influence because they had their own history to share. Their parents were both born in Finland. From them, I learned how to churn butter. I watched my grandmother make homemade cheese as my grandfather saved and restored their farm equipment. It was horse drawn and so forth, which was crude, but it never wore out. He told me the fewer the moving parts, the better."

Ivan mentioned how he got his first real job. "When I graduated from high school in 1970, I went to work at a mobile home factory. I got hired because the guy knew I lived in Erwin Township and that I was a good worker. Plus, when I told him who my godparents were, my godfather happened to be his wife's brother. When I started working there, they made pickup truck campers and toppers out of scraps of wood and metal. I worked there for eleven years. The good thing about that job was it taught me carpentry, electrical, plumbing, gas appliances, and skills for using different tools. I'm surprised what a person can learn. Blows my mind sometimes thinking about it."

I asked why he'd left that job.

"When they had that first gas shortage in the 1970s, it did a number on mobile home sales. So, I ended up, for the last four or five years, being the only employee. My job was basically putting sheet metal, trim, and lights on a wood frame. I did everything by myself. It was one of those jobs where there's no benefits, and pay isn't the best. But, boy, you're learning a lot. It came in handy in the future. They closed down in 1981, and I had a daughter at home and a baby on the way in May, and this was March. I don't remember getting panicky because I didn't have a job."

"It sounds like you didn't have time to be panicky."

"No. But then all of a sudden I had three job offers, and I had to decide which one to take. One was a beer-distributing job, and I wasn't too keen on that. Another one was heading up the maintenance at a housing complex, and the third one was maintenance and custodian for the local JC Penny store. After being outdoors in rotten elements, putting together mobile homes, I thought I'd work an inside job for a change. That turned out to be the best decision. I was busy all the time, which made the days go by fast. I loved it. For the first ten years the store was downtown, but then they moved onto the highway in a plaza, a modern new building. I'm not one who likes change, but it had nice new floors that didn't have to be stripped or waxed. I worked there nine years. Super busy. I also worked on computers even though I knew nothing about them. They installed them when the boss was out of town. To get them to work, I had to take a call from headquarters and learn how to program them. I said, 'Tell me what to do.' The computers were on a metal wire stand and had a mouse, something I wasn't familiar with. Well, I didn't know you had to have a mouse pad. Here I'm trying to move this mouse on this metal thing, and the thing was jumping all over, and the guy on the phone was getting upset. It was a nightmare really. I had to learn so much. Someone at JC Penny corporate said they wanted me to be cloned so I could also do work in the Ashland, Wisconsin, store. I went there to help a couple times. They weren't used to someone who worked. I mean, when their cash registers didn't work, I could troubleshoot them and get parts and fix 'em.

"Penny's was a blessing 'cause I had two kids," Ivan said, "and we got really good discounts on clothing. It was 25 percent off—we got that plus our 15 percent discount."

"That's when department stores actually had benefits," I said.

"Yes, plus a savings and profit-sharing plan. So, I ended up working nineteen years there, loving every minute of it. Then in 2000 they closed our store one year short of my twentieth year, so I didn't qualify for any kind of special bonus, although they did give me a lifetime discount. Problem is, ours was the only Penny's within driving range, so it didn't benefit me. When they closed, I took a

Iran Hellen, Director, Erwin Township Historical Society, Ironwood, Michigan

computer course at our local community college. That allowed me to get a job in the shipping department at Jacquard Fabric Products, which also makes Stormy Cromer hats. So, my work with the computers at JC Penny, along with the college course, allowed me to learn a whole new system—shipping products out, rather than checking things in. I worked there sixteen years until 2017 when I retired from full-time work. However, I did keep my two part-time jobs—a seasonal job at Rose Wreath Company making Christmas wreaths and doing maintenance and custodial work here for the township."

"Ivan," I said, "the amount of work you do is quite amazing."

"I didn't tell you about my volunteer work," he replied. "In 1998, I started getting involved in redoing the township hall. We began by moving historical items into it to turn portions of the building into a township museum. But once the number of items being displayed grew, people felt another location would be preferred."

"Is that when you found the old schoolhouse?" I asked.

"Yes, we began to look for a building and found a structure that was intended to be a residence but was instead being used as a storage building. We approached the owner to see if he was interested in selling it. The owner agreed to sell the building for $10,000 with the understanding it would be used as a museum and that the building would be moved off his property. Because we already had a site, we decided to move the building 2.2 miles to where it is now."

Ivan told me that now, two years later, after remodeling the building and developing the site, it was ready for the public. Named the Erwin Township Historical Museum, a project of the Erwin Township Historical Society, the sign on the front said "East End School—1915."

"Everything in the building is like it was originally," he said, "with the exception of a small addition for a meeting room, along with handicapped restrooms." To raise the money, they held several fundraisers. People who gave various amounts could purchase rooms, windows, and plaques in memory of loved ones. Ivan added, "Land was donated so it could be sold to help pay for some of the improvements. We received a grant to build a walking trail. A state grant to buy the computers and printers for a research library, along with a genealogy center. It is a big asset for the township."

I felt exhausted after following Ivan around and hearing his story. He was a man who simply wouldn't accept no for an answer when a project was rattling around in his head. Ivan was old school. He thought that work meant the backbreaking kind. I doubted whether he would ever consider newer kinds of jobs, those now heading to Ironwood, to be worthwhile.

After a few days in Ironwood, where I talked to and met several people, I headed to the Wisconsin border, which was only a few feet away from Ironwood. The Montreal River flowed between Ironwood and Hurley, though it was barely a trickle. I imagined that if I had the speed and enough energy, I could jump it in a single bound.

The first person I met that day was an attorney, Paul Sturgul, one of the first elder law attorneys in Wisconsin. Puzzled, I asked him what an elder attorney did.

"It's pretty simple. Elder law is a relatively new field of American law. It's a combination of traditional trust and estate law and planning for long-term care."

I asked Paul why there was a need for that specialized attorney practice in such a remote region as northeast Wisconsin.

"We have some of the highest percentages of elderly people in America here in the Lake Superior region," he said. "Neighboring Ontonagon County, two counties to our east, in the Upper Peninsula of Michigan, has the seventh-highest number of Americans over the age of sixty-five. Here in Iron County, Wisconsin, more than 30 percent of population is over sixty-five."

"Why do so many older people live near here?" I asked.

Paul, who had lived most of his life in Hurley, said, "This is an old mining area. It had its origins in the mining and lumbering boom of the nineteenth century. After the mines closed many of the workers who lost their jobs decided to stay. As a result, we now have a lot of elderly people, so I've been very busy with my work." He added, "I'm technically a native of the Upper Peninsula, although I was raised here in Hurley. I was born at the Newport Mining Hospital in Ironwood on May 24, 1948. It was the nearest hospital. My parents lived almost their entire lives in Hurley. They were both born in Ashland, forty miles to the west, but by coincidence they both moved to Hurley as children."

I asked about his heritage, where his family was from.

"On my father's side, my grandparents came to the United States from eastern Poland in the late 1880s and early 1990s, first to Scranton, Pennsylvania, and then to Iron River, Michigan, and then to Hurley.

"On my mother's side, my grandparents were born in southern Italy. My grandfather was a water boy on a railroad that came through the Lake Superior region. His uncle was sorta the head of the family because my grandfather's mother died giving birth to twins. So, he was an orphan who came to New York to live with his uncle who worked on the railroad. My grandfather was too young to actually work there except as a water boy. His uncle went back to New York, and my grandfather stayed in Ashland, where he worked in the sawmills. He married my grandmother, who was nineteen years younger than him. They lived in Brooklyn for around six months. My grandfather hated it because he had grown up in northern Wisconsin so they moved back there, and he again worked in a sawmill. Their first daughter, Viola, died of bad milk, my grandmother said, when she was about nine months old. My grandfather realized he wasn't going anywhere working in sawmills, so he went to night school and became the first Metropolitan Life Insurance agent on the Gogebic Range. He did very well selling to his compatriots and others. That's how I ended up in Hurley. My parents both graduated from the Hurley high school and met and got married. I've lived in Hurley almost all of my life, except for seven years as a law school undergrad at the University of Wisconsin in Madison and two years in San Francisco in the mid '80s."

I asked Paul why he went into elder law.

"I've always related well to the elderly. When I was in law school, my best grades were in trusts and estates and also modern American legal history. I had the good fortune of studying under J. Willard Hearst, the founder of the modern American legal history curriculum and the expert in the field. I enjoyed legal history and probate law. I've also been interested in social justice issues. But, like many lawyers, I initially practiced general law and took just about anything that walked through the door."

Paul leaned back in his chair for a couple minutes, as if remembering his early years practicing law. "I can tell you about my own experience, living as a single gay man in this small town far away from all the delights of a big city—especially with most of the townspeople being elderly. I often felt frustrated because I wasn't getting what I expected out of life. But gradually, I concluded that all of these elderly people had so many legal needs, what a wonderful responsibility and opportunity it was that I could be of service to them. I changed my attitude, and instead of being frustrated because life didn't offer me what I thought it should, I was able to realize that life expected a lot from me. My whole life came together, and that realization brought me to where I am right now. It's sort of an existential way of looking at my situation. To answer your question about social justice, I must have been five years old, and one of my early memories was of an elderly Italian immigrant woman who cleaned houses for a living. She lived down the block from me. She had one disabled child who had epilepsy, and I remember my grandmother saying to me in hushed tones, 'Old lady Cheto went on the county.'"

He asked her what "on the county" meant.

"My grandmother had referred to Mrs. Cristina receiving what was then known as 'old age assistance,' the forerunner of Medicaid, when people had to give the county a lien on their homes in order to get help. It was known as signing over your house to the county. That really struck me as a very strange concept in American law, and I wondered, *Why do people have to sign over their homes in order to get this kind of assistance?* Much later, when I realized my true vocation as an elder law attorney—which, at the heart of it, is Medicaid planning, helping people save their money when they need nursing home care—I came across what became of old age assistance liens. It is now called Medicaid estate recovery, which is currently mandatory on estates. So, a lot of what I did was helping clients and their families avoid losing their homes when they had the misfortune of needing long-term care."

That got me thinking of my own mother, who died thirteen years before my father. A year before she died, she and my father crashed their car while on the way home from Florida. Both of them required long-term care but never lost their condo, despite the many hundreds of thousands of dollars Medicaid paid to treat them. Though I wasn't privy to all their finances, I do know they received help from a lawyer in making that possible. I asked Paul whether that was what he meant.

"Yes, it has given me a great deal of satisfaction to help people navigate the Medicaid maze when they needed long-term care. I really enjoyed my work, and I've regarded it as service more than anything else. The money is a nice byproduct, but that's not why I did it." Paul added, "Not only does one have to be poor to get Medicaid, but then the state can claw back the Medicaid it's paid for by taking the person's home. It's just a very strange concept in American law. If the stated purpose of estate recovery is to help reimburse the Medicaid program, it fails at that objective because the actual amount collected is a minuscule percentage of the total Medicaid budget."

Paul talked about inheritance, saying, "It is a deeply held American value, especially to white families and middle-class African Americans. Behind the whole Medicaid program lurks a lot of racism. When LBJ proposed Medicare and Medicaid, Wilbur Mills—the chairman of the House Ways and Means Committee—said to President Johnson they'd go along with Medicare, even though they didn't like it, but that they were not going to allow the federal government to be in charge of financing the healthcare of poor people. By that, he meant largely but not entirely blacks. Because when Medicare came in during 1965, it led to the massive desegregation of Southern white hospitals. Before Medicare, there was a saying that the delivery room for expectant African American women was the hospital parking lot. They simply could not get in, nor could physicians of color get hospital privileges at white hospitals. Medicare led to the desegregation of hospitals in the South. That's a little known aspect of the Medicare program."

We then discussed the future and what Paul would like to see as it pertained to Medicaid. (Unlike Medicare, which is a federal program, Medicaid is run by the states.) He said, "I'd like to see the complete federalization of the entire Medicaid program to make it more like Medicare. I would also like to see a long-term care benefit funded by federal taxes that would not require Americans to impoverish themselves in order to get long-term care."

Paul said, "I came to my practice of eldercare by accident. I just happened to live in an area where there were so many old people, but this was a harbinger of what's happening now across all of America."

"Does that mean elder law practices are now moving to larger cities?" I asked.

"Yes. We have a dearth of professionals in rural America. At one time, lots of professionals who were brought up in rural places would go back to their homes to practice. You don't, as a general rule, see that anymore. There are programs through various organizations such as the National Health Corps where, if you agree to serve for a certain number of years in an underserved area, you can have your medical education debt forgiven. We've had National Health Service Corps professionals come to Hurley. The problem is, most medical professionals leave the area as soon as their obligation ends. Many Americans, especially older Americans, like to go to a healthcare provider whom they think will stick around for a while. And if they know that the doctor with sterling credentials who is coming to Hurley will leave after three years, then they'll go somewhere else. Even though driving far away is inconvenient, they will travel in order to have the same doctor. I remember around ten years ago that a person I knew had gone to a National Health Service Corps doctor and asked, 'How long are you going to be here?' The doctor said he'd be there forever, yet that particular doctor didn't even stay the full three years."

Paul Sturgul, Elder Law Attorney Hurley, Wisconsin

Paul Sturgul's story reminded me of the description of the two cities in the book *Wisconsin, A Guide to the Badger State,* written in 1941, as compiled by the Workers of the Writer's Program of the Works Progress Administration (WPA) during the Great Depression: "Siamese twins, Hurley and Ironwood were born in 1884 and grew rapidly into lusty infants on a diet of lumber and iron ore. By 1886 thousands of men were on the Gogebic Range, cutting timber and digging ore from small open pits. Hurley soon sheltered 7,000 residents and hundreds of transient lumberjacks and miners. 'The four toughest places in the world are Cumberland, Hayward, Hurley and Hell,' it was said at the time, and Hurley was the toughest of all. Lumberjacks and miners crowded its slab saloons; when dead drunk, they were methodically 'rolled' and thrown into the streets. Nearby were the stockades, shacks surrounded by high board fences, where prostitutes were housed.

"As low-grade Wisconsin ore was forced from the market, and Wisconsin forests were exhausted, Ironwood forged slowly ahead, becoming the business and commercial center of the two twin cities. Hurley's population fell as Ironwood's rose. By 1910, little remained of its proud boom days except a reputation for bawdiness and crime, which led Edna Ferber to choose it as the setting of her novel *Come and Get It.*"

This was the reputation of Hurley before the modern era, and it only got worse during Prohibition when fifty-one speakeasys were selling liquor after the government banned it. After Prohibition, during the 1940s, the number of taverns grew to eighty.

But as Hurley matured, after the 1950s, the strip clubs and the bars were relegated to a block along Silver Street, where they remain to this day.

Westward on US-2, the landscape changed to forests, farms, and small towns that evoked the feeling of a Norman Rockwell painting. In the picturesque town of Saxon, the steeple of the St. Ann Catholic Church stood out from the rolling hills.

After seven more miles, I encountered the view from atop Birch Hill, a spectacular wooded landscape that stretched on to the Bad River Reservation. Encompassing 244 square miles, it was the home of the Bad River Band of the Lake Superior Tribe of Chippewa Indians—a federally recognized tribe of Ojibwe people.

Just across the Bad River was the village of Odanah, once the location of the Franciscan Sisters of Perpetual Adoration's St. Mary's Indian School. It was part of a federal government program to take native children from their parents and place them in boarding schools with the goal of stripping them of their native culture. From 1883 until 1969, the St. Mary's Indian School used the federal government's 1819 Civilization Fund Act to instill "good moral character" and reprogram indigenous children. Richard Henry Pratt, a leader of the government program who also founded the Carlisle Pennsylvania Indian School, wrote in his book *The Advantages of Mingling Indians with Whites:* "That all the Indian there is in the race should be dead. Kill the Indian in him, and save the man." Once children were enrolled, the schools pursued the process of "assimilation" through a systematic "denigration and suppression" of Native American culture to get rid of any traditions that whites considered "savage." Students were required to have their hair cut, surrender their traditional clothing, speak only English, and give up their musical traditions. In most cases, the children were sent away to the schools. Bad River was different; their mistreatment happened on the reservation, and the group doing the reprogramming was at a school run by the church.

At the western border of the Bad River Reservation was Ashland, beautiful Ashland. As described by Webb Waldron in his book *We Explore the Great Lakes,* published in 1923, "On one side the towering concrete ore dock shut off the view. On the other stretched a wide, hill-circled bay. Along the shore, close at hand, a sawmill emitted early morning steam, and beyond it lay the roof of a town, and a bell was ringing."

In its past, before French and British fur traders arrived in the 1600s, many tribes, including the Chippewa, had called it home.

With seven miles of sandy shoreline on Chequamegon Bay, Ashland had its initial growth spurt during the late 1800s, due to its proximity to the Gogebic Iron Range. Iron ore was shipped out of Ashland until the last mine closed.

When I entered the city, the remains of the Soo Line ore dock were barely visible any more. Most of it had been torn down in 2013, except for the base, which the city was now turning it into a park. That was the main difference with Ashland compared to many former iron ore towns. Ashland had moved on and decided to embrace the future instead of living in the past. The city of Ashland diversified its economy by using its natural beauty to become a leader in applying sustainability best practices, caring for the environment, and promoting tourism geared to outdoor activities.

Ashland brought in Carver Harries, an artist, to head its regional Ashland Economic Development Center. He told me, "I was in a long-term relationship and living in rural northern Minnesota. My partner and I were thinking about leaving our day jobs and getting an RV and being self-sufficient, meaning we would both have businesses that we would run from our RV while traveling the country."

"What brought you back to Ashland?" I asked.

"My mom lived here. She was starting to have some issues with dementia, and I wanted to be with her during that chapter of her life. It was my impetus for coming back, but I didn't plan on staying."

"How did you notice that your mom was suffering from dementia?"

"At that time she was eighty-three. So, when my siblings first pointed out that she was having memory problems, I didn't see it. But when I started to pay attention, I saw it. We needed to make sure she was taking her medicine on time and getting nutrition and that she wasn't falling. And that fit in with me trying to get my business off the ground. I'd only started it the year before, so I had the ability to live in two different places without it affecting my relationship. Then, when she was napping or watching TV, I could work on developing my business."

"But then you stayed . . ."

"Yes, after my mother passed away five years later, I had decided not to stay, but things changed in my relationship. Plus, I had run out of money to keep my business going. I needed to find a part-time job to supplement my income, and Northland College offered me a position in sustainability coordination."

Carver said that he liked Northland College because it was a private liberal arts college with a focus on the environment and sustainability. So, getting a full-time job there perfectly matched his interests.

"I'd had a very eclectic career by then. I did everything my high school guidance counselor told me *not* to do as far as having security and a career. I had grown up in the 1960s when the path was to find an employer that offered health insurance, benefits, and a pension and stick with them until you retired. Maybe switch jobs once. Any more than that, and you're going to look flighty and undependable."

Since I had not followed the career advice my high school counselor suggested either, I wanted to know what jobs Carver, a fellow artist, had before his position at Northland.

"I had an immense number of jobs," he said. "Different fields. I didn't make any of those decisions about getting a job based on creating a career path or strategizing an estate or anything else. They were all based on relationships, living in many different places and experiencing several different things, which, as it turned out, was a very good nontraditional education for becoming a coach for other folks who wanted to be entrepreneurs. As an example, having been in the Marine Corps, I was able to talk to potential candidates about going into the military. I also worked in law enforcement, was a working artist displaying my art at outdoor art shows, worked at an animal shelter caring for pets, and worked at an independent bookstore."

"So, why did you choose to stay in Ashland?"

"With my mom getting older and my nieces and nephews graduating, I wanted to be here for them. Thinking about it now, I made a lot of choices based on what really ran through my entire life: connections and relationships."

"That must have been why you fit in so well with economic development."

"Exactly, economic development is where massive changes are happening. Traditionally, it was about creating jobs, focusing on manufacturing, transportation, and metrics; it was all about numbers."

I asked Carver whether now it was more about living where you wanted to be.

"Yes, instead of creating jobs to attract people to your community, which is one of those false goals, it's turned to creating quality of life for the people who live there right now."

I asked what did quality of life mean to him, to Carver?

"Quality of life to me is taking care of families, which includes access to quality childcare, availability of housing, access to healthcare and nutritious food, making sure your kids are safe in your neighborhood and in your schools, asking if the elderly who are trying to live independently have what they need. When you focus on those things for your workforce, then they become much more productive, and your entrepreneurs become more creative because they have the energy and the resources, financial and other services, to focus on traditional jobs or even a gig workforce or whatever is their passion."

To clarify, I said, "What I hear you saying is that people stay in a community when that community's quality of life standards match the expectations of those who are moving in."

"Exactly. Now when we attract people to move to our community, they see that our community values match what they are looking for. As a result, they're not moving to a job but instead to the life and experiences they dream about, especially the younger folks who are not as tied into owning things as some of the older folks may be, generally speaking."

Carver told me how his own skillsets matched the expectations of what economic development had now become in that area. "It's right up my alley because I'm about building the connections required by people, businesses, and nonprofits today."

Carver talked about entrepreneurs he normally met with in the center. "Meetings often begin with the person saying, 'I want to start a business, and I'd like you to coach me through the process of developing my business plan.' Once I know their purpose for the meeting, the first thing I have them do is take out a sheet of paper and at the top of the page write, *If this business is successful, what will it do for me, the owner?* Not for their family, not for their community but for them personally. It could be that they want to get rich, that they're going to take advantage of a lucrative opportunity. Maybe they think there is status in being an entrepreneur. Or they might want the freedom to determine their own schedule."

That was what Carver did. He challenged wannabe entrepreneurs to state up front what they wanted to accomplish. In one fashion, he wanted to build a sustainable community, one with real growth, not just in numbers, but in people's lives. It was a challenge that rural communities faced if they wanted sustainable growth and included topics such as childcare and access to it.

Carver felt that as a nation, we should treat childcare centers the way we treated schools. "Why would we treat infants to five-year-olds differently than we treat six-year-olds to eighteen-year-olds? It is an essential service because parents of young children are struggling. There are too few facilities. Grandparents are becoming more often pressed into service in providing childcare."

Carver said that Wisconsin's population was aging and shrinking faster than that of its neighboring states and even more so in Ashland County and the northern region. "How are we going to care for our aging population?" he asked. "Here our health industry is booming with more healthcare providers than we have a right to have for our eight thousand–person population." He pointed out that Ashland offered regional cancer care, an expanded surgery center, and a planned primary care clinic. "The only thing that's keeping us from growing our healthcare segment faster is lack of housing and childcare. We have a need for housing at every level from homes to apartments to condos to senior living. The problem is we don't have enough contractors, trade workers, carpenters, electricians, or other trades to build the housing. How do we attract people here to fill those jobs if we don't have enough available housing for them to live here?"

Carven Harries, Executive Director, Ashland County Development Corporation, Ashland, Wisconsin

One primary goal of the Ashland Area Development Corporation was to help the traditionally underserved communities within Ashland County, including women, Native Americans, people of color, and LGBTQ people. Its huge, 60,000-square-foot building housed several nonprofits and business startups, which was unique for an economic development agency.

I asked Carver what the center offered.

"We have revolving loan funds, so we can provide loans to businesses. We do the coaching and consulting. We can be the fiscal agent for new nonprofits that are starting up that can't apply for grants until they get their paperwork from the federal government that grants tax-exempt status. Other northern Wisconsin counties do not have this jewel like we have, which isn't looking to make money but instead exists to make businesses successful. It's a hybrid incubator. We are a 501(c3), so we depend on fundraising, in addition to help from municipalities. The building was originally a car dealership, then it became a fabric assembly center for Munsingwear, and after that, it was a picture frame manufacturer. Then we took it over. One thing that helps us the most is this building because we rent out space."

In addition, Carver said Ashland had another unique benefit: its location.

"I can close my office, lock my doors at the end of the workday, walk two blocks, and jump in the water of Lake Superior—the greatest, coldest, cleanest lake in the world."

16

I headed west to Superior, Wisconsin, in a roundabout way, taking Wisconsin Route 13, also known as Wisconsin's Lake Superior Scenic Byway. This 90-mile loop road went past the picturesque towns of Washburn, Bayfield, and Cornucopia, as well as the Apostle Islands National Lakeshore.

Washburn, population roughly two thousand, was the largest town in the Bayfield Peninsula. In 1883, its lumber business was booming. Located on a bluff overlooking Lake Superior's Chequamegon Bay and with access to its natural port, Washburn had a prevalence of sandstone outcroppings along the shore. Several quarries sprang up to mine this perfect building material, which was resistant to fire and more durable than wood. It became known as Chequamegon Sandstone, with a desirable combination of red, brown, and white colors. Some notable sandstone buildings housed the Bank of Washburn, the Bayfield Courthouse, the Washburn County Library, and numerous downtown businesses, along with several homes.

At the bookstore downtown that sold volumes of new and used, I squeezed past a guy who was deep into a series of Westerns. We didn't talk. I guess neither of us had a reason to speak. However, while I checked out, the person behind the counter, who was filling in for the owner, couldn't stop talking. With an armful, I got back into my car, which was now heavier than before I'd bookstored myself. With some books under the front seat and others beneath the lift gate, I headed to Bayfield, which was populated by summer residents and tourists who were in the middle of their summer reading. Many of them were waiting to take the ferry to nearby Madeline Island. For centuries, the island was a traditional spiritual center for the Lake Superior Chippewa, along with related tribes of the Anishinaabe that included the Ojibwe, the Odawa, the Potawatomi, and the Algonquin people. But that was before the white Europeans arrived in Bayfield. Nowadays, those taking the ferry to the island are mostly tourists with bikes, tents, backpacks, and even SUVs who were all heading for vacations and lake cottages on Madeline Island.

The entirety of the Bayfield Peninsula was a mystical region. Artists were in abundance with fine art painters, sculptors, writers, photographers, and musicians, many of whom showcased their talent in local art galleries, bookstores, restaurants, bars, and the yearly Big Top Chautauqua Concert Venue with its 900-seat arena and performing arts center.

I decided to drive up the coast past the small village of Red Cliff, the administrative center of the Red Cliff Band of Lake Superior Chippewa, a federally recognized Ojibwe Native American tribe. This 1-mile by 14-mile piece of tribal land snakes along the coast of Lake Superior with views of Madeline and the Basswood Islands at the top of Bayfield County.

From there, I zigzagged my way past the beachfront towns of Cornucopia, Herbster, and Port Wing before cutting inland, passing orchards and fruit farms to get back to US-2 heading west toward Superior, Wisconsin.

On the eastern outskirts of the City of Superior was Moccasin Mike Road, which once was a Native American path called the Osaugie Trail. It was a part of the Indian War Trail, used when the Chippewa battled the Sioux. When the trail was converted to a road in the 1890s, a local politician lobbied the county board to name the road after his father, attorney Michael Bright, Sr., who went by the nickname "Moccasin Mike." Trouble was, Wisconsin Point contained a Native American burial ground that held the remains of Chief Joseph Headman Osaugie—one of the signers of the 1854 Treaty with the Chippewa, which essentially ceded all the lands east of the Mississippi River previously held by the Chippewa people to the United States. This treaty full of legalese was signed by many Native Americans, who all used an "X" instead of a signature because none of signers knew how to read English and, as such, had no idea what they were signing. With the treaty signed, U.S. Steel lobbied the county to move the remains from the Native American cemetery to St. Frances Cemetery in Superior, where the bodies were then interred—a site designated by a stone marker that said, "Here lies the bodies from Wisconsin Point removed in 1918. They were removed by United States Steel, so they could build a dock on the point."

Nearly a hundred years later, in 2014, the following article appeared in the *Indian Country Today* newspaper, written by Donna Ennis, a tribal elder with the Fond du Lac Reservation, and titled "The Heavens Became Black: The Curse of Wisconsin Point." It quoted the following passage:

> On February 6, 1925, a reporter for the *Milwaukee Journal* named Timm Severud recounted a conversation he had with an attorney named John A. Cadigan who represented the tribe in a suit they brought against U.S. Steel. In the conversation Cadigan stated: "In the Fall of 1916, I was about my office when suddenly the door opened and a tall stern faced Indian entered. He asked if I was interested in the Indian claims to Wisconsin Point and I told him I was. With no further preamble he begins to tell me about his ancestry. 'My father,

> my grandfather, my great grandfather, the mightiest chief that ever ruled the Chippewas, and their fathers before them lie buried on Wisconsin Point. Their bones must not be disturbed. I tell you now that the day the white man enters the Point to dig up the remains of our ancestors will see this nation visit the most terrible fire in its history, swept by the most devastating plague and plunged into the bloodiest war the world has ever known.'"

The suit by the lawyer was rejected, and soon afterward, workers removed the remains. According to Cadigan, "That day about noon the heavens became black for a time with a peculiar cloud. It was explained when we picked up the evening papers to read about the devastating Cloquet (Minnesota) fire, truly the worst that this part of the country, if not the entire nation has ever seen. The same paper conveyed news of the sweeping wave of influenza (the Flu Pandemic of 1918), which inundated our nation and took so many lives. And to make the triple prophecy of the Indian complete, America and the rest of the world was in the midst of a world war (World War I)."

After reading that account, I felt relieved to hear that the Fond du Lac Band of Lake Superior Chippewa had been in negotiations to acquire fourteen acres of Wisconsin Point, home to the original gravesites, and that they had plans to create a "living history center" on the land. Currently a city park, Wisconsin Point was a three-mile-long natural sand bar with dunes interspersed with forests along Lake Superior. A lighthouse and the pier along the Saint Louis River channel were accessible to the public, offering views of lake freighters as they made their way upriver.

On that mild sunny day, I saw the *Stewart J. Cort,* a laker, steaming up-channel. She had loaded iron ore at an ore dock in Superior and would deliver it to the Cleveland-Cliffs steel mill in Burns Harbor, Indiana.

I continued along US-2 through Superior using the Bong Bridge to cross the Saint Louis River to Minnesota. It was named after Army Air Force pilot Major Richard Bong, the most decorated fighter pilot during World War II, born in Superior and raised in nearby Poplar, Wisconsin. While crossing the river, I looked out over the harbor at Duluth stretching along the expanse of the river and the lake. The city was squeezed between rocky bluffs and its waterfront, with steep streets heading up the bluff.

At my next stop, Morgan Park, a neighborhood of Duluth, I met up with Bob Berg. He took me on a guided walking tour of what was once a company town. Bob explained that Morgan Park had been developed by U.S. Steel, though during the initial design phase it was called Model City. When construction began a year later, however, in 1914, the company decided to call it Morgan Park as a tribute to J. P. Morgan, the founder of U.S. Steel, at the time the largest company in America. Though the steel plant was gone, it was once the dominant company in Duluth. Bob said, "The houses, businesses, and churches were built for the workers to keep them happy. There were no bars here; instead they were placed in Gary, the next neighborhood over."

Continuing, Bob said, "U.S. Steel wanted Morgan Park to be a town of happy workers, so they built nice houses made out of concrete, each with a garden, and in addition a community center, a shopping mall, a school and two churches—one protestant and the other Catholic. All of the houses were company owned and could only be rented by U.S. Steel employees."

At its peak, the U.S. Steel Duluth Works employed thousands of workers.

Berg, who grew up in Morgan Park, recalled the pollution from the cement factory. "There was so much cement dust that when we sat down at our picnic table, we had to dust our plates off before we put the food on them. My dad had to take Coca-Cola and wash the car; otherwise, he couldn't get the cement dust off the car. Growing up, I thought everybody's roof was gray, but later I learned our roof was actually dark green. Before my mother hung out clothes, she had to make sure which way the wind was blowing, or else the sheets would be full of cement dust."

Bob, a retired elementary teacher and local historian, told me, "I've always been interested in history and architecture. And I've been a member of the Duluth Preservation Alliance for nearly forty years." During his working days as a grade school teacher in Duluth, Bob had taught more than twelve hundred students. Now, in his retirement, he was still teaching but only to history buffs.

After the walking tour, Bob showed me around his house, pointing out the quality construction: double-decker porch, bay windows, patterned windows, and carved woodwork. All the while, he told me about growing up in Morgan Park while his father was employed at the steel plant for much of his working life.

I asked Bob why the plant had closed.

"In the early 1970s, the Minnesota Pollution Control agency told the steel plant they needed to stop the pollution by fixing the plant. But U.S. Steel didn't want to put that much money into the plant because after the end of World War II, demand for iron ore began to decline."

Bob went on to tell me that U.S. Steel had threatened to close the plant previously, so it was a surprise when they actually closed the steel plant in 1971, the cement plant five years later, followed by the coke plant in 1979. The closing of the plants had sent the Duluth economy into a tailspin with the loss of thousands of high-paying, full-time jobs with benefits.

I asked how the closure of the plant had affected the population of Duluth.

Fumbling through his desk, Bob produced documents showing that the population of Duluth had peaked at 107,000 in 1960 prior to the closures and fell to around 86,000 afterward. "Luckily," he added, "the homes in Morgan Park had kept their value because of the quality of their construction."

He said, "Closing the plant forced the city to diversify the local economy."

I asked whether there was environmental damage while U.S. Steel's operations were running at full tilt.

"Yes, the steel plant did cause a lot of air and water pollution. Even today, more than forty years later, they are still cleaning up portions of the St. Louis River."

On leaving Morgan Park, I jumped back on US-2, a route that ran near the tracks of the Great Northern Railway, now the BNSF.

The importance of building the Great Northern cannot be overstated when it came to developing land in the West. The railroad's expansion was spearheaded by James J. Hill. Known as the Empire Builder, he was one of the most fascinating people in American history. Yet, today, few people have heard of him. However, if you took an Amtrak train west from Chicago to Seattle, you would be riding on the *Empire Builder*, which was named in his honor. The Great Northern Railway ushered in a new era in the American West because it was responsible for developing the agriculture, timber, and mining industries that fueled the growth of the U.S. economy.

About an hour's drive from Morgan Park was Floodwood, a small city built along the Great Northern tracks.

Always a sucker for an interesting thrift store, I found one in Downtown Floodwood. There I noticed an inviting, painted log façade with an old-fashioned name. That was how I met the owners of Grandma's Treasure Chest. When I asked what had gotten them to open a store, the man sitting in a chair inside the store told me it was their retirement job. The wife, known as Grandma, ran the store, and the husband, whose name escaped me, had a second retirement job as a rural postman. We talked about Floodwood and its history during the lumber era—a time when the town's population boomed.

"After the lumber era," Grandpa said, "the population went down, and there were far fewer jobs."

During our conversation, I asked how their business was doing. Grandma said, "Not very good. We're thinking about closing it down."

I looked around at the selection of historic postcards, antiques, and knickknacks, thinking, *It would be a shame if the store closed because one more open space in the downtown would be disappointing to the town's leaders. It's what happens when a town's population goes down.*

Once I got back on US-2, thirty miles west of Floodwood was the small, unincorporated town of Blackberry, where the Mississippi River began to run parallel with the highway. There, the Mississippi River transitioned from the wetlands and the forests of the Chippewa National Forest on the west, through the town of Grand Rapids, to the lowland hardwood forest of Aitkin County where Blackberry was located.

At the corner of US-2 and Dove Lane, a tiny mom-and-pop restaurant with no sign had a "Welcome Fishermen courtesy of Miller Lite" poster tacked to the side of the building. I turned left and passed the Blackberry Seventh Day Adventist Church, where they were worshipping on the seventh day of the week.

I drove a mile and a half, past several farms, and landed on the property line of the farm at the end of the road. By happenstance, it sat on the eastern bank of the Mississippi River, which narrowly curved around the farmer's property. Although there was no public access, I was able to stop for a few seconds to capture a photo of the river at the bend. This important stretch of the Mississippi was the eastern portion of the Louisiana Purchase, a small, insignificant nub of land that stuck up like a thumb. It was incapsulated by a trickle of the Mississippi River, marking the easternmost part of the land in the Louisiana Territory. The Spanish took this territory from native tribes and sold it to France. Then King Napoleon Bonaparte sold it to the United States to fund his war with the British.

I returned to US-2, heading west, and five miles later the highway crossed the Mississippi. At that spot, a bridge abutment had been constructed across the river. When I reached Grand Rapids and passed the gigantic Blandin Paper Mill with its huge stacks of logs, I saw the Mississippi again as it flowed through the paper mill's reservoir.

17

On my way from Grand Rapids to Bemidji, an 80-mile stretch of US-2, I passed through the Leech Lake Band of Ojibwe reservation. In the center of the reservation was a railway village, founded in 1898 when a post office was established there. Though its population was now fewer than 150, it had a storied history. From 1901 to 1911, the federal government operated three separate Indian boarding schools in the same general area: Bena, Cass Lake, and Leech Lake. During the Great Depression, as part of the New Deal initiated by President Franklin D. Roosevelt, the Civilian Conservation Corps (CCC) established one of 148 Minnesota camps near Bena. The camps closed down with the outbreak of World War II when later in the war, from 1944 to 1945, the U.S. Army operated a POW camp that housed German prisoners of war in Bena. The camp was located near the Big Winnie Resort and General Store, according to Arnold Dahl-Winny, the fifth-generation of the Dahl family to own the resort. I had stopped by the gas station and convenience store to fill up my tank and had gone inside the store. There, I talked with Arnold and saw the historic photos that covered the walls.

On entering Bemidji, I couldn't help but notice the statues of Paul Bunyan and Babe the Blue Ox that sat on the shore of Lake Bemidji. Amazed by the size of the statues, I said, "What the heck?" or something similar to another person who was also staring at the statues. A guy who overheard me said, "Talk to Bill Batchhelder."

"Who?" I asked.

"The guy who owns Bemidji Woolen Mills."

So I Googled the store and found a post on social media saying it had recently celebrated its one hundredth year in business. I thought, *I better find Bill and talk with him.*

I did find the store and was greeted by another statue, one that depicted a chainsaw-carved lumberjack wearing a stocking cap and holding a giant ax. In the store, I located Bill in the backroom, getting ready to ship something out to a customer in another state. I introduced myself, showed him the map of my route, and pointed out that my route traveled through Bemidji and that I needed someone from Bemidji to sit with me so I could do an interview.

"That would be me," Bill said.

So, we walked out onto the sales floor where there were racks upon racks of all types of outdoor clothing, from jackets to hats, to boots, socks, and even underwear, though there weren't many of those unmentionables on display. Bill, who wore a pressed blue shirt, tan khakis, and a wide smile, gave me a firm handshake, and we sat down to talk. I asked Bill to tell me about the Paul Bunyan and Babe statues.

Bill said they were constructed for the winter carnival of 1937. Babe was transported into town on a Granules Implement & Fuel Company truck with the vehicle's exhaust billowing out through the ox's nostrils. Apparently, Bemidji, a Northwoods lumber town, had figured the giant statues would bring tourists to town. And, in fact, they did and still do, with the pair once featured on a two-page spread in *Life* magazine.

I asked Bill whether he was a local.

He replied, "I was born, raised, and even attended college in Bemidji, and I only left briefly—ever." He told me he grew up on Lake Bemidji, but early on, his father had moved the family to a small farm off the lake.

That got my attention. "Why?"

"My dad said living on a lake was too much work. He often said, 'We have a boat and a trailer, and we live in a state with ten thousand lakes where most have public access. We can launch our boat on a different lake every day without ever boating on one lake twice.'"

Looking around his store, I saw historic pictures on the wall, one with Bill and people who looked like employees working. That told me Bill's store had a long legacy. There were shelves of hand-stitched wool blankets, gondolas filled with colorful fleece beanies, and racks of plaid jackets, sweaters, and shirts. There was even a shop in the backroom where wool garments were made on site.

Bill, who noticed me looking at an old photo, said, "I started working in the store when I was twelve, back in 1972. Worked for my grandfather, my uncle, and my father. So, yeah, I'm very proud to have lived in Bemidji all my life. Even went to Bemidji State University after graduating from Bemidji High School. Working here was such a normal thing to me that I had no idea that my family was building a legacy. It's the reason I ended up owning Bemidji Woolen Mills. I purchased it from my father and my uncle in 1995. Twenty-five years later, in 2020, we celebrated our one hundred years in business. That means if I live to be ninety-two, I will have beat my grandfather's tenure by two years. I started when I was twelve, he started when he was fourteen, and they carried him out on a stretcher when he was eighty-nine years old. Died three days later."

"Holy cow!" I exclaimed. "How in the world did your grandfather keep everyone in line for that long?"

"Well, he did the estate planning for our family in 1959 when he incorporated Bemidji Woolen Mills, putting 49 percent of the stock in my father's name, 49 percent of the stock in my uncle's name, and he and his wife kept 2 percent so they would always have total control because they could side with one or the other if things went in a way he didn't see fit. When my grandfather passed away, the estate planning was already done for my dad, my uncle, and his wife. Because when you grew up in that generation of America, you had so much respect for your forefathers. . . . Even though they could have at any time thrown my grandfather out or said goodbye, they let him run the Woolen Mills from 1959 all the way up to 1992. My grandfather was the solid leader and was in retirement longer than he worked in his regular career. Then just a few years later, in 1995, my father and my uncle were ready to retire, and that's when I purchased the business."

"So, any regrets?"

"When I was younger, my first dream was to become a navigator on a B-52 bomber. At the time, they were stationed at the Grand Forks Air Force Base and were the war machines of the day. My grandfather was in the air force, so I felt it would be a noble profession for me. I was getting ready to take the test, and my father asked, 'What are you doing?' I said, 'I'm going to join the air force, Dad.' 'Oh, no, we're not going to let you join the air force,' he said. It was immediately after the Vietnam War, the military was demoralized, and a lot of bad things were happening in Vietnam. So, my father marched me down to the fire department, and I became a volunteer firefighter for the City of Bemidji Fire Department. I'm proud, more than forty years later, that I'm still a volunteer firefighter."

"Have you ever left Bemidji for an extended period of time?" I asked.

"Yes, for eight weeks I was lucky enough to receive a trip courtesy of Rotary International to live in Brazil for nearly two months. That was for young businesspeople who weren't able to be foreign exchange students in high school. It was called Group Study Exchange."

"What do you love about Bemidji?" I asked.

"There are so many amenities in Bemidji, they are hard to count,"

Bill actually used the word *amenities,* instead of the more common phrase "things to do." I noticed that Bill used precise, measured words when he spoke.

He described the area's natural history, cultural history, geological history, and four seasons. He also mentioned that he loved the river system for kayaking, canoeing, and fishing; the lakes for recreation; the forests for mountain biking and hiking; and the culture of the people who made significant impacts in the region. He said, "Being in one place at Bemidji Woolen Mills, I have talked to, met, and experienced world and national leaders, governors, sports figures, writers, authors, and musicians who were on the national and world scene."

I was impressed.

I asked him what had gotten into Bemidji because it was growing while other towns in rural areas were shrinking.

Bill said that in the 1960s, the '70s, and into the '80s, young people left Bemidji in droves. They couldn't wait to graduate from high school, get the heck out of Bemidji, and experience the rest of the world. And once they left, found work elsewhere, and began raising families, they didn't come back." He said some moved to places like Chicago, New York City, Europe, Texas, MIT in Boston, and Harvard, never to return except to occasionally visit their parents.

"So, what changed?"

Bill explained that starting in the late 1980s, community leaders realized they had to find a way to attract talent that would stay in Bemidji. After doing a study, they figured out what they needed in order to grow.

According to Bill, studies showed *people* wanted to leave the hustle and bustle of the city but not if they didn't have access to the arts, culture, recreation, health care, and good schools. "In Bemidji," he said, "people can live on a lake, yet still get to meetings anywhere, either in person by flying out of Bemidji Regional Airport or by telecommunicating with our high-speed broadband."

The results had been obvious. Population in the area soared as new people moved in and local young people saw the advantages of staying.

Bill Batchelder, Owner, Bemidji Woolen Mills, Bemidji, Minnesota

Bill told me he had always enjoyed the outdoors and figured if they made Bemidji more attractive to visitors who also enjoyed outdoor life, they would stay. He said, "Here, within a couple minutes, I can be fishing in one of our lakes or streams. I can put my key in the door and be on a lake in five minutes because I've got my boat hooked up, and away we go." He said the same for mountain biking. "If I'm in New York City, I'd need a weekend or a long afternoon to be able to do that. So, we started to tell people that here in Bemidji, we have one of the finest symphony orchestras in the state, that Bemidji State University is a great source for the arts, the hospital care is excellent, and we have a regional airport. Let's say a cardiologist and his wife come to town, looking around. We take their kids to the high school, one of the finest high schools in the state. We take them to Lake Bemidji State Park and the trail system to show them outdoor opportunities: snowmobiling, cross-country skiing, hiking, and mountain biking. That was how we as a community changed the narrative about Bemidji."

As I left Bill's store, I couldn't help thinking about my grandfather and my father, and their more than fifty combined years of owning our family's store. Just as Bill and his father before him did, my dad followed my grandfather into the family business. Though Bill's store by every indication was still a success, my father was forced to close his business because of the competition from chain stores. Bill's store sold many exclusive items while my dad's store sold common goods, major kitchen appliances and TVs, and the like.

My conversation with Bill was still on my mind when I arrived at Jim Aakhus's cabin on nearby Lake Bemidji—a cabin that had been in his family for generations. During our visit, we walked down the old, worn wooden stairs to get a close look at the lake. Over a homemade meal, we talked for a couple hours. I asked whether it was okay if I car-camped in his yard. He said that would be fine. Soon afterward, I retired to my car, leaned the seat back, and slept while listening to the sounds of waterfowl quacking on the lake. To me, they sounded like mallards because of the series of quacks and calls that started loud and progressively got softer.

Though I slept well, I did get some aches from sleeping in the car, the signs of getting older. The next morning, after taking a handful of pain relievers, I headed to the Mississippi Headwaters south of Bemidji—all the while thinking, *I'm getting too old to keep traveling like this.*

While there, I learned that the discovery of the Mississippi River headwaters had been a challenge that was solved in 1832 when the Anishinaabe (Ojibwe) guide Ozaawindib led a party headed by Henry Rowe Schoolcraft. Schoolcraft was actually sent by the U.S. government to negotiate a treaty between the Dakota Sioux and the Ojibwa. The discovery happened when Schoolcraft diverted the party to explore an area where people thought the river headwaters originated—a lake known to native people as Omushkos and to French fur traders as Lac la Biche, both meaning "Elk Lake." Schoolcraft renamed the lake Itasca, which combined the Latin words for "truth" and "head," *verITAS CAput.*

Later, in 1891, Itasca State Park was established.

There, I learned about one of the true heroes at the Mississippi Headwaters: Mary Gibbs, who in 1903 stood up to armed loggers who were intent on cutting down the pines surrounding Lake Itasca in order to build a dam. Without her resistance, the old-growth trees at the headwaters might have been lost. That led to Mary Gibbs being made commissioner of Itasca State Park, the first female state park manager in the United States.

I also found out that in 1933, during the Great Depression, the Civilian Conservation Corps employed thousands of young men to plant trees and build roads and public buildings throughout the forested areas of our country. In Itasca State Park, the CCC dug trenches and placed the boulders that defined the headwaters of the Mississippi. One lasting legacy of the CCC was the historic marker at the headwaters, which read: "Here 1475 feet above the ocean the Mighty Mississippi begins to flow on its winding way 2552 miles to the Gulf of Mexico."

By 1937, the park had been transformed into a popular vacation spot, as it has remained ever since.

At the headwaters, I watched as people of all ages, from tiny ones to oldsters, walked across the stones that marked the actual beginning of the Mississippi River, while getting wet up to their shins and loving it. I'd bet I shot more than two hundred photos as I stood there enjoying every minute.

18

Heading west and driving through Shevlin, I noticed that the land began to change. The heavily forested land began transitioning to flat, endless prairie. And to the west, in Fosston, I saw a sign with the town's motto, "Where the prairie meets the pines."

Along US-2, where the plains began, deserted farm homes reminded me how tough it was to live off the land. Dreams gone bust were evidenced by abandoned homesteads of people forced to give up their property to creditors. When I talked about the ramshackle homesteads to farmers and ranchers, they often said that they left the structures standing as a way to honor people who came before them.

The idea of free land for settlers, sometimes called "headright," started in colonial times. Then, during the 1850s, newspapers took the editorial position that it was the right of average citizens to own land. Horace Greeley, publisher of the powerful *New York Tribune,* stated that public land should "be so modified that every person needing land may take possession of any quarter-section not previously located, and that none other than a person needing land shall be allowed to acquire it at all."

Longtime supporters of homesteading, such as the Free Soil Party, asserted that "all men have a natural right to a portion of the soil; and that, as the use of the soil is indispensable to life, the right of all men to the soil is as sacred as their right to life itself." Those against the idea of homesteading, such as the Know-Nothing Party, opposed the movement because it would give free land to foreign immigrants.

For homesteading to become reality, a few things needed to happen. First, people in the West had to gain more political power. And the Southern states that supported slavery had to be taken out of the mix to ensure that the homesteading states would be anti-slavery. Those two issues were resolved when the railroads gained more influence, and the Civil War removed the Confederate States from the discussion. As a result, a new political party, the Republicans—who elected Abraham Lincoln in 1960 and gained control of Congress during the same election—passed the Homestead Act of 1862. The act allowed "any person who is the head of a family, or who has arrived at the age of twenty-one years, and is a citizen of the United States, or who shall have filed his declaration of intention to become such" the right to claim 160 acres of land, also called a quarter-section, for free. The claimant needed only to pay a small filing fee and live on and improve the land for five years. Yet, even though more than 270 million acres were claimed, resulting in the settlement of 400,000 farms, many felt the Homestead Act fell short of its intended goals. That was partly because the western-most areas of land were too arid for 160 acres to provide for a family. To solve that problem, in 1909 Congress passed an expanded version of the Homestead Act that increased the size of the westernmost land grants from 160 to 320 acres.

Past Fosston, I entered Polk County, named for U.S. president James Knox Polk, who in 1849 signed the congressional act to make Minnesota a territory. Erskine, a town west of Fosston, sat along the eastern shore of Cameron Lake. There I saw a huge monument (27 feet long and 6 feet wide) celebrating the world's largest northern pike.

Seven or so miles past Erskine was the tiny city of Mentor, population 104. The highway skirted the north end of town where a boat storage facility was located. From that corner, I took County Road 45 to the west, passing by farmland. The straight-as-an-arrow road that was flat as a pancake did not look like much at all. But I decided to stay on it for around ten miles, driving past Dugdale, a ghost town, where the paved road turned to gravel. There were five or so miles of hard rough road and, on the left side of the road, Pembina Trail Preserve. No parking lot was available, so I parked on the side of the road.

The trail was pretty much unmarked, but it didn't matter to me because I was in unspoiled nature. The trail, called the Pembina, was named for buffalo hide traders who used ox carts to move their goods. If you went there at dusk or dawn, you would likely hear or even see a mix of prairie chickens, sharp-tailed grouse, and deer, the latter more plentiful than any other critters. I found it remarkable that the Pembina Trail was part of other restoration projects that included the Glacial Ridge, two scientific nature areas, three federal waterfowl protection areas, and nearly a dozen wildlife management areas that were state owned.

I had been on the road for what seemed like forever. My psyche needed that alone time. Some of the best photos I'd taken so far on my journey happened while hiking its trails. And to think I was on the plains, not in forests or on lakeshores where I expected to capture the best images.

Back on US-2, heading west, I crossed over an oxbow along the Red Lake River and reached downtown Crookston. Here, native people and fur traders had once traveled on their way to favored hunting grounds.

Just west of Crookston, the land transitioned to the rich farmland of the Red River Valley, one of the most productive agricultural areas in the United States. Called the Breadbasket of the World, it has yielded massive amounts of sugar beets, potatoes, corn, and wheat. It was actually the floor of an ancient glacier lake known as Lake Agassiz, which receded eight thousand years ago and left behind rich, silty soil.

People who settled in the Red River Valley benefited greatly from the Homestead Act of 1862, in part because they were early settlers who got the best farmland.

At a celebration of the hundred-year anniversary of the act in 1962, President John F. Kennedy said in an address to Congress that the Homestead Act of 1862 was "probably the single greatest stimulus to national development ever enacted."

I decided to deadhead north to the town of Stephen to see Michael Douglas, whose agency sold crop insurance. I had heard of crop insurance before but had little understanding of what it was.

I asked Michael to explain what crop insurance was and why it was such a necessity for farmers.

Michael offered me a cup of coffee, told his wife who was out in the office to say to people who came in that he was busy, then leaned back in his office chair, relaxed, and said, "Risk management is extremely important, especially in crop insurance. Farmers have other inputs such as fertilizer, seed, and chemicals. But none of them guarantee they'll be able to afford to farm the next year. That's what crop insurance is, that no matter how bad the crop is, it guarantees they'll still be able to farm the next year." Michael made it clear that the farmers needed to do their own risk management and planning. And their lenders wanted to make sure the farmer had crop insurance backing. "As insurers, we give the farmer that base figure in terms of percentage of coverage. If everything goes to crap, the farmers know the amount of money they'll receive will enable them to farm the next year. It might not pay all the bills, but it will help them farm again."

Trying to summarize, I said, "To me, being a farmer means tossing the dice each year."

"They do," Michael said, "but with crop insurance, farmers limit their exposure in terms of absorbing all their loss. However, there is a crop insurance deadline of March 15 for the farmer to decide how much coverage to purchase. When you think about it, in mid-March snow might still be on the farmer's fields. The farmers need to gamble about what coverage they will need. For example, last year in the early days of the season when there was flooding, very little farming was going on. We have deadlines in crop insurance in terms of when the seeds need to be planted. In our area, small grains have to be planted by June 5th and row crops by June 10th. Farmers can still plant after those times, but they lose a percentage of their coverage the longer they wait to seed their fields."

I added, "I assume that when farmers seed their land, they don't know what price their crops will bring when it's delivered to the grain elevator."

"Kinda true. Farmers can contract ahead, which is what crop insurance can help them do. That way, farmers know they are guaranteed a certain amount. Roughly speaking, farmers are guaranteed two-thirds of what they've proved they can grow. And if they're new farmers, it's two-thirds of what the county averages are. That's roughly. Farmers generally can't guarantee themselves 100 percent of what their average is because the higher up they go in terms of coverage, the more expensive the crop insurance gets. Let's say a farmer can grow 10,000 bushels of wheat. They might presell 6,000 bushels ahead of time at the guaranteed price and the remaining 4,000 bushels after harvest at market price. So, yeah, farmers do have an idea of what price they will get. Now the question is, what will the farmers produce and how many bushels? The good thing about crop insurance is even if farmers don't produce what they thought, crop insurance will give them the amount of their contract."

Michael talked about his growing-up years on a family farm west of Stephen. "We're the fifth generation of Douglases to live on that piece of land. My grandfather and great-grandfather bought the quarter that we live on in 1917. My dad then added on to that. When I grew up, my father was farming mostly small grains and occasionally some type of row crop." He said his father also owned a John Deere dealership, in addition to farming, but he had seen the writing on the wall shortly afterward because Deere was in the process of consolidating its dealerships. With Stephen being such a small town, he would have likely lost that franchise, so instead of fighting it out with that giant company, he closed the dealership. Then, knowing he didn't have enough acreage to support his family, his father increased the size of his farm and dedicated all of his time to farming. He also took a seasonal winter job at snowmobile maker Arctic Cat, fifty miles from his family farm in Thief River Falls.

I asked Michael whether he had considered following in his father's footsteps and working on their farm. He had, but when he brought up the possibility, his father said if Michael wanted to farm, he had to find his own land, buy his own farm machinery, and find his own capital. So, instead of going into farming, after high school Michael enrolled at the University of Minnesota's Crookston campus. Within a month, though, his world fell apart: his mother was killed in a car crash. "I was only seventeen and kinda lost my way for a while. I dropped out of college. My heart wasn't in it. Plus, by this time my father had quit farming, so I went to work for the people who rented our land." That was how Michael kept his connection to farming. He also got a winter job at an auto parts store as a shelf stocker and a delivery person, and that led to his next job. "One day I was delivering parts to a local gas station repair shop, and the owner told me he needed another guy. So, I did that for eight years. We did mechanical work, sold tires—also big agricultural tires, which were expensive."

Michael described the harvest season of 1985, when the ground was very wet, and, as a result, the combines were losing traction. "We were putting rice tires on combines so that they could travel through the mud. But they didn't want to shut the combines down during the day. Me and my boss, we'd start putting on tires around ten o'clock at night. They were fairly easy to swap in and out because they're tubeless. However, they were so heavy we could only do three sets a night. My boss at the time was fifty, and he offered to sell me his business. But I turned him down because I didn't want to be changing out combine tires when I was fifty years old. By this time, Cheri and I were married and were starting to raise a family. So, I focused on looking for a job that could support them."

A year later, Michael got an opportunity he couldn't resist. Two CPAs bought out the local Farm Mutual Insurance agency and offered Michael a job selling crop insurance. "The two accountants knew me and my work ethic. They asked me if I'd ever thought about selling insurance." Michael told them it had never crossed his mind, but he did ask whether he could think about it. "So, I talked to Cheri, and we decided it was a little cut in pay to start, but the upside was pretty good. That was in 1986."

As with most jobs in the insurance business, Michael earned commissions. For the next twenty-two years, the business grew. But even though the accountants were licensed, they never sold insurance. Instead, they paid Michael commissions, but the amount was low.

"So I asked for a raise in my commission and was turned down. The accountants said that before they would give me a raise, they would sell the insurance themselves." Michael quit that job and wished them good luck. When they'd first hired him, the accountants had feared that Michael might go out on his own, so he'd been required to sign a noncompete clause, saying he couldn't compete within a 30-mile radius of their office. As a result, after he quit, he set up his first office in Oslo, 30.4 miles away.

Though Michael couldn't approach any of the agency's current clients, the clients were allowed to contact him. The accountants were now selling insurance and, fearing the loss of business, approached the agency's largest clients and asked them to stay with their office. Yet, each client made it clear that Michael was their agent because he knew the business, and they would follow Michael to his new office. The accountants then had second thoughts about not giving Michael the compensation he needed. After making several proposals, all of which Michael turned down, the accountants settled on an arrangement that would work for everyone. Michael would stay with them for two more years while receiving

Michael Douglas, Owner, Douglas Insurance Agency, Stephen, Minnesota

higher commissions than he'd originally requested. Then, after two years, the office ownership would shift to Michael.

Now, several years later, Michael owned a lake cottage near Bemidji. "As a funny aside, the pontoon boat I purchased is named 4 Percent, because if I'd gotten the 4 percent raise in commissions that I'd first requested, I would only have been able to afford the pontoon boat and not the lake home I eventually purchased." Since then, the business had grown substantially, and one of his sons was now working with him. In fact, during the last year he was able to purchase an additional agency in Middle River, Minnesota.

Changing the topic, I asked Michael what was key to keeping people, especially young people, in small rural towns?

"Here in Stephen we've seen a slight—not large but slight—increase in people being able to work remotely. Too early to know if it's a trend, but there are a few doing it here. Family is important, and that's the draw of living here. But here's the thing. Walk through the cemetery and look at the surnames and see how many people with those names are still living here. Very few. If every one of those families had one child who stayed here, we'd have a much higher population, instead of the roughly five hundred we currently have. Fifty years ago, more than nine hundred people lived here. I look at our area and can see there's some movement to moving back here because people want to raise their kids in a small town. We tend not to lock our doors. Like at our farm, growing up, we didn't even have keys to our doors. We never locked them. But now, if we're gone for an extended period of time, we'll lock the place up.

"Look at Bemidji. Since we bought our lake cabin there in 2009, its population growth in those fifteen years has gone from 13,000 to over 15,000. That begs the question, how big do you want to be? You don't want to grow too much because of the need to grow the infrastructure and hire more personnel to run the town."

From Michael, I not only learned about crop insurance; I also learned about perseverance, the need to stick to your guns by not caving when things got tough. A lesson I wished I'd gotten into my thick Dutch-Danish head when I was still in college. I learned one of Michael's sons, Steven, was an actor trying to make his way up the chain of live theatrical productions. He could have given up long ago but instead moved to New York City and took a series of part-time jobs to make ends meet. He was still continuing to chase his dream at the time when his father and I spoke. As I got into my car, Michael walked up. I rolled down my window, and he said, "I know my son Steven's got the talent. I've seen him act and heard him sing. I think he's got what it takes."

From Stephen, I headed north to Kittson County.

While driving through Hallock, population 906, I learned of this small town's importance on the prairie. Some scenes from the Coen Brothers' movie *Fargo* were shot in the downtown, and the inventor of refrigeration technology for semis, Frederick McKinley Jones, once lived here. Jones was the first African American to become a member of the American Society of Refrigeration Engineers in 1944 and the National Inventors Hall of Fame posthumously in 2007. Though I scouted the place out, I was unable to find a trace of either the movie set or the inventor.

From Hallock, I headed west and crossed the Red River of the North into North Dakota. Though the river looked to be a trickle, I heard that when it rose up, it was known to flood during the yearly snowmelt. I kept heading west for an hour, then turned south on North Dakota Highway 1, where a few miles later I saw on the horizon the strangest thing I ever remembered seeing out on the prairie. It was huge and, I had to admit, scary looking. But I needed to see it up close, and a mile or so before reaching Nekoma (population thirty-one), I turned down a road that seemed to lead to it. There was a cemetery to the right and a wind farm nearly circling it. Close up, I realized that the weird-looking structure was a pyramid four or five stories high with what looked to be receptors of a gigantic radar system receiver, long since removed. There were other old buildings around it. The sign said, "Stanley R. Mickelsen Safeguard Complex, a Cold War–era Defense Department project."

I caught the attention of a man mowing the lawn of the nearby cemetery and, while pointing at the pyramid, asked, "What in the heck is that?"

He said, "They put it there to defend our nation."

"That!" I was nearly yelling to get heard over the sound of his tractor with the mower attached.

"Yes! It was part of the Safeguard program. When the Soviets sent missiles loaded with nuclear bombs, it told the air force over in Grand Forks to send up anti-ballistic missiles to shoot them down."

I yelled, "Did it work!?"

He shouted back, "Never found out! Congress took the money out of the program and shut it down the day after it was completed!"

I hollered, "Must have cost a lot!"

"Billions!" he yelled back.

I bellowed, "Jobs, too?"

"Lots of 'em, ask the folks over in Nakoma! They housed them! Place has never been the same since!"

It was then that I noticed the man cutting the lawn was carefully manicuring the grass around a small grave of twins who had apparently died at birth in 1921. That small grave sat in the caring shadow of the parents, Alex and Julia Borho. Carved into the infants' gravestone were the names Mary and Joseph Borho, whom I thought were aptly named.

With my ears still ringing, I drove south to Lakota and turned west on US-2. Fifteen miles later, near a rest area, I could see Devil's Lake in the distance. I later learned it was a glacier lake and the largest natural lake in North Dakota.

It's filled with salt water, kinda like the Great Salt Lake in Utah, where its water was trapped without a natural outflow. So, the trapped water became endorheic, meaning it did not drain into the ocean. During the Great Depression and Dust Bowl days of the 1930s, Devils Lake receded and nearly went dry in places. In contrast, due to above-normal precipitation in the mid 1950s, the water surface of Devils Lake rose to its highest level in forty years, resulting in massive flooding. The lake levels receded enough to stop the flooding from the 1960s to the '80s, but from 1992 on, for eighteen years, it rose more than twenty-nine feet. In response, the state constructed emergency outlets to the Sheyenne River and built a twelve-mile-long earthen levee to protect the city of Devils Lake from flooding.

Across the highway from Devils Lake was the city of Devils Lake, population roughly seven thousand. It got its name from the Dakota language *mni-wak'-an,* which translates as "spirit water." But when American settlers from Europe arrived in the 1800s, they misinterpreted the name as "bad spirit," due to the lake's high salinity, which made it undrinkable. Because most of the settlers were strict Christians, they misconstrued "bad" to mean "of the devil."

Not wanting to be lured by the Devil, I drove through there quickly.

19

Rugby was where, in the late 1990s, I first saw the obelisk that celebrated the location of the Geographical Center of North America. I happened to be there while conducting interviews for the book I authored for the Presbyterian Church (USA). Though I didn't conduct any interviews in Rugby itself, I did meet with somebody affiliated with the Presbyterian denomination. We chatted over coffee and a slice of pie that I selected from the glass-domed pie holder at a café along US-2 near the obelisk.

I first met Kipp Johnson by phone in a circuitous way. It was harvest time on the plains, and I wanted to find a farmer willing to let me sit in what was called a buddy, grandchild, or banker seat—a seat that most combines had. Yet, to find a farmer who was currently combining, I needed a stroke of good luck. So, I called a rancher near Watford City who knew a jeweler in Minot, whose husband was a farmer but who had already finished combining. But the farmer knew another farmer near Rugby who was currently combining. I made the call, and he invited me to join him the next morning. It needed to be early but not too early. The sun had to dry the dew from the previous night so that the combine worked properly. But it couldn't be too late because once the sun got high, it could get hot out on the field. And knowing just when to start combining depended on . . . Well, let me put it another way. When Goldilocks put out the porridge, which got the interest of the Three Bears, for one it was too hot, for another it was too cold, and for the third it was just right. That was how the farmer knew it was the right time to begin combining. The moisture in the field could not be too wet or too dry; it had to be just right.

At the time, I was spending the night in Devils Lake, which was roughly an hour away from the Johnson Farm, a little east of Rugby. I figured Kipp would be out in the field around 9 a.m., but I did not want to be too late. So, I headed out of Devils Lake sometime around 7 a.m.

Once I arrived at the Johnson Farm, I met Kipp and his two brothers, Scott and Cory, who were fixing, filling, and checking things as they got ready to combine.

I hung around for a little while as things were readied, and soon Kipp drove up in his combine. "Jump in," he said, because they were going to be harvesting their wheat and soybean fields. Over the sound of the engine, he said, "We need to go a half-mile to get to the field."

That meant jumping onto US-2 and heading a little bit east at half the speed of the other drivers on the highway. Watching through the rearview mirror, I saw upcoming cars going much faster than us. I asked Kipp if the traffic bothered him.

"No," he said, "as long as they pass safely and don't go either too fast or slow."

"Too slow?" I asked.

"Yes, some drivers think by passing super slow, they are being cautious when, in reality, traveling at just less than highway speed is best."

Once we reached the field, Kipp turned on his GPS. "It's just one of many improvements that helped us compete. After all, a lot of hungry people are out there, and we need to do our part in feeding them." He told me of other modern inventions, like the ability of sprayers to put down exactly the amount of fertilizer and weed control mixtures that the crops could handle while protecting the environment. "When we get to harvesting our crops like we are today, we have exactly the equipment and personnel required."

Like a well-choreographed dance, the header on the combine scooped and cut the wheat plant and sorted the grain from the straw and the chaff. While storing the grain in an internal bin, the combine dispensed the straw out the back. In a later process, the straw was made into organic compost. In the meantime, a long pipe that enclosed an auger lifted the grain into a chaser bin towed by a tractor. Once filled, the chaser bin moved the grain into a semi that was hauling a grain trailer. All these processes were done simultaneously in a side-by-side manner. Though I was amazed at what I saw, to Kipp and his brothers it was just another day at work.

Kipp told me about his family and how they got into farming several generations ago. "Both sides of my family immigrated from Norway in the late 1800s. My mom's parents are buried fourteen miles north of Rugby near the now abandoned Marker Lutheran Church. Their homestead was just a little bit southeast of the church. My mom remembers attending a small school that was built out on the prairie not far from where she was raised."

The conversation switched to his dad's side of the family. Then Kipp noticed part of his header unit was not working right. He figured something had gotten jammed, which he said could happen when the header unit picked up a rock, usually while turning at the end of a row. He jumped out of the combine and made an adjustment. Within a couple minutes, he climbed back into the combine and continued.

"So, my mom's family was up by that Marker Church, and my dad grew up not far away in Overly." Kipp explained that his mother and his father had a lot in common. Both traced their ancestry to Norway and had been brought up Lutheran.

I asked whether he had ever been to Norway.

"Yes, I took my family there about ten years ago, and we actually got to see the home where my great-grandmother grew up. Her name was Inga. She and a cousin were able to come over to America." Their trip was made possible because his wife's aunt and uncle, who didn't have kids, had come up with the money to send her to America.

"Inga came from a family of eight to ten children, not sure exactly how many, but she was the only one who was able to come over. Unfortunately, she never got back to Norway and never saw her family again."

"So, how was it to be in Norway at the home where your great-grandmother grew up?" I asked.

"I learned a lot. She lived in a little log house with a sod roof built on the side of a mountain. She left because there wasn't enough work or food for their family. I can't imagine the journey she had getting over here, let alone leaving her family."

Kipp then took a cellphone call from a mechanic in town. They were working on one of the pieces of equipment Kipp had brought in to be fixed. I noticed that even though Kipp was totally focused on harvesting, at the same time he was also concentrating on his conversation with the mechanic. After Kipp hung up, without missing a beat he continued the story he'd been telling me before he took the call. "Once in America, Inga met Peter Johnson, my great-grandfather. They got married and had four kids, three girls and a boy. When I was in Norway, I met cousins I'd never seen, and one of them looked very similar to me. It was a little scary."

Kipp then told me that while he was in the family home in Norway, something brought the story of his great-grandmother home. "So, I'm looking around. There was a really cool stone fireplace against the wall. Hanging on the wall was a picture that looked familiar. It was like I'd seen that picture before. As I got closer, I realized it was a panoramic picture of the farmstead in Overly, North Dakota. Inga had mailed it to her family, basically saying, 'Mom and Dad, I made it to America.' My heart just dropped. I'm thousands and thousands of miles away, and here's a picture that is identical to the one that's in my Mom and Dad's house. I asked, 'Did you guys just put this in here because you knew I was coming?' And she said, 'No, it's always been here. Inga had made a duplicate copy.'"

I was asked whether the homestead in Overly was still there. "Yes, my uncle and cousins farm it now."

While combining an adjoining field, Kipp talked about how people were initially lured to North Dakota through various government acts. Much of what became North Dakota was settled through the Homestead Act of 1862. The government had provided land grants of 160 acres to people willing to improve the land, build structures, and plant crops. Then, after five years of working the land, the land was granted to the grantee. The number of acres granted increased the farther west a homesteader settled on the dry land of the western portion of the Dakota Territory. "Every state has its history when it comes to white Euro settlements. In the northwest corner of what would become North Dakota, the government had a challenge enticing homesteaders because the land is dry, and it seldom rains."

Just then Kipp's son, Isaiah, drove up. "My son is one year away from his master's at the University of Michigan. He's out here helping me today. He hasn't been around here very much the last couple years, so he's forgotten where things are and how to do certain jobs. But he's really good at driving a truck and helping me. I must admit, when he was a kid I never really got him into the tractor very often because he was so busy with everything at school and is really into sports. I wanted him to enjoy that because you only get so many years to do that. But the downfall is that he's twenty years old and needs to ask how to run certain pieces of equipment. That's when I think he gets a little frustrated with himself. As an example, when he got into the truck I told him to roll up the tarp. He asked, 'How do I do this one? I always use the electric tarp, and this one is manual.' 'It's not that hard,' I said, so I showed him once, and now he's good for the rest of his life. It's just comical. I just assumed that he knew how. And he said, 'Dad, you never showed me when I was young. That's one of your downfalls.' And I just thought, *Oh, man. I failed at teaching him how to roll up a tarp.*"

"So, Isaiah's going into hospital administration," I said.

"Yes, my son has a personality like me. I told him to remember that whether you're working with ten people or a hundred people, everybody's got a different personality, and you'll be the guy who has to figure it out. You'll also be the guy who has to lay the law down that says this has to get done, or we fail, and it's up to you to figure it out. I'm very proud of my son. I think he'll do well. He kinda knows what he wants to do. He's driven, so we'll see where it leads."

"How about your daughter?" I asked.

"Annika is doing fantastically at Concordia College. She's in her first year and wants to become a doctor. But when you tell her what to do, it's like, 'Dad, I'll figure it out. Just leave me alone.' She has been that way since she was three years old. Even when she was three, I'd say to her, 'Do you want me to help you get ready or pick out the clothes for today?' 'Dad, I'll do it myself.' She's always been headstrong. 'I'll figure it out and do it myself.' My daughter from the very get-go, she's always been determined. She wants to be a doctor. We need doctors, and we need administrators, and we need farmers, and we need teachers. I wish we could all be back in Rugby, but they don't always come back. We develop a lot of great kids, but a lot of them end up leaving. They end up being super successful, and I do attribute it to having a good upbringing and a good work ethic. This is a farm community, and you need to figure things out. My son has a four-point average at the University of Michigan, and he will do well. I'm so proud of my kids."

"What about Leah?" I asked.

"My wife has been a school teacher for over twenty-five years. She kinda retired last year, though is still teaching one class. College English." Kipp also mentioned Leah had taken another position at First Lutheran Church in Rugby, where she was on the staff for youth and family ministries.

Kipp looked at his GPS and made some sort of an adjustment, then glanced back at me and said, "And here I am, I'm doing the same thing that my great-grandfather did, just in a different style. I've got a big tractor with air conditioning that is the best in the world, but he had a tractor that he thought was the best. We're doing the same thing; we're trying to raise food to feed the world. Farming, like any industry or any job, can be very, very frustrating. It has its moments. This is the busy time of the year. Springtime, May, June, August, September, October. It is go, go, go. There's a lot that has to happen together to make it work. It's all about timing and watching the weather. In North Dakota we feel like we have a forty-eight-hour window because the snow leaves, and we gotta get it in before it rains, and all of a sudden it's June, and we think, *Whatever happened to the month of May?* But like every year, we get it in. It's a crazy industry, and you hope to get it all in and survive until another year. Automation is helpful in upping our production, but you still need people out there to drive the grain trucks."

"How about your brothers?" I asked.

Kipp Johnson, Johnson Farms, Rugby, North Dakota

"My oldest brother is 62, I'm 52, and my middle brother is 56. We're not getting any younger, but by farm standards we're still young farmers. Yet we're getting to that next stage in life. My oldest brother didn't have any kids, my middle brother has three kids with one son who wants to farm. In my case, my son and daughter are interested in doing something else, and I want to encourage them to do what they want. You have to have a passion to do this. Ten years from now, will my son want to farm? Maybe. I don't know."

"You're not going to take North Dakota out of him," I said.

"True. And I see that when he comes home. My dad started this farm back in 1967 when my parents moved to Rugby. He started something good, and we hope that it continues. We feel like we've done a good job up to this point. During our time here, running the farm, we've been very progressive farmers. One thing we started is the irrigation pit near our land along US-2, east of Rugby. Years ago, if you'd told me we'd have irrigation, I'd have said you're crazy. But I was able to get a permit, and as long as there is water in the lake, I can irrigate. The reason irrigation works here is that the watershed goes to the Mouse River and not to Devils Lake, which is thirty-five miles away and is a saltwater lake with no drainage. Without drainage, Devils Lake is like a coffee cup and traps all of its water."

Then Kipp took another call from one of his brothers, giving a report on the field he was working. After he hung up, he said, "Now where was I? . . . I think back to my ancestors who came here and how they survived. I get a kick out of people who complain about our winters, yet we get in our cars and turn on our seat heaters, or we get into our house and turn our fireplaces on. Our ancestors didn't have those luxuries. Then you see their homesteads and wonder how they survived. It's just amazing that they survived. There were no trees. And speaking of trees, whenever I journey to Ann Arbor, Michigan, to visit my son, while traveling through the beautiful forests of Michigan, I think, *My God, there are a lot of trees.* Thank God, he didn't put trees in North Dakota because how else would we feed these people? I went to Michigan to see things, but I couldn't see anything because there were so many trees."

"But in Michigan we have water," I said. "We're surrounded by it. When we want to see things we look out over the water since there aren't any trees in the water."

"As a farmer, we always say you survive because you have water. All the cities are built around water. The little water we get from April 1st until July 1st, it can be three inches, it can be four inches, or it can be nothing. The only thing that can save us sometimes are cooler temperatures, which can help a little bit, and our subsoil moisture from snowfall in the winter and rain in the fall. We have such a small window to make a crop, and if Mother Nature doesn't give us rain, we just don't know what we'll get. But she can also produce hail, tornadoes, hundred-mile-an-hour wind. There's no trees, nothing to stop it. There are just so many things that can happen when you harvest a crop."

When I left the Johnson farm, I took a few back roads to head farther west. I thought about Kipp and Leah and how they had not pushed their children into farming.

A lot of children were pushed or encouraged to do something they were not that interested in doing, in part because of tradition. For a good century in the plains states, farms passed from generation to generation. When a generation decided to do something else, the farm land was often rented or sold off to another farmer. Oftentimes, to the farm next door. Though a generational farm passed into other hands, the now larger farm would update its technology, allowing a farmer to farm more land and in the process become more productive. This enabled farms in the United States to compete with farms in other countries, resulting in fewer acres required to raise more crops. The downside was that the towns near the farms often shrank in population, resulting in fewer kids in school, fewer families purchasing groceries and other goods, fewer workers to both work the farms and work in stores, and fewer services available because with fewer people, the local commerce shrank. This revolving cycle made it less possible for children to stay around once they hit the age of adulthood.

It was a problem with no immediate fixes unless something dramatic happened to drive up population. I saw it in most rural places.

The opposite was true in areas near cities, especially large cities where burgeoning suburbs and housing developments use land that was once some of the most fertile in the country. You saw it in areas around my hometown in Grand Haven, Michigan, which used to have a massive number of blueberry fields and lots of acreage dedicated to vegetables. Lowlands with plenty of moisture, which were perfect for growing landscape plants. Wetlands that were great places to grow celery. Those fields had been made into either housing developments or commercial properties. Our county, Ottawa County, was once the largest blueberry producer in the country. Not anymore. There were still some blueberry fields; however, one by one, they had been sold off to developers.

20

As I continued driving west, the land and how it was used, changed. Fewer farms and more ranches. Flat lands became diversified with more hills and hollows. It was most noticeable once I got past Minot. I was heading west to get to the Bakken Oil Play in the western portion of North Dakota.

Historically, in the 1880s, the Great Northern was quickly laying down its tracks across the flat plains of North Dakota and heading toward the Pacific. By early 1886, James J. Hill, the "Empire Builder," had 8,000 men and 3,000 horse teams crossing the Mouse River, 40 miles east of what became Minot. Nothing seemingly was getting in their way until October, when they arrived at the spot where the Minot townsite was planned.

Though it was easy for the railroad to lay tracks to Minot, a difficult task was ahead. They needed to construct a bridge over the Gassman Coulee, but it was late in the season, and the cold winds and winter snows made continuing near impossible. The railroad had to build a tent city to house the workers during the upcoming winter.

If you'd ever been to North Dakota in the winter, as I had, you'd know what I meant. People in these parts talked about the howling wind and temps falling to well below zero as if it were bikini weather. A guy I knew said the wind only stopped blowing long enough to change directions.

By the time the Gassman Coulee trestle was completed on May 1, 1887, it had taken nearly a million and a half feet of lumber to get the job done. In the meantime, the population of Minot had grown to around five thousand, earning the town the title the "Magic City," a name that stuck.

If you looked to the south off US-2 just past Minot, you could see the trestle on the left. It was hard to miss. It was still fully operational, Like all of the tracks, trestles, and tunnels built by the workers on the Great Northern, it was overbuilt on purpose. It became the most reliable railway in the country. It still is, as the BNSF.

One thing that amazed me during my many trips to Minot was how few people knew the story about how their city began, even though they often drove under a bridge with a large sign announcing "The Magic City"—a city that grew to a population just shy of fifty thousand. Yet this city was truly magical, standing proud and strong along the Drift Plains more than a hundred miles away from any city close to its size. That distance made Minot a destination city for people in a radius of more than fifty miles in every direction. Minot, with its diverse economy, was the home of the Minot Air Force Base, Minot State University, a good-size hospital, and many stores and restaurants.

At the university, I stopped to see the concert hall where the Minot Symphony Orchestra performed. As I entered, something caught my attention and made me realize how much of an impact the attacks of 9/11 had on our nation. There, on a sign in gold letters above the concert hall doors, was the name Ann Nicole Nelson Concert Hall. Later, I learned that Ann Nicole Nelson was the daughter of Gary and Jenette Nelson, and that she had brought her parents and others much joy. After overseas study, she graduated from Carleton College in Northfield, Minnesota, and later took a job as a bond trader in New York City. On

September 11, 2001, while she was working at Cantor Fitzgerald, one of the planes hit the building she was in at the World Trade Center. She was among the nearly three thousand who perished that day.

I also learned that Ann's father, Gary S. Nelson, had passed away months before my visit. His obituary told me the kind of man he was. The youngest of eleven children, he was a rancher, an educator, and a businessman who with his wife, Jenette, raised their family in Stanley, North Dakota, fifty-some miles west of Minot. During his life, he served on many boards, volunteered as a firefighter, and was dedicated to helping others reach their potential. So, what started as an invitation to a concert grew into my better understanding of how a town the size of Minot could have a fine symphonic orchestra playing in a venue worthy of a major orchestra.

As I continued on my way west, the land changed from the nearly flat Drift Plains to a hilly terrain that was part of the Missouri Escarpment. This land's steep rise marked the dividing line between the Drift Plains and the Missouri Plateau to the west. North of the highway was the Souris River, winding through the valley and the Gassman Coulee.

The Bakken Formation was the third-largest oil reserve in the country. Though the Bakken produced a modest amount of oil for many years, after the development of horizontal drilling mechanisms and hydraulic fracturing in the early 2000s, the production of oil increased.

And with fracking came what has been called "the Bakken land grab." Once the potential of the Bakken formation was discovered, oil companies aggressively leased land from landowners, often at high prices, to secure access to drilling sites. The rush to lease land sometimes led to disputes over land ownership and the potential exploitation of landowners, particularly those less familiar with oil industry practices.

Driving through the Bakken, I saw single pumpjack rigs and large multiple pumpjack fracking fields. Called nodding donkeys, the distinctive up-and-down motion of the pumpjack resembled a donkey nodding its head as the jack pumped oil to the surface. It seemed like everywhere I looked, oil wells were mixed in with ranches and farms, along with grain elevators and rail tracks.

Although the Bakken oil boom brought significant economic growth to the region, including job creation and a housing boom, it led to rapid population increases and a lack of living spaces for oil workers. It also put a strain on local infrastructure.

Because some Native American reservations overlapped with the Bakken formation, concerns had been raised about potential environmental damage, along with a lower-than-market-value compensation for land leases. The result was a series of lawsuits.

Though farmers and ranchers benefited from oil drilling by selling the mineral rights of their land, the payment they received was just enough to help them break even. As a local rancher explained to me in confidence, "Land owners like me have no leverage. We can either sell land rights at the oil companies' price or let them go down the road and offer the deal to someone else." Another rancher said, "Mineral rights give me enough money to help make up for some of the losses during a particularly bad year."

21

It was New Year's Eve, 1998, when I first visited Williston—years before the latest oil boom. At the time, Williston had a stagnant population of around twelve thousand and was known by some as a Wild West town. Tired from a day of travel, I pulled up to a small motel. When the desk clerk looked me over and saw my attire and the satchel I was carrying, she figured I wouldn't fit in with all the rabble rousing that would likely happen as the New Year's clock ticked toward midnight. So, she asked whether I was there to sleep or to party. I said sleep. Hearing that, she called a motel across town and arranged for me to get a room there. She said that her motel had a bar, by midnight guns would be going off in the parking lot, and partying wouldn't end until the early morning hours. To this day, I still remember the kindness she showed me on that New Year's Eve.

During my route across America and back, I knew I'd be sure to return to Williston. As the largest city on the Bakken, it had grown exponentially since the late 1990s when I was there for New Year's Eve. It had now nearly tripled in size. This once Wild West town had developed so much, I couldn't even recognize it anymore. The one area in town that had stayed the same was the downtown. I stopped by the local indy bookstore, Books on Broadway, where I ran into the owner, Chuck Wilder, in a booth in the backroom coffeeshop.

I introduced myself, and without a moment passing, he said, "Time to sit down over coffee?" With that, he walked over to the coffee bar, which was reminiscent of the chrome counter of a New Jersey diner.

Chuck asked, "Black or room for cream?"

"Black," I said, and during the course of the next couple hours, we became friends.

The layout of Books on Broadway looked like a packed bookstore in midtown Manhattan where every square inch was used. Racks of books were on wooden bookshelves that didn't necessarily match. You squeezed through the store in order to rifle through the books. Atop the shelves were anything from antiquarian books to photos of Williston back in the day. Framed artwork was tacked onto walls, along with twirly wire racks with cards. All types of objects hung from the ceiling, including globes with lights, actual globes of the world, a toy biplane, posters of TV westerns, and even wind chimes. On the floor were unopened boxes of books, stuffed animals, and coffee table books leaning on upholstered chairs. In other words, a store someone could spend a lifetime exploring. Quite frankly, it reminded me of my studio back home where every flat surface was covered with stuff. So, Chuck's store reminded me of home, which might have been one reason I did not want to leave. So, I stayed until Chuck asked, "Can I get you something for lunch?"

During our conversation, Chuck told me he was an attorney by trade, but that he chose to take over the bookstore after his wife died several years back. Something told me he loved his wife dearly and was living on to make the business she'd founded a living legacy.

"I like to say we are an independent bookstore for independent minds," Chuck said. "This is a store where people come to share their ideas without any fear of judgment."

And come they do. While I sat in the booth talking with Chuck, a musician walked in, settled into the next booth down from us, and began strumming on his guitar and singing. Not only did he strum and sing, he was an excellent musician playing songs he had written. What a concept, a store where customers felt comfortable enough to share their artistic talent. Later, another guy came in. He had machined a part that would fix the espresso machine, which was making a whole lot of noise. It suddenly became quiet after he fixed it.

Amid all of the mayhem, Chuck said, "I'm from Williston, and I'm a local here. My two grandmothers were here when the railroad came through in 1887. One of my grandmothers was two, and the other one was five. My roots go way back. I've got a real love-hate relationship with this town. Parts of it can drive you stark raving nuts, but in general it's a good town."

A second later, Chuck was back on his feet, heading over to the checkout counter to answer a woman's question. She told him about someone she knew who had a goiter. Chuck solved her problem by recommending a book with old-fashioned remedies, which she purchased.

Back at our booth, Chuck grabbed my cup and poured me a refill. Sitting down again, he told me about the boom-and-bust nature of Williston. "When oil was discovered in Tioga in 1951," he said, "it was a couple years before I was born. That was the first oil boom. I was here during the second boom in the late '70s and early '80s. That was a boom and a bust. When that busted, the price of oil dropped from about forty-five dollars a barrel to roughly seven dollars a barrel within a couple weeks. That was very hard on Williston economically. The population when the second boom ended had been around twenty-two thousand and dropped back to about twelve thousand."

I told Chuck my story about being in Williston in the late '90s and witnessing one of the busts.

Chuck said that when the latest oil boom hit in 2013, the population grew from twelve thousand to more than thirty thousand. "When that happened, the city was in poor financial condition." He explained that Williston had been stuck with a lot of special assessments. The city had gone out on a limb to finance many infrastructure improvements, which included miles of paved roads and sidewalks. Chuck said, "Developers built two 700-unit trailer parks, called man camps. Those were a mess. It's good to see they have since been taken down."

Just then, Chuck got up to help another customer, a friend looking for a novel about the Old West. Chuck plucked a book off the shelf and told the man the gist of the story. They headed to the checkout together and talked for a while as Chuck rang up the sale.

When Chuck returned, he said, "One thing I remember about the latest boom was that it seemed different than the earlier booms. These guys started arriving from companies like Halliburton, and they came into the store and bought books. I thought that was kinda unusual because in prior booms, all those people were like high school dropouts. The ones who came in this time had college degrees, and they were readers. That's one thing with the boom that we're still in: I'd say it's still booming; it hasn't busted yet. It's more of a technology-driven boom. They're drilling into the Bakken Formation, which is a narrow strip of land, and the Williston Basin, which is more like a dish. There's all these layers in it. When oil was discovered in 1951, they were drilling into the Red River and the Madison Formation. They always knew there was oil in the Bakken Layer, but they could never access it because it was tight shale, and when they drilled down, they would just draw in a little bit of oil. Now the rigs are pulling a lot more oil out, and that is upping our capacity."

Just then, Chuck was called away by a neighboring business owner, and they discussed an upcoming event. As he stood there talking, something came to me that had slipped my mind. Chuck looked like a dad with his checked shirt and khakis, a friendly guy who spoke without judgment. I thought, *I'll bet he spends much of his days giving straight-from-the-shoulder advice. As if he was that kinda dad whom everyone in town could count on.* Chuck had told me earlier that an author who had done a signing called him from the road to say his books were stacked in a store a good hour away. And without the author asking, Chuck drove there to pick them up.

When Chuck returned, and after yet another refill of coffee, I asked what Williston was like when it was founded.

Chuck Wilder, Owner, Books on Broadway, Williston, North Dakota

"It started as a little group of log cabins," Chuck said, "put there in anticipation of the arrival of the railroad." He told me North Dakota had achieved statehood in 1889 and, by that time, "my family was into ranching. They were basically squatting on land." During the first few years, things went well, but by the time of World War I, farmers had experienced crop failures, followed by economic challenges in the 1920s. In the 1930s, Chuck said, "A time known as the 'dirty thirties,' the dust storms arrived. By the late thirties, there was a large outward migration from North Dakota to the West Coast."

He told me about Williston's rich history, which extended from the tribal days of centuries ago to Lewis and Clark's Corps of Discovery passing through in 1805 and 1806. Then an influx of fur traders established Fort Union Trading Post in 1828. For forty years until its closing in 1867, that post conducted trade with the Assiniboine and six other Northern Plains Tribes, exchanging buffalo robes and smaller furs for goods from around the world, including cloth, guns, blankets, and beads.

We then talked a bit about the confluence of the Yellowstone and Missouri rivers a few miles southwest of Williston and when Louis and Clark passed through on their way west in 1804 and their trip eastward in 1806. Fort Union had been built by John Jacob Astor at the confluence twenty years later as a commercial fur trading post. "Though Native Americans were warring a lot," Chuck said, "they saw Fort Union as a place where they could get beads, arms, and clothes, among other items. Fort Union was sort of a neutral area, and tribes would come in and trade. Then once they got a certain distance away, all hell would break loose."

Chuck told me that once Fort Union had run its course, the federal government purchased what remained and built Fort Buford two miles away. Although Fort Union had been a trading post, Fort Buford was run by the military. During its thirty years of existence, the fort gained notoriety in 1881 when Sitting Bull surrendered there after being in exile in Canada for six years.

In the time I spent with Chuck, his humility stood out. He was a friend to everyone he met, a good person to know who helped all who asked, in one way or another.

Next, I drove to Watford City, an hour's drive away. Like Williston, it was a town that grew once oil was discovered. This small ranching town also served as the gateway to the North Dakota Badlands, the Little Missouri National Grasslands, and the northern unit of Theodore Roosevelt National Park. It was a convenient place for me to stay. I found a room in a mom-and-pop motel where oil workers stayed, owned by a couple who lived nearby. The husband, Roger Maki, who once worked in the oil industry, said, "Drilling for our own oil is way better than importing it from overseas. That way, dollars are kept at home. I don't know what the fracking does in places like Pennsylvania where it's closer to the surface, but here we are drilling 10,000 to 12,000 feet down, a depth that doesn't threaten our drinking water."

During my stay in Watford City, I was invited to watch a branding operation at the Veeder Ranch, owned by Gene and Beth Veeder and their daughter, Jessie Veeder Scofield, and their son-in-law, Chad. Though they owned and operated a good-size cow/calf ranch, they still needed other jobs to help pay their way. Jessie was a singer/songwriter and author, and Chad worked in the oil fields. Few understood the hard work and dedication of America's ranchers. Jessie told me, "Much of ranching is about repairing fences, feeding cattle, and staying on the ranch. You can't go anywhere for much over a day. Right now, Dad helps out because someone has to be on the place to take care of the cattle."

Her dad, Gene, added, "Out here, life's conveniences, such as available healthcare and shopping, are oftentimes lacking. There was a time when people regularly visited rural places, but with cross-country air travel and interstates that get travelers from coast to coast without needing to visit small towns, many people have no idea what country living is all about."

When Jessie joined her father, Gene, in running the Veeder Ranch, they carried on a tradition that had begun more than a hundred years earlier. The ranch, located on the edge of the North Dakota Badlands, was near where Theodore Roosevelt once ranched.

While in the area, I spent much of my time at the North Unit of Theodore Roosevelt National Park, located roughly fifteen miles south of Watford City. In a nod to the past, when Texas Longhorns were raised in North Dakota, the north unit still had a small herd of longhorn steers. I took time to capture photos of the park's buffalo and bighorn sheep. While there, I thought about Theodore Roosevelt. Called the "father of the conservation movement," he said, "We have become great because of the lavish use of our resources. But the time has come to inquire seriously what will happen when our forests are gone, when the coal, the iron, the oil, and the gas are exhausted, when the soils have still further impoverished and washed into the streams, polluting the rivers, denuding the fields and obstructing navigation."

As president, Roosevelt used the power of the executive branch to create the United States Forest Service and establish 150 national forests, 51 federal bird reserves, 4 national game preserves, 5 national parks, and 18 national monuments through the American Antiquities Act of 1906.

To me, the beauty of the Theodore Roosevelt National Park North Unit was that fewer people visited the park than at some of the more popular national parks. As a result, in the park I spent less time with crowds. I especially enjoyed being in the park at sunrise and sunset when the wildlife were far more likely to be seen.

22

Heading west into Montana, I was reminded of a passage from the book titled *Route 2,* by Louise Erdrich and Michael Dorris. It described their cross-country journey along U.S. Highway 2, entering Montana from North Dakota. "It's a marvel how properly the state line is drawn because once across it we know we're in Montana. A feeling of unlimited space builds from the first mile, enhanced by the occasional swell and roll of land which imparts a sense that the car is sailing, flying low, over a boundless distance. The sky is big in Montana, unreasonably so, bigger than it has a right to be."

Though beautifully written, that passage didn't tell the entire story of crossing the state line into Montana. Actually, the one thing that stood out in the vast plains was a small casino appropriately named State Line Casino, one of the only structures in view of the state border. Just past the casino was the first mile marker, number 667, which gave motorists a pretty good idea of how large Montana was. The expanse of rolling hills was grazing land for cattle. In Montana,

US-2 is called the Hi-Line, which the Great Northern Railway also initially called the stretch of track from Havre to Whitefish. Since then, Montanans have referred to the entire northern region of the state as the Hi-Line Region.

After driving eight miles from the North Dakota border, I encountered Bainville, a whistle stop that served the farmers and the ranchers along the prairie when first founded in 1904. On the plains in this part of the state, people said the winds were so strong that a breeze that made a log chain stand out like the tail of a kite wasn't so bad, but when the end links started snapping off, one after another, a storm was about to begin.

I was driving in an area of the country where virtually all jobs had a connection to the Ag industry. Unless someone's family owned a farm, a ranch, or a business related to agriculture, it was very hard to make a living.

North of the Missouri River where Lewis and Clark camped on April 28, 1805, Meriwether Lewis mentioned in his journal the unique rock formations east of present-day Culbertson. ". . . the hills & Bluffs Shew the Straturs of Coal, and burnt appearances in maney places, in and about them I could find no appearance of Pumice Stone . . . the Bluffs in this part as also below Shew different Straturs of Coal or carbonated wood, and 'Coloured earth,' such as dark brown, yellow a lightish brown, & dark red &c." What Meriwether Lewis had noticed was lignite coal, and the burnt appearances were likely clinker, which formed when a burning coal bed baked any adjacent shale and clay stone. Apparently, Captain Lewis called any frothy-looking rock with numerous pores "pumice stone," which appeared similar to clinker but was not of volcanic origin. Lewis's journal entree was proof that he didn't know how to spell—something I could relate to as I tried to decipher my own hand-scribbled notes.

The town of Culbertson was created when the Great Northern Railway arrived in 1887. The first settlers raised horses for the U.S. Army Calvary, which was laying siege to native tribes. Once the need for horses ended, ranchers switched to raising cattle, which continued to this day. Later, when the U.S. government increased the size of homesteads from 160-acre quarter sections to 320-acre half sections, farmers and ranchers could raise more crops and cattle in arid eastern Montana. As ranches and farms grew larger, farmers constructed grain elevators, which boosted commerce as farmers brought more grain to Culbertson to ship to cities across the country.

West of Culbertson, I drove across the Muddy Creek, a tributary of the Missouri River and the eastern boundary of the Fort Peck Assiniboine and Sioux Tribes' Reservation.

I drove a couple hundred yards along US-2 and took a left on Indian Road, which was paved. I pulled off on the shoulder and got out my now nearly filled note pad. I had something to say and didn't want to forget what it was, so I needed to write it down right away.

I wanted to explain something about my mother and one of her beliefs. She believed with all of her heart that she was a descendant of a member of the Delaware tribe. Her belief was based on an old photo of an uncle dating back to the early 1900s. On the back of the photo was an inscription written in pencil saying that her uncle was part "Delaware Indian." Later on, after my brothers and I had left for college or our careers, she ramped up her investigation. For the next umpteen years, my mom searched her ancestry by going back home to Metuchen, New Jersey, where she was born and raised. This was prior to the use of DNA. Her investigation took her down deep rabbit holes that turned out to be misleading at best, crooked at worst. There were still stacks of books in storage that she purchased on her quest. Nothing would stop her. For several years, she continued to search, following any hint she could find. She was on a mission and could not be stopped. Once she traveled to a town near her hometown just to meet a man who said he had some answers. They met, and she received clues but nothing solid.

Twenty years later, after my mother died, I took a DNA test, convinced I was part Delaware. When the test came back, it was not only negative; it was alarming because everyone on my entire family tree, according to my DNA, was from the Netherlands, Denmark, Sweden, and Norway. Not a single suggestion of any Delaware tribe in my family history.

Since then, I've spoken to many tribal members, and apparently a lot of white Americans have believed they were part Native American. Native people called these people "pretendian," a pejorative colloquialism describing a person who falsely claimed to be part Native American or First Nation tribal member. My mother actually thought she was part Delaware and often headed off on one of her investigations to find her family's native heritage—which did not exist.

Nobody knew more about that behavior than Ramey Escarcega Growing Thunder, the director of the Fort Peck Assiniboine and Sioux Tribes' Reservation. I stopped by to see her at the reservation's Language and Cultural Department while in Poplar. She made time for me even though her PhD ceremony at the University of Montana in faraway Missoula, Montana, was being held the next day. Ramey's doctorate was in InterDisciplinary Studies: Cultural & Linguistic Anthropology, Native American Studies & Educational Leadership. The degree had been long in coming. And with Missoula being more than an eight-and-a-half-hour drive away, she had only a couple of hours to spare before she needed to get going.

Ramey told me, "What I do is for my people, though the last couple years have been hard. But I won't let that define me or kill me. I won't let that happen because of my ancestors. My father once told me that I needed to finish college in order to help our people."

Those words held a special meaning for Ramey because her father had died a year earlier. He was a leader who had served with honor in the U.S. Air Force and later on the tribal council. For two years he had suffered, and Ramey, his devoted daughter, was ever present during that time. She and her father had a special bond that played out when Ramey had donated a kidney to him several years earlier. Even while he was sick, he had continued pushing her to get her doctorate. And on this special day, her long drive to Missoula and thoughts about what it had taken to earn the degree were justifiably on her mind.

Born in Poplar on the Fort Peck Assiniboine and Sioux tribes' reservation, Ramey had lived there most of her life. She was married to a well-known artist whose works were featured in several major museums. They raised their children on the reservation, with the youngest about to graduate from high school.

Ramey's interest in language and culture came early in her life through her grandmother, who was a member of the Navajo Nation. "When we'd visit Grandma in New Mexico, which was a very long drive, we'd get there, and nobody would speak English. So, I had to learn the Navajo language. Grandma had sheep, horses, and cattle, so while there we were highly involved with the livestock. My

Dr. Ramey Growing Thunder, Dakota name Thawachin Iwichacu Win ("Takes Their Mind Woman"), holding framed photo of her beloved grandmother. Ramey is Director, Fort Peck Tribes' Language & Culture Department, Poplar, Montana

grandma was a rug weaver. She had this long stick, and she'd weave with it. Then we would go out and pick plants with Grandma explaining that you dye purple with a purple plant and yellow with a yellow plant. And we would pick the plants according to the color that worked when she dyed with it. She would then boil the mixture down, and we'd dye the wool. And she'd make her rugs, which she'd sell to supplement her income. Grandma taught me life lessons I still use today."

After earning her master's degree in Albuquerque, Ramey returned to Fort Peck to put her education into practice by teaching the Dakota and Nakota Sioux languages to native people who wanted to recover their language heritage. Much of it had been lost during the Indian boarding school era. Ramey had a special place in her heart for teaching children and developed a nine-week course for students during summer break. "Working with the youth outdoors gets them outside where we can visit sacred sites, hike the badlands. There's a different activity every day. I use those opportunities to teach about our cultural heritage. I try to get close to our ancestral teachings that the youth may have heard while growing up, through oral stories or in written family histories."

One of the most uplifting developments at Fort Peck Reservation was the return of the buffalo. Many Americans knew about the slaughter of the North American buffalo during the late 1800s. This led to the government's needing to provide ongoing help for the Plains Indians, who depended on the buffalo for sustenance. Ramey Growing Thunder told me during our visit, "They were our Walmart." They provided skins for tepees, fur for clothing, and bones for tools, digging sticks, cups, spoons, and even knives. Yet when the Europeans and later the Americans came along, they saw the buffalo as sport and nearly wiped them out—millions upon millions of buffalo—leaving the native populations with nothing.

No one had more comprehensive knowledge about the Fort Peck Reservation's buffalo than Robert (Robbie) Magnan, who had been the director of the Fort Peck Tribes' Fish and Game Department for more than thirty-four years. Yet, if you had asked Robbie during his earlier life whether he would be working there, he'd have thought you were crazy.

Robbie was born on the Fort Peck Reservation and lived with his family there until he was a sixth-grader. But then the family moved to Denver, Colorado, and that was when trouble began. "It was an era when a lot of busing was going on. A lot of conflicts there, and I got in a lot of fights with my black brothers, and things didn't work out right."

Could you imagine moving from the safety of the reservation in rural Montana to a large city like Denver during your formative years and being put in such a racially charged environment? During this time, Richard M. Nixon was president, the Apollo missions were still putting men on the moon, and people were shocked when they heard about the My Lai massacre in Vietnam.

Confrontations in cities were heating up as the government forced kids to be shuttled to school by buses, in an attempt to desegregate public schools.

At the time, Robbie didn't know the Denver School Board had instituted a plan in 1974 to bus students among its schools, resulting in many fights occurring between students. By the time Robbie entered eighth grade, his mother had had enough. "So, my mom sent me to the Immaculate Conception Indian boarding school in Stephan, South Dakota. I spent four years there."

I asked Robbie whether they had cut his hair.

"No. Those were my cowboy days. They didn't touch it. I wouldn't let them."

Established in 1886, the Immaculate Conception Indian Mission was a boarding school on the Crow Creek Reservation. Father Joseph A. Stephen was director of the Catholic Indian Missions from 1884 to 1901. The mission was known for indoctrinating young Native American children into the ways of the white European settlers. As explained by Red Cloud, war chief and leader of the Oglala branch of the Teton Sioux, "The white men made us many promises, more promises than I can remember. But they never kept but one. They promised to take our land, and they took it."

After graduating from the Immaculate Conception Mission School, Robbie moved back to Montana. There, he worked for the tribes as a police officer for two years before joining the military for a four-year hitch. Then he returned to the Fort Peck Reservation, where he resumed his role with the police. After serving a year, Robbie said, "A friend asked if I wanted to become a game warden. At that time I didn't know exactly what a game warden really did. But after joining the force, little did I know it would be the best job I'd ever have." A job Robbie had held to the present day.

"I tell people, I don't have a job, I have an adventure because there's always something new going on."

Being part of the Fish and Game Department allowed Robbie to help guide the reestablishment of the buffalo on the reservation, a responsibility of great honor. "When they first introduced the buffalo onto the reservation after a 137-year absence, I was fortunate to go pick up the first semi load in January 1990 when the tribe bought a hundred buffalo from Fort Belknap Reservation to establish the herd."

The herd was intended to exclusively be used by tribal members. "After a couple years of the buffalo being here, the tribes realized that keeping the buffalo was very costly. Wages for employees, the land to lease, the feed required, they told me that we had to find a way to make the buffalo pay for themselves." That was when the idea for the business herd began—a second herd of buffalo for non-tribal members who wanted to pay for the chance to hunt buffalo. As word got around in the hunting community, hunters from several states called. That was when the Fort Peck tribes had their first buffalo hunt. Those hunters told others about it, and soon more hunts happened. According to Robbie, "It got to be a real lucrative deal for the reservation. But a lot of our elders got upset that we were losing focus about why we got the buffalo back. People more and more were getting interested in having a cultural herd."

Around that time, the state of Montana sued Yellowstone National Park over the buffalo coming into Montana with brucellosis, a disease that could be fatal to cattle. That led Yellowstone management to agree to do an experiment to see if it was possible to get buffalo out of Yellowstone brucellosis free. Yellowstone then started a quarantine program to see whether they could get rid of the disease. After five years of quarantine, the park decided to release those buffalo because the quarantine process had worked. With that success under its belt, Yellowstone proposed that organizations that were able could apply to take the quarantined buffalo. As Robbie remembered, "At that time we thought, Gee, that would be great. We could have two herds using Yellowstone buffalo for cultural purposes and go back to the original group to have a business herd. That way, one herd would pay for the other."

After the tribal leaders decided to give that idea a try, it was up to Robbie to make it happen. "We got a plot of land to use and applied for a grant to build the first range enclosure for the cultural herd."

The importance of the buffalo to Plains Indians couldn't be overstated. They believed the Earth was shared with their animal relatives, especially the buffalo. Ceremonies and prayers began with the Lakota and Dakota Sioux phrase *Mitakuye Oyasin* ("We are all related") to express gratitude for the connectedness of life. The buffalo gave the gift of life by sacrificing its own: the flesh and blood of the buffalo were part of the flesh and blood of the Plains Indians. Post-hunt ceremonies were performed to thank the spirits for the buffalo that was killed, and the Plains Indians were thankful for the gifts the buffalo provided every day. Everything the Plains Indians needed for life, the buffalo provided from its body. The Plains Indians had more than 150 different uses for the various buffalo parts. They even used the bladder as a container to hold water. For the Plains Indians, the buffalo meant survival.

The story of saving the Yellowstone buffalo began with a photo. In 1894, there was a widely circulated photo of several Yellowstone soldiers standing behind eight buffalo killed by a poacher. That led Congress to give the army the power to prosecute people who killed wildlife inside Yellowstone National Park. But try as they might, saving the buffalo seemed impossible. And by 1916, park managers determined there were only twenty-three buffalo left in Yellowstone.

Years earlier, William Hornaday, the first director of the soon-to-be Bronx Zoo, was working on a plan to save the buffalo (also known as the bison; I used the word *buffalo* because that was the common English name used by Native Americans, in whose language the buffalo was called *iinniiwa* in Blackfoot, *tatanka* in Lakota, *ivanbito* in Navajo, and *Kuts* in Paiute). Hornaday—along with fellow conservationists who included famed naturalist Ernest Harold Baynes—founded the American Bison Society in 1905 with the mission of saving the buffalo from extinction. Theodore Roosevelt was the new organization's honorary president. Though apparently more buffalo existed than had been reported, those were domestic cattle hybrids and not purebred buffalo. The only known purebred buffalo were in the herd of Yellowstone buffalo.

The only source of purebred buffalo outside of the West was in the Bronx Zoo. But they needed to be moved to land expansive enough to allow for breeding to increase that herd. In 1907, the American Bison Society arranged for fifteen bison donated by the New York Zoological Society (now the Bronx Zoo) to be shipped by railway from the Bronx to the Wichita National Forest and Game Preserve in Oklahoma. And in Oklahoma and other sites, including the Wind Cave National Game Preserve in South Dakota, the purebred buffalo were gradually returned to their natural habitat.

With the preservation programs succeeding, the American Bison Society declared victory and disbanded in 1935. Yet, over the years, the herd of purebred buffalo in Yellowstone grew so large that it needed to be culled. Then the Fort Peck tribes got involved. As Robbie Magnan remembered, "Yellowstone couldn't release the buffalo to just any place because cattle ranchers feared brucellosis if buffalo infected their herds." With the Fort Peck tribes' experience in safely quarantining their own herd, they were a natural fit for working with Yellowstone to reestablish the purebred buffalo on tribal lands. Robbie said, "I went to the state and said that we would like to quarantine these animals, but I needed a couple years to put in a fencing system." Apparently, two other tribes, Belknap and Wind River, had also put in a request. But instead of giving the buffalo to one of the tribes, the state turned around and gave the buffalo to Ted Turner.

"We got up in arms," Robbie said. "We told them we had the facilities ready, but nobody mentioned it. We found out later it was all about politics." Montana governor Schweitzer agreed and spoke with Robbie, telling him Fort Peck should wait: "Build me another pasture with an electric fence, and I'll give you the second batch." Though Robbie was disappointed, he made a side deal with the Belknap tribe. "I said we'd give Belknap half of the buffalo once we got them, and they agreed. We built the electric fence so Schweitzer would give us that second group."

When the buffalo finally arrived at Fort Peck, there were sixty-eight of them. But then tragedy struck during the summer of 2012: a large wildfire burned 35,000 acres, including the Fort Peck buffalo pasture, and they lost eight adults and twelve calves. News reports said that after the tribes had fought for years to get the buffalo back, winds of 40 to 50 miles an hour had whipped the flames across the grasslands, and many buffalo were lost. As Robbie recalled, "They got burned up. But it proved one thing: the electric fence that the tribe had built will keep the buffalo contained." He was quoted in the media as saying, "The fire went through one pasture, the one that was 2,100 acres, and a temporary pasture we had put them in. About 90 percent of that pasture burned. The cow and calf never had a chance. The wind carried that fire so fast, they couldn't get out of the way."

Robbie remembered the call he made to Governor Schweitzer, explaining that they had to move the buffalo out of the pasture with the electric fence. The governor told him they had to do what they had to do, even if it meant losing several buffalo. To Robbie, the silver lining to the tragedy was that the fence was good enough to keep the buffalo in the pasture. "Lo and behold, we found out that the pasture was good enough to hold them. It holds them to this day. We found out we didn't need the more elaborate electric fence. The regular electric fence would work."

Three years later, the state's agreement with Ted Turner ended. The terms of the agreement were that Turner would keep the buffalo for five years and then give them all back, except for 75 percent of the calves. Turner got to keep those calves, and the state got all of the adults and 25 percent of the calves. Those buffalo were then given to Fort Peck after the state had reviewed several other proposals. As Robbie recalled, "By this time, Bullock was governor. He decided to give them all to Fort Peck. We did a good job with the first group, so he let us have them all. Then they decided to do a study of our quarantine program. They found out it was successful if you do it the way we did it. All of our buffalo tested brucellosis-free."

Robbie was then told that the state didn't want to do the brucellosis testing anymore, so Fort Peck decided to do the program themselves. It turned into another political fight lasting three years, but finally the state agreed to allow Fort Peck to do the testing. "At the time, we were raising bulls to give to tribes that wanted to improve the genetics of their existing herds."

Since the testing program began, Fort Peck has handled family groups, consisting of a male, a female, and calves. According to Robbie, "Right now, we have 115 buffalo in quarantine, and we're looking at giving away three family groups this coming December. We're also now working with Canadian tribes and plan to do our first international transfer."

Reflecting on his time with Fort Peck tribes' Fish and Game Department, Robbie said, "I've been with the tribes for thirty-four years. I want to retire, but I'm getting a lot of pushback on it, so I don't know. Our program has expanded economically to where we're in need of a processing plant. We are getting funding to build one. It makes me happy that they are confident that I can do it. We'll start small with custom cutting at first. Once we prove to our community that we can do this, then we will evolve into meat cutting for resale. We get a lot

Robert (Robbie) Magnan, Director, Fort Peck Tribes' Fish & Game Department, Poplar, Montana

of people who want buffalo meat steaks and roasts. We would like to eventually offer those cuts. Because the process is similar, we could also offer cuts of beef. Here in Montana, we brag that we have the best beef in the world because of the grasses they eat. We have what you call cool weather grasses. The growing season is April, May, and June. That's when we have good vegetation. But it makes me laugh. You've got the best beef, but do you consume it? No. They tell me if you go to Costco or Walmart and you buy their meat, most likely your meat comes from a far distance away. And you don't know what antibiotics or steroids they put into that meat. So, you're eating something you don't know where it came from or what's in it. If we do local processing and customers get their meat from a local rancher, they will know what they put in it. Right now, there's a big demand for grass-fed beef. We can do that here. We already do that with our buffalo. We sell buffalo that's only eaten grass from beginning to end. They're never pushed into a feedlot where they're traumatized. They are all out in the open for their entire lives. We could market over the Internet here and create good jobs. Not only processing jobs but also sales and marketing and distribution. That could provide a lot of jobs for our community. I like to start out small, then let it grow."

I asked Robbie whether he was seriously considering retirement.

"What I want to do is to continue to work. I'm not going to retire." And with that, he needed to head out to a conference several hours away.

Next, I stopped by then tribal chairman Floyd Azure's office. During his first term from 2011 to 2013, he was instrumental in handling the politics of establishing the cultural buffalo herd on the reservation. "I remember that time well," he said. "It was the first time I was chairman, and in the second month of my term we began to work out an agreement with Yellowstone to establish our cultural herd. We needed to clear the hurdles with both the Montana Fish and Wildlife Commission and the Montana Board of Livestock. Neither was initially in favor of us working with Yellowstone to establish our cultural herd."

Chairman Azure said that he and Robbie had represented the tribe at presentations in front of both organizations. "We were the only brown faces there." When the Fish and Wildlife Commission opened the meeting, Chairman Azure asked to speak after everyone who was objecting had spoken. "When our time to speak came up, we explained that our goal was to take the extra buffalo from Yellowstone and offer them to our own tribal members, along with sharing all excess buffalo with other tribes that wanted to have their own buffalo herds." He told me all the attendees were ranchers, with most of them ranching far away in the middle of the state. "It was puzzling because the cultural herd wouldn't be anywhere near where they ranched." The ranchers had a baseless fear that brucellosis would infect their cattle herds. Truth was, the only known cases of brucellosis had occurred in mountainous areas populated by elk. After that discussion, someone made a motion, and the entire board of the Montana Fish and Wildlife Commission voted in favor.

As Chairman Azure remembered, "That is when the fight began." At that point, the Montana Board of Livestock made an objection, saying that buffalo were not game animals and instead were classified as cattle. That objection took more than a year to handle, with the board eventually saying the request was not approved. Finally, the tribe members spoke with then Governor Schweitzer, who signed off on the request, saying he had the power to override the cattle board.

With that, representatives of the Fort Peck tribe met with members of the National Parks Department to arrange to transfer the buffalo to the reservation. Chairman Azure and Robbie Magnan, along with several tribal members, left early in the morning to drive the livestock trailers to Yellowstone where the buffalo were loaded. "We knew it would take a minimum of eight hours to drive the buffalo back to the reservation, so we got an early start. That created yet another controversy when we were accused of transferring the buffalo under cover of darkness."

Not long after the buffalo arrived, Chairman Azure and Governor Schweitzer drove up to the pasture where the quarantine facility was located to check on the buffalo. "As we traveled there, the governor received a call saying the Board of Livestock had filed an injunction demanding the buffalo be returned to Yellowstone. To his credit, the governor told the representative of the board that they needed the order to be signed by the judge in the jurisdiction of the reservation, which was not about to happen." The protesters mostly consisted of ranchers and farmers who came onto the reservation. One was a woman who owned a farm next to the business herd but had not noticed that the business herd had been grazing next to her wheat field for several years. "That one upset me. I told her the argument she made was null and void. We take care of our buffalo and our cattle herds and have never had any problems with either of our herds. Our quarantine facility had never been breached. In fact, our quarantine facility is better than the one owned by the state."

During my time at the Fort Peck Reservation, I was honored to photograph one of the brucellosis tests. It was incredible to see the thundering herd of buffalo run full speed into a holding pen. And as with the other tests before it, all of the buffalo tested negative.

Later, I attended the annual Fort Peck Indian Rodeo being held nearby. I was invited by my friend Grant Stafne, the former buffalo ranch manager, tribal council member, and at that time with the Bureau of Land Management (BLM). Grant took me to see the buffalo at the ranch and to witness a tribal member who won the lottery to take down one of those massive animals. Once cleaned, the buffalo would feed the tribal member's family for a year.

While at the rodeo, I didn't dare admit I'd never been to one before. I wasn't from the West, and in my part of the country rodeos were not part of our culture. However, in the Western states rodeos were huge. One interesting thing about the Fort Peck rodeo was its location, next to a hill that allowed tiered parking so attendees could watch from their own cars. And with the Fort Peck Rodeo being a smaller venue, it was a very intimate setting. The rodeo riders, the bull fighters, and the pickup riders were all world-class athletes. So, too, were the support people who were invaluable in protecting the safety of all involved, including the animals. From the opening anthem performed in their native tongue to the closing ceremony, along with all the action in between, it was an event I'd surely want to attend again. The feats that day included bull riding, saddle bronc riding, team roping, tie-down roping, and a wild horse race, which was pure mayhem. I was especially impressed by the bull fighters. Once called rodeo clowns, bull fighters were athletes of the highest order. Dressed in bright, colorful attire, they had the job of distracting the bull in order to keep the bull rider from being tramped or gored by a thousand-pound animal.

23

A simple observation, whether from an airplane or even Google maps, would show a casual observer that much of the land within the Fort Peck Reservation was brown, not green. That was because land along the flat plains of eastern Montana depended on water, mostly from rivers, aquifers, and snowfall runoff from hills, to raise crops. And because the land within the Fort Peck Reservation ran north of the Missouri, west of Muddy Creek, and east of Porcupine Creek, this land was not ideal to raise row crops. Instead, it was mostly used for cattle and buffalo grazing on grasses and raising hay.

While I traveled west along US-2, it wasn't until I crossed over Porcupine Creek that the highway began to follow the Milk River—a river made famous by Merriwether Lewis of Lewis & Clark and the Corps of Discovery. He described it in a journal entry dated May 8, 1805: "(T)he water of this river possesses a peculiar whiteness, being about the colour of a cup of tea with the admixture of a tabelspoonfull of milk. from the colour of it's water we called it Milk river. We think it possible that this may be the river called by the Minitares (Hidatsa) 'the river that scolds at all others' . . ." It was one of the landmarks the Hidatsas had told Merriwether Lewis to look for as they traveled west.

From my own observances, the Milk River was a gentle stream that twisted its way through the northern plains of Central Montana and southern Canada. This was among the most productive farmland in north central Montana.

Dr. Kenneth Ryan, former Director of Economic Development at Fort Peck Reservation, told me about a place along US-2, fifty miles west of Glasgow. He said to look for a small wooden shed and two large boulders displayed behind an iron fence. While driving, I thought, *How will I ever find something like that?* With sweeping plains uninterrupted for more than a hundred miles and many abandoned structures from the homesteading days, it seemed like I'd be looking for a needle in a haystack.

Dr. Ryan said it was called the Sleeping Buffalo Rock, it was on the National Register of Historic Places, and it was described as "a traditional cultural property, a powerful spirit helper important to the Blackfoot, the Assiniboine, the Gros Ventre, the Cree, the Chippewa and other native peoples of the Northern Plains." Just as I was about to give up, there it stood. And it was just as Dr. Ryan had described.

Stopping at the small parking lot along US-2, I looked closely at the largest boulder. He was right; it was a boulder shaped like a sleeping buffalo. One of those historical signs was posted next to the shed, describing what I was looking at. It said that for countless generations, stories of Sleeping Buffalo Rock had been handed down among the tribes of Montana and western Canada through their oral traditions.

One tale involved five warriors who were stalking a small buffalo herd seemingly resting on a ridge overlooking the Milk River. The warriors were hungry and weary from their travels. Two of the warriors were assigned the task of approaching the buffalo. As the pair moved closer, the buffalo remained motionless and appeared to be easy prey. The young warriors motioned to the others to join them. As they cautiously approached the herd, they discovered the supposed buffalo were actually boulders.

There was another historical sign a little west of Malta. It said that on July 3, 1901, the infamous outlaws Butch Cassidy and the Sundance Kid, along with a hoodlum known as Kidd Curry, robbed a Great Northern Railway train carrying a load of legal tender. Though the banknotes were unsigned and therefore useless, the robbers stole around $40,000 in spendable currency. Still, it became one of the most successful train robberies in U.S. history. The gang eventually became known as the Wild Bunch and, until they disbanded in 1903, continued to pull off heists. Though George Parker, "Butch Cassidy," and Harry Longabaugh, "Sundance Kid," headed to South America to elude capture by Detective William Pinkerton and his agents, the fate of Harvey Logan, "Kid Curry," was not as clear. He may have died by his own hand in Parachute, Colorado, in 1904; might have been killed by a wild mule in South America in 1909; or perhaps died from some other means—nobody knew for sure.

I'd been on the plains for days, and although I loved the unending horizon, finding things that broke up the trip was welcome. Yet, nothing prepared me for what I saw next. Just as I approached the town of Harlem, there, sitting high on a bluff, was an abandoned church with a stuccoed exterior that had taken on a pink color. From another person who also stopped, I learned it had been boarded up since 1964. A sign by the side of the road said it was called the Sacred Heart Catholic Church, which was built in 1931 as a Jesuit mission to the Fort Belknap Reservation, on whose ground it was located. On the lot beside the church was a cemetery with grave markers colorfully decorated with flowers, some real and others plastic but all respectfully placed. The graves were adorned with assorted memorabilia, from toys to crosses to baby shoes, all left by people to celebrate the lives of those who had passed.

The building itself was deteriorating due to the harsh weather and lack of care, in part caused by persistent poverty, along with neglect and other challenges, which had doomed nearly half the local population to living below the poverty line. The tribes didn't have enough money to feed and clothe everyone, let alone invest in local structures.

Dang, I thought, as I left the pink church parking lot. *I'm nearly out of gas.* I pulled out my map, looked for logical places where gas might be sold. *Here I am in the middle of nowhere with a plug-in hybrid that averages 60 miles per gallon. A gas gauge I seldom check because, let's face it, with a 10-gallon capacity and a range of 500 to 600 miles, the car generally has enough in the tank to get wherever I'm going each day.*

I'd filled up west of Williston, and my next stop was Havre, which I mentally calculated to be a 300-mile drive. So, why now? I remembered, as I sat there, that I had taken a few side trips: to the buffalo ranch near Poplar, north to the old military base near Glasgow, and a bit of a stretch of Old US-2 west of Saco to Lake Bowdoin and back. Thinking about it more, I had traveled quite a distance when I counted the side trip miles. I thought, *The Fort Belknap Casino is only few miles away. Surely, they will sell gas there.*

I drove the five miles to the casino, and, yes, there was a gas station of sorts—a self fill-up pump outside the convenience store. I swiped my card, and the purchase was approved. But when I reached for the hose, it wasn't attached. So, I walked into the store and barked something to the guy behind the counter who was busy checking someone out. He looked up and grunted a reply that didn't sound promising.

I got back in my car, figuring it was only a few more miles to Harlem. Once I got there, the Conoco station was open, but the pumps were closed. I checked with the woman inside, who said it would be fixed later on. So, I grabbed a slice of pizza from the warmer oven and got back in my car, figuring there must be gas in Chinook. Calculating that the drive was twenty miles, off I headed. And just to the east of Chinook, I could see another station, Conoco, off in the distance. I got there on fumes and finally filled up.

24

Havre looked to be at the bottom of a bowl. It was. From all directions, when approaching Havre, you were going downhill to get there. That was probably why the town was originally named Bullhook Bottoms. And without James J. Hill and the Great Northern Railway, it would have remained so. It was a name railroad builder James J. Hill hated. To get the money and the commerce the railroad would bring, a group of town folks formed a committee to give the town a new name in order to please J.J. Hill. After many disagreements that included at least one brawl, the committee decided on a name with French origins, the common heritage of the citizenry. They settled on the name Havre, which in French meant "haven" or "harbor."

Havre was where I met local historian Emily Mayer. And without her willingness to share her knowledge, I never would have known about C. W. "Shorty" Young—a rags-to-riches and back-to-rags-again story. He was broke in 1894 when he arrived in Havre and died broke in 1944. Though Shorty didn't invent Havre's racketeering, he certainly benefited from it. Emily told me Shorty was "a lovable man who could also be a scoundrel, and he pretty much ran the town back in the early years of the 1900s."

Having grown up in North Havre on "the wrong side of town," Emily had early on decided to become a historian. She said, "There were two other historians in Havre who were better than me. They both were quite old. At the time, there were no historians in this area who were my age or younger."

I asked Emily how she was able to establish herself at such a young age.

"I knew that to become a historian I needed to do good work, the actual research. Several others were interested in local history, but very few took the time required to go through all the old records like I did."

Havre was the largest city between the towns of Williston, North Dakota, and Billings, Montana, and Great Falls, Montana. With a population just under ten thousand, Havre served the needs of people living in the north-central portion of Montana with its college, hospital, shopping, and business services. It also had a large railroad yard for the BNSF railroad with a twice-daily stopover of Amtrak's *Empire Builder* passenger train. Havre was a very important destination along the Hi-Line.

During my three-day visit, Emily gave me a personal tour of Havre and the surrounding areas.

Havre was a route for smuggling alcohol to Canada during Prohibition and, as such, was the home of many nefarious characters. As we walked through the downtown area, Emily pointed out the purple squares in the sidewalks. "These were the skylights for the underground activities by outlaws like Shorty Young, who portrayed themselves as businessmen." She told me when the businesses first started, they operated under canvas tents. "Over time, they built wooden buildings like other Western communities. But as happened in many towns, a fire in Havre destroyed a good portion of our downtown in January 1904. Yet, because merchants still had stock to sell, they dug out basements, covered them, and connected them with passageways to other businesses that had similarly dug out their basements. They operated like that for a number of years until they got the financing together to build stone and concrete structures."

I asked Emily what kinds of businesses were located underground.

"There were saloons selling banned alcohol, gambling joints, dancehalls, opium dens, and bordellos."

She said it was from 1918 to 1920, when Canada had its prohibition. As a result, Canadians were importing alcohol from the United States. And with the Canadian border being so close, much of the alcohol smuggled into Canada came from Havre. Moving along, Emily told me the tables turned in 1920 when a nationwide Prohibition began in the United States just as it ended in Canada. That allowed the Canadians to begin smuggling alcohol into Havre. And with the maze of underground passages in place, it was easy to get from one business to another, all while avoiding detection by the authorities. It was a successful, effective way to hide alcohol and illegal substances.

During my visit with Emily, she took me to many places that made Havre special. Driving her classic Chevy pickup with a cracked windshield and double-stacked headlights, she told me so many stories that I wondered, *How in the world does Emily remember so much?*

Walking along the downtown streets, in rapid-fire sequence Emily told me who owned which business and who had worked there and when. Then we toured residential areas, and she described the history of each house and owner.

We next headed to the cemetery where Emily took me from one grave to another, and, as before, she reeled off information about each grave from memory. She knew who each person was, what the people did, and, in some cases, who they cheated or cheated on.

Next, we took a series of road trips—one toward the Canadian border to see some of the bootlegging routes and another trip south to the Bears Paw Mountains to see the Rocky Boy Tribe's Reservation.

We hiked the Wahkpa Chu'gun Buffalo Jump site where thousands of buffalo bones revealed how Native Americans had efficiently been able to kill buffalo for several hundred years.

As we drove, we talked about the Hutterite communities in Hill County and how ingenious they were in using technology to grow produce and other crops that they brought to market. Emily said, "A lot of people don't like them because they feel they take advantage of the system by not paying taxes as a religious order. However, I, for one, like them. They are nice people who stick to their traditions and keep to themselves. They're really savvy in how quickly they adapt to state-of-the-art equipment. The Hutterites are good for the economy and generally buy locally."

Emily said three presidents had visited Havre: Franklyn Roosevelt, Harry Truman, and Bill Clinton. "I attended the event when Bill Clinton visited, and a lot of people came to see him. Even Republicans came."

Emily Mayer, Local Historian, Havre, Montana

We talked about the local economy. "Almost every person I know works a second job," Emily said. "'Cause they have to. I know one person who works three jobs to make ends meet. And she's a hard worker. But that's the way it is around here."

That turned our conversation to the topic of living in rural America. Emily said, "I keep hearing people from cities that say there's nothing out there. There's plenty here. I just wish they'd come to see us so they can appreciate this part of the country. We're all Americans, and I think we would do better if we got to know each other just a little bit more. Some people here say that people in big cities don't understand us. I say, they don't understand us, and we don't understand them. Some say they view us as simply flyover country. . . . One thing I love about living here in Havre is the beauty of the landscape. You go up north toward Canada, and you've got that incredible prairie, you go west and you've got Fresno Reservoir, which is the closest thing to a beach we have."

The more we talked, the more we both learned. Emily heard about my area of the country, and I discovered more about the hill country of Montana.

When we returned to Havre after all that driving, there at the train depot was the Amtrak *Empire Builder,* sitting on the track near the statue of James J. Hill. He looked proud of his accomplishments, with one hand grasping his vest and other holding his hat, welcoming everyone who had just arrived. I thought, *Heck, I had Emily to show me around, not some statue of a wealthy robber baron, acting smug.*

25

From Havre, I headed west to Chester, passing through several water stop settlements along the way. This portion of the route was a perfect demonstration of how water stops were required, how they worked, and what became of the settlements that formed near many of them. In the days of steam locomotives, water stops needed to be located every six or so miles. At each stop, it took the railway crew a good hour to fill the tender, which sat between the steam engine and the crew in the cab of the locomotive. The crew consisted of an engineer who drove the locomotive and a fireman who tended to the firebox, making sure that a steady supply of coal or wood fueled the steam engine.

The first railroad stop was north of Beaver Creek where the railroad tracks crossed the Big Sandy Creek, a tributary to the Milk River. As far as I could see while walking through the area, no permanent settlement had formed there.

Next was Burnham, where the only indication of its being a water stop was a third set of tracks running a few hundred feet and then ending without reconnecting to the other sets of tracks.

Then came Kremlin, which was still a settlement. The area around Kremlin was known for its chocolate loam—soil that was excellent for growing wheat, rye, oats, barley, and flax without irrigation. One explanation of its name was that in 1910, several of its homesteaders were Russian. Another explanation was that local farmers saw prairie mirages that looked like the Kremlin in Moscow. Though the town grew for a decade, in the 1920s drought and recession forced many homesteaders to leave the area.

Next stop was Guildford, also established by homesteaders in 1910. It was thought that with more than 800,000 acres of productive chocolate loam soil, it would become a large city. And from 1915 until it closed down in 1951, it had a flour mill that milled Golden Grain Flour, a popular brand. Now, with the mill long gone, the population steadily decreased and was down to fewer than 150.

Hingham, called "the progressive city—a city built on the square," developed as a grain storage and shipping center along the Great Northern Railway. For a town with a population of around 130, I thought it looked to be doing okay.

Rudyard, after building two grain elevators, quickly grew into a grain shipping center and shipped more wheat than any other community between Havre and Shelby.

The next encampment was Inverness, population seventy-seven. What began as a section house in 1909 soon became a thriving community that included a school, a church, a grain elevator, a hardware store, and a grocery.

Many homesteaders who settled in the area came from Minnesota and North Dakota, and for a few years farming was okay. Then an extreme drought happened in 1917, and by 1918, many homesteaders gave up and moved away. Those who stayed bought up more land and built larger, more economically sound farms than the 160-acre homesteads they first farmed.

The last town before Chester was Joplin, a station house on the Great Northern Railway. Homesteaders began arriving in the spring of 1910, and by 1915 the town's population exploded. The Joplin Commercial Club coined the phrase the "Biggest Little Town on Earth," which was still attached to the town.

The town of Chester began in 1891 when the Great Northern Railway constructed a 50,000-gallon water tank, a windmill, and a section house and eventually added a coal dock. The town grew so fast, it was soon larger than Havre.

When I arrived in Chester, the first place I headed was the local newspaper to meet its owner, Paul Overlie. He talked about the declining population that he said happened because of the success of the farmers. "When I was a kid, the average farm was around two thousand acres, and someone could get by on a section or two. The average farm today is probably five thousand acres. We once had around two hundred family farms. Now we have about a hundred." He noted that it took fewer people to farm more acres because farm equipment and farming techniques had gotten a lot more efficient. Although it kept food prices down, fewer people were required, which led to a loss in population.

Paul said he'd been in the newspaper business for more than thirty years, with the last twenty in Chester. He saw the population declining yet still believed in the possibility of renewed growth as more people were able to work remotely. Paul said, "It could happen as more people become attracted to the kind of small town living we have in Chester."

I asked Paul why people liked living in Chester.

"Most of the people I know who move here are outdoorsy types who enjoy hunting, fishing, and camping." He added, "If people aren't interested in doing those kinds of things, Chester might not be for them. Chester is small but safe; people here don't lock their doors. It's the way we live around here. Little things matter. If you get stuck in a ditch, people around here pull you out."

Paul suggested I stop by the lumberyard and speak with Damon Lalum, its owner.

So I drove a couple blocks away to Western Lumber & Supply, where I found Damon at the front desk. I asked whether he had a little time to talk, and he said he did, though if customers came, he'd need to give them his attention.

I asked whether he could tell me about his growing-up years.

Damon said, "I was born here, went to college in Bozeman and worked construction in Phoenix for ten years. But when my parents, who owned the lumberyard, decided to retire, I moved back here to raise my family."

I asked how many in his high school class had stayed in town. Thinking about it for a minute, Damon said, "Let's see, out of my twenty-five classmates, only four of us are still here. Two of them are farmers who took over the family farm, one who married someone local, and me, who moved away and then came back. We are an Ag town, so our jobs here are as farmers, at companies like the grain elevator, or in stores that sell to farmers such as our one remaining local grocery store."

I asked about his family ties to Chester.

"My parents were second generation and were both from Chester. They grew up here and stayed here and never lived anywhere else." Pointing around the store as he spoke, Damon said, "My father started working here in the lumberyard in the early '80s and then purchased the store in 1999. He owned it until 2013, when I bought it from him. We only need two workers plus myself to run the store, and we are the only lumberyard within our area. We cover over 95 miles of US-2 and all the way north to Canada."

I looked around his store. It was well stocked with a large assortment of products, from lumber, which was out in the yard, to hardware, tools, and small items like nails, screws, bolts, and that type of thing. Then Damon had to help a customer load his pickup.

When he returned, our conversation shifted to area employment and how farms as they got more efficient needed fewer workers. I had heard several people in towns along the prairie mention parents who have "the talk" with their children—about how staying where they grew up might not be the best idea if they wanted some sort of future that didn't involve agriculture. So, I asked Damon if he'd had that talk with his own parents.

"My brother got a technology job and moved to Boise, and my sister went into the medical field. She moved to Bozeman, where she's doing well. Neither of them had any intent to come back to Chester, and neither did I, to be honest. I told my parents I was not interested in the lumberyard. So, yeah, we did have 'the talk,' and they wanted us to go away to college. And I was the only one who came back."

I asked Damon what had changed in Chester since his growing-up years.

"The area has definitely declined in population. You don't notice it so much based on the number of people around, but you do notice it in the school and church enrollment. We used to have five churches with really good attendance. Now all five of those churches are struggling. The number of students in school has also declined. When I graduated in the late '90s, there were probably 110 kids in high school, and now we're roughly half of that. A few of the businesses have also declined, like the implement dealer, which used to have a huge inventory of tractors and combines. Now they pretty much just have a maintenance facility. We used to have two grocery stores; now we have one. In town, the big employers are the hospital, the school, and the county. Outside of those, everything here is based on agriculture."

Next, I asked how the farms had changed. He replied, "Twenty years ago, a farm could get by on a third of the acres that they do now. All of those farms have consolidated. So, what used to be three is now one. Therefore, a third as many people are running the farms, resulting in the population slowly decreasing."

"How about economic development here in Chester, would that help in growing the population?"

"It's hard to think of any kind of growth that wouldn't be agriculture-based in some sort or fashion. Because that's all we have around here. For one, we don't have a workforce; everybody here either has a job already or is a farmer. Being away from the freeways and the airport, it's hard to see anything developing here. I'd be happy if we can continue with what we have. In terms of people coming back, there just isn't the kind of dining or entertainment or even a movie theater here that would make people want to move back. All those things are what people want. As an example, our hospital has trouble attracting doctors and nurses. And if they are single, the dating pool here is pretty thin."

Damon added, "We moved back so that our children could spend more time with us. We both worked long hours in Phoenix, so the kids were in daycare a lot. We moved back for our children. Since both sets of grandparents already lived here, the kids could see their grandparents more often. Also, there is less stress. Chester is a less stressful place to live than Phoenix, where driving was miserable. We felt that when you spend two hours a day commuting, it's unfair to the children."

The roads that headed north of Chester were rough, ruddy, and graveled. My car kicked up a good amount of dust that blocked my rear-view mirror. Around fifteen miles north of Chester was where Jeff Mattson farmed. From one of his fields, I could see the grain elevators near Damon Lalum's store. His farm shared the same zip code as Chester, yet it took me a good thirty minutes to get there.

Jeff was a fourth-generation farmer. His farm was homesteaded by his great-grandfather. He said, "When my grandpa was young, he watched as they plowed the field behind a horse."

I asked how wide his plow was back then.

"A foot-and-a-half-wide."

"What you using now?"

"Our drills are sixty to eighty feet wide, and our sprayers are a hundred twenty feet, which travel twenty times faster than a horse."

"These days, what are you pulling them with?"

"A Cat tractor with track drive. They don't make them anymore. They sold the tractor division to AGCO and consolidated it with a lot of other brands under the Fendt name."

Jeff talked about his family history. "My great-grandfather had three sons. My grandfather was the oldest and, as was the custom, took over the homestead while his two brothers took over nearby farms. My dad was the oldest son, so he took over the original homestead. When his brother came back from overseas after serving in the military at the end of World War II, he joined my father, and they farmed together for a number of years. I've taken over from them. I have an

Jeff Mattson, Farmer, Chester, Montana

older brother who works in computers and a cousin who's older. He's an athletic trainer and a teacher in southern Montana."

During Jeff's college years, he majored in music. "When I started college, I wanted to be a music teacher, but after taking several classes, I didn't love music as much when it was a job. I worked in agriculture in the summer and took odd jobs in the winter. Ended up taking over the farm, and now here I am."

"Just like me," I said. "Went off to college to study music, left music school when studying music became a pain." I told Jeff that I also lacked the passion for teaching music and ended up leaving school and working in the family business, which lost out to the chain stores a few years later.

So, here I was, talking to a dry land farmer on a field in the flatlands of north-central Montana that could use some rain.

I asked, "How are you staying productive these days?"

"We start by fine-tuning our farming methods. Do it every year. It's like we're in a race to stay productive in the world that keeps trying to catch up with us. We weigh choices, when to upgrade the equipment or take advantage of land made available when another farmer quits or retires."

Jeff's farm sat in the shadow of the Sweetgrass Hills, the 7,000-foot-high mountains that separated the plains of Montana from Alberta, Canada, and were among the most isolated peaks in the country.

I asked Jeff what he typically raised.

"When I took over the farm twenty years ago, the crop was mainly spring wheat or winter wheat. It was half wheat and half idle ground, which you'd keep clean for the next year's crop. Since then, we've transitioned into two-thirds crop and one-third idle. Our crops these days are winter wheat, summer wheat with some durham, Austrian peas, chickpeas, mustard, barley—in other words, we grow quite the smorgasbord of crop varieties. It's all on a rotation to protect the land."

I asked what it was like when he first started to farm.

"I first started when I was little. Helped my dad and uncle. Back then, you had your crops, and you'd spray when needed. They would fertilize some when it first became the norm. You would pull a plow or a shovel that would turn the dirt to kill the weeds. You'd do that over and over, all summer long. Nowadays, it's chemical follow, or 'chem-follow,' so you control your weeds with chemicals. You're no longer pulverizing the ground by turning it and stirring it all the time and not breaking things apart. You're keeping more biomass, more roots, more plants in the ground, keeping things alive and together as much as possible. Same with seeding. Now we're going into minimum tilling and no till, so rather than tearing everything up and then trenching in a crop, you don't touch it. Instead, you're kinda knifing it in, and everything is still standing except that one little slit where you just cut it and drop your seed in. More and more often, we're treating soil like a living organism where the less you disturb it, the better. We constantly make improvements as we learn."

"Anytime someone hears the word *chemicals,*" I said, "they go, 'Oh, my god, are you trying to kill me?'"

"Yeah, when people hear we are using chemicals, they think we're covering acres and acres with them. Though in essence that is true, those same people have lawns or have a garden or a little plot of grass that they water, mow, and chemically fertilize. What they put on that one little plot, we spread over a large acreage. It's like taking a dollop of mayonnaise and putting it in your mouth; you get a concentrated amount of product. But think about spreading that same amount of mayonnaise across your entire floor or your driveway, and you don't even know it's there. And with each increase in knowledge and research, we use less and less. Even five years ago, when you would chem-follow, you'd spray every square foot of land. Now I have my sprayers equipped with a technology that senses the weed and the chlorophyl in the plant and absorbs it with its infrared light, and where it makes that gap in the light, it replaces that with a spray from a single nozzle. So, rather than fogging for ten feet and hitting one plant, now the sprayer is off the whole time and only sprays where it finds a weed. Before it was available, a full load of spray would do 240 acres. Now that same load of spray will take care of 900 acres."

"How about GPS?" I asked. "How does that work out for you?"

"GPS has made a huge difference. Anytime you have to cover an area that's a half-mile wide, you can get your process down so you are working in centimeters, rather than just eyeballing and driving it. In essence, everything is more efficient. Your time, your fuel, your wear and tear—across the board, GPS has made a huge difference."

From Jeff Mattson's farm, I headed farther north to the Whitlash-Aden border crossing, one of the least-crossed borders to Canada. Averaging just two crossings per day, it was the only border crossing with an unpaved road.

I first visited the crossing in 1998 while writing the book about the Presbyterians. What attracted me to the area was the small country church in Whitlash. The border guard and his young family were members of that church. Back then, before 9/11, the stations on both sides of the border looked like a couple of trailers in a mobile home park. The only difference was the lift gate at the border line. I remember asking about security: "What if someone drove through or around the gate?" The border guard said someone breaking through the border would soon be caught because the area near the border was so remote. The only people living anywhere near the border were likely ranchers, and ranchers noticed anything that seemed out of order.

This time when I revisited the same border crossing, the American border station had been replaced by a large, secure-looking structure. The new barrier gate was far more intimidating than the previous flimsy one. Yet nothing else in the area had changed much at all. The road was still unpaved, the border agents were still accommodating, and the traffic through the border still amounted to fewer than a handful of crossings a day.

On this latest trip, I wanted to walk from the American side into Canada to take some photos. I didn't want to drive my car across the border because of the amount of photographic equipment I carried, which might have triggered a search. The border guard on the American side was very accommodating and phoned the Canadian side to make sure it was okay and that I would be allowed to take the walk. They soon worked it out. The Canadians agreed just so long as I stayed on their side for only a couple of minutes. Otherwise, they would need to fill out paperwork noting the visit. Afterward, I was able to say I walked into Canada at one of the least-trafficked border crossings in the country.

26

My room that night was in the town of Conrad, Montana—another railroad town. Here, I would climb from the foothills to the core of the Rockies with my intended destination Glacier National Park, all the while hoping my plug-in hybrid was up to the task.

In Conrad, I stayed at a small, low-priced motel with an attached casino, gas station, and convenience store. I imagined if I got caught in a blizzard and the roads were closed, pretty much everything I required to survive was right there. I planned to travel back and forth for a couple days to explore the eastern portion of Glacier National Park, the fifth-largest national park in the contiguous United States.

It took me around two hours to drive from Conrad to Glacier National Park's St. Mary entrance. I passed through a semi-arid shortgrass prairie that included ranch lands much of the way. Only when I'd nearly arrived at Browning did the mountains of Glacier begin to stand out. This wide open space had vistas of a long, gently rising landscape, where the road ahead looked like an unrolled ribbon going on and on as it disappeared into the distance. Here the weather was unforgiving, and ranchers living in the area were as tough as the climate.

The road to Glacier passed through the Blackfoot Nation, one of the country's ten largest reservations, where buffalo were beginning their comeback after near extinction more than a century ago. While driving along the vast expanse of the prairie, I imagined what it must have been like when all of the land was roamed by millions of buffalo.

In Browning, I stopped by the Museum of the Plains Indian to learn more about the history of the Blackfoot people. While there, I asked how the Blackfoot got their name.

I was told there were a couple of explanations. One was that French fur traders noticed the bottoms of many tribal members' moccasins after they had walked through a prairie fire and ended up with blackened soles, thus called them *pen-wa,* which in French meant "black foot." The other explanation was that the name came from the tribe's long association with the buffalo, whose hooves were black.

Wandering through the museum, I saw displays that showed many tribal nations and that the tribe's members came from multiple bands. The traditional lands of the Blackfoot—or Niitsitapi, in their native language—stretched along the eastern foothills of the northern Rockies from southern Alberta and Saskatchewan through northern Montana. The tribe had four bands: the Kanai (Blood Tribe), the Siksika (Blackfoot), the Piikani (Peigan), and the Amskapi Pikuni (Blackfoot). Only the Blackfoot lived in Montana; the others were in Alberta.

I asked about the relationship between the Blackfoot and the buffalo.

One of the museum docents explained that the Blackfoot were a nomadic tribe that followed the buffalo, which he said was their main source of food, hides for clothing and shelter, and horns and bones for tools. He added that the loss of the buffalo and much of their land was due to incursions by white settlers, along with the government's mass killing of the buffalo. This was intended to starve indigenous people who resisted government orders to leave, and from that point on, life got hard.

I also learned that the Blackfoot had migrated to the West from areas along the northern Great Lakes. They were fast learners, after withstanding an attack by the Shoshoni in 1730, a tribe that rode horses. Soon the Blackfoot obtained their own horses from the Flathead, the Kutenai, and the Nez Perce. Then later, in the 1800s, they traded buffalo hides for horses and guns with the newly arrived white settlers.

In 1870, the Blackfoot suffered a terrible tragedy when American troops slaughtered two hundred members of the Peigan band, mostly women and children. The Peigans were a friendly tribe—not the hostile group the troops were supposed to be pursuing. The incident was known as the Marias Massacre. In their defense, the commander of the American troops said he had permission to kill Indian people for things they "may" have been guilty of in the past, the present, or the future—the worst excuse for murder I had ever heard.

By the winter of 1884, the cherished buffalo in the region were nearly extinct, and tribes had to depend on the U.S. government's Indian Agency for food and other necessities. They were also forced to live on reservations by the government through the signing of a treaty in 1895, a treaty that the tribes didn't understand—written in legalese, not a form of communication they knew about or could even comprehend. The land of the Blackfoot once covered vast areas of Alberta extending to the Yellowstone River along the North Dakota border. The treaty reduced their land to include only land along the foothills of the Rockies from northern Montana to Alberta. Gone, too, were many of their spiritual sites, having been repurposed for other uses and no longer being in areas the tribal people could visit.

After I visited the Museum of the Plains Indians, I decided to travel near one of the most sacred places that once belonged to the Blackfoot Nation. Chief Mountain (Ninaistako, in the Blackfoot language) was viewable along Montana Route 17, also known as Chief Mountain Highway. Its distinctive flat-topped peak could be seen from up to one hundred miles away.

To the Blackfoot Nation, Chief Mountain was sacred and thought to hold ancient knowledge, along with stories of creation. It was believed that if the mountain were to be destroyed, the Blackfoot People would cease to exist.

The base of the mountain also served as a sacred gathering spot for sweet grass ceremonies, prayer-flag placement, and other rituals. It was the site of ancient burials as well.

In an agreement, the Blackfoot Reservation retained legal jurisdiction over the mountain and the responsibility to jointly manage it with the National Parks Service. Due to increased recreational use by tourists, resulting in landslides and vandalism of sacred objects, the Blackfoot Nation's ritual use for ceremonies would take precedence, and tourists were asked "to enjoy Chief Mountain's distinctive profile from a distance"—which was exactly what I did when I viewed it from the turnout on Chief Mountain Highway.

Next, I doubled back to the Many Glacier entrance of the eastern portion of Glacier National Park to the Waterton-Glacier International Peace Park. It had lofty, angular peaks, knife-edge ridges, and dense forests with glaciers nestled in many of its highest peaks. The park was bisected by the Continental Divide where streams flowed in multiple directions—northward to Hudson Bay, eastward to the Gulf of Mexico, or westward to the Pacific Ocean. This land of many species had grizzlies, black and brown bears, moose, elk, and mountain goats.

The Many Glacier Hotel was closed at season's end, so I walked its grounds before hiking the trail around Swiftcurrent Lake. There, I met a hearing specialist named David from Kalispell by way of Seattle, who'd moved to Montana to be closer to Glacier. Before making the move, he'd sold his home and practice and purchased an existing practice, which he was able to grow ten-fold in two years. I asked him about the population increase during the last decade in Flathead County. He said he was lucky the practice he'd purchased did so well because otherwise he wouldn't have been able to afford to live anywhere near Glacier. Housing costs were high, due to people from Washington State, Oregon, and California moving there, David had to purchase a home half the size of his house in Seattle—and that was nearly a decade ago. Yet, he was still glad he'd made the move.

Just after speaking with David, I spotted a grizzly along the trail. With bear spray ready and the bear noticing me, I was happy when the bear retreated. Bears, even grizzlies, were not fond of people and generally avoided contact with humans. It was important to be prepared yet even more crucial to remember what was posted on signs everywhere: the park was their home, not ours.

From Many Glacier, I headed back to Conrad for the night, figuring I'd start the next day fresh at the Saint Mary Visitor Center, the eastern terminus of the long, scenic Going-to-the-Sun road. Around dawn the next morning, I stopped by the visitor center and found out it was the final day that it would be open that year. The woman I met at the visitor center was from South Carolina, and her husband worked as a park ranger, a summer assignment the couple enjoyed. With it being the last day in the season, she and her husband were preparing to leave the next day to go back home. They planned to get jobs during the off season with the hope of returning next summer to the park. They lived in a small, tow-behind trailer and were part of a growing trend of young people who chose experiences over career. They said their jobs supported a lifestyle of enjoying the outdoors without their needing to settle down. As I left the visitor center, I thought, *What would we do without those who were willing to work for next to nothing for the National Park Service? Such great people. I hope the federal government knows how special they are.*

The Blackfoot People called the mountain landscape in and around Glacier National Park "The Backbone of the World." But a man from Brooklyn, George Bird Grinnell, became the single most important person to lead the effort of creating

Glacier National Park. He coined the phrase "The Crown of the Continent" in describing the landscape. When he passed away on April 11, 1938, the *New York Times* called him the "father of the modern day conservation movement."

The crown jewel of Glacier National Park, Going-to-the-Sun Road, ran diagonally through the park for nearly fifty-one miles. It passed alongside glacier lakes, old-growth forests, and sheer mountain cliffs and was one of the first National Park Service roads specifically intended to accommodate automobiles.

Before the Going-to-the-Sun Road was built and the park was established, people often contemplated but seldom attempted to explore the rugged Glacier area, and they rarely had significant success. The promise of mineral deposits and oil fields drew some of the first adventurers to the area thirty-odd years before the park was established. The prospectors settled briefly in mining camps and filed almost two thousand mineral claims. The dilapidated remains of unprofitable ventures such as the Cracker Lake Mine and the Butte Oil Well testified to this era of Glacier's early history.

Crossing the Continental Divide through the Marias Pass, the Great Northern Railroad obtained a right-of-way through the mountains that later formed the southern boundary of Glacier. James J. Hill and his son Louis Hill, who ran the Great Northern, saw Glacier National Park as the "playground of the Northwest" and built hotels and chalets that would attract visitors.

In 1921, construction began at both ends of Going-to-the-Sun Road, originally called the Transmountain Highway. But the road needed to cross twenty-one miles of the Continental Divide, which required accurate mapping. At that time Frank A. Kittredge, director of the Bureau of Public Roads, led a team of thirty-two men who climbed three thousand feet in elevation to get to the survey sites. They walked along narrow ledges and used ropes to hang over cliffs to take many of the measurements. Going-to-the-Sun Road was completed during the summer of 1933, after more than twenty years of planning and construction. In 1952, the paving was finished over the entire fifty-one-mile road.

Driving along Going-to-the-Sun Road on the last day it was open allowed me to be one of the last hikers to climb to Hidden Lake Overlook at Logan Pass. During that hike, two young boys, so excited to make the climb, ran past me as their parents slowly climbed the increasingly difficult path. I thought, *I hope those kids don't fall and break their necks while running where they should be walking.* Then I remembered that when I was their age, I had done the same as them, and my parents would have said what I was now thinking. Funny how age changed one's perspective.

Once I arrived at the overlook, I took out my camera to capture the beauty, to celebrate that I'd completed the hike to the destination, and as proof I'd actually made it there. When I got back to my car after the hike, I was tired and sat for a while before driving the remainder of Going-to-the-Sun Road. I used to be invigorated when I completed a hike, but now that my body was no longer as capable, I thought, *I sure wish I was twenty years younger.*

After leaving the park, I headed to Kalispell. While I registered at a small motel—one of the few places my budget allowed—the front desk manager said he was born and raised in the area but couldn't find an affordable place to live. He spoke of the farms and the ranches being replaced by housing developments for the wealthy.

"I remember those days," I said. "It used to be just fine to own a house elsewhere and to stay at motels while away. But with tax laws favoring people with money, those days had passed." We talked about how unfair our system of taxation was and that individuals with a lot of money no longer gave a damn about regular people.

I said, "I remember when the wealthy donated land to the public, but now the billionaire class spends their extra money on riding rockets into space." He agreed, saying, "Take a drive to Whitefish and look at all the houses sitting up on the mountains. They are the ones who have made it darn near impossible for workers like me to get a place I can afford."

The next morning, the car parked next to mine was missing its hood and one of its doors. Inside, the interior had been covered with pink cloth. I spoke with its owner as he added a couple quarts of oil and asked what was up with his car. He said, "I was heading to Cut Bank, need a place to live. Don't get paid enough to cover the rent around here. Fresh oil and a few gallons in the tank should get me there."

I offered him a ride because I was heading back to the east, not all the way to Cut Bank but close. He didn't want it, so I left. To this day, I wonder if he made it there.

Someone had told me about a monument to the east called Camp Disappointment. It meant crossing back over the Continental Divide. Two hours or so later, after I'd logged more than a hundred miles, one of those historical signs greeted me near—of all places—a whistle stop called Meriwether. It said,

> The monument on the hill above was erected by the Great Northern Railway in 1925 to commemorate the farthest point north reached by the Lewis and Clark Expedition, 1804–1806. Captain Meriwether Lewis, with three of his best men, left the main party at the Missouri River and embarked on a side trip to explore the headwaters of the Marias River. He hoped to be able to report to President Jefferson that the headwaters arose north of the 49th parallel, thus extending the boundaries of the newly acquired Louisiana Purchase. The party

> camped on the Cut Bank River July 22–25, 1806, in a "beautifull and extensive bottom." Deep in the territory of the dreaded Blackfoot, the men were uneasy. Lewis wrote, "game of every discription is extreemly wild which induces me to believe the indians are now, or have been lately, in this neighborhood." Lewis could see from here that the river arose to the west rather than the north, as he had hoped. Disheartened, by his discovery, by the cold, rainy weather, and by the shortage of game, Lewis named this farthest point north Camp Disappointment, the actual site of which is four miles directly north of this monument.

The sign failed to say that it was also where Meriwether Lewis shot and killed two Blackfoot tribal members during their one and only serious incident with native people. It is no wonder why, when you climbed the hill, the monument had been spray-painted with various phrases, including one that said, "This is Pikuni Blackfoot land," in large black letters.

I headed back west, and on US-2 at the Marias Pass was the monument dedicated to John Frank Stevens, who was hired by James J. Hill to find a route for the Great Northern Railway to cross the Marias Pass. Hill was fond of saying, "What we want is the best possible line, shortest distance, lowest grades, and least curvature we can build. We do not care enough for Rocky Mountains scenery to spend a large sum of money developing it."

Given those orders, John F. Stevens proved to be tougher and more determined than anyone hired for that job in the past. Stevens knew that to find a railway route through the Marias Pass, he would need to employ someone familiar with that land. When the Blackfoot wouldn't help, he hired a Flathead who was living with the Blackfoot.

It was December, and the snow was deep when Stevens and his guide set out on rawhide-strung snowshoes. When they reached a place called False Summit, several miles east of the pass, the guide couldn't go any farther. At that point, Stevens went on alone. Later, he said it was by chance that he walked right into the Marias Pass. Once he found it, he continued far enough west to make sure he had crossed the Continental Divide. He turned back and stayed the night at the summit. The deep snow prevented him from having a fire, and he decided not to lie down in the extreme cold. He walked back and forth all night to keep from freezing to death. The temperature that night was forty below. At daybreak, he walked back to where he had left the Flathead, who during the night had let his fire run out and was almost dead from the cold. Together, they returned to their starting point along Badger Creek. John Stevens, a modest man, said he was able to complete the journey "because he was strong," as if he were unaware of the importance of his accomplishment.

Although the mountain pass had been well known to area tribes, with the Salish, the Kootenai, and the Blackfoot frequently crossing it to hunt buffalo and raid their neighbors, the pass had been unknown to non-Indians. And when the railroad was completed in 1893, it became the shortest link between the Mississippi River headwaters and the Pacific, making the Great Northern the most efficient and profitable means of transportation in the country—a railroad route still used today.

To the west of Kalispell was a region of lakes, streams, forests, and mountains to the Kootenai National Forest and the Idaho Panhandle National Forest. Just past Libby, Montana, the Kootenai Falls Swinging Bridge crossed the Kootenai River downstream from the falls.

As someone with an extreme fear of heights, when I hiked to the swinging bridge and looked at the rushing waters below, I thought, *No way.* Instead, I watched as, one by one, people crossed the swinging bridge. A young couple approached the bridge, hand in hand, and gingerly walked to midspan when suddenly they had a long embrace—from my vantage point, it looked like the man may have proposed. Next came a young lady who took a video selfie while walking across the bridge. Then came an elderly couple. He was game; she wasn't. He began crossing, and reluctantly she followed. From her timid actions, I could tell she was scared. A few minutes later, a young woman crossing the bridge began to jump up and down, causing the bridge to swing even more. Finally came a family of three, the mother holding their toddler's hand. All of a sudden, the child shouted, "Wheee!" as they crossed. Seeing them having so much fun, I decided to cross the bridge myself. And truthfully, it was a lot of fun. As I stood at midspan, the view was breathtaking. Once on the other side, I hiked along the opposite side of the Kootenay River.

When I walked up the footpath back to my car, a retired couple from Omaha, Nebraska, joined me. The man had taken a buyout after a long career with Ma Bell. He said there once were more than four thousand union jobs where he worked. But following cutback after cutback, the facility was down to a handful of workers. He said there were similar stories all across the country as people switched from landlines to cellphones. Now, in retirement, they had recently visited the beaches of Key West and were on their way home from a week in the mountains of Glacier National Park. They left me with words of wisdom: that life was less about the work one does; it was all about experiences one enjoyed.

Just before getting back in my car, I noticed a small gift shack near the parking lot. The woman who owned it told me her shop had been open to summer visitors for six years, and she'd spent winters running a bakery in nearby Troy. Now in her sixties, she recently told the bakery she would no longer work winters.

She had worked enough, ever since age twelve. Smiling, she said now it was finally time for her to get the winters off.

US-2 followed the Kootenai River west from Libby, Montana, to Bonners Ferry, Idaho. As the highway wound its way down the mountain to Bonner Ferry, the landscape began to change. The land flattened out, and there came Ponderay, Sandpoint, and Lake Pend Oreille.

When renowned mapmaker and fur trader David Thompson first saw Lake Pend Oreille in 1809, he became the first white man on record to discover the large, deep glacier lake. He called it *Pend Oreille,* which in French means "an ear pendant"—what the lake's shape looked like to him. Years later in his memoir, he wrote, "The impression of my mind is, from the formation of the country and its climate, its extensive Meadows and fine forests, watered by countless brooks and Rills of pure water, that it will become the abode of civilized Man, whether Natives or other people."

That evening, I was in a local supermarket getting supplies when a young man from the Kalispel tribe saw that I was wearing a hat with an image of the Indian Medicine Wheel. After following me to my car, he asked whether I knew what the medicine wheel meant. After assuring him that I did, he said, "Thank you for honoring my people." My heart melted.

The next morning I left Ponderoy along US-2, following the Pend Oreille River past Idaho's border into Washington State. To keep my promise to seek a rural route, I avoided Spokane. I took backroads and eventually caught up to US-2 west of Spokane in the bedroom community of Reardan.

27

If railroad owners hadn't wanted to build a line from Spokane to the Columbia River, the following small towns wouldn't exist today: Reardon, Davenport, Telford, Creston, Wilbur, Govan, Almira, Hartline, and Coulee City. The towns closest to Spokane had benefited over the years as bedroom communities while the towns farther west were still Ag dependent.

While passing through Wilbur, I was welcomed into the home of Jerry and Helen Metcalf, who shared their story with me. Helen answered the door because Jerry, hobbled by a leg injury, was resting in the living room. I went through my usual routine, opening the map of my route to show them where I had been and where I was going. Then I leafed through my copy of William Least Heat-Moon's

Blue Highways to let them know my intended use of their story and how it would appear in my upcoming book.

Though Helen and Jerry lived in the small rural town of Wilbur, their worldview was large. After looking over my route, Jerry said, "Our youngest daughter and her family had a house near Boise." He pointed at that location on my map. "She was a principal in a school there. But it got so congested that it made her commute longer, so she moved here to Wilbur where she is the principal of another school. Her husband is an electrical engineer just like I was. He works on power plants and power systems and travels for work to states like California, Oregon, and the coasts, yet is often able to work remotely out of his office here." Jerry then pointed at Seattle on the map. "Our oldest daughter is in France, teaching after graduating from the University of Washington in Seattle. Just to show how technology has changed things, she sends us pictures over the Internet that we view here on our iPad. Our other daughter is in Japan right now, and we're getting pictures from her while she's there."

"It's hard though," Helen added. "The pictures come in late at night when I'm getting Jerry's medicine set up for the next day."

The Metcalfs had lived in Montana before moving to Wilbur in 1967, when Jerry's job for the Bureau of Reclamation assigned him to the enormous project of building the third power plant at the Grand Coulee Dam. They told me Wilbur was a convenient place to live because it sat on US-2, which gave them access to goods and services in Spokane, an hour's drive east. Jerry commuted twenty miles north to his job at the dam. As she had when they'd lived in Montana, Helen supplemented the family income by giving piano lessons at home. I didn't think of it at the time, but I could have asked Helen to play something on their piano during our visit. After all, it was sitting right there in the living room.

I asked Jerry about his job on the dam.

"When we came here in '67, our crew was initially working on the generators, fixing problems. My work on the third power plant lasted until about 1980 when my job shifted to other projects for the Bureau of Reclamation."

Jerry's work on the Grand Coulee Dam piqued my interest. I had first visited the dam in 1998 while writing the book about the Presbyterians. At the time, I had just finished interviewing the president of what was then Whitworth College, now Whitworth University, a private Christian college affiliated with the Presbyterian Church. The day I visited the dam, I had been on my way to Seattle to do more interviews and had diverted north to see it. I still have the photos I shot that day.

Though much of the country had changed since my last visit, towns along US-2 in this part of Washington State looked exactly as they did back then.

I asked Jerry about the purpose of the third power plant, as opposed to the initial dam buildout.

"They wanted to move more water out of the Columbia River and into the Columbia River Basin for irrigation and to boost the electrical output."

"So," I said, "it gave the dam more oomph."

"Yes. You could say that. The original units were quite a bit smaller. There were nine units, which was excess capacity at the time the dam was originally constructed in the 1930s. The third power plant was conceived as the result of an international treaty between the United States and Canada, which recommended that we add one dam down here and four or five dams in Canada."

I asked how the job was for the crew working on the dam.

"It was a challenge but less vigorous because it was an add-on to the initial dam project. In addition to the power plant, we also had to modify the water flow. So, we built an extension to the dam that diverted the water to a channel five hundred feet wide, which fed water to the power plant. Banks Lake reservoir in Coulee City, as an example, has six pumps, which fed into a canal that took the water down to the lake that was created by damming the north end."

I asked whether the new buildout had helped with the irrigation in nearby places like the farms and towns along US-2, or if it mostly benefited towns farther away.

"Local irrigation came during the original buildout," Jerry said. "The new irrigation capacity reached out farther because there's more water. The new dams are referred to as treaty dams to differentiate between them and the original dams. Those provide the extra storage capacity and more water capacity here. And they reach to the Tri-Cities area of Kennewick, Pasco, and Richland at the confluence of the Columbia, Yakima, and Snake rivers, 130 miles south of here and 150 miles south of the dam. Also, to Moses Lake."

I asked whether the irrigation also helped the apple growers in Wenatchee. Jerry said it did.

The phone rang, and Helen went to answer it. While she was taking the call, I asked Jerry, "How long have you had Parkinson's?" (Earlier, I had noticed a twitch that made me wonder.)

"Since 2010. I started picking up signs in 2020. Part of my ability to move and do things has been affected by it. I've been fortunate not to have a full case of it. But it's there. I take medicine for it, and I've been successful in maintaining control of it. I go for treatment in Spokane, an hour away."

By then, Helen had come back into the living room. "Did he tell you he fell in 2000? He was out running in the winter before church on the Sunday before Thanksgiving. They didn't even think he was going to live. They had to fly him to the hospital. He's had surgery on his eyes because there was a brain injury that caused other damage. We think he may have developed Parkinson's after that. The knee injury is unrelated. There's a friend at church who had brain surgery.

He shook a lot. And Jerry doesn't shake. He does have restless knees. He has medication for that as well."

Noting that they had to travel to Spokane for treatment, I asked, "Is it hard to get doctors to open practices here?"

"I was on the hospital board for eight years," Helen said. "We had a clinic here, but it was sold to a hospital in Davenport. We really have trouble getting doctors down there. They would be attracted to the outdoor sports here; then their families would come and say they didn't like being so far from Spokane. We had specialists who would come once a week."

Our conversation shifted to how farms have changed over the years.

"When we got here, there were a lot of fences," Helen said, "because a lot of sheep farmers were here at that time. But that all disappeared after we arrived. Not much cattle farming here. A lot of cattle farther west in Hartline and Elmira. A lot more dry land there, which is more conducive to cattle than farming."

Jerry added, "Lately, it's drier here because of problems with the wells. That groundwater can be depleted. There's a lot of activity in this area. In Wilbur, going south, they have wells that are depleting the groundwater. The amount of groundwater is way down, so the wells are not as effective as they once were. That's because of an increase in irrigating using groundwater. They are currently working on a project that would get more irrigation from the dam. It's still in the preliminary phase. It's been decades of activity to try to fix it."

Helen weighed in. "When we first moved here, farms generally had the farmer, a son who was going to take over the family farm, and at least one farmhand. Now there's just the farmer, and to make a decent living, the farmers are swallowing up a lot of smaller farms. There's been a lot of consolidation here."

"Is the consolidation because the farmer is getting older and none of the kids want to farm and as a result moved away?" I asked.

"Yeah. The farming techniques and equipment have changed dramatically. Farmers used to rely on sheep to cut the weeds down. That's why the fields were fenced off—for the sheep. But they were not like the sheep farmers in Spain and Portugal who raised sheep for their wool. The farmers here saw sheep as equipment, and when better equipment came along, they got rid of the sheep. We have a picture here of the evolution of farm equipment. The first tractors had big metal wheels and a steam engine pulling a hand-fed thresher. That shows how farming has changed over time."

"What do you think will happen in Wilbur in the future?" I asked.

"As an example," Helen said, "look at Davenport and all the empty buildings there. They used to have three pharmacies; now there's one. They used to have several banks; now only one. Everyone hopes somebody will open a store that sells lumber. We have a new neighbor who's remodeling their house, and you see them

Helen and Jerry Metcalf, Wilbur, Montana

leave on Sunday, and they take all day to get back with a load of building materials. We used to have a lumber yard here in Wilbur. Very few younger people move here anymore unless they're taking over the family farm. Reardon is definitely a bedroom community of Spokane. You can really tell it's growing. It used to have a tiny grocery store, a bar, and a restaurant. Now they have a fabric store, plus a lot of chain stores. But the people who live there, they go to Spokane for everything because they work there. When our kids were growing up here, there were two classes for every grade. Now there is one small class for each grade."

When I first drove into Wilbur, I had noticed the statue of a pig, so I asked about it.

"Oh, you mean Wilbur the Pig," Helen said. "The chamber has it. It was built for a parade. They've needed to have him refurbished. It's one of those quirks in these towns. You're not accepted as a resident until you've been here for generations. You are still seen as a newcomer. We've been here since 1967, and some think we're still newbies."

That night I stayed in a small motel in Davenport. The Metcalfs were right. There was only one grocery store without much of a selection. It was drizzling, which may have influenced my attitude. When I arrived at my motel, a sign in the window said, "Manager out, your key is in your room, we do not have any other reservations, I have gone fishing, wish me a good catch, leave your key in the morning in your room, we will not offer coffee in the morning, have a great day."

The next morning, I continued heading west through the towns of Govan, Almira, and Hartline. Next came Coulee City, I turned right for the Grand Coulee Dam and kept on US-2 to cross Banks Lake Reservoir. Both the dam and the reservoir irrigated crops. I passed by the Cozy Motel with its fancy cement outdoor tables and benches to match. The place did look cozy, but it was too early to stop.

It was just west of Bank Lake at a rustic camping area where I met Chad, the vagabond from Mt. Baker, Washington. He was holed up in a campsite above Banks Lake. Cool like a block of ice melting next to his campfire, he told me to call him "the Dude." I asked, "How long have you been on the road, Dude?" He simply said, "Months."

I looked at his car. It was a wreck, a piece of crap with one door missing and a tire leaning against the car, which was on blocks. He seemed not to care about much of anything.

"How are you keeping fed?" I asked.

"Odd jobs, scrubbing dishes and the like." Then he said the strangest thing. "I'm a trust fund baby." And without saying anything further about it, he asked, "Did you see that storm that rolled in last night?"

"I didn't, was down the road in a motel with the shades drawn and air conditioning on." Still wondering what was up with the guy, I meant to say "Dude" but didn't. I simply asked, "What does a trust fund baby do?"

"Not much of anything."

We stared at each other for an uncomfortable amount of time. Then I said, "See ya," and I left. I might have mentioned I was heading to Wenatchee, but I can't remember if I did or whether it would have mattered much.

28

I left Wenatchee early to cross Stevens Pass before it got dark. But when I reached Cashmere, fifteen minutes later, something pulled at me like a magnet holding onto paper clips. There was this guy sweeping the sidewalk in front of a ministry called the Henry Building. I stopped. He invited me inside.

His name was Max Church. He said he was born in Wenatchee in 1954. He'd just retired and was trying to figure out what to do next.

I asked, "How long have you lived in these parts?"

"I've lived here all my life, worked in the timber industry, in the woods, for twenty-five years as a logger. That was thirty years ago. I was a pretty conventional logger and had to travel a long way to find work."

I thought, *How odd. I met a conventional logger west of Fort Kent, Maine, weeks earlier, and he said much the same thing about traveling a long way to find work.*

Max said, "Later on, I took a job rigging, hauling timber mostly. Then I spent a couple years in Williston, North Dakota, during the oil boom. Then I came back here and found work as an electrician, commercial and residential. Retired a year ago."

I asked, "What brings you here?"

"The Lord, if you want to know bluntly. The building was purchased by a couple who wanted to do work for the Lord. He had them buy this building, and they did, and they are. It's a place for gathering, for groups. They don't have to be Christians. It's a place where people meet, get together. It's active in blessing the community. Just before you drove up, I was here, inside, at a men's meeting. It was used yesterday evening, and it needed a little cleanup. I occasionally volunteer here. That's what I was doing when you saw me sweeping the sidewalk out front."

"What else have you been doing in the community since retiring?"

"I'm used to working hard. Enjoy working. I worked for good people. I liked what I did, and I enjoyed working with those people, and I miss a lot of them." He hesitated, then finally said, "But there's more people, always new people to meet. So, this is a good place to do it. It's a small town environment, and the people who live here love it."

I mentioned that when I first drove through Cashmere twenty some years earlier, it seemed like the highway went right through the middle of town.

"Yes, the highway used to go through town, right through the downtown. It's like all those other towns, like Wenatchee and East Wenatchee—the highway used to go right through those towns. But with the bypass, people need a reason to get off the beaten path to stop here."

Remembering when I'd driven through years ago, I said, "It seems like there are fewer orchards in Wenatchee than years ago."

Max thought about it for a few seconds, then said, "Wenatchee was agriculture, apples, fruit trees mainly. But for the past forty years, housing developments are replacing most of the orchards. Because when I was a kid, living in Wenatchee, I can remember orchards all the way down to Wenatchee Avenue, near the center of town."

I looked around the room. It was nicely decorated with plenty of meeting spaces, soft chairs and tables mostly. A kitchen, more like a nook for guests to pick up food. A small alcove where I could imagine a musician or a group playing.

Max Church, Cashmere, Washington

"It's a very nice meeting space," I said. "Feels comfortable."

Max nodded in agreement and said, "What I like about it are the relationships that are formed here. To me, that's what life is about. It's about relationships. And this place promotes relationships with the One who created us. And that's what happens here. The Lord blesses and uses the place, and there are some amazing testimonies dealing with relationships that are spoken here."

Max then asked whether he could pray for me, "to bless your trip and to keep you safe."

That immediately took me to another place, long ago. When I was on another trip twenty years earlier, a man from my hometown called me at least once a week, asking whether he could pray for my safety. Something I would never forget. The man had since passed, but he lived well in my memory.

And when I left, Max followed me outside, grabbed his broom, and began sweeping again.

From Cashmere, I drove west to Leavenworth. Before the arrival of white settlers in 1885, native tribes had long used the confluence of the Wenatchee River and Icicle Creek for hunting and salmon fishing. Then came the white man and the train, and the population exploded to more than five thousand. The town continued to thrive into the early 1900s when miles of irrigation canals were dug to establish fruit tree farms.

But in the 1920s and '30s, the town economy crashed when the Great Northern Railway moved its roundhouse and headquarters to Wenatchee and rerouted its rail lines to bypass Leavenworth. Then, during the Great Depression, the fruit business suffered. In the 1960s, though, Leavenworth gambled and won the jackpot when the town converted its architecture to look like a Bavarian Village to attract tourists. It worked, and today visitors come by the millions.

After I passed through Leavenworth, the Wenatchee River began to change from calm waters to rushing rapids. At a highway turnout, I spotted a couple sitting next to their RV and looking as if they didn't want to be there.

I stopped to check on them, and that was how I met Jim and Carolyn Owens.

With the rushing water of the spring thaw tumbling through the pass, the sound was deafening. I could barely hear Carolyn when she yelled, "We've been sitting here for three days! No cell service! Nobody will stop!"

"What about the cops?" I shouted back

"Nope, they drive on by!"

We talked, or rather yelled, for a while as I wondered what I could do to help.

I barked my name, and she hollered back, "I'm Carolyn, he's Jim! We live in Republic, Washington, northeast of here, fairly close to Canada!" Looking over at Jim as he sat there scowling, she said more quietly so only I could hear, "He's pissed, I'm having a panic attack. He says there's a wrecker coming, I told him to walk to where he could get cell service. He wants to wait, and, as I said, I'm having a panic attack."

Because I suffered from panic disorder, I asked how I could help. Though Carolyn said she didn't need any help, I did give her some advice to think about. I explained how slow, deep, steady breathing could calm the attacks. But with the loud rushing water that made it darn near impossible to hear, my words were lost on her. With that, I switched my attention to her husband.

Jim, who still had a Southern flair to his accent, said he was raised in northeast Tennessee and joined the service in 1959, spent three years and four months with the army, and had an extension because of the Bay of Pigs. I asked him when he'd met Carolyn, and he said, "Right after I got out of the service, I met my wife here in Washington at Fort Lewis, and we ultimately got married." Soon after marrying Carolyn in 1965, he became a firefighter for the city of Everett.

"Tell me about that job," I said loudly. At that moment, it seemed as if the sound of the rushing water was getting more furious. Listening later to the audio recording, I found Jim's words hard to decipher. Even though I had clipped a lavaliere mic to him, I could barely hear him say: "I spent thirty years most of them as a driver, pump operator, and ladder operator. I was also in Hazmat for the last few years of my career there."

The sounds of the rapids and traffic, a lot of it semis, passing by interrupted our conversation multiple times. I noticed through one of their RV windows that inside, they had a lot of Native American beadwork and a cross hanging from their rearview mirror. Jim said, "Those things are Carolyn's," so I shifted my attention back to her.

"Yeah, I'm the beader. I also like rockhounding." She added, "I love how the Native Americans pay so much attention to detail, along with their way of beading. Especially the Navajo."

That reminded me of my own time twenty-five years ago on the Navajo Nation reservation, when I wrote about and photographed my own observations. My recollections were very similar to what Carolyn had experienced. From my visits to the Hubble Trading Post National Historic Site in Ganado, Arizona, and the Navajo Gift Shops several miles away in Cameron, I remembered the colorful blankets, bracelets and pendants, antique beadwork, and beaded moccasins.

Having their RV on his mind, Jim joined in again with memories of vehicle breakdowns.

"Seventy miles from Dallas, Texas, we were going down a two-lane road when all of a sudden we started smelling this really bad odor—reminded me of Johnson's floor wax. I look in the mirror and see a big fog coming out of the back of the rig. So, I pulled over, and there was a high-pressure fuel leak coming out of the engine compartment. A wrecker came eventually, and we got towed to Irving where it was fixed. Had another problem a few years back, a slider went out near Spokane."

Once again, Carolyn, entered the conversation. "If you get him going on the mechanical stuff, you'll be here all day." Now she got serious, emotional, telling me they had been sitting in the same spot for more than three days and that Jim had walked a few miles to finally get a cell signal and contact a towing service. The wrecker driver had promised he would get to them within a few hours, yet here it was more than a day later. "This is really scary. I don't know why this man is doing this because he knows how old I am, and he knows I have heart problems, and he knows I'm going blind. So, where is he? People think panic attacks are fun. They're not fun."

After hearing Carolyn's anguish, I decided it was time to continue toward the pass to find a cell signal so I could call 911. At Coles Corner, a few miles after the Wenatchee River split off from US-2, I was finally able to make the call. The county dispatch, unaware of the problem, told me they would send a cruiser right away. Then I decided to continue my journey west, all the while thinking about what I'd just learned about resilience from Jim and Carolyn. In spite of a situation that was out of their control, they'd decided to soldier on. There was no talk of going back home, none of that. Instead, they were able to talk about their past trips and some of the adventures they'd had while touring the country.

A while later, I reached the highest point of US-2 at the entrance of Stevens Pass Ski Resort.

From the brochure sitting by the ticket booth, I read that the ski area had a base elevation at 4,061 feet and a peak elevation at 5,845 feet. It also said the resort received an average winter snowfall of 450 inches and attracted skiers from across the Pacific Northwest. Although US-2 was kept open year round, motorists were warned to prepare to install chains when road conditions warranted because the area was prone to avalanches and road closures.

Just past the ski area was a break in the concrete barrier. There, a dirt road named Tye headed into what looked like a gully and passed a small wooden sign that said, "Wellington." I surmised it was the original path of the railroad, perhaps eventually leading to the Iron Goat Trailhead. This six-mile-long, looping trail started in the former townsite of Wellington, now named Tye—the site of the worst railroad disaster in U.S. history.

I had originally heard that the railroad took a series of switchbacks to make it over Stevens Pass. Yet, because the grade was steep, and it required so much coal to fire up the engines, a tunnel was built. Construction started in 1897, and the tunnel opened in 1900, but from the beginning it was

Jim and Carolyn Owens, stranded in their RV along US-2 west of Leavenworth, Washington

plagued with ventilation issues. Tragedy nearly happened when a train broke down inside the tunnel in 1903. As a result, the railroad decided to electrify specially designed locomotives to pull the cars through the tunnel. The tunnel electrification project took until July 1909 to be completed. Although powered by a hydroelectric plant generated by the Tumwater Dam project, quite often the system broke down, leaving the job of pulling cars through the tunnel to steam locomotives.

It was during the winter of 1910 that the unthinkable happened. On February 23, 1910, near the east entrance of the tunnel, two westbound trains, one carrying passengers and the other, mail, were halted by avalanches at Wellington station. Five days later, a few passengers, afraid to stay on the train, decided to walk through the tunnel along the tracks to Scenic Station. On March 1, after several small avalanches, a gigantic avalanche struck the two trains and swept both trains and half of the town down the steep rocky cliff, leaving few survivors. It took a day for the rescue parties to arrive and a few weeks to locate all the bodies and clear the tracks of wreckage. When all were accounted for, ninety-six were dead. After the disaster, the small Wellington encampment at the tunnel entrance was renamed Tye.

I decided to hike the path toward the original Cascade Tunnel, now closed from a landslide in 2007. Though I couldn't reach the tunnel opening, I could see it from where the path ended. It gave me an eerie feeling to know so many people, on two separate trains, had been at that spot before they met their demise. The photo I took showed how thick the overgrown forest was, along with how water-logged the path to the tunnel had become. A few months after I left, I learned the tunnel had since been capped. to keep people safe

Doubling back to US-2, I drove over the pass to Scenic, at one time known as Scenic Hot Springs. It was near the western trailhead of the Iron Goat Trail where I had found the west entrance of the new Cascade Tunnel, which BNSF trains regularly used. I hiked in to where I heard the muffled sound of a train whistle. I waited as the whistle got louder, and soon came a west-bound BNSF train. I took out my camera and captured the train as it emerged from the tunnel. I must say, I was very fortunate to have taken that photo and smiled all the way back to where I'd parked my car.

As I continued west on US-2, Skykomish was the next town past Scenic, which sat right around where the highway leveled off. Looking about the town, I stopped at the Great Northern and Cascade Railway museum with its 7-1/2" gauge railroad and souvenir shop. There, I saw an amazing display of railroad memorabilia.

From Skykomish, I drove past a series of railroad towns: Grotto, Baring, Index, Big Bend, Gold Bar, Startup, Sultan, and Monroe.

US-2 skirted Snohomish, where I turned north on Washington Highway 9 and headed to Mount Vernon. I spent the night there—though it wasn't as simple as that. I pulled into a motel parking lot, and things seemed strange. Even the name of the motel sounded spooky. I felt as if someone were watching. I went into the lobby and asked the clerk whether it was a safe place to stay.

Dumb question, I thought as I said it. *Of course, what else can he say other than it's safe?* I was tired, the day had been long, and I just wanted a room. Yet, that feeling remained. So, I decided not to stay, but because I had a reservation, I went back into the lobby and told the desk clerk to cancel my reservation.

"No problem," he said. "Of course, I will need to charge you a twenty-five dollar fee for canceling."

"What?" I said. "I haven't even been to the room. I asked you if it was safe here, and you said it was. But looking at some of the people hanging around the lot, there is no way I'm paying that fee."

The clerk gave me a look, with a glint of "I got you" in his eyes. "The cancellation fee remains. If you leave, that's fine, but the fee is what we'll get."

"I'll cancel it at my end with a simple call to the credit card company," I said.

"We'll object at our end," he said. "You won't get a nickel back. Guaranteed."

With that, he looked the other way, much as a restaurant server would ignore a diner by appearing too busy to look in the diner's direction. I headed to the lot and called the issuer to cancel the charge. With a confident thought of *I got you,* I drove five or six blocks farther to an area that looked and felt a whole lot safer. While registering there, I met a well-dressed—make that, fancy-dressed—man who was talking about his sheep.

"Sheep?" I asked. "Did I hear you right?" I mentioned his manner of dress as my reason for asking.

"I own a company in Seattle, Queen Anne neighborhood," he said. "In my work I have a lot of stress, and sheep help ease it."

Now more puzzled, I asked, "You keep sheep in Seattle in that upscale area?"

"No, I have a farm ten miles away in a valley just north of Big Lake," he said, pointing east.

I asked whether he could show it to me. He agreed, took my card, and said he'd call when he was heading that way. I waited and waited, no call.

Two hours later, as the sky darkened, he called. Said he'd fallen asleep and wouldn't be going there until the morning. "Would you like to go then?" he asked.

But I had to say no. I'd already made two appointments for the next day, and one was early.

29

The next morning as the sun rose, I drove to Anacortes, a city on Fidalgo Island in Puget Sound. There I met Alice and Jim Doggett on their boat, which was moored at a local marina.

Anacortes' livelihood once depended on the lumber industry of the Pacific Northwest. That all changed when the Anacortes Veneer Corporation ramped up its operations in the 1930s during the Great Depression. As an employee-owned company that offered good-paying jobs, at one time many people in Anacortes worked there. But that ended when chipboard replaced plywood. And, after several iterations, what was once the city's largest employer went out of business.

The area was originally home to the Samish people, who fished for salmon and raised inland crops. Yet, as was often the case, they were shoved out of the way to western Fidalgo Island and other Puget Sound islands to make room for so-called progress: for example, two giant oil refineries across Fidalgo Bay on the meadows of March Point.

Now a vibrant community with artists' studios downtown, restaurants serving an extravaganza of food, and marinas along its shoreline, Anacortes was also the part-time home of Alice and Jim Doggett.

When I arrived at the marina, I quipped to Alice, "What do photographers never do?" to which she responded, "Take their own pictures."

We then joked that a photographer's memory wall had only a couple of photos on it. That led to our mutual experience of not being included in our own class reunion photos because we were the ones who took them.

Alice added, "Photographers are always judging the quality of what they're looking at. So, when you look at yourself, you think, *I see myself, and I don't want to look like that.* That's just our own critique."

When I first contacted Alice, it was through social media while I planned my 10,000-mile journey. I had noticed her photography and also noted that she and her husband, Jim, lived near Bend, Oregon, along the path I was taking. However, when I contacted Alice and gave her my travel schedule, she said at that time of the year they would be living on their boat at a marina in Anacortes. I decided that if not in Bend, I'd visit them while they were on their boat.

In my mind, Alice was a giant because her landscape photography was so spectacular. But when I met her, she was very petite with a clear and direct voice. And like me, she liked to laugh. Jim, who was a perfect match for Alice, was more specific and spoke less like an artist. In fact, right away he said, "I'm not an artist," to which Alice responded, "Jim understands the technical things more than I do. I get kinda lost in all of that."

I asked Alice how she got into photography.

"I got lucky. I was doing graphic design before I did photography. It turned out I have a good eye for composition. At the time I was designing magazine articles. Photography was one of those things that kinda came naturally. I did web design for a while, and I got into aspects of color and lighting. Lighting is what photography is all about. I got seriously into photography about ten years ago." She added, "People ask, 'What's your favorite picture?' and I always answer, 'The next one I take.'"

As we sat in the stern of their boat, Alice noticed a great blue heron on the dock. "I gotta tell you about the herons. I like nature. This spring our boat has had herons on the top of it, and they often make a mess. We also have river otters that climb the stairs and get in the boat and make a mess. That leads to a lot of messes that need to be cleaned up. When we drove home last time, an elk ran into our car. The elk hit the side of our car at eleven o'clock at night. Scared the bloody hell out of us. And you couldn't pull over because there's no shoulder. And it was pitch black. I think wildlife are taking back their spaces. This is our life of adventure."

"You mentioned adventure. Explain."

"I wanted to buy Jim a boat for our first anniversary. Not a big boat, a rowboat. Something we could put on top of the car. But when I saw how expensive that was, I thought it would be best as a joint venture. That got us shopping for boats, and we ended up with a much larger boat."

Jim added, "We kept that boat for a year, traded it in for a 29-footer. Kept that for about three years. Traded it in on a 37-footer with the idea of doing some serious cruising, which we did in 1983. Went down to Mexico, then sailed from there to Hawaii and back to western Washington. All were sailboats."

"Any interesting situations?"

"We got our butts kicked off Coos Bay, Oregon. We ran into some really heavy weather. Called the National Weather Service in Portland and wondered how long it was going to last. Asked what they recommended, and they advised that we go to harbor and wait it out. Which we did."

Alice looked at Jim as if there were more to the story. "What Jim didn't say was at the time, we were 125 miles offshore, and the wind was 50 mph. What we did was try to stall the boat. There's a procedure when you have a sailboat to drop the sails so you don't go anywhere. But we still drifted a hundred miles toward shore because we were like that for twenty-four hours. That's when we called to see what the forecast was. We did all the things that they tell you to do. We were getting too close to shore. It was almost nightfall, so we ended up motoring into Coos Bay. By the time we got there, it was dark, and there's a lighthouse there. We had a list of ports but not a map showing statistics. We had intended to stop on the coast to get charts. As we entered the port, we found out we needed nine feet of draft. I am the helms person. I looked at the depth finder, and it was only eight feet. So, I took the wheel and turned and luckily found a dock. It was so windy, we were there for three days. There was a bridge nearby that we needed to cross to get supplies. It was so windy I could hardly walk. When we finally left, we were with another sailor who had also docked because of the storm. He was a bush pilot in Alaska, and he had never seen weather like that either. It was so rough we nearly capsized on the way out."

I asked about how the two of them met and what their growing-up years were like.

"We met at work," Jim said and went on to tell me he was born in Seattle. When he was nine and in the fourth grade, his family moved across the Cascades to Wenatchee. "My father was a trucking company manager, my mother was a cook at the high school." After Jim graduated from high school, he attended the local community college for a year, then went into the army and spent a year in Vietnam while the war was still on. "I was a platoon leader but kinda got turned off to the whole thing after a while." After serving out his three-year stint, he returned home and enrolled at Eastern Washington University in nearby Chelan. "I got a degree in business administration, worked for the Forest Service during summers to pay for school, got offered a job shortly afterwards with Ma Bell in Seattle. At the time, I was two years into an MBA."

Alice, though, was raised in Bellevue across Lake Washington from Seattle. "My mother had MS and was in a wheelchair, so she couldn't work. We lived in a house on the beach. My dad wanted her to be able to see Lake Washington outside her window."

"How about your father?"

"My dad was a service manager at a shop that fixed calculators. Mechanical ones before the electronic ones were invented. His job changed to copy machines after calculators became handhelds."

"So, he worked in Seattle and commuted from Bellevue," I said.

"Yes, the house he bought there was only twelve thousand dollars. It was before things got built up in Bellevue. I had an hour's ride on a school bus to get to school. It was a wonderful existence. I loved being outdoors. Because we lived on a beach, we didn't have to go far to be outdoors. I stayed there through high school."

"What did you do after high school?"

"After I graduated, I worked for my dad just to make a little money. Another guy worked there who was in charge of the copy machines. He was in the process of moving to San Francisco, and he really needed a secretary, so he talked me into moving there. That was in '65 or '66. Right before Haight-Ashbury. I just put myself in a car and moved down there. I had a friend there who I stayed with until I got an apartment. I remember when we went to the movies, we had to wear white gloves, and people were smoking in the theater. Within a year, Haight-Ashbury started. Everybody was suddenly wearing loose clothes, and all the high fashion of that era, it was somewhere else. It was a time when everything changed. Totally. I lived there for six years. I left when my mother was dying, and I lived with my parents again. Didn't stay long before moving into an apartment in Bellevue. At the time, Jim lived in Seattle. We met while we were both taking classes. I was learning how to be a computer programmer, and he was studying advanced computer language. We got married a few years after that."

"It was during the era when AT&T, Ma Bell, had a monopoly in the telephone business," Jim said. "We both worked there. We've been married fifty years as of last June."

"At that time, we were in a rental house," Alice added. "Jim had this vision of living someplace with a white picket fence. This during the gasoline crisis of 1973."

I remembered those times. The 1973 energy crisis was what they now called an oil shock, one that caused energy prices to spike and resulted in fuel shortages, long lines at gas stations, and OPEC refusing to sell crude to the United States. The oil embargo was in response to our country supporting Israel during the 1973 Yom Kippur War. Even though OPEC lifted its embargo in the spring of 1974, it left economic damage throughout the United States and around the world. Economists said it was one of the factors that led to "stagflation," when inflation was high, and the economy stagnated.

As a result, Jim and Alice ended up on Bainbridge Island in a little house within walking distance of the ferry terminal.

As Alice remembered, "The ferry took us to the office in Seattle. We stayed in that house for a long time, then bought an empty lot and had a house built on it. We lived there for almost twenty years. That's the house we were living in when we went offshore sailing down the coast to Mexico. The reason we went offshore sailing is that the company we worked for, Ma Bell, wasn't doing so well. So, they were encouraging people to take leaves of absence."

"We had a house we bought," Jim added. "It was during a time of cheap housing when you could write a check and buy it. That was in 1983 when AT&T was getting ready for the breakup."

After an eight-year-long lawsuit that was settled in January 1982, AT&T agreed to break up its local businesses into seven smaller regional operating companies that became known as "Baby Bells." The process took two years, and when it ended in 1984, AT&T retained ownership of its long distance service, Bell Labs and Western Electric.

"I was gone almost a year and a half," Alice recalled. "So was Jim. I was guaranteed a job when I came back and kept my healthcare insurance while I was gone. At the time, that wasn't such a big deal. It was before medical care became so expensive. My mother had a doctor and a dentist who came to the house. That

Alice and Jim Doggett, next to their boat at a marina in Anacortes, Washington

doesn't happen anymore. People were nicer then. In almost every aspect, people were more aware of being nice to the people around them. Our values were built on a whole different platform."

"So, it sounds like you are saying it is all about neighbors."

"Yes, exactly. We had a community there, and we all knew each other. We lived on a lake with probably a dozen houses there."

"But now you live much of the year in Oregon."

"Yes. We sold the waterfront house in 1992 and purchased the house in Oregon. In the meantime, the company gave me a buyout, a year's worth of salary and cashed out my pension. I was in my forties at the time. I felt I needed to take it. So, all of a sudden I was unemployed. A very weird time. I remember how hard it was not to have interactions with people at work. I had no sense of who I was. I lacked confidence, thinking, *What in the heck am I doing?* I didn't want to get another job, so I ended up refinishing the interior of the sailboat we had at that time. We had friends who moved to Sun River, Oregon. It sounded like a good place to be. We ended up moving there, and I got a job doing marketing for a construction company."

In the meantime, Jim was flying to Phoenix for work. He described the so-called "1992/93 winter from hell when we got 180 inches of snow. We had snow up to the first-floor gutters. I retired in 2002. We kept the house in Oregon for seventeen years and decided to sell it because it was too large, and we were now living on Social Security, along with investments."

After selling the house, they couldn't find a smaller, more affordable house so they began looking in the Bend, Oregon, area. They ended up finding a home in Sisters. "We've been there since. We try to go back and forth between the marina in Anacortes and the house in Sisters. However, with boating getting so expensive, it's only a matter of time before we get out of boating."

When Jim and Alice talked about their lives, they mentioned never having kids. Instead, they were living a life of adventure. I asked when they had first noticed they had that spirit.

"Probably right after we got married, when we got that boat on our first wedding anniversary. We didn't know how to sail. Jim had a book, and that's what we used to learn how to sail. We've been places that few boaters go. We've been in this marina for over twenty years. Back then, there were an awful lot of people like us who learned from one another. We all took care of our own boats. But now a lot of boat owners have a paid crew. So, you just don't have the same camaraderie about common issues because if you're not doing it yourself, it's not the same."

From Anacortes, I drove fifty miles up the coast along Washington State Highway 11, passing the bays of Fidalgo, Padilla, and Samish and through the city of Bellingham. I followed the coastline of Bellingham Bay to the northwest—all of the land I drove through had once been part of the Lummi Indian Reservation that spanned the entire Puget Sound in Washington State and British Columbia.

The Lummi people were known as the people of the sea—*Lhaq'temish,* in their native language. For centuries, they established villages along the coastal areas in warmer months and in the inland forests in colder seasons. They lived in multi-family, cedar-plank longhouses and fished, hunted, gathered, and harvested along the freshwater streams and estuaries. Because salmon migration was cyclic, their lives revolved around the life cycle of the fish—they moved in sync with the salmon, and their catch depended on the size of the annual salmon runs. Thousands of years of observation allowed the Lummi to develop ways to create everything they needed from their catch, including clothing, tools, and shelter. They also invented ways of capturing salmon that were unique to the Lummi people.

They knew their way of life would change with the arrival of white European settlers, and they signed the 1855 Treaty of Point Elliott. In exchange for the Lummi ceding all but a small portion of their vast reservation to the U.S. government, they received the right to fish in their "usual and accustomed" places. Yet, over time, it became increasingly difficult for the Lummi to gain access to their traditional fishing sites, in part because of the many commercial fishing operations. They sued the government for breaking the agreement, and in a 1974 landmark legal case known as the Boldt Decision, the right of the Lummis and other tribes in Washington State to harvest salmon was affirmed.

Residing within the boundaries of the Lummi Reservation was artist Jayne Baron, who lived in a bus she had converted into a home and a studio. She worked in several media, from oils to watercolor to photography, and her studio was a colorful, art-filled space. Being a fellow creative, I was always interested in seeing other artists' work spaces. Some artists could only work in an organized space, while others, like myself, had trouble being creative without things being cluttered. In Jayne's case, I'd describe her space as comfortable and lightly organized, reflective of her warm personality and welcoming spirit. Immediately, she poured a cup a herbal tea, saying, "Try this. Tell me if you like it."

Knowing I was there for an interview, she asked whether I had specific questions. I didn't, I explained, "my interviews are more like a conversation."

And talk we did, for a couple of hours. We hit on a variety of topics from her art to her life to our shared Dutch heritage. She said, "I like to see and understand the whole picture, the big picture, and I think I have subconsciously orchestrated my life in a way to get the broad view through a wide range of experiences." I asked her to explain more simply. Clarifying, she said her life was at "a significant milestone" because she was about to turn sixty and was making the occasion a celebration. She explained that as an artist, she was used to working alone but was getting ready to do something different. "I have never been a person to celebrate myself, let alone host my own birthday party."

"Never?" I asked.

"Never ever," she replied. "Growing up, I might have had some decent parties." But hosting her own party seemed "audacious" to her and, in ways, "funny."

With that, she offered me a piece of traditional Dutch licorice. "It's not just about having a big celebration, it's about my identity." She had been a "really slow starter," having had so many other obligations in her earlier life.

"I always had a feeling I'd live a long life," she said, and at age fifty she'd figured her life was half over. But now she was entering her seventh decade and said that with all the advances in science, perhaps she could live to be 120. That got me thinking about my older brother, who was convinced he would live to be 151. I didn't share that thought with Jayne, however, because even 120 was a stretch. I didn't want her to think I was crazy. So, instead, I switched the topic and asked, "Ideally, what does a true life look like?"

Contemplating for a minute, she finally said, "For me, freedom to thrive, to have time for deep, meaningful relationships, and to enjoy new adventures."

"What prevented you from acting sooner?"

"Probably a combination of lack of confidence and the need to earn a living."

Bingo, I thought. Exactly what many creatives experienced. Confidence came from affirmation by friends and colleagues. Money because making a living as an artist was difficult at best. The same feelings I had in my own life as a creative. And though I was a fellow creative, I could not draw a stick figure if my life depended on it. Which was why I needed a camera to make my art.

"So, what would you most like to do?" I asked.

"I love to create beautiful environments. I'm kind of a homebody, and my personal environment is important to me. Most of my money in the past has come from gig work. I've been a caregiver, a pet walker, a house sitter, an interior and exterior painter. You can say I'm a Jayne of all trades."

I sensed Jayne felt as if time was running out, and doing odd jobs was getting in her way. I thought of how old Grandma Moses was when she started to paint—seventy-seven, if I wasn't mistaken. At any rate, for sure older than Jayne. But I didn't say anything. It would have been unseemly.

At this point, she changed the tenor of the conversation. "I'm very idealistic. I have been anti-money because it's the root of all evil. I've had to work through that. I actually limited myself by not being willing to play the game. . . . I don't want to set myself up to keep struggling for the rest of my life."

My mind wandered as I looked out the window and saw the beauty of the surroundings. I thought, *There is much to like about living in the woods within a short walk of Bellingham Bay.* Jayne then told me about her bus and all the work involved in making it her home.

"I bought the bus off Craigslist at the end of 2016. I was in the excitement of a new relationship, and we talked about working on it together and traveling the country. He dropped me the next day. So, I continued on without him. It was a lot of work, from removing the seats to the finishing touches. It's been almost exclusively my solo project. With practically no income and no knowledge or experience, it's been an incredible challenge for me and a very satisfying accomplishment."

I asked about the painting of the exterior.

"The exterior went through stages. It was in camo for a while when I wanted it to hide, be invisible. Then I wanted to celebrate it as a caravan with an Old World feel, a celebration. I was inspired by the Dutch folk art called *hindeloopen* with Tibetan designs and pure whimsy. At some point, I plan to incorporate African and Native American designs into the sides."

I wondered about the challenge of living as a working artist and how she had managed the high cost of housing.

"I'm here in this bus because the overhead is really low. I couldn't possibly live anywhere else. Even getting a room somewhere would be more expensive than here." She added, "I have an aversion to the rat race. Nine to five just doesn't work for me. I've made my intentions clear to everyone I know. Proclaiming to the

Jayne Baron, artist, in front of her bus near Bellingham, Washington

world that my art is important now. Making a living with my art, at the moment it's scary as shit."

And when Jayne said that, I thought, *Yes, scary as shit.*

Having journeyed north to Bellingham, I now would head south. My challenge was trying to navigate past the sprawling metropolis of Greater Seattle and stay away from the interstate highways. To do this, I had to double back to Bellingham and take Washington Route 9 south to US-2, then head east to Monroe. From there, I'd follow the foothills south through the Cascades and Mount Rainier National Park, then onward to Yakima with a planned stopover in Ellensburg.

One of my stops, the Sunrise Visitor Center in Rainier, was a good place to take photos of the mountain's northeastern side and hike the many trails in the shadow of its fabled snowcapped peak. The peak was visible from several areas around Sunrise. Sunrise Road had some of the most spectacular views in the park. Then the drive from Sunrise to Ellensburg took more than two and a half hours, so I had only a few minutes to get settled in my motel room before heading out to visit a friend twenty miles away in Cle Elum.

30

Jeff Osiadacz was known for many things, especially for being blunt and direct. When I first met him, he was drinking coffee. So, whenever I was nearby, I always called to meet him for coffee. As usual, when my name came up on his phone, he answered in his deep baritone voice, "Mr. Dirk, where you at?"

Knowing he would be up for coffee, I asked, "Where you going these days, the Cottage or the Sunrise?"

"I don't go to the Cottage no more. That woman I can't stand is still there, so I'm at the Sunrise these days. Better food, coffee's fine. When you getting in?"

The first time I met Jeff, he was sitting on his "stump" (his term for a barstool) at the Cottage Cafe. Since then, he rotated quite often from the Cottage Cafe to the Sunset Cafe and back again to the Cottage Cafe. Jeff grew up in nearby Roslyn, where his family had worked the coal mines. This area of Kittitas County, called the valley, included the twin towns of Cle Elum and Roslyn, which had a long history of coal mining. Because the money was good, the jobs were passed down from generation to generation. Jeff was the last generation of coal miners. Mining began its long, slow decline in the 1940s and ended in the 1960s when the last mine closed. The closings caused a loss of population, with Cle Elum going from around 2,500 to fewer than 1,800 and Roslyn going from a high of 3,000 to around 850. Jeff lived through those hard times, and, as he said, "I was born and raised here in Roslyn. My first job out of high school was working in the Number 9 coal mine where my family, my dad, my grandfather, three uncles, all of them worked the mines. In 1962, they decided to close the mines. I got laid off, then I went to work in some gyppo sawmills around here."

"Over the years," I said, "you worked a lot of jobs."

"I did. Jobs were scarce then. When you're raising a family, and I had four kids and a wife, you did what you had to do to keep money coming in."

"So, you started in the mines, went from there to a sawmill. What other jobs do you remember having? By the way, what's a gyppo sawmill?"

"A small independent operation, not a company logger. Gyppos don't have benefits, but it did get me into logging, and after that, I managed to find a job working in the woods, logging, setting checkers, fastening steel cables around logs so they could be dragged out of the woods. It was big money back then, $2.50 an hour. It was hard work."

I nodded, trying to imagine how hard people worked. But I could see Jeff in his younger days working hard like that. He was a good-size guy with a hardened face and a strong upper body, even now in his late seventies.

"What did you do after that?"

"I graduated up to where I was helping to build logging roads, driving logging trucks, dump trucks, and running some heavy equipment."

The young lady who was waiting on our table asked if we wanted a refill. Jeff gave her some sort of sign, which apparently meant we wanted a pot of coffee. After she dropped off a pot, I said, "I heard you once were a cop."

"Yeah, when the logging started closing down around here, I was lucky enough to get on with the police department, spent six years doing that up in Roslyn. I was also a relief officer for Cle Elum, and I was a reserve deputy for the Kittitas County Sheriff's Department. Then for a while I was acting chief up in Roslyn. Like I said, you just had to do what you had to do to feed the family. Jobs were scarce back then. Plus, I also got a divorce. Things kinda fell apart."

"What happened after that?"

"I moved to Ellensburg and worked in a packing house down there. On the kill floors, cutting locker beef and stuff like that. Then I wound up working for Safeway for three years. Got laid off there because they were cutting back on man hours."

"That's a lot of jobs and lots of disappointments."

"Yeah, it seemed like everything I grabbed ahold of I ended up with nothing. Everything was short term. Somebody said the other day, 'Why did you have so many jobs?' I told him it's necessary, everyone around here is seasonal. You might work for two months, you might work for six months, you might work for a year. You just don't know. In this area, when you're raising a family, you take whatever jobs you can find."

Earlier, Jeff had told me he used to live in Alaska and that he drove a truck up there.

"When were you in Alaska?"

"Around '85. Driving hot oil tankers. We'd go to Kenai, load up with hot oil, take it up to the batch plants in Anchorage. I played music a little bit, done it for over forty years. I got started with an old, broken-down Silvertone guitar when I was much younger. I still sing and play on occasion. While in Alaska, I got to meet and play music with some of the big names, like Buddy Knight, who was Merle Haggard's bass guitar player, and Johnny Collinsworth, a lead player for Glen Campbell. I got to meet a lot of fantastic musicians. Had a lot of fun up there."

"Why did you return?"

"My dad had a towing service down here in the wrecking yard. He had a stroke, and he couldn't run the towing service, so Mom got on the phone and was singing the blues that nobody was down here running the business. So, I left Alaska, came back down, and ran my dad's business for a while till he passed away. Then my nephew took it over 'cause I'd had enough of it. I didn't want it no more."

Thoroughly engrossed in Jeff's story, I asked, "So, what did you do after that?"

"I went to work for Suncadia Resort up here, big golf resort with lots of condos. I was with them for ten years. That was my last regular job. Now I help do maintenance at a laundromat."

Jeff said that living costs had gone way up since Suncadia Resort had opened. Having a four-star resort and conference center with around two thousand condos, several restaurants, and three golf courses surely made it more difficult for locals to find affordable housing. Jeff struggled himself, going from rental to rental. He had needed to "couch hop," staying with others between having his own space.

It was a constant on my route, whether in New England, in upstate New York, in the Rockies near Yellowstone and Glacier, along the shores of the Great Lakes, and near most any lake in northern Minnesota. These once-rural places where people did back-breaking work to get ahead now were suffering as the disparity between the rich and regular folk widened. In Cle Elum, things began to change with the building of Interstate 90 in the mid 1960s as people in Seattle and other coastal areas discovered the beauty of the land east of the Cascades. Cle Elum, being the first town of any size east of Snoqualmie Pass, was an ideal spot for vacation homes. Suncadia was the first resort of any size, with construction that began in 2004.

Jeff Osiadacz, leaning on the front fender of a Mack truck in Cle Elum, Washington

Interestingly, Jeff's own work career mirrored the development of the upper valley region of Washington State as he went from working the coal mines, being in the timber industry, working in retail grocery stores, being a musician in the entertainment field, and finally working at Suncadia Resort. Over several pots of coffee at the Sunset Café, we talked, even disagreeing on a lot of things, politics included. We never let that get in the way of our friendship. Plus, we both drank our coffee black, which was worth something.

Later that evening when I returned to my motel in Ellensburg, I met a guy in the parking lot. Mark, in his mid '70s and from Philly, was driving a black 1993 Buick Century with an odd-looking rack holding his mountain bike. Retired from a career managing apartments, he now was vagabonding, rotating between camping and staying in cheap motels. He told me he enjoyed riding his mountain bike along pathways in national forests. He'd been all over the country and planned to keep going because "retiring does not mean inactivity or lack of enthusiasm for travel." When I asked him whether he still returned home, he said, "Home is now the open road." He further explained that he was using the money he got from selling his house to pay for his travel. "I've still got a sister in Pennsylvania just in case I head back east and need a place to lay my head."

I thought about what he said, wondering if I could ever do that. Whenever I was on the road, I looked at the places where I'd traveled and evaluated each one's livability for me. But every time I'd come to the same conclusion, thinking, *It's kinda nice living in a condo in a beach town near the sandy shores of Lake Michigan.*

The next morning I got up early, filled a couple of Styrofoam bowls with cereal from the doodad with the twirly handle, and grabbed a cellophane-wrapped bagel and a single-serve cream cheese in a squeezie thingy. Motel travelers will know what I mean.

As I approached my car, I noticed Mark's car was missing. It would have been nice to speak with him again.

To get to the Oregon border and avoid the interstates, I jumped on what locals called the Old Road. Now named the Yakima River Canyon Scenic Byway (Highway 821), it stretched from just outside Ellensburg to the fruit groves of Pomona.

In the early days, despite Ellensburg and Yakima being only forty miles apart, it was pretty near impossible to make that trip. It required hiking a series of rugged winding pathways worn by many centuries of Native Americans passing through miles of rocky canyon ridges.

The first railroad to connect Ellensburg with Yakima was the Northern Pacific in the spring of 1885, which cut through the canyon along the western side of the Yakima River.

Constructing a road through the Yakima River Canyon was an entirely different matter. There wasn't enough room for a road bed on the western side of the river, where the rail tracks were located, so they needed to use the eastern side. It was far less level, and the road needed to be cut through the canyon's rocky walls.

The road through the canyon first had a gravel surface in 1924, then, in 1932, it was paved, and tunnels were blasted through the basalt cliffs. In 1963, a major realignment of the highway bypassed the tunnels, allowing more traffic to flow through the canyon. Finally, in 1967, the state put the Scenic and Recreational Highway Act into effect to highlight the beauty of many scenic drives.

Because I had an early start, I didn't run into a lot of traffic driving along the byway. That allowed me to stop to take pictures and do some hiking. The views were spectacular as the byway passed through its many rocky curves and switchbacks. Near the top of a particularly steep climb, I passed a mountain biker peddling to the top of a long hill. When he reached the top, he stopped to take a short rest. And that was how I met Cliff Crego, a man in his seventies who was a composer, a former conductor, and the founder of the ASKO Musical Ensemble in Amsterdam. He was also a teacher, a poet, a translator, and a nature photographer. For a good hour at the top of that ridge, we had a wide-ranging conversation on a variety of topics. Cliff told me he lived part of the year at his base camp in the "rugged and snowcapped alpine summit Wallowa mountains," where he could look down at the high desert of northeast Oregon. He also spent some of his time in the Netherlands and the Swiss Alps.

Cliff enjoyed riding his bike across multiple Western states during the warmer months, when the weather was good for camping. During the winter, he skied in remote areas. I mentioned where I was headed, and he said, "Whatever you do, don't take US-20 from Bend to Burns. I peddled it, and it took me three days. I had to sleep by the side of the highway with semis continually passing by. One nearly hit me. Don't go that way." As Cliff warned me, I thought, *Darn, that is the route I'm taking.* After our conversation ended, we became friends over social media and occasionally spoke by phone when he and I both had good cell service.

As abruptly as the Yakima River Canyon Scenic Byway had begun, it ended. The mountainous landscape leveled off, and the massive orchards near Pomona came into view. In an area famous for its Washington State apples, the final stage of the year's harvest was still in progress as trucks carried freshly picked fruit to local cold storage warehouses and shipping centers. The busyness continued through Selah, where I picked up highway US-12. Union Gap sat in a valley along the Yakima River just north of Rattlesnake Ridge. At the top of the ridge were two boulders, one carved to mark the Battle of Union Gap (Pa Ho Ti Cute—"Two Buttes") that took place on November 9 and 10, 1855. It was the second engagement of the Yakama War, a war that had been brewing for quite a while.

At the time of the Lewis and Clark Expedition in 1805, Meriwether Lewis and William Clark encountered the Yakama people for the first time along the confluence of the Columbia and Yakima rivers near present-day Richmond, Washington. It was the Yakamas' first contact with the white man. Lewis and Clark named the people Chim'-nah-pum, which was the name of the village at the mouth of the Yakima River.

Soon after the Yakamas met Lewis and Clark's party, white fur trappers arrived to trade, and then white settlers appeared, looking for land to farm. To accommodate the settlers' growing need for land and resources, Washington Territory governor Isaac Stevens negotiated the Yakama Nation Treaty of 1855 with the Yakama, who, along with fourteen other tribes, ceded eleven million acres to the U.S. government in exchange for hunting and fishing rights, awards of money and provisions, and reserved land where white settlement would be prohibited. But soon after the treaty was signed, the U.S. government demanded that the tribes move immediately and sent solders to enforce the order. Because of that broken promise, Kamiakin, the Yakama chief, encouraged the tribes to fight. Soon other tribes joined forces with the Yakama for the beginning of the uprising known as the Yakima Indian War, which lasted from 1855 until 1858. (*Note:* Yakima vs. Yakama. Yakima was the white man's word; Yakama, the Native Americans' word.)

The first battle occurred on October 5, 1855, at Toppenish Creek and ended with the retreat of the U.S. calvary. Then on November 9, on the bank of the Yakima River at Union Gap, a far larger U.S. force surprised Kamiakin and his warriors. Outnumbered two to one and nearly surrounded, Kamiakin's warriors retreated to the safety of a Catholic mission twenty miles west along the Rattlesnake Ridge near Tampico, Washington.

War raged until September 5, 1858, and ended along the Spokane Plains, where Kamiakin and his warriors were defeated. Afterward, the Yakama and the other tribes were placed on reservations. By then, Kamiakin had fled to Canada. However, twenty-four other chiefs were captured and executed, some hung and others shot. Kamiakin was the only chief who refused to surrender.

As Kamiakin said,

> "We wish to be left alone in the lands of our forefathers, whose bones lie in the sand hills and along the trails, but a pale-face stranger has come from a distant land and sent word to us that we must give up our country. Where can we go? There is no place left. My people, the Great Spirit has his eyes upon us. He will be angry if, like cowardly dogs, we give up our lands to the whites. Better to die like brave warriors on the battlefields, than live among our vanquishers, despised. Our young men and women would speedily become destroyed by their fire water and we should perish as a race."
>
> —Kamiakin, Head Chief of the Yakama Nations (1800–1878)

Heading south along US-97 toward Wapato, I passed through some of the most fertile farmland in the nation, due to water provided by the Yakama Reservation Irrigation District. But few of the area landowners were Native American. That was because after Congress passed the Allotment Act of 1887, also called the Dawes Severalty Act, land was divided among individual tribal members. The act allowed tribal members to sell their land to whoever they wanted to sell it to, resulting in people who were not Native American purchasing what was once owned by tribal members.

Land around Wapato was known for its apple and cherry orchards, vegetable crops, fruits, and berries, along with hops for breweries. From my vantage point along the highway, I saw massive stacks of apple cartons next to apple storage and wholesale facilities.

With a population of roughly 4,500, Wapato was among the oldest Hispanic communities in Washington. But it wasn't always that way. In the early 1900s, the people attracted to the town were of Japanese descent, making it the second-largest Asian population after Seattle in Washington. In the 1920s and '30s, however, anti-Japanese sentiment grew because of discriminatory actions by the state and organizations such as the Anti-Japanese League, resulting in many farm workers of Japanese heritage moving away. Then, during World War II, when Roosevelt's Executive Order 9066 consigned everyone of Japanese descent to internment camps, the rest of Wapato's Japanese-American population were interned. During the war, they were replaced by Germans from a POW camp south of town. After the war, there was a shortage of workers, and Hispanic migrant workers under a guest worker program that was negotiated with Mexico began working the fields. Now, more than 80 percent of the population in Wapato were Hispanic.

The road to Toppenish passed through an area of Yakima Valley farmland irrigated by the Yakima River Basin Irrigation system. And just like Wapato, the population of Toppenish was 80 percent Hispanic and was located on the Yakama Indian Reservation. Toppenish was the largest city on the reservation and home to the Yakama Nation Tribal Offices, the Cultural Center, the Tribal School, and Wildlife and Fisheries. Called the City of Murals and Museums, Toppenish had eighty historical murals painted on buildings throughout the downtown.

From Toppenmish to Goldendale was a fifty-mile drive, where the land went from farmland to high desert to forest.

As I drove through the forest north of Goldendale, I happened upon St. John the Forerunner Monastery and Bakery. It was such a surprise seeing anything there, much less a monastery with an attached bakery, that after I drove on by, I swung back around to take a closer look. Inside, three young women with head dressings and robes were quietly doing their work. One was stocking shelves, another was ringing somebody up, while the third was at the espresso machine, making a customer a latte. When I asked one of the women about the monastery, without a word, she pointed to a stack of brochures along the counter while continuing to go about her business.

Just then, a couple walked in, apparently also their first visit. We struck up a conversation as we looked over a display of jams, sweet bread, and baklava. The man—whose name escaped me, but it could have been Richard, Roger, or something similar—mentioned they were on a mystery adventure that his wife, Julie, had put together and he followed. She, I believe she said, was a retired teacher; he, a radio journalist. They had driven in from northern Oregon. As I ordered an espresso, they ordered sandwiches. We talked about the monastery. They'd read that a local doctor had donated several acres of land with the stipulation that it become a women's monastic community within the Greek Orthodox tradition. A priest was assigned from Greece to head up the project, and the monastery had since grown to twenty nuns and novices.

In the brochure I picked up at the counter, I read about the monastery's daily routines. The women rose at 2:00 a.m. for daily prayer and began their work at 4:00 a.m. After a break for lunch and daily devotionals at 1:00 p.m., they worked until 5:30 p.m. and had Vespers service and dinner starting at 6:00 p.m. before they retired to their cells around 9:00 p.m. As a haven for the Orthodox faithful since its establishment in 1995, the monastery was thriving. At the same time, I wondered, given their routine, whether the nuns and the novices were getting enough sleep.

On US-97 south on the east side of the Cascades, the traffic was lighter than on the west side. That gave me time and space to pull over anywhere along the highway to explore.

Just before I entered Goldendale, home of the Goldendale Observatory State Park, the terrain transformed from densely forested to rolling hills of prairie. Traditional sources of income changed from lumbering to farming.

I had heard about the observatory, so I took the first road into Goldendale and followed it to the downtown area. The Observatory State Park was north of there. Noted for its large public telescope, the state park sat atop a tall hill. Formerly a dark sky park, it should once again receive that designation now that the observatory's multimillion dollar reconstruction was completed. Within the park, several telescopes were available to the public. There I met Troy Carpenter, the park manager. He described the newly updated solar sky observatory, which had technology that allowed visitors to view images of the stars at night and the sun during the day. Troy, another observatory guest, and I had coffee between the day exhibit and the nighttime viewing. We talked about this and that, because none of us had ever met one another before. Troy had big plans for the park, more technology, and the like. The woman was just passing through and was headed the next day to Burns, Oregon, for a job she'd just taken. I was heading south to get to where US-97 intersected with US-20, and I planned to drive through Burns on my way east.

As I drove south, four mountain peaks were visible: Mt. Hood, Mt. Adams, Mt. Rainier, and Mt. St. Helens. In that general area, the landscape opened up to reveal the vast Columbia River Gorge surrounded by lush fields of alfalfa hay.

Just before I crossed the Columbia River, I reached the unincorporated town of Maryhill, population fifty, founded by Sam Hill. To learn more about Hill, I headed east to the Maryhill Museum of Art, a castle overlooking the Columbia River, built for Hill's wife, Mary.

I learned from the docent at the museum that Sam Hill was born in 1857 to a Quaker family in North Carolina. When the Civil War began, the family, who were pacifists and against slavery, moved to the safety of Minneapolis. Educated in Ivy League schools to be a lawyer, Sam returned to the Twin Cities to practice law. He was such an excellent attorney that he won several cases against the Great Northern Railway. That impressed the Great Northern's principal owner, James J. Hill, so much that the railroad hired him as its top lawyer. While under James J. Hill's employ, Sam Hill met the Empire Builder's eldest daughter, Mary Hill, and married her. To prevent confusion about the possibility of the two being related, Mary's married name became Mary Hill Hill. The newlyweds received a large wedding gift from Mary's father, and for the first few years, their lives went well.

But as the years passed, Sam Hill's manic behavior got the best of him. He quit his father-in-law's employ and decided to go it alone and move to Seattle. Around this time, 1900, Mary and Sam were having difficulties in their marriage, so Mary moved back to the safety and security of her parents' mansion in St. Paul, Minnesota.

That set in motion Sam's world travel, allowing him to become friends of royalty. A globetrotter by nature and fluent in German, French, Italian, and Russian, he visited Europe fifty times, went to Japan nine times, and traveled throughout the American West, which he adopted as his home. Sam seldom lived with his wife and daughter. He was a man of ideas with the money to bring them to fruition, with some being successful and most others not.

Hill founded the Seattle Gas and Electric Company, the Home Telephone Company of Portland, and a golf course in Maryhill, to name a few endeavors. His most notable projects were the Peace Arch along the U.S.-Canada border, a private subscription library named the Minneapolis Athenaeum, the Maryhill Art Museum, and the Maryhill Stonehenge, commemorating those who died in World War I. Just down the hill from the Maryhill Stonehenge was the burial place of Sam Hill himself. The docent went on to say something along the order of Sam Hill being a manic, compulsive, eccentric friend and dreamer. Not her exact words, but close.

I learned that part of Sam Hill's legacy was the Maryhill Loops Road, the first asphalt paved road in the Northwest. Hill was quoted as saying, "Good roads are more than my hobby, they are my religion."

After a day of exploration and learning, I decided to stay just across the Columbia River in Biggs Junction, Oregon. There, I managed to snag a room at an off-season rate overlooking Maryhill. The woman who checked me in handed me a coupon for half off at the breakfast spot across the parking lot. On my way into the parking lot, I saw that the restaurant was closed for the season.

I mentioned that the restaurant was closed, and the woman said it was not her fault. I asked why she had given me a coupon for a half-off breakfast at a place that was closed, and she said, "It is part of our routine. Got a complaint, take it to the owner."

I asked whether the owner was around. She said he lived out of state and had never been to the motel. I surmised it was simply the investment of a one-percenter who had far too much money and had decided to burn part of it on a venture that could never pay off.

The next morning, I picked up a truck-stop breakfast sandwich with a paper cup of weak, watered-down, scalding hot black coffee.

Just south of Biggs Junction was a sign warning motorists that the next gas station was ninety-four miles away, which prompted the car ahead of me to turn around and head back to the truck stop it had just passed. Thinking about it, I decided to backtrack as well and instead take a parallel road to US-97 that passed through the Fulton Canyon. The road twisted through the canyon walls until it reached the peaceful irrigated high plains a few miles in. It was so windy in the canyon that whenever I left my car to shoot a photo, the wind nearly blew my doors off and about knocked me off my feet.

Sherman County, Oregon's least populated county, was known as "the land between the rivers," with the Columbia River to the north, John Day River to the east, Deschutes River to the west, and Buck Hollow to the south. Many of Sherman County's earliest settlers saw ranching opportunities on the Columbia Plateau, where the dry, rolling, bunch grass hills were perfect for raising cattle.

Later, in the 1880s, homesteaders began arriving by steamboat, stagecoach, and wagon. Farmers settled on nearly every quarter section, plowing the grass and fencing their fields in order to receive government patents to raise crops such as golden winter wheat.

In Sherman County, not much had changed. Some small towns were relegated to ghost town status, and Moro, Wasco, and Grass Valley all now had populations under five hundred.

Eighty miles before I reached Bend, I approached Madras, a town that sat in a basin nestled in the high desert with panoramic views of the Cascade Mountain Range. Settlers had first arrived at the dawn of the twentieth century, and the population rapidly grew once the Deschutes Irrigation Project was completed in 1946. The dry farmlands turned green and began producing some of the world's finest mint and seed crops. Now Madras was a commercial hub with some light manufacturing and tourism and a multicultural population proud of its Native American heritage and its rich Hispanic history. Madras more than doubled its population to 7,500 from the mid 1990s to 2020.

As dusk approached, I stopped by the Peter Skene Ogden State Scenic Viewpoint to see its vertical basalt cliffs and tall river canyons. I walked along the juniper tree–lined footpath, then crept closer to the low stone barriers overlooking the canyon below. It was the scariest overlook I'd ever visited. As one who was deathly afraid of heights, I was not alone in my fear. I looked down at the canyon and saw signs warning pet owners to keep their dogs on leashes, due to many instances of dogs jumping over the barriers and plummeting several hundred feet.

There, I met Mike the Oxygen Guy, who sold and installed durable medical equipment. He was taking a smoke break close to the overlook. I asked whether he'd heard of any instances of dogs jumping to their deaths. He had. He said in one case, a guy and his date were taking her dogs for a walk. The guy threw a ball for the dogs to fetch, and because it had too much velocity, the ball bounced over the wall. Both dogs jumped over the cliff.

"It was in the news," he said.

"Was he charged?" I asked. Mike said he was but couldn't recall the outcome.

By the time I left the overlook, shadows were long, and I still had more than thirty miles to go.

But then, three miles later, after driving up a mountain ridge, I entered the town of Terrebonne, the entry to Smith Rock State Park. I just had to see it, even though it was nearly dark. A favorite of rock climbers, the steep cliffs always attracted crowds of people. I hiked quickly from the upper lot to the top of the cliff. From that viewpoint, I could barely make out the people hiking along the paths below. Though that was a good perspective, I needed to get to the bottom to see the deep river canyons from down below before it got totally dark.

Named one of Oregon's Seven Wonders, the park's peaks, rock spires, and canyons were made of compressed volcanic ash rising six hundred feet above the Crooked River. The park offered breathtaking views, hiking and mountain bike trails, and world-class, rock-face climbing. Once it was the traditional homeland of the Tenino and Northern Paiute tribes, but white settlers began to arrive in the late 1800s.

I spent an hour in the park and wished it could have been an entire day. It was pitch dark as I drove the final twenty or so miles to my motel in Bend.

31

In Bend, I was greeted by a motel employee who had worked the front desk for more than thirty years. She ran the place like a drill sergeant, barking orders she'd obviously memorized. "No hot water in the shower, it's lukewarm. Forgetaboutit getting hotter. Towels are scruffy, get used to it. Use them to defoliate your skin, looks like you could use it. No morning breakfast, get it at the restaurant next door. The ice machine closes at ten, go to the gas station down the road. Park your car by your room. Don't bother me later, I'm going to bed. Check out by ten. Don't expect to see anyone before you leave. Oh, and by the way, welcome to Bend." And with that, she handed me my key.

The next morning I headed to the Deschutes Historical Museum in the historic Reid School building. I needed to find someone knowledgeable to speak with about the area, but when I arrived, everything was in a state of flux. They were working against a deadline to get a new display up and running. I first approached the volunteer manning the counter, but she didn't have time to help. She suggested I speak with the museum director, whom I could see was up to her eyeballs putting together the exhibit. She did take a couple of minutes to speak with me and was very kind and apologetic. She first suggested I return on another day. But when I told her I was driving through and wouldn't be around, she tried to figure out something else. I asked whether there was a board member who could speak with me. "Perfect," she said, and soon I had the name and phone number of one of the board members, along with her recommendation that he was the best person for me to interview. And that was how I connected with Les Joslin.

Bend had grown from a population of 20,000 to more than 100,000 in the last fifty years. Everything was hard for me to locate, but I did find my way to Les's house on a hill with a view. Something that was quickly disappearing as housing developments popped up pretty much everywhere.

With a warm smile, Les greeted me. I apologized for the last-minute connection.

"Not a problem. I have an hour or so of time."

By way of introduction, I unfolded a map showing my 10,000-mile journey. Les looked it over, saying there were a lot of familiar places and that he'd been to many of them.

"So, where were you born?" I asked.

"Chelsea, Massachusetts, at the U.S. Naval Hospital. My father's career had him stationed near there at Davisville, Rhode Island, with the Seabees." As he talked, he pointed out each location on my map.

"When and how long was he stationed there?"

"He got transferred right away. It was 1943, during World War II. I was only six weeks old when my mother and I followed him. She got on a train full of troops, and we rode from Boston to Los Angeles. We lived with an uncle in Long Beach for a while. My dad wasn't sure where he'd be stationed after he was transferred to the West Coast."

I said it sounded like everything was super-secret back then. Les said that it was.

"Seems like you followed him through his career."

"Yes, his career usually involved medical facilities at naval stations or actual naval hospitals."

"What was your father's name?"

"Leslie Hugh Joslin. He was from a dirt farm in Batesville, Mississippi. Real squalor. Managed to work his way up and out of that situation, joining the CCC in '33 during the Great Depression. The next year, with a dollar in his pocket, he went to a New Orleans navy recruiting station and joined the navy in 1934. My father served in the navy from 1934 until 1974. It was someplace to go. He could go somewhere and be paid, get something to eat. He was a hospital corpsman and eventually made chief petty officer. Then gradually he was promoted to ensign and all the way up to captain. There were no admirals in the Medical Service Corps at that time. So, he went as far as a person could go."

I asked what his father did after that.

"He wound up as commanding officer of the naval dispensary in Seattle. Then he was the administrative officer at the naval hospital in Oakland."

Les told me that his father had sat for the photographer and pinup artist Earl Maran, who was famous for his images of celebrities of the era—including Marilyn Monroe, Betty Grable, and Judy Garland. "He came around and painted portraits of patients, asking my dad, 'Would you like to have your portrait painted?' My dad said, 'I've never had that done.' Ten minutes later, he had a portrait. It captures his rather serious demeanor. He had a lot to be serious about."

"So, at a certain point you went off to school?"

"I graduated from high school in Monterey, California. I went to four high schools. Went to the University of California. After a year and a half there, I transferred to San Jose State College, where I graduated. Worked my way through college with the U.S. Forest Service. Five summers."

Les met with a navy recruiter in Memphis where his father ran the naval hospital, before his fifth season with the forest service. "They wanted me to be a naval pilot or a flight officer. I wasn't fond of airplanes, so I said I'd be interested in another sort of duty. They had this program, one that they seldom recruited for because there was only one per squadron. Air intelligence officer. I thought, *That sounds like me.*"

I asked how long it took to get that position.

"I was sworn in the next day to the naval reserve and to go on active duty whenever they could find me a slot in aviation candidate school." Which, Les told me, was required before he could go to air intelligence school. "Long story short, after finishing air intelligence school in Colorado, I wound up on my first operational assignment with an A6 Intruder squadron, Attack Squadron 75, based at the naval air station in Oceana, Virginia."

I asked whether he'd served in Vietnam.

"We were scheduled to deploy for a tour of duty to Southeast Asia. But at some big meeting, they reshuffled the deck, and I wound up going to the Mediterranean for a six-month deployment on the *USS Saratoga*."

"How did you meet your wife, Pat?"

"We met on the island of Corfu when we made a port call. We were supposed to go to Istanbul, but they were having anti-American riots there. The navy figured five thousand Americans walking around in white uniforms wouldn't be a good idea. So, they diverted us to a little-used port on the Greek island of Corfu in the Ionian Sea."

Les told me that every squadron had a hotel room on the beach for officers and that junior officers were assigned as the "queen for the day," the person responsible for keeping the hotel room "squared away." On the last night in port, Les was the queen for the day.

Les Joslin, at his home in Bend, Oregon

"I was snoozing away in an upper level room and woke up when I heard some giggling from down below. I looked over and saw this tanned, slender girl waving at me. It turned out to be Pat, her and two of her friends. All three were from England on a trip to Athens, and they worked as radiographers in a hospital in Bern, Switzerland. I started talking with her, and we ended up taking a walk around Corfu. A couple of months later, we were at port in Italy. I caught a train and visited her in Switzerland. Then, at the end of the deployment, I took some leave and visited her again. We decided she'd move to the United States because I was going to eventually get orders to return to shore duty to teach at the Air Intelligence School in Denver. She was a skier, and she liked the idea of living in Colorado. So, we got married. We've been married for fifty-three years. During my naval career, I had two assignments in the United Kingdom, then in D.C., where I eventually retired. There's no avoiding D.C. when you're in naval intelligence."

"How did you end up in Bend?" I asked.

"We had been scouting around places to live in the western United States when I retired. We found Bend. It was a nice size and had great access to several forests. We sold our house in Northern Virginia and moved here. That was 1988. We decided to have our house built in Sunriver because of its history as Camp Abbot during World War II and the vision of making it a planned community. We had a place to move to and have been building our life here in Bend ever since."

Sunriver had experienced its troubles early on, having survived two economic crises. But by 1988, when Les and Pat purchased their lot and built their house, things had turned around, and the building boom was going full throttle—even though Bend was in a downturn.

"When we first came here in 1987 to look around, we looked at Bend, and we looked at Sunriver. Bend was pretty down in the dumps. We thought Sunriver was really nice, it was booming with a lot of things going on. We built our house there, knowing if we didn't like it we could always sell. We lived there, off and on, for a few years. Then, when Bend began to boom, we purchased land and built our house here."

Though retired from the navy, Les, with an urge to do more, took up teaching, went back to working for the U.S. Forest Service, and became a firefighter, an author, and a volunteer at the Deschutes County Historical Society.

Of particular interest to me was Les's belief in staying active. "Instead of viewing retirement as the end of something," he said, "I looked on it as the beginning of something else."

eastward bound

I had finished my trek west, had headed south, and now it was time to go back east. This was a big deal. I'd turned the corner and now would return to Maine by a different route. Thoughts that hit me as I made the halfway point were, first and foremost, that I'd been away from home for a long time. But was I ready to go home yet? No. I still felt there were so many people I needed to meet. So much more to learn from those who lived *out there.* Much more to see. Halfway points were like that. Yet, still, I felt lonely being out there. Alone. These were the random thoughts of a solo traveler with roughly five thousand more miles of road to cover.

1

Once I hit the outer city limits of Bend, the only thing that separated me from the town of Burns was high desert land stretching for 130 miles into the distance. Looking out at the landscape, I thought that if someone wanted to hide a body, this would be the place. There were ranches, landing strips for ranchers who had planes, gun ranges, dirt tracks for off-roaders, ghost towns, and sagebrush. Open grazing land for ranchers with permits, hollows and valleys for cattle. Finally, a rest area appeared called Sage Hen with a pathway that led to the stone marker that said, "In memory of Harry C. Smith, citizen road builder, erected by Harney County Good Road Club," dated 1910.

For centuries, the Northern Paiute tribes, a nomadic people, had established seasonal homes throughout central-southeastern Oregon, northern Nevada, northwestern California, and western Idaho—an area of more than five thousand square miles. The Paiutes first encountered white Europeans in 1827 when they met Peter Skene Ogden, a fur trader and a map maker with the Hudson Bay Company. His mission was to explore areas near the Snake River. In his journal, he described the endless amount of "wormwood" (sagebrush).

Ogden also wrote about the vast numbers of native people whom he called "Snake Indians" (Northern Paiutes): "[We] descended into a level plain and found 2 camps of Snake Indians who can give little assistance in provisions . . . Indians numerous but not troublesome."

In 1843, U.S. Army officer John Charles Fremont arrived to survey and map an emigrant route to Oregon, which later became known as the Oregon Trail.

From the 1840s through 1869, settlers traveled by wagon train more than 2,200 miles from Independence, Missouri, to Willamette Valley, Oregon. In their doing so, the drumbeat of white European settlers continued.

By the time the transcontinental railroad was completed in 1869 and ended the stage rush, an estimated 350,000 people had traveled west by wagon train. Though initially most emigrants started out for California, many opted for Oregon instead when they heard news of the Donation Land Act of 1850. It entitled certain white settlers and Indians of mixed blood who arrived in Oregon Territory between December 1, 1850, and December 1, 1853, to be granted 320 acres (640 acres for married couples).

As more and more immigrants arrived, the Northern Paiute people were limited in how they could live. As a tribe that lived in small groups and moved often, due to their nomadic lifestyle that followed seasonal animal migrations, they found it difficult to get used to the meat and the fresh-grown foods the government supplied to them. Their original diet typically included mountain-grown pinyon nuts, grass seeds, roots, freshly caught fish, and animals from communal hunts.

As competition for food with the new immigrants grew, so too did hostilities. It resulted in the Pyramid Lake War of 1860 and the Owens Valley Indian War from 1864 to 1868. In 1869, an agreement between the warring parties led to the establishment of the Malheur Reservation, which set aside 1.8 million acres for the Paiute people. But like virtually all agreements with the government, it didn't last. The result was the Bannock War of 1878, which the Northern Paiutes lost.

In retaliation, the U.S. government broke the agreement that had reserved land for the Paiutes and opened it up to ranchers for grazing cattle. In addition, the surviving Paiutes were forced to march more than three hundred miles to Fort Simcoe and Fort Vancouver, Washington. During their five-year internment in Washington, many Paiutes snuck away, and those who didn't were allowed to leave. When they were released, some returned to Harney Valley to find that their reservation had been turned into land in the public domain and was no longer available to the Paiutes. To survive, the remaining Paiute people established a temporary encampment on the outskirts of Burns. Over time, the Wadatika Band of Northern Paiutes improved their situation, purchased the land, and converted it to federal trust status, which has since become their reservation.

Ten miles west of Burns, I saw a BLM Wild Horse facility—one of seventeen such facilities across the West that specialized in offering permanent, off-range, corral adoption and purchase centers to place wild horses and burros in private care.

Wild horses were removed because their overpopulation caused damage to range land, destroying the fragile vegetation by spreading weeds, harming wetlands, and reducing the land's ability to support native wildlife. With so little grassland on parts of the open range, hungry wild horses grazed the grass to the ground. Due to overpopulation, the horses also risked starvation, especially in winter. Wild horses roaming have remained a problem still in search of a solution.

2

On entering Hines, the town west of Burns, I noticed a tall smokestack standing alone and not attached to any other structure. Seeing such an oddity, I decided to stop to photograph it. A guy in a pickup drove up, rolled down his window, and said, "Betcha didn't know there once was a lumber mill there," as he pointed toward a vacant piece of property.

For the next few minutes, he told me about the Edward Hines Lumber Company. That the company had platted a town and named it Hines. The company was "Oregon's first "made-to-order community" and "one of the first scientifically planned cities in America." He said the company built the first 150 homes with no two adjacent houses being the same color or design. But "they hadn't figured on the Great Depression in their equation, so the town nearly failed. If not for World War II and the demand for lumber to supply the war effort, it would have become a ghost town." He went on to talk about business booming during the Baby Boom years and then tanking during the 1970s, when housing sales slumped. "The company paid a good wage but not good enough to suit the union. That's when the layoffs began and the mill closed."

I looked around and saw good commercial activity. "Town seems to be doing okay now."

He said, "Yup," rolled his side window up, and drove away.

That evening when I found a motel that looked a little dated, I asked the manager if I could check out my room before registering.

That's how I met Crystal Short, the motel manager—a young woman with a warm, disarming smile and a kind demeanor, who handed me a key and said, "Check it out for yourself." After a quick inspection where I made sure the bathroom was clean, the mattress was firm, and there was no evidence of bedbugs, I checked in. The room was fine, so I stayed.

Later that evening, I wandered back into the office to get some ice. I asked Crystal if she lived in the motel. She did, along with her husband and two children.

I told her about my journey, showed her the map of my 10,000-mile route, and asked if she had time to talk." She asked, "About what?"

"About you."

"Me?" she said, looking surprised. "I'm only thirty-one, and I haven't accomplished very much yet."

"It's really easy, I promise I won't take too much of your time, and we can stop any time a guest comes into the office."

With that, I said, "Tell me where you were born and about your early life, leading to your job here."

"I was born in Tillamook, Oregon. Lived there till I was two. Was raised by a lot of different people. By my grandpa's ex-wife for a while and my aunt till I was seventeen."

"After that, did you split?" I asked.

"Yeah, I ended up running away from that situation because my aunt isn't a good person either."

"Where were your parents in all this?"

"My mother was really young when she had me and was still in her partying stage. My dad was in and out of prison. I mostly saw my mom after living with my grandpa's ex. She had me until I was eight. I think she made the choice to send me to live with my aunt because it was better for me, because of where she was in her life. I haven't seen my dad since I was five."

The way Crystal talked, without emotion but just matter-of-fact, made me realize her life early on was not what she had wanted. Who would have?

"You kinda were repeatedly dealt bad cards," I said.

"Yeah. I don't really talk about it too much."

"It's unfortunately a common situation," I said.

"I know." Her voice trailed off. There was a short period of silence before we said anything else.

Dwelling on what Crystal had said, I thought, *She was married and had two children. Something good must have happened to get her to where she currently was.* So, I asked, "You were seventeen and you left. What did you do?"

"I met my future husband. He was in the same situation as me."

I smiled. She smiled back.

"And you're happy?" I asked.

Still smiling, she nodded.

Looking directly into her eyes, I said, "You figured out a way to be happy."

With confidence she said, "Yeah, I wanted to break the chain of our bad family stuff."

Digging further, I asked, "How about school?"

"I went to high school, and then I did some college. I was trying to, but I had a kid already, and college didn't work out very well."

"So, what type of jobs did you work?"

"I have worked a lot of different jobs. I had a paper route. Worked for an alternative medicine doctor where I helped with paperwork. I've worked in a food truck at a gas station, serving food mostly. Moved to Burns and worked at the hospital here, serving food. Me and my husband were painters with Sage Country Farms, painting those sheds that you see all over people's yards. We did that for a while. That was a really rewarding job. Now I'm here."

Knowing she had two kids to support, I asked her whether the jobs she worked had benefits.

"When you work the kind of jobs I've had, there are no benefits."

From the exasperation in her voice, the same emotion I'd heard from so many others on my journey—and knowing how difficult it was to make ends meet when working hourly jobs—I asked how living in Burns was impacting her income.

After a pause, Crystal said, "Out here, it's a little more difficult, I think, because it's such a small town. They don't have a lot of resources out here."

I asked about the schools and opportunities for education for her kids.

Pausing again a few seconds, she said, "Where I went to school, there were a lot of kids. Here, there are only around eight hundred students in the entire

Crystal Short, motel manager, at work in Burns, Oregon

county. I'd like them to have more options when it comes to schooling. Because out here, it's just about one school and one school only. And if you don't like the way it's going or feel they are not teaching your kids enough, you don't have another option. It puts a lot of pressure on the parents when they rely on the school to help mold their children's minds and teach them the basics, such as reading, writing, and math."

We also talked about how hard it was to get hospital care when the nearest town of any size was more than a hundred miles away. Crystal told me about a local woman who had a stroke, and it took the air ambulance an hour to get there. Fortunately, she survived, but getting ER cases to the large city hospital was a concern.

What impressed me so much was Crystal's spirit. After her upbringing, her life could have turned out so differently. Sitting there late into the evening, I met Crystal's husband and her kids. Then, knowing she needed to get up early to deal with checkout time, I headed back to my room.

The next morning, I drove farther east and passed through part of the Burns Paiute Indian Reservation. Known as Old Camp, it was formed when homeless Northern Paiutes gathered in Burns to claim the ten acres they were allotted in 1887. Officially recognized by the U.S. government in 1972, the descendants of the Wadatika who once controlled more than 50,000 square miles of territory from central Oregon to the Payotte Valley north of Boise, Idaho, now owned only about 14,000 acres, all within the boundaries of Harney County.

Keeping my route rural required me to get past Boise in a mostly indirect manner. Rather than stay on US-20 out of Burns, I instead took Oregon-78 east, otherwise known as Steens Highway. It connected to US-95, called ION Highway as it headed north. The closer I got to Boise, the busier the traffic got, even though I skirted the city to its south. There were few people living along that route. Instead, it was a high desert prairie that occasionally passed through rough, mountainous terrain and cattle-grazing fields. Just before crossing the Owyhee River, I reached Rome, which had a gas station and a restaurant, the first I'd seen of either since leaving Burns. My destination for the night was Mountain Home, Idaho—still 150 miles away. I stopped to fill my tank at the Rome station, checked out its small convenience store, and walked over to the adjoining RV park and motel cabins to stretch my legs as I ate an apple.

At Jordon Valley, population 130—which was like an oasis on the prairie—I followed US-95 north. Just past a small roadside park was a fairly large rodeo. And beyond Sheaville, population less than ten, the highway crossed into Idaho, where a sign said, "Gas 26 miles." At a viewpoint, I stopped to shoot photos of the mountainous landscape that stretched on for miles. I eventually crossed the Snake River and found my way to Mountain Home. Although it was a longer route than going through Boise, it was a more relaxing way to reach my night's destination in a one-star motel where the microwave didn't work, and there was no hot water.

The fifty miles along US-20 from Mountain Home to Fairfield was a desolate drive. Still, the landscape had a special beauty with mountains to the north and south. US-20 stretched like a ribbon from a lowland desert plain to a high prairie, eventually reaching the irrigated Camus Prairie. There lay the only town along the route, Fairfield.

Just as I got back onto US-20, there was a sudden rainstorm, turning what had been a sunny day now mysteriously dark. As the clouds intensified, the rain poured down in torrents. I couldn't see anything. I tried to pull off but couldn't figure out where. Fortunately, the storm passed quickly, and within minutes the sun came back. A short while later, though, a second storm hit. It was more manageable but sure did get my attention. I thought, *This is the Western prairie, and storms come up quickly. When they do, all hell can break out.*

Near Picabo, population one hundred, I passed over Silver Creek, a favorite hunting spot of Ernest Hemingway, who owned a home in nearby Ketchum. It was where Hemingway committed suicide during the summer of 1961.

As I drove along the highway to a higher elevation, I saw the vast ocean of lava flows and islands of cinder cones in Craters of the Moon National Monument and Preserve. I decided to stop.

Entering Craters of the Moon, I looked around and wondered whether I'd left the planet. The park ranger at the entryway said the landscape had been created by volcanic eruptions that occurred when cracks in the earth formed 15,000 years ago. She said something about volcanic fissures and fluid basaltic lava from which gases could escape.

After I listened intently, my mind was about to explode. Now I wished I were fluent in science, but I'd flunked every science course I ever took. When she said the volcanoes in the park were not dead, though, that made sense.

3

Arco, initially named Root Hog, was first established in 1879 to the south of present-day Arco along the Big Lost River. Later, local ranchers decided to move the town closer to a stagecoach crossing to the north. Then, when the railroad tracks were laid east of town in 1901, the town was moved again.

While poking around Arco, I learned about its connection to nuclear power. When the first nuclear reactor was being tested, the lab decided to do its initial test in Arco. On July 17, 1955, for about an hour, Arco was the first town in the world to be lit by nuclear power. That was when the nearby National Reactor Testing Station (NRTS) fired up Argonne National Laboratory's BORAX-III reactor. As the need for nuclear power and its technology grew, the NRTS changed its name to the Idaho National Laboratory (INL). Many INL employees still lived in Arco.

To find out more about the area, I stopped by the office of the local paper and talked with Tom Cammack, the second-generation owner of the *Arco Advertiser*. "We moved here in 1971," he said, "when my dad bought the paper after he sold a newspaper in northwest South Dakota. He, my mother, my brother, and I have been here continually running it. Lost my brother in 2018, and that left it all to me."

Tom said the paper published its first edition in March 1909. "Since it first opened, it has had several owners and was once owned and operated by two-time Idaho governor C. A. Bottolfsen. The city park is named after him." He pointed to a framed photo on the wall. "He still watches over our day-to-day operations."

Tom told me Bottolfsen was born in Superior, Wisconsin, and had relocated with his family to Fessenden, North Dakota, which was where he started his career in the printing industry. Then he moved to Arco and became owner and publisher of the newspaper in 1912, turning it into one of Idaho's largest weeklies. He said, "After Bottolfsen entered politics in 1921, was elected governor of Idaho in 1938, and elected again in 1942, he didn't have much to do with running the paper. Though he's buried in the cemetery here." Tom pointed toward the cemetery, just down the road from where we were sitting.

I asked Tom whether the paper was printed in Arco.

"When we moved here in 1971, the paper was being composed here and printed in Rexburg, Idaho, ninety miles away. Winter, summer, fall, you name it, we made that trip before we finally put machinery in here. Our trade is printing. We bought a news press two years ago in Gunderson, Colorado, and have been using it to print the paper since then. When we bought the paper, there was a kitchen table and a refrigerator in here, along with a busted linotype. Machinery from one end of the building to the other." He exclaimed, "It was a mess!"

"What are you using these days?" I asked.

"We're pretty proud of our equipment. We still have a hundred-year-old, hand-fed press that we use occasionally. We can do letterpress with it. We have modern digital stuff, too. The newspaper is printed on a web offset press. We have one small offset press, but we mostly print digitally. Our newspaper is a weekly."

"How about local coverage?" I asked. "I heard a lot of papers have stopped covering local government and school board meetings."

"Not here," Tom said. "We cover council meetings and have reporters cover the stories and take the photos. We have two office staff: a graphic designer and an office manager. Most of our circulation is in Custer and Butte counties. We are a subscription model, so we don't put our content online."

"How have you seen your subscriptions changing? Are there fewer of them?"

"We noticed a big reduction right around the early 1990s when we got on board and put a website up. That about dropped our circulation in half. We've been clawing back since then. We print about 1,250 papers a week with more than 900 going out in the mail. We only print a paper version. We do have a static webpage where people can subscribe."

"How's that working out for you?"

"We won't get rich with the paper; we provide a service. I'm in the process of selling the business to my graphic designer. I'll still do printing, but I'm leaving the operational headaches to someone else. Printers never seem to retire. They're kinda like undertakers. My dad worked right up to ninety-three years old."

"Any difference in how people are accepting the news these days?"

"Our news is accepted very well. It's getting the younger generation to expand their horizons and begin looking again at the paper. We do have some very dedicated subscribers, generational people. And a lot of the new people moving to town will subscribe."

I asked Tom whether he'd noticed people from other places buying second homes near Arco.

"Absolutely, predominately up north in the mountains toward Mackay and that area. There's a lot of California money up there."

The topic switched to Tom's home life. "So, do you have any children?"

"Yes, they're on their own now. My eldest son lives in Georgia. He's a service tech for an irrigation company. He's an Iraqi war vet and liked it when he was stationed in the Georgia area. He was able to see other places while in the military."

I asked whether his son saw his future in Arco?

"No. You just don't make a livable living here. Doing what I do, none of the kids were interested in picking up after me."

"That's totally different from other generations," I said.

"Oh, yeah. My brother and I never questioned what we were going to be when we grew up. For us, here at the paper, Facebook has been a killer. Unsubstantiated little tidbits there. It is filled with non-sourced news from local people. In the news business, we get at least two sources before reporting. Putting up unsubstantiated news can create turmoil in seconds."

"How have you seen the town change over the last fifty years?"

"When we moved here, it was a pretty booming town. We come from a very small, four-hundred-person town. Back then, there were a lot of stores, rather than all these holes up and down main street where the buildings used to be. They were once functioning businesses. Not so much anymore. Because you got your

Tom Cammack, publisher, in front of his newspaper office in Arco, Idaho

big box stores and your 'get it yesterday in the mail' situation. People can go sixty miles down the road to the Walmart or to a dollar store in Idaho Falls."

"So the population is down?"

"Yes, the big kicker was when the navy moved out in the late '70s, early '80s. They used to train the nuclear navy out here at the nuclear site, and then they discontinued that. I worked at the print shop at the test site for over a year out there. Security was very lax back then. It's crazy now because you have to jump through so many hoops. I couldn't do that again. Craters of the Moon has been a good thing. Anyone who goes there will come through Arco. They have around 250,000 visitors per year. We get a lot of campers here as well. We've seen a small uptick in businesses starting. More encouraging are local people buying and rejuvenating existing businesses. A lot of them are dual employment; they'll have another job and start a home-based business. You have to have a pretty good job to support a business in Arco. We did have a barbershop open up here. We have a hospital here and a very well-run clinic. We have a dentist from Idaho Falls who sets up here a couple days a week."

I asked about the Ag business in Arco. I said it seemed to be evenly split between farmers and ranchers.

"Yeah, it's a pretty even split. It's predominately seed potatoes, alfalfa and barley, and wheat. We also have a lot of cattle and sheep ranchers. There is a lot of surface groundwater irrigation. It comes down from the mountains. There's an aquifer that empties out at Thousand Springs in southern Idaho a hundred miles away."

Tom told me about the site of the SL-1 reactor. "It's twenty miles east of here along US-20. It is where two soldiers and a sailor died in 1961 after the reactor had been shut down over the Christmas holidays. They were doing the startup procedures when all of a sudden the reactor suffered a steam explosion. It's the only reactor accident in American history that resulted in deaths. You should stop there on your way east."

That night I stayed in a cheap, dirty, broken-down motel somewhere near Arco. In the office was a woman who had written a four-page, single-spaced communication to each guest listing the rules of the place. Of special note were the rules that applied to the rusted-out, coal-fired grill. Guests could use it but had to follow these rules: They had to buy charcoal briquettes from the motel office, which was closed more often than it was open. They could not use any accelerant other than what was sold at the office. After use, the wire grill had to be scrubbed with an approved tool, sold in the office. The inside of the grill had to be cleaned with an approved device, sold in the office. The meat used on the grill had to be purchased at an approved meat market, located next door to the motel. All hotdogs, buns, or rolls and fixings had to be purchased at the convenience store on the other adjacent property next to the motel.

I didn't do any of that. Instead, I bought a hand-cut sub sandwich across town.

When I returned to the motel, a group of Texans stood outside cooking burgers on the grill. To make conversation, I asked if they had purchased the essentials for their dinner at the approved market. They hadn't. It might have been Bobby Joe something, who drove a white dually pickup that appeared large enough to eat my Prius Prime for dinner, who said, "No, sir." Five of them were standing or sitting near the grill, using words like *sir, madam,* or *gal* in their conversation. Over a case of domestic cans of beer, they talked about the weather in Texas near where they lived, a hundred or so miles from Dallas. Each of them wore a hat: two had cowboy hats, and the other three, ball caps. The beer cans were on ice, hopefully sourced from the motel office because, if I read the list correctly, they were supposed to purchase it at the convenience store down the way. After the Texans got loud, I retired to my crappy room to watch TV on a fourteen-inch screen, which, given the high cost of the room, was expensive entertainment.

The next morning I drove from Arco to the west entrance of Yellowstone National Park. Along the way, I felt like John Colter who allegedly walked there—although I did it from the comfort of my car. To explain, Colter was a member of the Lewis & Clark expedition who left the party when it got to the Pacific. He was said to be the first white man to travel through what eventually became

Yellowstone. Yet, historians were still split over whether that story was true. But that didn't matter because Native Americans had been hunting and gathering in and around Yellowstone for at least eleven thousand years before the white man ever arrived. Yet, one thing was for certain—on March 1, 1872, when President Ulysses S. Grant signed the Yellowstone National Park Protection Act, which turned the land into a public park, that legislation led to the creation of the National Park Service.

As I entered Yellowstone from the west entrance, I had in mind the other national parks I had visited earlier in my journey. They all had unique features. But in my opinion, Yellowstone offered visitors such a vast variety of experiences that it surpassed all other parks: geysers, forested mountains, high-altitude lakes, dramatic gorges, waterfalls, overlooks, and rivers.

Yellowstone National Park lay within a lava plateau between the rugged Northern Rockies and the steep Big Horns of the Middle Rockies. Someone could stay in Yellowstone for a lifetime and not see all of its more than two million acres. Though buffalo were once nearly extinct, Yellowstone now had more than 6,000 of them. There were 10 wolf packs, more than 1,000 grizzlies, and roughly 600 black bears. Signs throughout the park said, "Danger, Do Not Approach Wildlife," meaning Yellowstone was their home and not the home of its millions of visitors.

Yellowstone also had roughly 300 species of birds, 16 species of fish, 5 kinds of amphibians, 6 species of reptiles, and 67 species of mammals.

During my drive along the Grand Loop Road, I could see Porcupine Hill Geyser, my first geyser sighting. For the next ten miles, there were, in rapid succession, countless geysers, basins, springs, pits, and pools until finally the big show, Old Faithful. It was set to go off within a half hour. I found a parking spot and walked to the observation deck, like a half-circle stadium with benches—each with a perfect view.

As I sat waiting, people around me were talking, not just with their own parties but with others as well. Travelers had come from all over the world. A couple from the English Midlands sat next to me, describing their recent visit to New Zealand and their decision to see Old Faithful on the way home. A family from Japan directly behind me got so excited, they could hardly control their joy. I could understand them intermittently as they drifted back and forth from English to their native language, but their laughs and giggles didn't need any translation. Two young ladies from California to my right were celebrating their college friendship. They had just driven seven hours all night without sleep from Glacier National Park. A good hundred or so people all waited for a less-than-two-minute show.

Then it started with a gasp and a rumble. Soon a sudden burst of energy erupted as the geyser shot boiling water upward like a chugging locomotive building up steam. And as quickly as it had started, it ended. Everyone around me was silent, experiencing the moment when something powerful and predictable had erupted. With only a few hours of daylight left, I had so much more to see before bedding down for the night.

I drove from Old Faithful to the overlook of the West Thumb of Yellowstone Lake, roughly twenty miles. On the way to West Thumb, I turned onto Gull Point Drive, which took me to waterfront views of Yellowstone Lake—the largest lake in the park. Gull Point was a great place to hike on trails along the lake's rocky shores and through an area of old-growth forest. From the vantage point along the lake, I saw several 10,000-foot mountain peaks: Mount Stevenson, Top Notch Peak, Hoyt Peak, Avalanche Peak, and Silver Tip Peak.

I stopped several more times for short hikes—once to LeHardy Rapids, which, during spawning season from early May through mid July, was where you might see Yellowstone cutthroat trout leaping the rapids. Farther along, I took the short, easy hiking trail through a dense stand of conifers to a beach on Yellowstone Lake.

Next, I drove inland from the lake on a paved road leading to Lake Butte Overlook where I could see the Grand Teton Mountain Range. At the top, I walked to the actual overlook. That, for me, was stressful because my fear of heights was hitting me pretty hard. Then along came two Iranian guys who had absolutely no fear. One climbed up the steep hill above the overlook and danced at the summit. Watching them made me shake from the top of my head to the tips of my toes.

That night I was lucky to find a campsite. The ranger stationed there warned me that grizzlies can pop open a car like a drinker flips a tab on a beer can, at the smell of something as faint as a single potato chip at the bottom of a sealed bag. Yet, the campers nearby were roasting hotdogs on sticks and melting marshmallows to squish between graham crackers and chocolate bars. The silence of the night was deafening, though I knew if I got out of my bag while it was still dark, I could be eaten alive. Living in a beach town on Lake Michigan, we didn't have animals that could kill you. At home, I could sleep on a sandy beach and stare at the stars. Here, it was different. A Fig Newton stored in plastic wrap was enough to make a person into a meal.

I survived the night.

The next day I explored the northern portion of the Grand Loop Road. I stopped at Mammoth Hot Springs in the morning and the Grand Canyon of Yellowstone in the afternoon. Since it was early in the season, snow blanketed the woods, and the lakes were still covered in ice. At Mammoth Hot Springs, it looked like a field of hot springs that had been turned upside-down.

The Grand Canyon of the Yellowstone was created by the force of the Yellowstone River cutting through lava flows and glaciers to form a 20-mile-long canyon. The colors of its rock walls were caused by oxidizing iron. I hiked along the canyon rim to the overlooks along the upper and lower falls. At Artist's Point, named for painter Thomas Moran, I glimpsed the river flowing beneath the colorful, eroded canyon walls.

I returned to my car even later than I'd planned, and I still needed to drive to Powell, nearly 120 miles away. To get there, I skirted the northern portion of Lake Yellowstone while taking in short views of Lake Butte, Avalanche Peak, and Top Notch Peak. I waved at the Yellowstone Park sign as I exited onto US-20. Soon I reached the Buffalo Bill Reservoir and could see the lights of Cody in the distance. I had an appointment there the next morning, but first I needed rest, which came like providence in a motel room in Powell with knotty pine walls and handmade log furniture.

4

The next day I passed on a motel breakfast of gooey gravy over warm biscuits. "Stick to your ribs" food was not worth the pain. I'd noticed that motels out here offered either biscuits and gravy or Belgian waffles hot topped with maple-ish syrup. So, instead of the goo they were serving, I hot-footed it to the coffee stand in the parking lot next door for a latte and a bagel.

As I drove from Powell to Cody, by happenstance I saw the remains of a Japanese World War II internment camp tucked in the irrigated farmland by the side of the road. Now named the Heart Mountain Interpretive Center and National Historic Landmark, it was where 14,000 Japanese Americans were confined during the war.

Rooted in decades of anti-Japanese and anti-Asian hate speech, the internment of 120,000 American citizens of Japanese descent was triggered by the bombing of Pearl Harbor on December 7, 1941. Immediately afterward, the U.S. government imposed mandatory curfews on Japanese nationals and Japanese American citizens, and all were required to carry identification. As the war heated up, people on the home front deepened their hatred of anyone with Japanese ancestry. On February 19, 1942, President Franklin Roosevelt issued Executive Order 9066, ordering the detention of all persons of Japanese descent. I thought about FDR. In my mind, he was one of our greatest presidents, but my feelings could have been based on my being Caucasian.

Signs posted all around the park told the story: Construction at the internment camp began in June 1942, and the barracks housing, mess halls, latrines, administration, and hospital buildings were erected in sixty-two days. There was little regard for quality construction, so freshly cut green lumber shrank and was seldom straight, and black tar paper covering the walls offered little to no insulation. The 30 blocks of barracks each had 24 buildings designed to hold 550 people. Only two buildings in each block had showers, sinks, and laundry tubs. Each urinal and shower was communal, leaving detainees with no privacy. Families of up to six were consigned to live in single rooms, each with a pot-bellied stove, a single lightbulb hanging from the open ceiling, an army cot, and two blankets for each internee. The entire complex was surrounded by barbed wire with guard towers. At times, the frigid Wyoming winter temperatures dropped to 30 below, and water pipes froze solid.

The War Relocation Authority (WRA) provided meals for the detainees with the food budgeted at 32 cents per person per day. To get adequate food, many internees were forced to grow their own crops. The nearby Shoshone Dam had been started by the CCC, whose members went off to war, and was completed by the internees. The internees' labor helped transform a section of Wyoming's Big Horn Basin into productive farmland. Local farmers still say to former internees when they visit, "You people showed us what could be done on this land."

In a brochure I picked up at the park, I read that in December 1944, the Supreme Court ruled detention to be illegal. Even so, the last internees weren't released until November 1945. Yet, despite being incarcerated and forced to live in wooden barracks, more than 750 internees volunteered to serve the United States in the armed forces with more than 15 giving their lives for our country.

On release, internees were given only twenty-five dollars and a rail pass to the destination of their choosing. After the war, former internees suffered greatly due to people's hostility, housing shortages that occurred as soldiers returned from the war, and businesses that were not willing to hire them. Asian Americans who'd had businesses before the war could not go back to them after they were shuttered.

After entering Cody, I stopped to see a man I had interviewed twenty-five years earlier. Now retired, Reverend George Pasek lived with his wife in a newer, yet modest, ranch home in a quiet neighborhood. For the next few hours over several cups of coffee, we talked about his life.

George, who had lived a very vigorous life after his retirement, went on to coach the road cycling team at the local high school and started the ski team at the middle school. He did that for eleven years, until one day it hit him: he was slowing down. "I couldn't keep up anymore," he told me. "I wound up being five miles behind the other bicyclists and thought, *If something goes wrong with one of the team members, it would take me ten minutes to get there.* So, I stopped coaching. I was seventy-six years old and thought, *Now what?*"

It was a common thought for retirees who had worked hard for their entire lives: the "Now what?" question.

So I asked, "What did you do?"

Reflecting on his life as a minister and his work as a coach, he said, "What coaching did for me was what I needed when I retired from the ministry. As a minister, I had spent much of my life taking care of others. I had wanted to stay busy and found coaching young people satisfying. But after that ended, now there was nothing. So, for a year, I kinda just took care of things around the house. But then seven years ago, at age seventy-seven, I got my horn out. I hadn't seen it for twenty-five years. Put the mouthpiece in, and I lasted about three minutes."

At that point, I believe I mentioned to George something about learning how to play a French horn when I was in college while studying music. That the damn thing was too hard for me to get a note out of, and I had given up on trying to play it. I had instead tried to play a trumpet, which worked better for my type of embouchure, the position of my lips on the mouthpiece.

George agreed, saying he realized he had lost the ability to blow hard into a wind instrument, a French horn, which took a lot of stamina. Rather than give up, as I had, he went over to the local college and took lessons. Soon he had regained his skills by first redeveloping his embouchure and his ability to blow into the instrument with enough volume. Before long, he was playing in the college band, and after about six months he was told, "You gotta play in the symphony." He'd been doing that ever since.

George said he was born in Scotland, North Dakota, in 1939, twelve weeks after the beginning of World War II when Germany invaded Poland. At the time, his father was a drafting teacher in a school in South Dakota. Because of a big demand for draftsmen in the ramp-up to the war, George's family moved to San Diego so his father could get a job at an aircraft plant. He did so well that he eventually worked his way up to senior designer.

Then in 1950, when the Korean War started, George was ten and interested in the Cub Scouts, where he learned backpacking, camping, climbing, and all kinds of outside activities. "I played French horn in junior high, had braces in high school, so I couldn't play then, took it up again in college. Majored in music—why, I don't know. Then to the University of Washington for grad school but didn't want to be a music teacher. That was when I remember hearing a group of Japanese children sing 'Jesus Loves Me This I Know' in Japanese." George was so moved by it that he enrolled in a new program at the university, ethnomusicology, the study of music of different cultures, especially non-Western ones. "I was one of the first three grad students to take that course of study. It was like heaven."

A month later, though, he overheard some people talking and asked, "What's up?" That was how George learned about the Cuban Missile Crisis. "I got my draft notice in November, my draft physical in December, and on January 15, 1963, my mother's birthday, I was in the army."

George remembered getting on the train in San Diego, bound for Los Angeles for processing. He looked at his mother and noticed she was crying. "She thought it was the last time she was going to see me." He spent three years in the military and hated every minute of it. As George recalled, "One day they said, 'The captain wants to speak with you.' He offered me a position as a member of the infantry of an elite counterintelligence unit. I was Special Agent 1247 and served in Germany, where I chased enemies." This was after the Berlin Wall had gone up, and things were tense. It was the hottest time of the Cold War. The Soviet Union had taken over the Baltic countries, East Germany and Poland. "I spoke German pretty well. So, my assignment was with a senior agent.

"These days people say, 'Thank you for your service.' You have no fucking idea. I don't want to be thanked for the stuff I did. There were things I did that I don't want to be thanked for—things I did that I wouldn't do now, but then it was absolutely imperative that they occurred. Do you see tension between what I did there and what I am now? I live with that every day. Every day I think about that. What could I have done? You couldn't have done anything different because it was a different time, and it was dangerous."

Back then, the Soviets had military liaison missions in four parts of then-divided Germany: United States, France, Britain, and Russia. Each of them had a mission to the others and to their officers and their intelligence officers. They wore uniforms, and their job was to gather intelligence. Some of the work was clandestine, and some wasn't. The Russians had vehicles where the license plates had their military liaison mission numbers. And every GI in Germany had a card with a picture on the front and a license on the back side with a telephone number. If intelligence officers saw the license number, they'd call that number with the date, time, and direction of travel.

As George remembered, "There were two of us. We were positioned near the Autobahn in Stuttgart, so we got a lot of calls. There was an office with a big map, and they kept track of where those guys were who we were monitoring. One time the phone rang, and we were told to check out a car that was off the Autobahn. It was at one of the largest military bases in Germany, and the car was in a place it wasn't supposed to be. I grabbed my briefcase, which had my 38 Special, plus a camera and other devices we used for surveillance. We jumped into our 1964 Plymouth Valiant Slant 6, which would go a good hundred miles per hour. We went screaming out of there, taking a road we thought they might be on. All of a sudden, we saw a black Mercedes that our map showed was over the boundary. We pulled up beside it on a two-lane road. The driver rolled his window down, while holding up his badge of credentials. Then he reached down in his briefcase and pulled out his

45, jacked a shell in it, and stuck it out the window. He said, 'Pasek, cut him off.' The doors flew open, two officers and two agents. I positioned myself behind the engine block for cover. Our pistols were drawn, and we were all screaming, 'Don't shoot!' in four different languages. One of them was a colonel. He raised his left hand, put his pistol on top of the car. And it was over. We talked a little bit—they spoke very good English, and we spoke very good German. I smoked a Soviet cigarette and about turned green. They were scared. No papers, no reports, because they had been caught. They had violated the status of forces agreements. But we were in the wrong because they had diplomatic immunity. So, they turned around and left.

"We went back to our quarters and never said anything. We didn't talk. Neither of us did. We pulled up in front of the senior agent's house, and he asked, 'Do you want a drink?' Got to his house, and his wife came to the front door. She took one look at him and asked, 'What happened?' He said, 'Bourbon.' I woke up the next morning with a pillow under my head and a blanket over me. I've never told anybody that. My first wife never knew it. We came that close to it being the end. Tears are not for me. I would not have had my son Tim, my daughter Toni, my other son Carl, or Katrina. I've thought about that every day for sixty years. I finally told my son. He went to the Coast Guard Academy, became an officer and a helicopter pilot. I felt like he needed to know before he deployed."

Another time while in Germany, George was told about some soldiers being accused of homosexual activity. He was assigned to go out there and investigate. When he came back and reported to his senior agent, he was told, "'I want that report on my desk tomorrow by 8 a.m.,' as he thumped on the table. I typed the report up. Out of less than two hundred people, there were twenty to twenty-five who had engaged in homosexual activity. After I turned in the report, that company was gone in two days. Sent back to the U.S. and assigned to a different company. You see, back then, homosexual activity was one of those blackmailable things, from the military's point of view. So, fast-forward sixty years, my wife wanted me to serve on the board of directors of a family-planning clinic here. Title 10. So, I did, and it's open. We welcome everybody, and it's become more and more rainbow, and I'm fully supportive of that. Do you see tension between what I did back then in the military and what I am now? I live with that every day. Every day I think about that. What could I have done? I couldn't have done anything different because it was a different time, and it was dangerous."

I asked George where he had pastored in churches after becoming a minister.

"My first parish was in Grand Island, Nebraska. It was very conservative but wasn't fundamentalist. Pastor drank his booze out of a coffee cup." While serving that church, George recalled one of the funerals. A farming family had lost its patriarch. When the procession went to the cemetery, the pallbearers put the casket on a frame with straps attached to lower it down into the grave.

"And we're out there in the grass, and we're leaving and the family is bringing up the rear. There's a little boy about six years old or so, he turns and looks, then runs to catch up to his mother, then he does it again. He turns around and looks. The third time he does it, I think, *There's something wrong.* He shouts, 'Are we just going to leave him like that?' So, I ask his mom whether she minds if I take him back to the grave so he can watch what happens next. I told her we would catch back up at the church for the lunch. She agrees. So, I take him back. We approach the casket, funeral director in black, the sexton of the cemetery in Carhartt's. I explain to them why we are there, and the funeral director acts like we shouldn't be there, but the sexton, he is on board. To the boy, I explain we are taking away the fake grass because the people don't like to see the open hole, asking, 'But you'd like to see the open hole, wouldn't you?' And he says, 'Yeah.' The sexton explains how the frame worked and the little lever there. 'Do you want to push the lever and let your grandpa's casket down into the ground?' The boy says, 'Yeah.' So, he actually does it. Next, we hear the diesel start up on the Caterpillar front loader's big bucket, which has got all the dirt. This is a little kid who probably has ten Tonka trucks, and they're all yellow. The operator leans out of the cab, holds his hands up, so I pick the boy up and pass him up. The operator takes the little guy's hands and lets him dump in the dirt. He passes the kid back to me.

"The story's not over. The sexton hands the boy a shovel. 'Do you want to pat the ground with it?' He does. The little boy says thanks, and away we go. Back at the church, we walk into the parish hall, and they're eating their lunch. The little boy walks in and announces with a big broad grin, 'I buried grandpa!' Job's done. And when that little boy makes his announcement, his mommy pops out of her chair, rushes to him, throws her arms around him, picks him up, and says, 'You all, I am convinced we'll feel the everlasting arms of the Divine surrounding us, and we will hear no matter what.' But how many times didn't the job get done? And we couldn't do the job for a whole lot of reasons. I said, 'Job well done, good and faithful servant.'"

After George was the pastor in Grand Island, he went to Ouray, Colorado, to serve a small Presbyterian church in a town of six hundred people, right along the Million Dollar Highway—yet pretty isolated. While there, George became an EMT. "We were forty miles from the hospital. I was there six years. I was a climber, so I was able to spend time on the mountains nearby."

While in Ouray, George retired for the first time, only to take another call at the two churches he served in Greybull and Shell, Wyoming. That was when I first met George more than twenty-five years ago. We had not stayed in touch, but when I was in the area, I checked with the pastor of the Greybull church, who gave me George's contact information. And when I first emailed him after all those years, he put in his reply subject line, "Not dead yet."

Retired Presbyterian minister George Pasek, in his backyard with his French horn in Cody, Wyoming

Spending time with George again allowed us to catch up. Though he now only occasionally filled in at a few of the Presbyterian churches, he was more comfortable attending churches that mirrored his beliefs. "So, we found a United Church of Christ church, which was more in tune with our politics. But the preacher served his Jesus light, and I liked to eat. I don't want Jesus to be heavy duty and mean. Meaning, for example, when Jesus was thirteen years old and walking with his buddies, and the girls were going to the well, and one of them showed an ankle, you can't tell me Jesus didn't say, 'Wow!' If he didn't, there would be something wrong. Because if he didn't, he has nothing to say to me. After that, we began attending the Episcopal Church here. I'm a refugee. I'm very welcomed, but there are things about the Episcopal Church that I cannot do. I'm a Presbyterian. We get our group together, and we make decisions together. There we have the bishop and the rector; the rector has all the power. They have a vestry, but they're 'yes' people. They have me on their worship committee, and they're always saying, 'We're so glad you're here.' They pray, 'We're so glad you're here tonight, good conversation, eternal God, you're the one you're going to be after it's all gone.' You can guess what kind of prayer that might be. And they'll say, 'How'd you learn how to pray like that?' It comes from heaven. I'm a very religious person without being formal in the language. How did

I get that way, how did I stay that way? Every once in a while, I'll say it comes from my life experiences. I can't stand organized religion anymore."

After my visit with George, I headed back to Powell to stay the night. Because I was hungry and needed a cheap place to eat, I found a convenience store and bought a sub sandwich wrapped in plastic, a small bag of chips, and a diet whatever that had an extra button to put in a squirt of more flavor—vanilla, I believe. Day-old donuts were fifty cents, so I grabbed one of those as well. All the while I thought, *If I were a one-percenter, I'd have stayed in one of those "air b and b's" and have dined at a place that uses fancy folded white fabric napkins, been served standing rib roast with fine wine. But for me to travel, I need to eat a gas station sub and nearly break a tooth on a day-old donut, all the while knowing I have the best job on the planet because I get to experience what's out there. Beats digging ditches, a job I am not qualified to do.*

Early the next morning I decided to take scenic route 14A as I headed east. I took that route because Jim LaBlanc, the owner of the Dancing Crane Coffeehouse on the Bay Mills Reservation, had recommended I stop to see the Medicine Wheel sacred stone monument if I was able to get anywhere near Medicine Mountain while traveling through Wyoming.

To get to Medicine Mountain, I drove through several small towns, passed over the southern tip of Bighorn Lake, and saw the Yellowtail Dam. It was named after Robert Yellowtail, then chairman of the Crow tribe. He had been against damming the river and flooding the Bighorn Canyon because the Crow people held the lands as sacred. The dam and river project acquired 12,000 acres of land from the Crow tribe with an agreement that specified water rights and ensured protection of surrounding areas as their reservation and as private property. Because the dam regulated the flow of water into the Bighorn, the river became legendary as a world-class trout fishery. That led to its designation as Bighorn Canyon National Recreation Area in 1968. Since then, more than 200,000 yearly visitors have enjoyed boating, fishing, camping, and other outdoor activities there.

From the Yellowtail Reservoir, I drove to a higher elevation to the Bighorn National Forest where I saw the turn-off for Medicine Wheel. Once in the parking lot, I began to hike the trail that skirted the side of the mountain. All the while, I thought about what Jim LaBlanc had told me when we talked earlier in my journey. He had explained the meaning of the medicine wheel in the native culture. I was wearing the hat I'd purchased at the Dancing Crane Coffeehouse. The symbol of the medicine wheel on the hat had stimulated a conversation with the young man I'd met at the Idaho supermarket. I kept thinking about what the medicine wheel meant, the importance of the Four Directions. The Father Sky, the Mother Earth, and the Spirit Tree. The cycles of life. Each of the Four Directions—East, South, West, and North—was represented by a different color.

That was on my mind when, all of a sudden, I saw that the trail was blocked by a large pile of snow. I was about to turn back, but a guy wearing sneakers appeared on the other side of the snow pile. He catapulted over it as if it were no big deal.

"How do you do that?" I asked him.

He replied, "I work for the Forest Service and put out wildfires. I need to stay limber."

As he caught his breath, I asked a few questions about where he worked and where he was from.

"Yellowstone by way of Chicago."

"Why Chicago and why Yellowstone?" I asked.

"I graduated from the University of Chicago. I studied environmental sciences. I want to make a difference in fighting wildfires while doing my part in combating fires that result from climate change. It's a really big deal to me."

"What's your age? How long have you been at it?"

"Twenty-two, graduated in the fall. Living in Forest Service housing in Gardiner, Montana, 'cause there's no affordable housing near Yellowstone."

"So, you commute in?" I asked.

"Fifty miles each day."

And with that, he ran off like a gazelle.

At that point, I realized the trail would be too difficult for someone my age, so I walked back to my car. All the while, I thought about what he had told me. I wished I'd gotten his name. To me, he was a superstar. A young man . . . Hard to say more, only that he impressed me.

As I continued to drive along US-14A toward Burgess Junction, snow began to blow across the road, banking on both sides. Then I went south past Antelope Butte to Shell, past the Presbyterian church where I had met George Pasek more than twenty-five years ago.

I needed to keep going, to get to Worland, a town where I had a personal connection.

When I was growing up, my mother's side of the family lived in Metuchen, New Jersey, where her father managed the local A&P food market. He was a lifelong collector of rocks, which he polished and made into jewelry. When my mother's parents reached their retirement years, they decided to move to where my mother's sister lived, in Worland. It was a perfect place for a man who enjoyed nothing more than wandering along mountain roads looking for the best rocks to polish. My grandparents loved their time in Worland so much, they were buried there. So, whenever I passed through Worland, I always stopped by the cemetery and put a small pebble on their grave as a remembrance of my grandfather's hobby.

It was a long haul from Worland to Casper, where I planned to spend the night. To get there, I needed to follow the Bighorn River to Thermopolis, which was billed as the world's largest mineral hot spring.

Three miles from Thermopolis, I pulled off the road into a parking lot that sat next to the Bighorn River and read a historical sign that told the story of the Wedding of the Waters. Here, the Bighorn River met the Wind River, one of the few places where a river changed its name in midstream. The sign said early explorers arriving at the river, in what was now the state of Montana, named it the Bighorn for the bighorn sheep that were found along the river. However, its headwaters were at Wind River Lake in the Rocky Mountains, near the summit of Togwotee Pass (pronounced TOH-guh-tee), and the river gathered water from several forks along the northeast side of the Wind River Range in west central Wyoming.

After joining with the Bighorn River at the Wedding of the Waters, the river ultimately merged into the Missouri River, which eventually emptied into the Gulf of Mexico.

In time, people realized there was actually only one river with two well-established names. To prevent confusion, it was decided that the river upstream would be called the Wind River and the river downstream, the Bighorn.

One of the most fascinating things about the Wedding of the Waters was the wildlife. Because of the warm thermal spring water downstream in Thermopolis, the river remained free of ice all winter. Similarly, the warmer waters released from the Boysen Reservoir upstream let the aquatic vegetation stay viable during the winter. Because of the warm water and available plant life, waterfowl and trout stayed during the winter, which made them prey to the bald eagle, which, with a ready source of food, also remained all winter. Mammals such as mule deer and marmots were able to live along the shoreline rather than moving inland, and bighorn sheep used the Wind River Canyon during the winter as well, making the area around the Wedding of the Waters a special place.

After my grandparents on my mother's side moved to Worland, Wyoming, they would visit the Wedding of the Waters. While he was there, my grandfather Jorgensen—who, in addition to being a rockhound, was a published poet—penned the following poem:

Down in Wind River Canyon,
where the Wind River waters flow,
To the wedding of the waters,
At the Big Horn and below,
You travel between canyon walls,
Look up at an azure blue sky,
An awesome sight. Tis God's creation,
and you ponder the how and why.

I drove south on US-20 until it entered Shoshoni. For the next nearly one hundred miles, from Shoshoni to Casper, I didn't see a single traffic signal. Along the way were non-irrigated, arid desert plains, mostly cattle and horse pasture with a little cropland, growing mainly hay.

There were two tiny towns on the way to Casper: Monte, population close to zero; and Hiland, population ten. When I stopped at Hiland, other than a couple of empty buildings, the only businesses left were a two-pump gas station, regular and diesel, and a small convenience store.

Then, all of a sudden, after I'd driven through miles and miles of flat, arid range land, there came an oddity that sneaked up on me called Hell's Half Acre. And sure enough, as if the devil had ascended, stabbed a knife in the earth's crust to open the planet to its very core, and I could see to China, there was this miniature version of the badlands with a steep rocky canyon surrounded by desert. Luckily, it was protected by a high chain-link fence, possibly to prevent people from taking death-defying selfies. It was described in a travel brochure as "a large geological formation that encompasses over 960 acres. This geologic oddity is composed of deep ravines, caves, rock formations, and hard-packed eroded earth."

Similar to the Buffalo Jump in Havre, Montana, Native American tribes used the ravines to drive thousands of buffalo over the cliffs during the time when buffalo were plentiful. This was before their near elimination by the government in a move to starve Native Americans into submission.

In Casper, I found a low-priced motel along a busy road. The people were nice, and the room was fine. Nothing more or less. I tried making conversation with the woman at the front desk, but her tone was curt and her responses, brief. I asked about a reasonable place to eat, and she handed me a list, saying, "It depends what you want." I didn't know. I'd been driving all day, it was getting late, so I picked up something fast.

The next morning at the motel breakfast bar, I grabbed some cereal, a biscuit, and an overripe banana and headed east to Douglas, where the Jackalope had been created. Two brothers in town named Douglas and Ralph Herrick had just completed a mail order course in taxidermy. They were off hunting and bagged a rabbit. Douglas, returning home to their taxidermy shop, tossed the hare's carcass onto the shop floor, and it slid next to a pair of deer antlers. Seeing the humor of a rabbit with antlers, they decided to mount it that way. Over time, the Jackalope became a legend as people from across the country purchased souvenirs of the critter in various forms: postcards, wooden cutouts, keychains, stuffed and mounted trophies, and other versions as well.

5

From Douglas to the Nebraska border was the route of the Wyoming Central Railway, a shadow company for the Chicago and North Western Railroad, which was based in Chicago and by law could not operate in Wyoming. By forming a shadow company and using a different name, the Chicago and North Western Railroad was, in 1886, able to expand into Wyoming. Railroad towns formed along the line from the Nebraska border a hundred miles to Douglas: Van Tassel, Wyoming, and to the east Node, Lusk, Manville, Keeline, Lost Springs, Shawnee, and Orin. Even today, the former tracks of the Wyoming Central Railway, currently the BNSF, made that same run. Many of those towns had shrunk in population so much that they lost their post offices.

As I drove through Shawnee, I noticed a man on a ladder working on an old schoolhouse. I decided to check it out, and that's how I met Doug Stark, who had been working all day, trimming windows. Some people in this world just had to do something positive about problems that existed. Doug had heard someone was going to buy the old schoolhouse and tear it down to build a new home. That was when he and a few others arranged a land swap so the person could build on a different lot. Once the swap was made, the group decided to renovate the old schoolhouse so that people could meet there.

Doug, who'd spent his working life away from Wyoming in the business world, decided to move back after he retired. "My wife and I were born nearby but didn't meet until we were both in school at the University of Wyoming in Laramie. We came back in a circuitous way. After living in other places, the last twenty years in Omaha, Nebraska, where I was CEO for a large company, we missed the ranch land where we grew up, so coming back was an easy decision."

As he wiped his brow, a kindly look came across his face. "So, we're a little bit of an anomaly because we were gone for a long time, and then we came back."

Doug had retired five years earlier, and he and his wife, Denise, were now living on a small ranch north of Shawnee where, he said, "There's not another neighbor for miles." Getting the mail was a challenge because the post office in Shawnee had been closed for years, in spite of the town still having a zip code. Instead, they picked up their mail in Lost Springs, five miles away, which had a bar that was closed, a community center, and an old post office that had been replaced by a set of cluster boxes. "Our address is listed as Shawnee, Wyoming, but our post office is in Lost Springs, and between the two cities, there's only two people. Just a bunch of ranchers who live near here."

When asked whether they raised cattle, he said, "Now and then," adding, "My father-in-law's ranch is next to us, and he runs cattle and sheep. They're well into their '80s and still work their operation." The area had only a few sheep producers, but there were still a lot of sheep in Wyoming, even though their numbers were dwindling.

"We came back because we like the rural lifestyle. We were from here originally, bought the ranch thirty-some years ago, and built a small home on it once we moved back."

Beyond the old schoolhouse, the green pastures and the picturesque landscape were a place of beauty. It was a shame that in most rural places, the kids didn't stay. Doug and Denise had two grown daughters who didn't live in Wyoming anymore. One lived in Ann Arbor, where she worked at the University of Michigan as a researcher. The other lived in Fort Collins, Colorado, and was raising a family.

Just then, a mile-long BNSF train began passing by the small hill where we stood. The rumble of the coal cars contrasted with the solitude of our location. I could tell Doug wanted to get back to work. It was getting late, and I was sure he wanted to get home before it got dark, so I asked if he could describe the project.

"As you can see, we're restoring a hundred-year-old school. My wife actually went to school here forty-some years ago, so she was motivated for us to help a small group of community folks who also went to school here." He told me it was

Retired executive Doug Stark, volunteering his time to fix an old schoolhouse near Lusk, Wyoming

the only school in the state of Wyoming that still had its original bell. "We have a new roof on it, we've painted the outside, and now we're putting on new windows, which I'm trimming out today."

There was still work left to do, though. The electrical system needed to be completed before the sheetrock could go up. Plans were to use the schoolhouse for historical purposes, family gatherings, and community meetings. People who lived nearby were excited to see the old schoolhouse coming back to life. Doug said, "I've had two people stop by today to take pictures. It's a pretty location, sitting on top of this little knoll. I noticed there was even playground equipment in back, including an old merry-go-round. I'm not sure if it's legal anymore, though it probably is grandfathered in."

Doug talked about why they loved living on the ranch. "We have wildlife near our house all the time. Two nights ago, we had a bull elk on our property. It's very gratifying to live out here."

As I drove away, I could see Doug moving his ladder to the next window, which I guessed would make him a little late for dinner.

Thirty miles from the old schoolhouse, Lusk (population 1,500) had lost 25 percent of its population since 1950. The town was located in Niobrara County, an area of mostly ranches and farms in a high-desert environment.

I remembered my first visit in the late 1980s and the town's history and importance as a railroad water stop. That was why I felt drawn to the town. The first time I passed through Lusk, I was on my way to see the Crazy Horse Monument and Mount Rushmore. On that January day, the temperature was way below zero. Now I felt glad to return when the weather was nicer.

Lusk got its name from a man named Frank S. Lusk, who convinced the railroad to build a new leg of its Texas Trail, which at the time had its terminus in Ogallala. And because Lusk knew the railroad would prefer to lay its tracks through a town, he plotted out a townsite where his cattle ranch was located.

When I stayed in a motel in Lusk, being a bottom feeder in terms of the price I paid for a room became a bonus. The room—the cheapest I could find—was way underpriced. It had a perfect bed, a big-screen TV, a bathroom with a walk-in shower, hosts who cared enough to carry on a nice conversation, and a coupon for a deluxe breakfast at an outdoor food wagon with all the trimmings. I sat in the early morning sunlight, overlooking a garden with people who were much better dressed than me. *Pinch me,* I thought. *Have I gone to heaven, or am I still in Wyoming?* Heck, the coffee was even served in fine china. I did not want to leave, but alas I did.

On the way out of Lusk, I saw one of six remaining Redwood Water Tanks. Built by the Wyoming Central Railway in 1886, it stored water for steam engines that ran the spur from Chadron to Fort Fetterman.

Van Tassell was a border town with a population of around fifteen. It was named for R. S. Van Tassell, a cattleman who had huge landholdings in Wyoming. Before his death at age eighty-six, he staked out land where he thought the Union Pacific would lay its tracks outside Cheyenne. He cashed in when the value of that land grew. When Theodore Roosevelt visited Cheyenne in 1908, he wanted to ride horses 50 miles to Laramie. Known as a skilled horseman, R. S. Van Tassell guided Roosevelt on his famous 50-mile ride.

6

Two miles past Van Tassell, I crossed into Nebraska. The only things I could see from the welcome sign at the Nebraska border were the stretch of highway ahead and signs for two ranches: Ellicott Ranch in the foreground and the Gray's Angus Ranch in the far distance. Known as the Pine Ridge Escarpment, though the land appeared barren, it held a lot of history. This was where the Lakota Sioux made their final stand at the end of the Great Sioux War of 1876, also known as the Black Hills War. The war was caused by the U.S. government's desire to obtain ownership of the Black Hills. There, Chief Crazy Horse fought and eventually died.

It got me thinking about that stretch of US-20. As it passed through the western portion of northern Nebraska, it could very well be dedicated to Chief Crazy Horse, the spiritual leader of the Oglala Lakota Sioux. To me, the land felt spiritual.

The drive from the Nebraska border to Fort Robinson was fifty miles. Built in 1874 to oversee the Camp Red Cloud Agency, which consisted of the Oglala Lakota Sioux, the Northern Cheyenne, and the Arapaho tribes, Fort Robinson was essential to the U.S. Army. The tribes had earlier been moved from their traditional home along the North Platte River as part of the 1868 Fort Laramie Treaty. It stipulated that native people live in agencies, the predecessors of modern-day Indian reservations. Agencies had Indian agents who had been authorized to interact with the tribes on behalf of the government.

It was at Fort Robinson on May 7, 1877, where Crazy Horse led 1,100 followers to surrender after suffering a defeat at the Battle of Wolf Mountain on January 8, 1877. Before the battle, as was the custom during winter, the Lakota Sioux had bedded down in their camp, waiting for warmer weather to arrive. They didn't realize the army was still pursuing them because, at that time, battles had not been common during winter weather.

When Crazy Horse's band was attacked, their horses were starving, which forced the warriors to fight on foot in three feet of snow. The band quickly ran out of ammunition and had to resort to using bows and arrows.

After the battle, scouts and couriers from Fort Robinson arrived and promised Crazy Horse that if he brought his band in, they would all be treated well. On their arrival, though, old rivalries and misunderstandings between military officers and many of the Lakota Sioux erupted into open hostility. The army arrested Crazy Horse to prevent continued disruption, and in the ensuing scuffle, he was stabbed and mortally wounded. Crazy Horse died on the evening of September 5, 1877.

Similarly, in late November 1876, the U.S. Army attacked the Northern Cheyenne in "the Dull Knife Fight." The battle began when an Indian scout located a large village of Northern Cheyenne camped at the source of Crazy Woman Creek, around thirty miles northeast of present-day Buffalo, Wyoming.

Colonel Ranald S. "No-Finger Chief" Mackenzie led a contingent of a thousand troops, a third of them Pawnee warriors, from Fort Robinson to locate and attack the Cheyenne village. Within a few days, Mackenzie's troops found the camp near Crazy Woman Creek along a fork of the Powder River. At the time, the Cheyenne were celebrating a victory over the Shoshone. At the first light of dawn, Mackenzie's troops attacked, surprising the Cheyenne and forcing them to leave their buffalo robes, blankets, and other warm winter clothing behind. Though Dull Knife's warriors put up a good fight, they eventually had to retreat. In their absence, the U.S. Army destroyed the village, along with seven hundred head of cattle. Without food and provisions, the Cheyenne had two choices: surrender or die. They picked the former.

Once the Northern Cheyenne were in custody, the U.S. Army decided to remove them from their traditional homeland in the Great Plains and transfer them to the Southern Cheyenne and Arapaho Agency in Indian Territory (in present-day Oklahoma). On their arrival, the 937 Northern Cheyenne were suffering from malnutrition, cultural alienation, and diseases that included measles, dysentery, and infections, which, in many cases, resulted in death. After being denied permission to return north, more than 350 Cheyenne broke out of the reservation. Their leaders, chiefs Dull Knife and Little Wolf, moved northward through Kansas. Once in Nebraska, they formed two groups: Little Wolf and his group went north to Canada to meet up with Sitting Bull, and Dull Knife and his followers headed for the Red Cloud Agency in Nebraska.

When Dull Knife and his people arrived in present-day Chadron, Nebraska, an army patrol intercepted them and escorted them to Fort Robinson. There, the 149 men, women, and children were taken into custody and confined to military barracks. Dull Knife asked the military post commanders to either allow them to join Chief Red Cloud at his agency or let them remain in their northern Plains homeland. The army refused that request and pressured them to return to the Indian Territory reservation in Oklahoma. When the Cheyenne refused to go, the commanding officer of Fort Robinson, Brigadier General Henry T. Wessells, denied them food and water.

In desperation, on January 9, 1879, with six inches of snow on the ground, the Cheyenne broke out of the barracks where they were being held, shooting several guards in the process. At the same time, they lost a good number of their warriors, and many of their women and children were recaptured. The remaining Cheyenne fled west in an attempt to reach the limestone bluffs. During the pursuit, the army killed around twenty-seven Cheyenne and mutilated the body of Dull Knife's daughter. On reaching the bluffs, the Cheyenne separated into smaller groups. Over the next few days, the soldiers continued their pursuit and captured several Cheyenne. Others were killed or died from exposure. Their only food consisted of dead cavalry horses.

Two weeks later, on January 22, 1879, at a camp north of Fort Robinson the soldiers found the largest group of surviving Cheyenne along the shore of Antelope Creek. At the time, they were trying to reach the Sioux in South Dakota. Wessells pleaded with them to surrender; however, the Cheyenne responded with gunfire, killing three soldiers. The soldiers mounted a charge, firing on the Cheyenne who had taken refuge in a buffalo wallow. When the fighting ceased, twenty-eight Cheyenne were dead or dying. Only nine survived, all women and children. The dead were buried in a mass grave called "the Pit," in what was called the Fort Robinson Massacre.

Dull Knife and some of his family had separated from the rest of the Cheyenne and escaped, fleeing eastward instead of to the west. Eventually, they found refuge with the Sioux in South Dakota, who hid them on their reservation.

Four years before the end of the Sioux Wars, in 1886, a tent city sprang up east of Fort Robinson to prepare for the arrival of the railroad. It was platted as a townsite and named Crawford, in memory of Lieutenant Emmet Crawford who had recently been killed while pursuing Apache leader Geronimo in Mexico.

Crawford had a reputation as a Wild West town, where nearby Fort Robinson soldiers mixed with gold miners and cowhands, often ending up in fights. Like many "fort towns," Crawford soon established businesses essential to local ranchers. These included a bank, multiple general stores, two lumber yards, a furniture store, a meat market, a blacksmith shop, a wheelwright, a livery stable, two restaurants, three drugstores, a hardware establishment, and flour and feed stores, along with several saloons. Whenever the number of personnel at Fort Robinson increased, so too did the businesses in Crawford.

Over the years, Crawford had been host or home to Lakota Chief Red Cloud, former desperado David (Doc) Middleton, poet-scout John Wallace Crawford, frontierswoman Calamity Jane, military surgeon Walter Reed (who conquered yellow fever), and President Theodore Roosevelt, who delivered a speech while visiting Crawford on April 25, 1903.

East of Chadron, I began driving north to Wounded Knee, South Dakota. I had to admit, my feelings were mixed. Whenever I'd mentioned to people along the way that I was heading to Wounded Knee, several of them described experiences that made them never want to return. Some talked about overenthusiastic vendors, others spoke about the sanctity of the site, and still others said that the experience wasn't worth crossing such barren land.

I had doubts about what I'd heard from people who visited Wounded Knee, based on my friendship years earlier with Sidney H. (Sid) Byrd, Hoksila Waste in the Dakota Sioux language. I had met him in the late 1990s as I drove across the country doing research for my book about the Presbyterians. Later, I visited him at his home in Arizona where he'd retired. During our visit, Sid handed me a signed copy of his book *Betrayal at Wounded Knee Creek,* where he told the story of the massacre of innocent Sioux tribal members. His book was one of the first written by a Native American. My goal during this trip was to verify the information in Sid's book through the storytelling of someone at the Wounded Knee memorial. Sid had passed in 2016 at age ninety-seven; at the time, he had lived in Flandreau, South Dakota.

I had felt a need inside me to learn more about the reason for the massacre. How could a sacred dance that provided hope for a people who had suffered horribly result in so many deaths? A people who had somehow survived the diseases brought by white settlers—smallpox being the worst, having decimated upward of 90 percent of the Lakota. The belief in Manifest Destiny (a phrase coined in 1845) drove nineteenth-century U.S. territorial expansion, granting white settlers a God-given right to take fertile native land and push the tribes onto reservations whose land was not close to equivalent. In addition, the near extinction of the buffalo deprived the tribes of the food, warmth, and shelter that the U.S. government had promised.

So many reasons for the massacre, with none making any sense.

I was both worried and excited as I drove through Whiteclay, a small unincorporated town on the Nebraska side of the border. Then I grew more scared than worried while crossing into South Dakota and entering the Oglala Lakota Nation with its welcome signs. In Pine Ridge, I passed by the historic Pine Ridge Episcopal Church, built in accordance with the Peace Policy of President U.S. Grant. The Catholics followed in 1880, the Jesuits started a mission and a school in 1884, and the Presbyterians came in 1887. Were the churches complicit in somehow causing the Wounded Knee Massacre in 1890? After all, the churches had claimed thousands of Christian converts at that time.

I turned east on US Highway 18, with the Wounded Knee Massacre site still sixteen miles away.

Wounded Knee, on the Pine Ridge Indian Reservation in Ogalala, Lakota County, South Dakota, had a population of 364. Though the entire county lay within the Pine Ridge Reservation, roughly 66 percent of the population was Native American because the Dawes Act of 1887 allowed tribal members to sell their land to non-natives. It was arid terrain with rolling hills.

Driving toward the small parking lot across the road from the burial site, I saw a weathered, stenciled, red-and-white sign with a message spelled out in all caps:

> "THIS MEMORIAL IS FREE TO PUBLIC VISITORS GOOD WILL DONATIONS AT YOUR OWN DISCRETION, OGLALA SIOUX TRIBE"

Exiting my car, I headed right for a metal, raised-letter sign posted next to the parking lot that told the story of the Massacre at Wounded Knee from the Lakota people's perspective. It was such a moving account, I copied it below in its entirety.

Dec. 29, 1890, Chief Spotted Elk who the U.S. Army called Big Foot, with his Minneconjou and Hunk papa Sioux Band of 106 warriors, 250 women and children, were encamped on this Flat, surrounded by the U.S. 7th Cavalry (470 soldiers), commanded by Col. Forsythe.

The "Messiah Craze" possessed many Indians, who left the vicinity of the Agencies to "Ghost Dance" during the summer and fall in 1890. "Unrest" on the Pine Ridge Reservation was partly due to the reduction of beef rations by Congress, and to the "Ghost Dancing" of Chiefs Sitting Bull, Hump, Spotted Elk, Kicking Bear, and Short Bull. The Sioux were told by Kicking Bear and Short Bull that by wearing "Ghost Shirts," the ghost dancing warriors would become immune to the whiteman's bullets and openly defy the soldiers and white settlers, and bring back the old days of the big buffalo herds.

On Nov. 15, 1890, Indian Agent Royer (Lakota Wokopa) at Pine Ridge called for troops, and by Dec. 1, 1890, several thousand U.S. Regulars were assembled in this area of Dakota Territory.

On Dec. 15, 1890, Chief Sitting Bear was killed by Lt. Bullhead of the Standing Rock Indian Police. Forty of Sitting Bull's braves escaped from the Grand River, and joined Chief Spotted Elk's band on Deep Creek, to camp and "Ghost Dance" on the south fork of the Cheyenne River. Chief Spotted Elk was under the close scrutiny of Lt. Col. Sumner and his troops, and on Dec. 23, 1890, they were ordered to arrest

Spotted Elk as a hostile. However, Spotted Elk's band had already silently slipped away from the Cheyenne country, into the Badlands, heading for Pine Ridge.

On Dec. 28, 1890, without a struggle, Chief Spotted Elk surrendered to the U.S. 7th Cavalry (Maj. Whitesides) at the site marked by a sign five miles north of here. The Band was then escorted to Wounded Knee, camping that night under guard.

Reinforcements of the U.S. Cavalry (including one company of Indian Scouts) arrived at Wounded Knee from Pine Ridge Agency on the morning of Dec. 29, 1890. Col. Forsythe took command of a force of 470 men. A battery of four Hotchkiss guns was placed on the hill 400 feet west of here, overlooking the Indian encampment. Spotted Elk's Band was encircled at 9:00 a.m. by a line of foot soldiers and cavalry. Chief Spotted Elk, sick with Pneumonia, lay in a warmed tent provided by Col. Forsythe, in the center of the camp. A white flag flew there, placed by the Indians. Directly in the rear of the Indian Camp was a dry draw, running east and west.

*The Indians were ordered to surrender their arms before proceeding to Pine Ridge. Capt. Wallace, with an Army detail, began searching the teepees for hidden weapons. During the excitement, Yellow Bird, a medicineman, [*** This should be two words. Please check original]walked among the bravest, blowing on an eagle bone whistle, inciting the warriors to action, declaring that the "Ghost Shirts" worn by the warriors would protect them from the soldiers' bullets. A shot was fired, and all hell broke loose. The troops fired a deadly volley into the Council warriors, killing nearly half of them. A bloody hand-to-hand struggle followed, all the more desperate since the Indians were armed mostly with clubs, knives, and revolvers. The Hotchkiss guns fired 2-pound explosive shells on the groups, indiscriminately killing warriors, women, children, and their own disarming soldiers. Soldiers were killed by cross-fire of their comrades in this desperate engagement.*

Surviving Indians stampeded in wild disorder for the shelter of the draw 200 feet to the south, escaping west and east in the draw, and north down Wounded Knee Creek. Pursuit by the 7th Cavalry resulted in the killing of more men, women, and children, causing this battle to be referred to as the "Wounded Knee Massacre." One hour later, 146 Indian men, women, and children lay dead in Wounded Knee Creek valley. The bodies of many were scattered along a distance of two miles from the scene of the encounter. Twenty soldiers were killed on the field, and sixteen later died of wounds. Wounded soldiers and Indians alike were taken to Pine Ridge Agency. A blizzard came up. Four days later, an Army detail gathered up the Indian dead and buried them in a common grave at the top of the hill northwest of here. A monument marks this grave.

"Ghost Dancing" ended with this encounter. The Wounded Knee battlefield is the site of the last armed conflict between the Sioux Indians and the United States Army.

As I finished reading the sign, up stepped Aloysius Little Moon, a member of the Lakota tribe who, at thirty-one years of age, had worked a variety of jobs for the last thirteen years at the Wounded Knee National Historic Landmark. He asked whether I'd like him to tell the story of Wounded Knee, which I welcomed.

Aloysius began by saying, "Open your ears so I can tell you. I want to share the story about Wounded Knee so you have a better understanding of what happened here."

After reading the sign and hearing what Aloysius said, along with what I'd learned about the U.S. Army's mission of destroying the native people on my way from Lusk to Wounded Knee, I simply wanted to hug him and apologize for what my people had done to the tribes. It was a very emotional time for me.

Together, we climbed the two-track, dirt-and-gravel path up the hill to the burial site. As Aloysius and I walked through the arched opening, he said, "The archway was built in 1969, and it still has bullet holes in it from 1973," referring to the takeover of Wounded Knee on February 27, 1973. It was when roughly two hundred members of the American Indian Movement, led by Russell Means and Dennis Banks, declared Wounded Knee to be the Independent Oglala Sioux Nation as a protest against corruption in tribal leadership, along with the failure of the U.S. government to honor native treaties. A 71-day siege took place, the longest civil disorder in the history of the U.S. Marshal Service. During that time, two protesters died, and several others were injured. The protest ended when the protesters surrendered after government officials promised to investigate their complaints.

The takeover drew the public's attention to the federal government's injustices against Native Americans and their rights to sovereignty. New legislation was also passed that included the Indian Freedom of Religion Act of 1978, the Indian Child Welfare Act of 1978, and the Native American Graves Protection and Repatriation Act of 1990. Even though the 1973 protest had happened twenty years before Aloysius was born, he spoke with great pride that it had happened at Wounded Knee.

Rather than follow Aloysius right away, I hung back for a few seconds to place my fingers in the bullet holes. I wanted to get a sense of what it must have felt like being there as the protesters' own government tried to kill them. As a student during the 1970s, I had witnessed the Kent State massacre—not in person but through television and newspaper reports. It was real to me then, just as Wounded Knee felt real during my visit.

As we walked through the burial site, Aloysius said that he often did maintenance work in the cemetery. "Every year I repaint the archway. I tell people, 'When you are here, don't write on it because it takes time for me to fix it.'"

Motioning for me to follow, he pointed at a single grave just outside of where the mass grave was located. "This is my great-grandmother's grave. Whenever I am here, I stop to say thanks for what her memory meant to me." Noting that Emma L. "Little Moon" Morrison had been born in 1892 and died in 1967 at age seventy-four, I realized she had died before getting to meet Aloysius. A second inscription on her monument said, "Wife of John J. Morrison," who, when I researched that name later, I discovered had died in May 1981 at age eighty-six, but his name did not include Little Moon nor did it say he was buried there—which made me wonder whether Aloysius's great-grandfather was Native American.

We next walked to the edge of the hill that overlooked Wounded Knee Creek. "See the tree line over there. When I was about five years old, my grandmother took me up there to show me where the Hotchkiss guns were located. She said, 'This is where the Seventh Calvary sat, and it was just a big old hill. And that was what made it unfair. They came here December 28, setting up the night before the massacre.'"

When Aloysius pointed at the massacre site, I thought about when I was little and my parents took me to the Gettysburg battle site. The vantage point the army had at Wounded Knee reminded me of the U.S. Army defense line at the final battle site at Gettysburg where Picket's Charge occurred. Within minutes, more than eleven hundred Confederate troops died there, and more than four thousand were wounded. It was a decisive battle for the Civil War, just as the massacre at Wounded Knee was the decisive battle of the Indian Wars.

Aloysius then pointed at the valley that Wounded Knee Creek flowed through. "My grandmother took me down there and let me sit there. This is where they were camped." The Native Americans had camped there—378 Lakota men, women, children, and elderly—on the night before the massacre. Spotted Elk (Big Foot, as the army called him) was sick and had placed a white flag of surrender next to the tent that the army's Colonel Forsythe had given him. When I saw, laid out before me, the position of the Hotchkiss guns and where the army had made the Lakota camp, it felt premeditated. It got me thinking about the twenty members of the 7th Cavalry who had received the Medal of Honor shortly after the massacre. The army now wanted to take the medals away in what was called the "Remove the Stain Act," which had passed previously and was attached to the final defense policy bill. However, Congress deleted it in the final compromise bill. Though Congress officially apologized in 1990 for the massacre, it failed to rescind the medals.

As we continued to talk, Aloysius told me that before the massacre, Colonel Forsythe had said, "These people are not to reach Red Cloud Agency. This is the last place they are going to see." Aloysius said, "When it happened, they set off the gunfire from here," He pointed at the hill overlooking the campsite. "Boom

boom, and they shot over here." He pointed at the campsite. "They hit the first teepee, and it hit the ground, and that's when all the elderly started running. They yelled, 'They're here! They're here! White man, he's here, and he's going to kill us!' Soon, more boom, boom, boom. They came down with bayonets on top of their guns. They came through here," he pointed at the plains between the hill and the campsite, "and they ran over that way," toward Wounded Knee Creek. "'Kill them, kill them, if you see any more, kill them, too.' What did they want? They wanted what is here in Wounded Knee."

It was as if I were watching the reenactment of the massacre from up on the hill where the cemetery was now. I simply could not imagine what the tribal members thought. When we were growing up, we played cowboys and Indians, but those games were with neighborhood friends, and the guns and the bows we played with were toys. The toys were symbols; they were not real. We were playing the way that we saw Hollywood actors fight onscreen. Though we might have been fooled into thinking the actors were real, they were simply acting according to a script. Unknown to us, when a scene ended for the day, they took a limo home. What happened here at Wounded Knee was real. It actually happened. It was not ancient history; for God's sake, the automobile had already been invented.

Aloysius next took me to the monument in the middle of the cemetery and said, "Here is the mass grave. They were all killed by the 7th Calvary. Fourteen years before, they were the calvary that was led by Custer. He and all his men died at the Battle of Little Bighorn. The massacre here happened because of what happened at Little Bighorn. It was revenge by the 7th Calvary for that battle."

I asked about the monument in the center of the cemetery, when it was built. I thought, *If this had happened in Washington, D.C., the monument would dominate the tourist business. But here, in a place where few people visited, it was a ruddy old cemetery with gravesites that needed upkeep, a lawn in patches that could use irrigation, and in an out-of-the-way place where vandals probably outnumbered tourists.* I thought that at the time but certainly did not say it. Rather than say anything, I let Aloysius talk.

Aloysius told me the monument had been built after the massacre when survivors vowed to honor the memory of the dead. Ten years after the massacre, the Wounded Knee Survivors Association was founded. Two of the founding members—Dewey Beard, the last survivor of the Battle of Little Big Horn, and Joseph Horn Cloud, whose father, Chief Horn Cloud, had died at Wounded Knee—raised the money needed to build the monument. It was erected next to the mass grave in 1905. It featured an urn atop the monument, which was carved with the names of several of the people buried there. Looking at the monument, I found the names hard to read. Years of harsh weather had worn away the carving.

Next, we walked over to a grave outside of the mass grave enclosure. With a sigh, Aloysius said, "Here is Lost Bird. She made it out of here. She was just a baby and lived." For the next few minutes, he told me her story. Her name was Zintkala Nuni, but she became known as the Lost Bird of the Wounded Knee massacre. She was found beneath a blanket under the frozen body of her mother, three days after the massacre. When Leonard Colby, the brigadier general in the Nebraska National Guard, heard about the live infant being found, he decided the baby would be a nice trophy to have. So, he posed as a Seneca Indian and gained possession of the baby. He brought the baby back home to his wife, Clara, who was a women's suffragette well known in Washington, D.C., circles.

Because they didn't have children, her husband adopted the baby, and Clara took on the job of raising Lost Bird, whose name had been changed to the adopted name Zintka. Then Leonard Colby cheated on his wife with the young nursemaid Maud Miller, who was helping to raise Lost Bird. Maud got pregnant by Leonard, and he soon took her as his mistress. After trying to save her marriage for more than a decade, Clara gave Leonard Colby her permission to seek a divorce.

Though Clara believed in Lost Bird and continued raising her, as time went on Lost Bird became hard to control. This led Clara to enroll her in an Indian boarding school, which attempted to "take the Indian out of" the young Lakota woman. Zintka ran away from boarding school, joined a Wild West show, and searched for her roots in South Dakota. At that time, she moved onto the Lakota Pine Ridge reservation but had problems being accepted because of her learned white ways. Zintka got pregnant, and her father placed her in the Mitford Industrial Home, a severe reformatory school. Zintka's son was stillborn, and she eventually returned to Clara Colby and married Albert Chalivat, a young friend of Clara's. Zintka discovered that her husband had given her syphilis, then incurable, and the illness left her an invalid for nearly a year.

Zintka moved to Hollywood and worked as an extra in Westerns, where she met and married Bob Keith, a Hollywood cowboy. She got pregnant and had a son. Then Zintka left her husband and joined Buffalo Bill Cody's Wild West Show. She next married Dick Allen, a calliope player and a clown with the show who also had a young son. The Allens, now with two small children, left the Wild West Show to work in vaudeville in San Francisco. Zintka lost her youngest child to an illness and gave up the other to a Native American woman who was in better circumstances. Her husband's continuing ill health meant she had to find a way for them to survive. Zintka and Dick Allen left vaudeville and moved in with his parents in Hanford, California. Zintka, Lost Bird, died in Hanford, California, on February 14, 1920, of influenza, during the Flu Epidemic of 1918. For many years, Zinkta lay in a California grave until a group raised money to move Lost Bird's remains and rebury her on July 11, 1991, at Wounded Knee. Aloysius showed me her grave just outside

Aloysius Little Moon, kneeling at the gravesite of Lost Bird at the Wounded Knee Memorial on the Pine Ridge Indian Reservation in South Dakota

the mass grave site, where she would be close to her mother's grave. Although her gravestone said she had died in 1919, that date seemed inaccurate.

After learning more about Lost Bird from Aloysius, I asked him to pick a place in the cemetery where he would like me to take his picture. Without hesitation, he chose to kneel beside Lost Bird's grave. After all that Aloysius had said about Lost Bird, I knew she had become very important to him. Her story certainly made an impression on me. Even now, I think about her. Had she been left with her people, she would have had a much better life. Instead, she suffered her entire life, trying to find her identity.

As we walked back down the hill to the parking lot, Aloysius told me, "It's important for everyone to know the real truth of what happened at Wounded Knee. How else will the truth ever get out there? The only truth they know is written in history books, and the history books don't really tell something that Wounded Knee tells itself. What this is really all about is my invitation for you to return to Wounded Knee each and every year. I just want to make sure everybody who comes through the archway has a better understanding about Wounded Knee."

I shook Aloysius's hand, while inside I felt overwhelmed. Aloysius, in the period of an hour or so, had in many ways changed me. As I drove away, I felt angry.

A mile or so from the Wounded Knee Massacre site, I needed to pull off the road and reflect on what I had witnessed. So, I took out a note pad and began to write. Looking at the plains that stretched out beyond, I thought about Aloysius and what he went through each day. To me, the most meaningful trait Aloysius possessed was his dignity. Before meeting him, I watched as visitors took advantage of his good nature and stiffed him when it came time to leave a tip. Yet Aloysius still said thank you and asked them to return. I knew how little he made, yet for thirteen years, he had been present almost every day, greeting people much as he had greeted me. As we walked from place to place, he told me about the many deaths of family members he'd endured. He said Pine Ridge was one of the most challenged reservations, that it had a high crime rate, poor housing, lack of good hospital care, and few, if any, good-paying jobs. I could only imagine what Aloysius faced in his own life. Yet, his smile was infectious, and his demeanor was kind. When he told me to return to Wounded Knee each year, I knew he meant it. All of this I wrote in my note pad to keep the memory fresh.

7

From the Wounded Knee Massacre site, I decided to head to the Nebraska Sandhills.

I had heard that ranchers once thought the Sandhills were totally unproductive land, unfit even for raising cattle. One story I'd heard was about an inventive rancher named E. S. Newman who decided to try to raise cattle along the banks of the Niobrara River but certainly not in the nearby Sandhills, which had no noticeable source of water. However, to the surprise of Newman and the cattle ranchers who followed, when the free-range cattle wandered into the hills, they found plenty of water and also grass and shelter. Since then, the Sandhills have become one of the most productive cattle-raising lands on earth. Over time, the Sandhills acquired a thicker, more stable covering of grass, and the rolling hills developed lusher vegetation, which made the region even more productive.

To view some of the ranches, I decided to cruise through two hundred miles of rangeland within the Nebraska Sandhills. South of Gordon, Nebraska, on Route 27, the road that led to Ellsworth, I passed by a church that seemed oddly out of place because I'd seen no signs of any people living nearby. Thinking about it, I decided to turn around and head back to that church.

I pulled into the empty parking lot, hoping the church door was open. It was. I saw a woman vacuuming the floor and asked whether she had a couple of minutes to sit and talk. Then I explained my purpose, showed her my map, and said, "I would like to interview you, and the conversation will not include any politics or religion." She stood up with an indignant, yet kind and questioning, look and said, "But we are a church. We talk about religion here. It's what we do. . . . Plus, I'd rather not put my name out there."

Not to be deterred, I asked whether the minister was around. "In his study," she said. "I'll get him." She returned a few minutes later with a young man who introduced himself as Trent Fugitt. I repeated what I had told the woman who didn't want her name used, but instead of mirroring what she'd said, Trent replied, "That's great, I'd enjoy a conversation that didn't include religion."

Knowing where I was and its demographics, I said, "You are a young pastor, if I might say, and I know that mostly older people live around here. Where did you come from? Where was your home before you got here?"

"Well, we moved here in January 2021," Trent said. "I was born and raised in Denver, Colorado; went to school in Fort Collins; moved to Colorado Springs when my wife and I got married; and have been around millions of people my entire life. And might I add, I've never felt a community as close and as strong as where we are now. We have three buildings on this property, and the closest building from this property is five miles away. And yet I feel closer to the people here than I ever did back in Colorado. What that's done for our family—it's given us not just the friendships in the community, but we truly do consider everyone within this thirty-mile range to be family."

The woman who didn't want her name out there said, "I moved to this area about twenty-one years ago, but we need young people as well as older people to serve our churches. . . . Our house we moved into, it's just off the highway. We used to drive by this church, and I was drawn to it. Where we live is halfway between my husband's family and my family. Even though where I live there's a church just down the road, it never felt comfortable to me. I wasn't drawn there. I believe this is where God wants me to be."

Trent added, "My wife and I were interested in going wherever God wanted us. We interviewed at a couple of other churches, and for each of those places, God made it very clear to us we weren't supposed to be there. He had something else for us, and when we came here for the first time, it was exactly where God wanted us to be."

When I thought about it later, I realized I always found it interesting when someone said, "God told me." It did resonate with me because I often used the words "I have a feeling I'm supposed to be somewhere or do something or meet someone or be someplace." Those were the kind of words I tended to use. When I was with Native Americans, they used the word *Creator* similarly. I'd also heard people say, "Higher Power." All of those terms resonated with me because I did feel there were things not yet explained that we were not supposed to know, that we would find out later, and that my britches were big enough to accept a lot of similar words and what people meant by them. Even in Exodus, when the burning bush spoke to Moses, the being said, "I am who I am," and added, "Say this to the people of Israel: 'I am has sent me to you.'"

At this point, Trent said, "You can look at demographics, and the age demographic of a church's congregation is roughly plus or minus fifteen years of the pastor's age. A lot of the younger families in this community didn't come to church because the pastor was not the right age. So, it bodes well for this church."

To that, the woman said, "This church is in the middle of nowhere, per se. This is the second country church that I've known in my whole lifetime that has been out where you wouldn't expect a church. Church is more than just church. It's a place where people have meetings and socialize, and I think that is where our potlucks come from. Because you can get together with people and have face-to-face conversations. Nowadays it's all about technology. Some say there are no jobs for kids, and they want to move away. A lot of it has to do with technology. It doesn't take tons of people to do the work that it used to, and it's all because of technology. People want to live out in the middle of nowhere but don't necessarily want to do the kind of work that is done out here. In other words, a lot of people don't like physical work."

Trent added, "A question we get is, 'You're a church that's thirty miles away from the closest town. Where do you draw people from?' The answer is, we have thirty miles' worth of land either way where people don't have a church to attend. So, they come here. We have people who travel quite a distance. Some travel up to an hour on back country dirt roads to get here because this is their community. There are churches in town, but we are not town folk. We are ranchers who have created a community outside of a town, and this is a church for that community of people."

"I've heard of traveling ministers who used to go to people's homes before there was a real building," the woman said. "Where I grew up, I'm pretty sure that the church came first, then the school building. That's the way they settled, and it's funny that you talked about the Kincaid Act because I live in the old Kincaid house. Where I grew up over in central Nebraska, there used to be a picture in the Pizza Hut that said, 'Here's a picture around the square where they had the drawing of the people getting their Kincaid Act slips.' I don't know if that picture is still there, but it was in Broken Bow, Nebraska, on Highway 2."

I asked Trent how the church had started.

"The church was formed here back in the 1950s. It started as a traveling Sunday school group. It didn't have a Sunday worship–type service. It was strictly a Sunday school. I think the Sunday school built the initial building. Once the community grew enough and stabilized in the number who attended the Sunday school, the worship service was begun. The sanctuary is relatively new and was built in the 1980s. This church has a very good history of longevity with its pastors. I'm probably only the fifth or sixth pastor since the '50s. The last guy was here for fifteen years. The guy before him was thirteen years. You have roots here, you stay here."

At this point, I started talking about country folk versus city folk. "I know people in cities who don't understand what it's like in the country. They don't need to go there anymore. They source locally, they fly over, and if they happen to drive across the country, they take the interstate. They never check out anything because they're glued to the wheel."

Trent could relate to what I said. "A family who lives another forty-five minutes away, back in the hills, is one of our closest neighbors. They had a grass fire, hay bale fire, on their property last fall. By the time they got the call out to emergency, there were already fifty neighbors around them who came and suppressed the fire. That's the type of community we have here. That's what we came into in 2021. Because back in Colorado, you get home from work at 5:30, you open your garage door, you pull in your car and close your garage door, then you get out of your car. You live next to a thousand people in the neighborhood, but you don't have a clue who they are. Here, you know the people because you live in this community, and they love you, and you love them. You see someone broken down by the side of the road, and you help them. That's the glue holding this community together."

The woman agreed with Trent. "Just like he's saying about community. In one of my other jobs I work with a lady who comes from New York. She says she really doesn't like it out here. I get the impression she hates Nebraska. Well, her husband, who's fairly young, had a stroke. She had to take him to a hospital in Colorado. But she didn't think she could go because of the cost. However, within twenty-four hours, they had enough money for her to go and spend two weeks over there with him. That was because this community pulled together. I told her that's why I love this place. I saw this while growing up. Even though I'm a country girl and have always been a country girl, and I grew up on a farm, now I'm in ranch country, and just like where I grew up, the community people are there for you. This lady grew up in New York. If something like that happened there, I'm pretty sure she wouldn't have had any help. I don't think her neighbors would have helped her at all. We have compassionate people out here."

I asked Trent about his earlier life and how it differed from here.

"I've been in church ministry all my life. I knew from a young age that I wanted to work in a church. The churches that we've had in Colorado are still lightyears behind the community out here. In Colorado Springs, we had the Air Force Academy and three other military bases within five miles, so it was a very transient community. At times, the mindset was 'I'm not going to bother putting too much into getting to know you and starting a relationship with you because the odds are you will move in two years when the military transfers you.' Here, in the Sandhills,

Trent Fugitt, pastor, Pleasant Point Community Church north of Ellsworth, Nebraska

there are generational roots. So, if you don't like your neighbor, that's tough because you're going to live next to him for the next eighty years. And your kids will live next to their kids for the next eighty years. There's been this type of mentality that we have to get along. We have to get to know and love our neighbors, not just because we live next to them but because we're going to help each other. Why would we be out here doing this work by ourselves when we can have this community? Yeah, there's different ranches, different ways of doing ranching. But at the end of the day, when you pull back and look at it, you're all doing the same thing, so why wouldn't we have a community to help each other, learn from each other, and grow on each other? Things like, 'Hey, this is working for me. What's working for you?' There's a deeper sense of community here than I've ever seen anywhere else."

Trent talked about the work he did before coming to the Sandhills. "Before I came out here, I was working at a nonprofit ministry in Colorado Springs. I was putting in fifty to sixty hours a week, thinking I was working full time. But I could have done that job in three or four hours a day; the other hours I was wasting my time, sitting in a cube in my office building. I wasn't even able to spend much time with my kids. When I starting working at home, I was able to get closer to my kids. And since moving here, we've gotten closer yet."

As I drove away, I thought about all of the wonderful people I'd met while writing the book about the Presbyterians. The man from California who'd sold everything he owned to buy a semi so he could help those without much who lived in the mountains of West Virginia. The woman I met who'd helped the homeless in the streets of Los Angeles. The young lady who'd helped the kids who had experienced the gun violence in a Denver suburb. I thought, *There are so many good people out there, all around the world, who help others. Some do it as part of their religion, yet others without any faith connection do it as well.*

I knew Ellsworth was about a half-hour's drive away, yet a couple miles from the church in a very remote location on a hill, I saw a pickup with its hood raised. I asked whether I could do anything to help. I told them I knew nothing about cars, let alone trucks. With me being a writer and a photographer, I had no actual skillsets, other than knowing how to sharpen a pencil and get a photo in focus. The older one—I believed, the father—pointed to his phone, indicating that he didn't have signal. At the same time, I noticed a younger guy, whom I assumed was the son, under the hood with a confused look on his face. Though I knew they were in a pickle, I could tell they were ranchers. I knew that ranchers were used to fixing things on their own and that they probably did not want to rely on someone else for help, especially a guy with out-of-state license plates driving a Prius.

I'd been on the road that day and hadn't seen any other vehicles for more than an hour. I threw out some ideas—none of them helpful. "Could I give you a ride to Alliance?" I asked. I knew there were auto shops in that town, so perhaps I could give them a ride.

The father said, "Nope." He looked at the mess of stuff in my car and figured there was no room.

"How about if I run and get you something?"

"Nope."

The way he scratched his head told me he did not believe someone like me would know enough to even pick up a part.

"How about if I give one of you a ride to your ranch, so you could find what you need?"

"Nope. Roads are rutty, two-lane dirt, and you would need to drive nearly ten miles in each direction. No way your car could make it."

"Let me give it a try," I said.

The son peeked around the side of the hood. "I know I have what I need in my barn."

"Let me take the stuff off the front seat and floor to make some room," I said. "I promise, it will only take a minute." With that, I grabbed a large paper sack from my back seat, scooped up everything in front, and threw it in the bag.

The son jumped in and motioned which direction I needed to go. "Look for the break in the road and turn right."

Rather than let him sit there without saying anything, I started asking him questions. And all of a sudden, he started talking. He told me about his growing-up years, how he and his brother had started a business that recycled tires. I asked how it was going, and he turned silent for a minute, then said, "My brother died a few years back. He was only thirty-five. He had gone into the house to fix lunch and slumped over dead, dying instantly. That was four years ago. And a month later, my mother died from cancer, and a month after that, my grandfather died."

"How did you cope?" I asked.

"Not well. Life sorta stopped." He added, "I'm gradually getting better."

I asked his age.

"Thirty-three."

I told him my son had died.

He asked when.

"Four months ago."

He asked how.

It was something I hadn't shared very often because it was hard for me to talk about. Finally, I said, "Alcoholism, he drank himself to death."

We had formed a bond, a bond of brokenness. Our conversation had awakened sad and painful memories in me. Of a little boy who rode his brand-new bike with training wheels from the bike store a block to where his mother lived. It had been a brutal divorce. I feared my son had gotten in the middle of it. Though I paid child support until he was of legal age, the father-son bond had never formed. Then, with his adulthood, came a series of drunken-driving offenses. The last time we talked was when I took him to his court appearance for yet another DUI. On the way there, I learned that he'd had not only one offense; there were several of them. I got angry and said, "You are no longer a drinker." We didn't speak again, and ten years later he died an alcoholic who had decided to drink.

We got to the ranch. The son got the tools. We slowly drove back, talking about this and that. The father greeted us with his billfold open, asking how much he could pay me.

"Over the past five years as I have wandered about the country, on at least six occasions a rancher stopped to help me," I said. "It's about time I could help a rancher."

When I reached Ellsworth, a signpost told the story of the legendary Spade Ranch. This 500,000-acre ranch once had a herd of 60,000 cattle; it still existed but was now split into a few smaller ranches. Ellsworth was once a company town, consisting of a post office, a general store, a school, hotels, and houses for cowboys who worked on the Spade Ranch. One of the cowboys was Veldon Morgan, who passed away in 2022 at the VA hospital in Hot Springs, Nebraska, after a ten-year battle with cancer. He was eighty-six years old.

Veldon and his son, Wade, owned the store now named Morgan's Cowpoke Haven, which was currently in Wade's hands. They sold hunting and fishing gear, guns, knives, and ammunition, along with saddles and other riding supplies.

Though you wouldn't know it from walking around Ellsworth, it was once a mecca of activity. It was a cattle shipping point for the Spade Ranch when the Chicago, Burlington, and Quincy Railroad chose the railroad siding for a depot and water stop in 1888. Now the only remaining business was Morgan's Cowpoke Haven and its attached post office, along with a few outbuildings just behind the store.

I had intended to meet Wade Morgan while visiting the store, but I learned he had left town for the day. Still, I was able to talk to his live-in girlfriend, Jolyann McKinney, who tended the store when Wade was away.

I asked Jolyann what had brought her to Ellsworth and found that it had happened in a circuitous fashion that took a few decades and involved two marriages and divorces, three children, several jobs, and living in multiple towns in Nebraska, Wyoming, Colorado, and Washington State. But when she met Wade eight years ago, after a fashion she fell in love with Ellsworth.

"So, Wade asked me to move down here, and I said, 'Okay, that's cool.' Then I learned living here would be an adjustment because if there were twenty-five people within several miles, it would be a miracle. And I'm talking cats and dogs and goats in that total. Even though I grew up on a ranch, we had a town nearby. That was probably the hardest thing for me to get used to, the solitude."

"What else has surprised you about living here?" I asked.

"People who come in and ask things like, 'Don't the trains bother you?' That's because we have a train come through just about every fifteen minutes and even worse on Sundays."

Having been across the plains watching the abundance of trains myself, I said, "If I'm not mistaken, it's the BNSF mainline."

"Yes, I believe it is. But, actually, I don't even hear the trains anymore. I mean, we'll be sitting and watching TV, and unless the screen door's open, we hardly can hear the whistle. Though when they have an engine in the middle, you know it's going to be a two-mile-long train. But, like I said, I barely even hear it anymore. They'll go by at nighttime, and we do hear the horn in the distance."

Changing the topic, I asked, "Do you get a lot of hunters, campers, and sportsmen passing through?"

"Yes, hunters of all types. A lot of deer, antelope, turkey hunters, and whatever."

"I bet they think of this as their second home."

"Probably, yeah. We get people from all walks of life. The postcards and stuff that you see on our ceiling here, those are all from people who have visited this store. We've had people from Australia, England, and many other countries. They come from all over. If they visit the store, we always ask them to send us a postcard from their hometown."

Looking up at the ceiling covered in postcards, I also noticed a very old photo on one wall. Asking about it, I said, "There's truly a legacy to this store."

"Yeah. It's one of the neatest pictures that we have. It is of this store, showing the train depot and a water tank and the hotel that sat across the street. Other than the store, none of those buildings are here anymore. Back then, the steam locomotives stopped here when they needed water. That's what this store was originally. It was built to get supplies to people living on the Spade Ranch. It was like a half-million acres, it was that big."

"Is the Spade Ranch still in business?" I asked.

"Yes, our friend Lindsey Bixby had it with his dad for a while a few years ago. They owned it half and half. Lindsey sold their half to some people out of Oregon, and they moved here and brought all their cows here. Good people, they are really nice. As a matter of fact, they were here last night. Clay Bixby, he still has the other half. I've never been out there, so I'm not exactly sure how the divides are. Yeah, it's a lot of acreage."

Just then, someone came in.

"Hello there, can I use your bathroom before I shop?"

Jolyann told him, "I'm sorry, our bathroom is out of order."

"How far away is a bathroom for the public?" he asked.

"Alliance, thirty miles away, has some there."

He walked out of the store, saying, "I'll stop back tomorrow."

"How do people find out about the store?" I asked Jolyann.

"People come here from all over. We even get business from the Internet. My son helped me put the store up on Facebook. I don't do a lot with the website because we're pretty busy doing our stuff. But every once in a while, I do get on there. Usually, people will take one of our cards from the counter, and sometimes they pass it on. We get calls from everywhere, with people asking, 'Can you send me this?' or 'Do you have this or that type of thing?'"

"So, you've been here eight years," I said. "Would you trade those eight years for any other eight years you've had?"

"No, I would not. It's very quiet here, and there are relatively few problems. No crime. It's a good thing, too, because our closest sheriff is probably three hours from here. And that's on a regular day, he might get here in two hours to three hours. The state patrol, they stop by a lot, but our actual sheriff is in Rushville. So, any kind of problems that we have, we use the sheriff. The Sheridan County sheriff is our go-to, which is fine. We can take pretty good care of ourselves."

"I get it. You do have a gun shop, after all. So, future wise," I asked, "do you see this being your home for a long time?"

"I do. I don't think Wade will ever move from here. He's in his sixties, and he's been here all of his life. It's what he knows."

"So," I asked, "how is the closeness of the rancher community here? Not as far as getting along because I know they have to do that. But how is it here as a community?"

"It's really like no other place. You can actually go across the street and borrow milk, eggs, or whatever from your neighbor and just pay them back with the same. People are here to help you. I can go across the street and ask my neighbor to help me, and she can do the same. And the postmaster can just leave work when necessary because I also work for the post office and am allowed to help. I'm her assistant. There's been times when both she and Wade are gone, and I watch both places. I just have to remember not to carry a gun into the post office. They do have rules against that. The community here, you couldn't ask for better people. They are willing to help. Brandings are a good example. People come from all different ranches to help one person brand. And it's a vice-versa thing."

"Are you finding fewer young people who want to live here and work the ranches?"

"We had probably two or three people who moved here and went to work for one of the ranches and then didn't stay."

I asked Jolyann whether ranches needed extra workers other than during branding and calving time.

Thinking about it, she said, "It depends on how many herds of cows they have. You utilize them for the branding and the haying and the calving and the fence fixing. There's a lot of stuff that goes into it. We have a friend who has an amazing number of cows, and he has a horrible time keeping help. Because there is so much to do, and it requires so much time. Younger people don't want to do physical work. Half the people don't know how to do anything, and they're almost a burden when they come out here. They don't know how to fix the fence, they don't know how to run the tractor, and they have no idea what they're doing in the hayfield. The worst thing about it is you can't get the kids who were raised here to stay here. I think it's because ranching and farming is not an easy task. If you're looking for a paycheck, you better look somewhere else. Every day when you get up, it could make or break you. People don't realize that. Farmers need a lot of equipment, and they need to run it around the clock. I know that's part of the reason a lot of people don't stay here anymore. The machines have changed so much, they need only one person to run them."

I asked whether the age of farmers and ranchers was a worry.

"Yes, and their kids don't want to take it over. My dad, that's all he ever did. Bringing cows, raising cows, and now he's retired. But they still have the land that they always had, so he continues to take in cows. He's basically still doing everything that he did before. He just calls it retirement."

Later on, I returned, and Wade was there. I sat down with him and Jolyann. This time he mostly talked, though Jolyann weighed in from time to time. I asked Wade about how his family had ended up in Ellsworth.

"We moved here in 1970 when I was a kid. Before that, we lived fifteen miles from here on the Spade Ranch. My dad worked for the Spade. While we were still out on the ranch, my dad started making groomers for horses. After that, he invented a bit for training horses. We sold quite a lot of those, many to other stores. Then this store came up for sale, and we moved the operation here. The building was pretty dilapidated. It had been hit by a semi-truck in the front, so we rebuilt the front of it. Dad was a pretty good carpenter, self-taught. Before we bought it, it was a grocery store. That first summer we lived in a camper out front. At the time, there were old gas pumps in front. I bought the store from my father in the mid '90s. I've sold guns since '93. Also, at one time, saddles. I've always done leather stuff. My grandpa did, and my father and myself. My grandpa made a lot of saddles, but he repaired more than he made.

"All my life we've lived in the Ellsworth area," Wade said. "When I was born, Dad was working for the Spade Ranch, for Lawrence Bixby. Lawrence took it over from Bartlet. Lawrence was Dad's hero. He took care of my dad, too. So, we lived out at the Spade Ranch when I was born in 1962. Then Dad decided to go out on his own, and we moved to Hay Springs. Dad leased some land up there to raise some cattle. Unfortunately, he lost most of the calves. It was a hard winter, and the cows were eating pine needles, which killed all of their calves. That's when they moved out to my grandparents' about fifteen miles north of here. I was around two at the time. I still go out there to cut firewood. We moved here in 1970, when I was eight. I started the fourth grade in the school here. It has since closed, but my daughter went there. The kids from here now go to Hyanis, which is silly because it's thirty miles away. Some drive themselves to Alliance for school."

"It must be hard to keep young people here," I said.

"It is. A few stay. One family near here, their kids stayed after their dad died at a young age. Both of those boys stayed on the ranch. But they are an exception. They really are. It's one of the few times that kids have stayed and kept the ranch together. Two brothers getting along for several years. Key is, they don't live in the same yard. They live four or five miles apart."

I asked Wade to tell me about his kids.

"Two daughters. They helped me here for years. One of my daughters lives in Chadron, and one's in Gering, so we are in an exact ninety-minute triangle. It's ninety minutes to Brittany and ninety to Randi. They live ninety minutes from each other, isn't that weird? It's awesome, I love it. Brandi puts together seed sales for Simplot and puts all the orders together for farmers, and Brittany, she runs a restaurant at Peterson Drug named Must Love Coffee. I just put a chair lift in her place because her son is in a wheelchair. Good practice. We live upstairs here, so maybe someday I'll need to put in one here."

"Your store is in such a remote location," I said. "How did you build your business out here?"

"When I first bought the place, it was a little tough. I mean, we had to scrape to get by. But we went to gun shows, a lot of them. Every other weekend we'd hit one, and that kept us in business, kept the money flowing. Because there aren't a lot of people who come here. I wouldn't trade it for anything, but if you're relying on that traffic coming here every day, it just doesn't. You'll get it eventually, but it's a lot slower. The good thing about it here is if I want to test guns, I can walk out back and shoot them. You can't do that in most gun stores. There are people living around most every gun store. We also do a class here to teach gun safety. That's a huge part of selling guns. It's the NRA program. Now we have constitutional carry here, which doesn't require any instruction. But do people know what to do when they get picked up by a state patrolman? They don't know. There are no instructions. You're supposed to tell them, 'I've got a gun.' They don't learn that on their own. Also, we instruct people about safe storage of the gun, cleaning of the gun, everything works together. If the gun doesn't work properly because it's dirty, in that class we go through a lot of that stuff. But it all goes together for your self-protection when using a firearm. Very few will take that class if they don't have to. Another thing, we give instructions on what to do when crossing state lines because there are differences from state to state. I'm an instructor, and I'm licensed."

"A lot of people think ranchers make a lot of money," I said. "They don't understand that you can be land rich and cash poor."

"Yeah, unless you sell it. Other than income from cattle, and it takes a lot of land to run a cow-calf operation. Just a cow and calf, used to be thirteen acres per cow-calf in this area. I think it might be a little better now, maybe twelve acres per cow-calf. I don't know that for a fact, but I would almost say it's probably better. Our water is higher than it used to be. To me, it looks a lot greener now. So far, we're having a fairly good spring here. The grass is pretty tall. For the last fifteen or so years, we've had good rain. In 2011, it was horribly dry. Not a drop of rain. The water table was way low here. So, it varies. We see a lot of difference here from year to year. So, we're not the ones running the show here, even though we might think we are."

I told Wade about a rancher I knew in Wisconsin who said he needed only a quarter-acre to raise a cow-calf because they had a lot of moisture there. We both agreed that was quite a difference from the Sandhills. I asked whether they had a lot of wildfires in their area.

"An old timer once told me he could remember when there wasn't any grass on the top of these hills. The wildfires were uncontrollable. They didn't have fire trucks then. Everything was done on horseback, so the rider had to carry any

Wade Morgan and Jolyann McKinney, in front of Morgan's Cowpoke Haven, Ellsworth, Nebraska

water that he could. They would carry a water tank that could spread the water between two horses, and that was how they put fires out then. They saved these hills. Man did that. They made these hills better. Actually, here in the Sandhills, man improved the hills, and there aren't very many places where you could say that. They had to save that grass. Without it, the sand would be exposed to the wind and blow around. You can dig a hole anywhere here, and you won't hit a rock. If you find one, someone put it there. You can look at a map and see where these Sandhills are by the amount of standing water. There are a lot of little lakes. Once you cross the Niobrara River, you're pretty much out of these Sandhills. The ground is different north of the river. It's mostly farming because the soil is richer. More dirt than sand. In the Sandhills, most of our rivers and water are under us in underground streams. On the Spade there are two or three aquifers or, better said, artisian wells. That water tastes great."

It was getting late when I left Ellsworth for my planned destination, Valentine. Heading east, it took me more than two hours to get to my night's stay. The roads to Valentine cut through the gut of the Nebraska Sandhills. Had I left earlier, I could have stopped at the towns along the way, instead of viewing them from a moving car. As I passed by Willy Lake, I barely saw it because the sun was sinking quickly. And once I got to Mullen and turned north, it was totally dark. With an hour to go before I'd get to a warm bed in Valentine, I knew that when I arrived at my lodging, I'd be tired.

The next morning I arose energized and decided to head south before driving east. During checkout, I met the woman tending the motel desk. She had a deep Southern drawl, uncommon for someone in Nebraska. I asked her if she was from the South.

Tersely, she said, "Never left here."

"But you sound like a Southerner," I said.

Once again, an abrupt response: "Nope, never left here."

"Oops." That's all I could say.

8

From Valentine, I decided to make a quick drive through a portion of a large area of the country known as the Corn Belt. For my purposes, in my 10,000-mile route, the Corn Belt was defined by the National Centers for Environmental Information of the National Oceanic and Atmospheric Administration (NOAA) as an area that stretched from just east of Valentine to the location of the movie set of *The Field of Dreams*. That place, according to my calculations, was about 575 miles away via rural roads. To get there, I needed to do two things: get up super early and hit the road, and drive through a lot of small towns connected by farm fields where mainly corn was grown.

For my journey that day, I took Nebraska Route 12, known as the Outlaw Trail Scenic Byway. It was an area of the country where the federal government housed a garrison of the U.S. Cavalry from 1879 to 1906 in Fort Niobrara Military Reservation, which was established after the Great Sioux Wars of 1876. The fort was created to monitor the tribes on the Great Sioux Reservation and ship beef and supplies to the Rosebud Reservation. In 1890, the calvary embarked from Fort Niobrara to respond to the "Pine Ridge outbreak" and massacred the Lakota at Wounded Knee.

I continued east along the Outlaw Trail Scenic Byway toward Butte, passing through the small towns of Sparks, Norden, Springview, Burton, Mills, and Naper. In Butte, I left the Outlaw Trail and headed north into South Dakota, then turned east on US-18 to avoid Sioux City, instead driving past the cornfields and small towns of South Dakota and Iowa. Finally, the road crossed the mighty Missouri, which was squeezed down to a trickle by the Fort Randall Dam just outside

Pickstown. Though the dam generated enough hydroelectric power to supply more than 200,000 households and helped irrigate the Missouri River Basin throughout much of South Dakota, the problem with building the dam where they did was that it forced Native Americans off property that was once part of the Standing Rock, Cheyenne River, Fort Berthold, Crow Creek, and Lower Brule reservations.

Nearby were the ruins of Fort Randall, which served as an important outpost for operations against the Sioux from 1863 to 1865. Its primary purpose was to maintain peace between American Indians and white settlers, as well as among the tribes themselves. Soldiers at Fort Randall guarded against incursions by Dakota warriors after the Minnesota Sioux Outbreak of 1862 and later interacted with the Poncas, along with the Santee, the Yankton, and the Teton Sioux. The fort's most famous inhabitant was Sitting Bull (Tatanka Iyotake) of the Lakota Sioux when he and his band of 158 Hunkpapa Sioux camped south of the fort and were kept under loose surveillance from July 1881 until November 1883. From there, they were moved to Fort Yates, in present-day North Dakota.

Most of the fairly flat land along US-18 in southeastern South Dakota was agricultural, split nearly fifty-fifty between livestock and crops. In this part of South Dakota, the Pick–Sloan Missouri Basin Program built many dams and hydroelectric plants for irrigation and flood control near the Missouri River. Then the geography shifted ever so gradually from the plains to the heartland, where rolling terrain sloped gently toward the Missouri and Mississippi river valleys. Most of its original forests and tall grass had been turned into fields planted mainly with corn and soybeans.

While driving through northwest Iowa, I noticed some similarities with my own area of the country. Just as the Dutch had settled West Michigan in 1847, so did the Dutch settle northwestern Iowa that very same year. Both had their roots in the Calvinist reformation, and both had two factions: the very conservative Christian Reformed Church and the more moderate Reformed Church of America. In northeastern Iowa, especially in Sioux County, I saw many churches from both denominations.

Pressing on farther east, I traveled through Palo Alto County to enter the north central Iowa counties of Kossuth, Hancock, Cerro Gordo, and Floyd.

During World War II, the town of Algoma in Kossuth County was host to a German POW camp. As one of more than 150 such camps, it had a clear mission: to hold German prisoners who had been captured during the war. The Algoma POW camp was a base camp that oversaw 34 branch camps in other Iowa communities and surrounding states. The Algoma camp housed ten thousand prisoners from mid 1943 to mid 1945, when the war ended. The prisoners were given work, some doing construction and others helping out on farms.

Charles City was nicknamed Chuck City and went by the motto "America's Hometown." However, when the Ho-Chunk Native Americans lived there, they were anything but welcome to stay once white settlers arrived. The government decided to move the tribe first to Minnesota, then to South Dakota, and finally to their current location in Nebraska, where the Winnebago Indian Reservation was established by treaties signed in 1865 and 1874. Also known as the Winnebago, the Ho-Chunk tribe had previously lived in central Wisconsin and northern Illinois. The General Allotment Act of 1887 resulted in the loss of about two-thirds of the tribe's reservation by 1913.

Beginning in 1903, Charles City also benefited when Charles W. Hart and Charles H. Parr developed a two-cylinder gasoline engine and set up a manufacturing plant there to build farm tractors. Soon their tractor, the Hart and Parr, became a household name. In 1929, when the country sank into the Great Depression, they were absorbed by the Oliver Tractor Corporation, then in 1960 were purchased by the White Motor Corporation, next by ARCO, and by the early 1990s, the plant was closed, resulting in two thousand workers losing their jobs. While driving near the downtown area of Charles City, I saw a large, empty, 23-acre lot that was a decaying slab of concrete. The town, which once had a population of more than 10,000, was now fewer than 7,500.

I took a short hike in the local cemetery and noticed the graves of Charles W. Hart and Charles H. Parr, who had remained friends until they died and now were buried within feet of each other.

After almost endless fields of corn and soybeans, near West Union the geography gradually changed to pine-forested hills, cliffs, and rivers. Though I loved the plains, eventually they wore on me, so I welcomed the change in scenery.

I had decided to visit the *Field of Dreams* movie site, north of Dyersville, because I wanted to see the actual field where the movie had been filmed. However, I didn't know what to expect. Had the field been commercialized? Would a large crowd be there? Were others similarly excited?

At the location, I saw a drive-up ticket window. I asked the woman working there about the price of admission, and she said it was free.

"Free?" I asked. "But you have a ticket window, so there must be a cost."

The woman said, "Free, but donations are accepted."

I asked what the suggested donation was, and she said, "It's up to you."

I asked what people normally paid. Same answer: "It's up to you." I said, "You must have some idea of the amount people pay." She replied, "It's free. Donations are up to you." "But I want to pay," I said. "I came a long way to get here, and I don't want to be a pest, but how much would you personally suggest?" Once again, she said, "It's free. Pay what you want, or don't pay at all. It's fully up to you." That made me feel guilty. I then asked in another way: "What did the person in the car before me pay?"

"Ten dollars."

So I paid ten dollars, and she said, "Have a nice time."

A small walking bridge took visitors to the field. It reminded me of a major league ballfield with the well-manicured, green, grassy field. The difference was its intimacy. It resembled a neighborhood ballfield with a small set of wooden bleachers and a chain-link backstop. Balls, bats, and gloves lay scattered about, tempting anyone who wanted to play some pickup ball, throw a pitch, or run the bases to do so. It was as if everyone there had become a child again. It was just plain fun.

Looking past the outfield, I saw a fully grown cornfield with corn stalks so high you could get lost back there. I walked into the cornfield with its tall, tasseling corn, but about six feet in, a sign said, "If you pass this point, you are fined $100." Before I walked out of the cornrows, though, I grabbed an old ear of corn that had fallen to the ground and stuffed it into my pocket.

While at the field, I met several people. A man and his son from Washington State: one from Yakima, the other from Bellingham. They were on a road trip across the country, stopping at historic baseball sites. A few days earlier, they had visited the Hall of Fame in Cooperstown, New York. The father, who taught school, proudly said they planned to go to a Seattle Mariners game the minute they got back home.

There was a couple from North Carolina who were originally from Iowa. They had been married not far from the field and had come back for a nostalgic visit. A family from Illinois was there on a day trip. The father wanted to show the kids the field, and the mother, who initially looked disinterested, grew excited when she saw the joy on the children's faces.

It reminded me of the time my father took me to a Detroit Tigers game at Briggs Stadium just before it was renamed Tiger Stadium. I still remember walking up the ramp into the grandstand and seeing the bright-green field, hearing the roar of the crowd, smelling the hotdogs, and hearing vendors yell, "Peanuts! Popcorn! Cracker Jacks!" I watched as the vendors threw perfect pitches of those snacks to fans in the stands.

One thing I remembered the most about my family's yearly trips to see the Detroit Tigers was that my dad had absolutely no interest in sports. He did it for his kids. Thinking about it now, years after he'd passed, I realized I had the best dad a child could have.

That night I stayed in a small, yet pleasant motel in the town of Guttenberg, which was a short walk away from Lock and Dam number 10 on the Mississippi

River. There, I watched a boat named *Lexington* out of the Port of Paducah, Kentucky, on the Ohio River as it headed upriver, all the while wondering how in the hell had that ship made it all the way up to here?

9

The next morning I decided to backtrack a bit and head northwest seventy miles or so to the small town of Spillville, which had the distinction of being the host, for the summer of 1893, of the Czech composer Antonín Dvořák. Ever since I was in music school, I had wanted to see where the composer of one of my favorite symphonies, *From the New World Symphony,* had summered. At the time, Dvořák was under contract as the director the New York City–based National Conservatory of Music of America, a post he held from 1892 to 1895. The conservatory was founded in 1885 by a Gilded Age socialite named Jeannette Meyers Thurber, who wanted to make a name for herself by hosting the great composers of the time. To get Dvořák to agree to come to New York, she had to make some contractual guarantees—one being that Dvořák would get the summers off. Although he wanted to head back to Bohemia because he felt homesick for his native country, his assistant, who was of Czech descent, recommended that Dvořák instead go to the assistant's hometown in Iowa, which had many Czech immigrants. That was how Dvořák found out about Spillville.

When I arrived in Spillville, I stopped by the Bily Clocks Museum, which had a display dedicated to Antonín Dvořák. During his time in Spillville, Dvořák was in the most productive period of his career. He felt so much at home in Spillville that while living there, he composed his Quartet No. 12 in F Major (*The American*) and his String Quintet No. 3 in E Flat Major. He also enjoyed walking along the Turkey River and playing the organ during mass at St. Wenceslaus Church.

Once inside the Bily Clocks Museum, I asked the person working that day for an interview, saying it would only take a few minutes. Instead, I was told to come back another day because, though there was only one visitor, the museum employee was way too busy to sit down and talk. I asked when it would be convenient and was told, "Next week." "I'm just passing through," I said, "and I'm unable to stay in the area that long." After visiting so many museums during my travels and knowing that museum personnel were often busy, I asked if I could speak with someone on the museum board because people who served in that capacity were often retired. However, I was told, "The town owns the museum." So, I asked where the town hall was located. "Two blocks away, can't miss it."

I headed to the town hall, which was part of the city garage, and met the mayor, Tom Stroube, who happened to be driving into the parking lot in his pickup when I arrived. He had a few minutes so we sat down to talk.

Tom told me that beyond his mayoral duties, he also owned a lawn-care business. I asked what made him run for mayor.

"I'd been on the city council for around ten years," he said. "When our previous mayor ran for state senate and won, he had to resign, so he handed off the job to our mayor pro tem, who served for a year in order to finish the previous mayor's term. But she wanted nothing to do with staying on as mayor, so I decided to run and was elected. That was a year and a half ago."

In the City of Spillville, a very small town, two local farmers, the brothers Frank and Joseph Bily, began making ornate, hand-built clocks in 1913. Without any self-promotion, these craftsmen received national attention. Clockmaking was purely a spare-time activity they did after finishing their daily farm chores. The clocks were crafted with elaborate wooden façades intertwined with finely detailed statuettes, which became even more complex as their skills developed further. The brothers had no interest in selling their clocks. During a span of thirty years, they built more than twenty clocks and eventually donated them to Spillville, with the understanding that they would not be sold or even moved.

I said that it sounded like an odd request. Tom agreed, especially because the museum was becoming a drain on the community, which itself was shrinking.

I wanted to know a little more about Tom, so I asked whether he'd been born in Spillville or had moved there.

"I moved here in 1979, I believe, or was it 1980? At any rate, one of those years. My dad and my stepmom still live here in town. My parents were divorced when I was eight, and my mom lives in Longmont, Colorado. I've got one older sister, three younger brothers, and a younger sister. My one brother and my sister live out in Longmont, and my other brother lives down by Durant. The other two—one lives in Calmar, the other one lives here in town. I have two boys: one is eighteen, the other fifteen. I was a golf course superintendent for eighteen years at the golf course out here. I got sick of members who thought they knew better than me, telling me how to take care of the lawn while they were just walking through, playing. That's when I decided to start my own lawn-care business, Turkey River Lawn Care."

As mayor of Spillville, Tom was responsible for helping to oversee the management of the Bily Clocks Museum. Like other mayors before him, he'd hoped tourist dollars would keep the museum afloat. Yet, over the years, fewer people had visited the museum. Tom said, "We pulled records from the 1940s and '50s, and there were like forty or fifty thousand people going through the museum every year. Now we struggle to get ten thousand."

That surprised me. I had heard about the museum years ago and had wanted to visit it if I ever was nearby—less because of the clocks and more for the Antonín Dvořák exhibit. After all, he had lived in the upstairs of what became the museum during the summer of 1893. I asked about Dvorak and about Spillville itself as being a welcoming town.

"Dvorak wanted to be somewhere that reminded him of home," Tom said. "We are a quaint little Czech village. When Dvorak was here, everyone was Czech, so there wasn't a language barrier like there was in New York. There are still quite a few Czech people, though not many can still speak the language. You know, a couple sentences here or there. The locals who have lived here forever, they would probably give you the shirt off their back if you needed it. That's just how it is around here."

"How have things changed since then?"

"Back then, there were small family farms but not many now—which is sad. My opinion, the big operations are pushing the little guys out. Big corn, big dairy. If you're not milking a hundred cows, you can't even make it anymore. Used to be there were probably twenty family dairies within fifteen miles from here; now there are probably five, if that."

I asked where the kids in town went to school.

Tom said, "They either go to South Winneshiek Community School six miles away in Calmar or the Catholic school, which has buildings here in town and in Ossian, but they have been merged. Schools around here were getting so small, they couldn't stay open. They used to have two other schools. After graduation, the kids go off to college. There aren't a lot of kids who stick around because there is no industry to speak of, and they're not going to come back to work on the family farm because they're not there anymore. You don't see many kids who come back after they find jobs somewhere else. It's sad. I wish there were more businesses with real jobs."

"What are the opportunities for growth here in Spillville?" I asked.

"Not a lot. There were opportunities for businesses to move in around here, like in Decorah, a nearby town. A big box retailer wanted to build there. Instead, they decided to build over the bridge in Wisconsin because the Decorah city council turned them down. Another big box store was going to build there two years ago, and the city council also shut that project down. I've been told that it will kill the small businesses in town by letting big corporations come in. If someone's going to buy from the lumberyard in Decorah, they're going to buy it there, and those who go to big box stores will go to those places, no matter what their city council says—whether it's two miles or fifty miles away. The thing is, they turned down two businesses that would have increased the tax revenue for the city and county. The only reason they shot it down was because they didn't want it. Plain and simple. The idea that it was going to kill the small businesses didn't make sense. That's hundreds of jobs that this area could have used. Plus, jobs that often go to older workers, workers who can no longer do physical work. Heck, I shingled my dad's roof last year, and that was difficult. I'm not a young man anymore."

Tom said Spillville had no unused property and didn't have space to expand. Year by year, the population shrank as families grew smaller, and their kids, who were looking for well-paying jobs, left mainly for work in the cities. With fewer kids, the schools had to consolidate with other districts. "Heck, we don't even have a gas station here anymore. And to get groceries, we need to drive a good ten miles."

I asked Tom about the kids in town and what happened after they finished school and left town.

"You don't see many kids who come back after they find jobs somewhere else."

I asked Tom whether he still enjoyed living in Spillville.

"Oh, yeah. I worked on the road for a while when I was young and found I don't like big cities and all the noise or all the people. It's good not hearing sirens and the rush of traffic. Rural Iowa is way better than living in downtown Chicago. I ran into a couple of people who had moved to the area from a large city, and they

Tom Stroube, Mayor, Spillville, Iowa

couldn't sleep because it was too quiet. They were upset because they couldn't hear any cars and instead heard crickets chirping. I said, 'Yeah, that's what happens.'"

After my time with Tom, I went back to the museum. But when I returned, the person at the museum was speaking with someone else. As I waited, I struck up a conversation with a man carrying leaflets who was from the nearby town of St Lucas and was promoting the museum there. He asked, "Have you been to St. Wenceslaus yet?" I said I hadn't.

"It's just up the road," he said. "In fact, there are two Catholic churches in Spillville, the German one and the Czech one."

"Isn't this a Czech town?" I asked.

"It's actually both."

I had assumed a small town like Spillville would have only one Catholic church. Clair Blong, the man with the leaflets, said there were two. We got into a conversation. I learned that Clair had been born in a nearby town, had moved away for college, followed by a government career, and then moved back to the family farm after he retired. I immediately liked Clair because of his thirst for knowledge and his warm, outgoing personality. I suggested we take a walk outside and sit at the picnic table so we could have a private conversation.

Clair told me he'd spent four years at Loras College in Dubuque, then two years in Milwaukee, working on a master's in political science. "That was kinda my big city experience." But then he moved to Washington, D.C.

"Talk about big city experience," I said. "If D.C. isn't big, I don't know what is."

"Yeah, forty-two years with the federal government. But mostly on location for the Department of Defense and later with FEMA. D.C. was fine because I could get out of town for my job."

Clair said he'd been in a unique situation with the Department of Defense, working for twelve years in Colorado Springs as the FEMA person involved in Disaster and National Security Emergency Planning. "People think that the military does all of this, but so much is FEMA." As an example, Clair said they would tackle "what if's," such as what would happen if a water system didn't work during an emergency or what to do in case of a nuclear attack. "A lot of planning goes on behind the scenes that the public doesn't know about."

Clair later worked at the National Defense University. "That was a fun experience. They do not study textbooks; they are all senior people in the government. People who are about to be promoted to general or admiral. We didn't just talk about countries like China or Russia. We would get on a plane, go to that country, and speak with their senior leadership."

Ten years ago when Clair retired, he moved back to the family farm. There, he learned farming had changed. The land had been rented to a big operator, someone who had modern equipment in order to increase production. "To

Clair Blong, inside St. Clement's Catholic Church, south of Spillville, Iowa

succeed at farming today, you need two hundred thousand dollar sprayers and half-million dollar combines. Things that a 160-acre farm can never afford. So, the whole idea of the small family farm is fiction." Clair said the only time a farmer needed help was during spring planting and for fall harvest. Temporary jobs that lasted a week or two at the most.

"So, you get to enjoy the farm without having to work it," I said.

"Exactly. Our farm is in a mixed area of fields and forest. The wooded area abuts against a state wildlife area, so we get to see more wildlife than when I left in the early '60s. Back then, they hunted and shot everything. Now we are focused on the environment and outdoor sports like fishing. You might say it's all cornstalks, but wildlife has become a big income generator." Clair was now seeing tourists in the area, which was why he became involved in the museum in St. Lucas near his farm.

I said I'd heard that people were now into experiences more than just owning things.

"Yeah, I agree. Used to be the only thing that attracted people were church dinners. Now we host events at the museum."

We shifted our conversation to the Germans and the Czechs and why they were initially attracted to Iowa. Clair said, "They moved to areas that were similar to where they came from."

I asked whether the Germans and the Czechs got along with one another.

"Not initially. That's why there was St. Clements south of Spillville, where the Germans worshipped, and St. Wenceslaus in the center of town, where the Czechs worshipped. Because the Germans didn't want to worship with the Bohemians." Both churches were built in the late 1850s and early 1860s because the Germans and the Czechs arrived around the same time. But by the 1940s, the German church had closed, and everyone worshipped together at the larger, more ornate Wenceslaus Catholic Church.

Clair told me what it was like growing up in an agricultural area. "I decided early in life that I wouldn't make a good farmer. The manual labor didn't appeal to me. Watching other farmers looked torturous." He said seeing farmers working day and night wasn't for him. But now, after coming back fifty-some years later, he disagreed with the famous author Thomas Wolfe who said you can never go home again.

10

After I left Spillville, my next stop was Effigy Mounds National Monument, which was fifty miles away. A patchwork quilt of farms, dairy, and crops led to its perch atop the Mississippi River between Harpers Ferry and Marquette, Iowa. Clair Blong had told me the easternmost portion of Iowa got a good amount of rain, making irrigation optional when raising corn or soybeans, the primary crops of Iowa farmers. It got me to thinking, even daydreaming, about the many square miles of crops that a lot of city folk see only as perfect squares when flying from coast to coast. Just as I was about to reach my destination, the hills turned hillier, the steep inclines steeper, and trees more plentiful. And, all of a sudden, there it was: Effigy Mounds National Monument.

In my part of the country—Ottawa County, Michigan—there once were ancient mounds, but almost all of them were plowed under when farmers turned their land into farms. I remember once after a night in a downtown Grand Haven bar, the local theater manager asked whether I would like to see an ancient Indian mound in the theater basement. It was probably around midnight, the theater was closed, and it was spooky dark inside.

As I recall, he opened a door behind the refreshment counter, and we climbed down a set of creaky stairs. A single lightbulb hanging by an electrical cord lit up the space below the theater. There was no floor; it was all sand. It was cold and got colder the farther into the open foundation we walked. The theater atop the foundation had a sloping floor so patrons' seats did not have a restricted view. However, the opposite was true in the space below the theater: the sloping floor above made the headroom shrink the farther we walked. The mounds were located in the underground space below the theater stage. Then, with the light dimming the closer we got to the mounds, I saw an unmistakable image that certainly looked like the mounds built by Woodland people many centuries earlier.

Now, these many years later, I still wonder whether those were burial mounds or if the theater manager was mistaken. But it did make a permanent impression that I carry in my memory. Unfortunately, the entire theater sans the marquee was torn down to make room for a condo project. But still, there was a question in my mind: What's underneath?

At Effigy Mounds, I parked in the lot at the visitor center. The signs pointed toward the paths to the mounds, only a short hike away.

At one time, countless thousands of Native American burial mounds were in Iowa. The number decreased when white settlers migrated to the state after the passage of the Homestead Act of 1862. During that time, America was an agrarian society, and most settlers, with 160 acres provided by the act, needed to make use of as much property as they could. As a result, many burial mounds were plowed under to make room for crops. A recent University of Iowa census of ancient burial mounds estimated the current number stood at roughly 1,500 statewide.

That was part of what made the Effigy Mounds National Monument special; it had two hundred Native American burial mounds within the borders of a single park. The Group Loop was a nearly two-mile trail that began and ended near the visitors' center. The trail passed through Little Bear Mound Group, several mounds grouped together depicting various animals and shapes. Built during the Late Woodland Period from 1,000 BC until approximately 900 AD, it was a prosperous time for Native Americans. Along the Upper Mississippi River, their land extended east to Lake Michigan. The land was associated with Effigy Moundbuilders, a regional cultural phenomenon. The earliest mounds were in the shapes of bears, buffalo, birds, and turtles, among other animals. In the later part of the period, the shapes were more practical, such as conical, linear, and rectangular. It has remained a mystery why the shapes changed so drastically.

I met a couple from Minnesota who were taking the same hike. We talked. She was creeped out; he was intrigued. She said, "Let's turn back," and he said, "Go ahead." All three us of kept trudging along, and soon I was back at my car. They asked where I was heading next. I said I was going to take the St. Feriole Island Bridge to Prairie du Chien, Wisconsin. They were driving south, possibly to Cedar Rapids, Iowa.

Once in Wisconsin, I decided to follow the Upper Mississippi River north. It was an area of the river where, before the 1930s, water levels were unpredictable, and the river was vulnerable to spring flooding and late summer drought. Then dams and locks were built in order to maintain a consistent nine-foot navigation depth.

Having just passed through rural Iowa, with its easy-going way of life, I was unprepared to face the traffic along such an iconic road with its herds of Harleys and solitary RVs hugging the center line. A road where everyone seemed to be in a hurry to get to god-knows-where, in order to weekend in the glow of a fire pit with hot dogs on a stick. At least, that was where I surmised they were headed. I wanted to roll down my window and yell, "What in the hell is so important that you need to drive so aggressively before relaxing in a tent?" I took turnouts to escape, only to find it was darn near impossible to get back on the road. At one point, I tried pulling into a fast food parking lot, only to be met with a group of bikers intent on intimidating me. I said to a guy pulling a trailer, "I bet you don't get more than ten miles on a gallon," as I thought, *My car gets nearly sixty*.

I had anticipated a nice, slow, steady drive up the Mississippi but instead found such a rush of traffic that it was an unpleasant ride. Finally, when I got to LaCrosse, I'd had enough. I veered onto a series of backroads, eventually ending up three hours later in a motel with a bed and a bath somewhere near Baldwin, Wisconsin.

11

Baldwin, a village in St. Croix County, Wisconsin, with a population of just over four thousand, was on the eastern edge of the Minneapolis–Saint Paul metropolitan area.

Known as the "Biggest Little Town in Wisconsin," it had recently become the retirement home of Jim and Nancy Benson, whom I'd originally met in Bemidji, Minnesota.

The thing that impressed me the most about Jim and Nancy Benson's relationship was that for the entirety of their marriage of sixty years, Jim had written a poem to Nancy each morning.

I asked Jim how he'd met his wife.

"I met Nancy, my lifelong sweetheart, while we were students at Erskine High School. After graduation, we both attended and graduated from Bemidji State University. We got married during my senior year in college."

I asked how they got by, once they were married.

"Nancy got a job teaching in the Bemidji school system, and I took a teaching job back home in Erskine. After three years, I resigned to go to grad school at the University of Wisconsin-Stout in Menomonie. That's where I earned my master's degree, while Nancy supported our growing family by taking a teaching job."

Jim told me that he earned his doctorate at Penn State, which was when he returned to Stout to begin his career in the university's technology department. Later, he became the dean of Stout's School of Industry. He then went on to be president of Dunwoody Institute in Minneapolis, before ending his career in the education field as president of Bemidji State University.

As for Nancy, after raising their five children, she returned to college where she earned a master's degree. She was hired by Chippewa Valley Technical College to start a learning center that became the first in the nation to run on the medical model of diagnosing, prescribing, treating, and assessing the results for each person they served who required job training.

I asked Jim how his family ended up in Erskine in the first place.

He said, "When my grandfather first arrived to homestead, he got 160 acres of solid white oak timber and had to clear the land with axes, saws, horses, and fire—the tools of the day. It was grueling work."

He told me his grandfather's neighbor also had 160 acres. When the neighbor quit farming, Jim's grandfather bought him out. And as other homesteaders left farming, his grandfather bought them out as well. In his heyday, Jim's grandfather was farming six hundred acres with horses.

"But think of clearing the land, six hundred acres of forest land, then farming it with horses," said Jim. "He had a dozen kids, three or four hired men, a gigantic barn, and hay that went all the way to the ceiling. On one side was the cow barn; on the other side was the horse barn. He was the very first person in northern Minnesota to have a two-story grainery." Jim said that when they were little, they had a one-cylinder engine tractor that went "Puff puff."

"I still own a little chunk of the farm," he said. "I have 101 acres. I rent it to a guy who has a field six miles to the south. His farm address is Holly, close to Morehead, which is over sixty miles away. So, I asked him one day, 'How many acres are you farming?' 'I'm not that big,' he said. 'But I am farming 27,000 acres.' It's very rich farmland, butting up against the Red River Valley. That's where my grandfather Bensen started. Now there's nobody farming unless they've got two or three of these monster, million-dollar combines."

"If the demographics hold to where they're going," I said, "there will be fewer farmers living out here and, with that, a smaller population to support area businesses." I noted that very few people these days wanted to farm or live where farmers lived, but that they, like Jim, didn't mind inheriting farmland and letting someone else farm it.

As for Jim's growing-up years, he said, "I grew up on the family farm. Dad worked the farm until he got hit with a rheumatic heart condition. By the time I was in high school, my father was no longer able to farm. So, through junior and senior high school, my brother, who is a year younger, and I basically ran the farm. We milked the cows by hand and played high school sports. But after I went off to the university, we sold all the cows and rented the farm."

I asked Jim what he did after retiring from Bemidji State University.

"During my retirement years was when I had the most fun," he said. "I worked with various community groups in Bemidji and helped start a program called Leads 1.0, which involved planning from the future back to the present, rather than the other way around—planning from today to the future."

He told me that by planning from the future back to the present, all the hopes and the dreams were flushed out, and nothing was impossible. It was much better than the other way around, where barriers got in the way of achieving future big ideas.

During that time, Jim and Nancy lived in a lake cabin near Bemidji.

I asked Jim why they moved from Bemidji to Baldwin.

"Our kids told us that when we turned eighty, we had to move so we could be closer to where they lived. But we were having so much fun in Bemidji, we

Jim Bensen, retired president of Bemidji State University in from of his home in Baldwin, Wisconsin

delayed the move until we were eighty-six years old. We have a son in Menomonee. When I left Stout, he came in as a professor, and he's now retired. We have a kid on the West Coast who's retired. Number-two son is a principal in Amery, twenty-five miles north of here. He's still working, but his wife is retiring this year. My son who lives next door has spent twenty-five years with Walmart in logistics at the distribution center in Menomonee. He recently left them and is now the head of the Coca-Cola distribution center out of River Falls. So, they live here, and all the grandkids are gone, and they have a daughter in North St. Paul. So, four of our five kids are here, and that's why we decided it was time to move—not pull the plug on Bemidji because we can still visit there as often as we can."

Just then Nancy arrived home, and sitting in the usual place was that day's poem. I thought, *I wish I could be as romantic as Jim.* I left with a joyful tear in my eye.

From Baldwin, I continued north to the intersection with US-8, where I headed east. The number of farms decreased as the forested areas grew more plentiful.

Weyerhaeuser, named after lumber baron Friedrich Weyerhäuser, was about where the thick forests began. Born in the then independent Grand Duchy of Hesse in 1834, Weyerhäuser emigrated to Pennsylvania in 1852. The sale of their small family farm in Germany allowed Weyerhäuser to travel farther west where he first made his mark in Rock Island, Illinois, working construction on the Rock Island and Peoria Railroad. Next, he got a job at a sawmill and worked his way up from night foreman to yard manager to salesman. All the while, he saved every bit of money he could to purchase the assets of the sawmill when its financials tanked. From that point on, Weyerhäuser leveraged his money, and by the time he died in 1914, the headline in the *New York Times* said,

> F. WEYERHAEUSER, LUMBER KING, DEAD, Left $30,000,000 Earned in Career That Began in Poverty in an Illinois Lumber Yard. Made His Fortune in the Great Pine Forests of Wisconsin—Work His Only Amusement.

As I drove toward Escanaba, Michigan, I passed through portions of the 1.5-million-acre Chequamegon-Nicolet National Forest. Rhinelander, with a population of 8,200, was the largest town before I crossed the border into Michigan.

Rhinelander had always been at a crossroads: the confluence of the Pelican and Wisconsin rivers during the lumbering era had helped move logs downstream; two rail lines—the Chicago & Northwestern and the Minneapolis, St. Paul, and Sault Ste. Marie Railways—converged there; and US-2 crossed WI-37 to bring tourists dollars to the area.

The town was originally called Pelican Rapids, but the citizens renamed the town Rhinelander after Frederick W. Rhinelander, top executive of the Milwaukee, Lake Shore, and Western Railroad. Ever since the lumber boom ended, Rhinelander had transitioned to outdoor recreation because of its 232 freshwater lakes.

In Rhinelander, I stopped at a coffeehouse with outdoor seating where I met a reporter writing a story about rural America. We chatted for a couple of hours about the what if's, what for's, and what now's.

Back on the road, I passed through a heavily forested region and the mining towns of Norway and Vulcan, where the remains of the iron ore Vulcan Mine on the Menominee Range were turned into a museum. It closed in 1945. The Menominee Range had mostly deep shaft mines with only a few that were open pit. Once the open pit mines were closed, the pumps were turned off, and the pits turned into lakes. The Cyclops Mine north of Norway had since become Strawberry Lake and was now a popular public park.

12

From Hermansville to Escanaba, I passed several small, lumber-era towns where land was converted from forests to agricultural use. In 1914, Congress passed the Smith-Lever Act to educate rural Americans about advances in agricultural practices and technology. Through those skillsets, Americans' agricultural productivity dramatically increased.

Bill Cook was the former Upper Peninsula Extension Forester & Wildlife Biologist for Michigan State University's Extension Services. A mouthful.

I stopped by Bill's house west of Escanaba, and we talked about what led him get into forestry in the first place.

"For a forester in the U.P.," I said, "you must have grown up near forests."

"Nope, born in Champlain, Illinois. I don't often admit that to people because I'm not fond of flatlanders, even though I have a whole nest of cousins in Chicago." Bill went on to say, "My grandparents lived in Des Plaines back then. It was actually open fields before the interstate system was built, so when we went from Madison to Des Plaines on old US-12, I still remember the bridges and the two lanes. Those bridges aren't there anymore, with some replaced by modern ones, and many of the simple roads were replaced with four lanes.

"We lived in a little trailer park south of the campus where my dad was going to school. Rainbow Court. I remember stories about the trailer. My cradle was in a drawer in a small cabinet. There wasn't enough room for anything else. My sister had a drawer, and my brother had a drawer, but it apparently didn't hurt us any. There's an old picture when I was just a toddler of a tree that my dad had planted. That was my dad's propensity, to plant trees wherever he lived. Even though he knew he wouldn't be there forever, he planted one anyway."

Then Bill leaned back in his chair, gave a sigh, and told me about other memories of Champlain, this one recent. "We had a tragic loss of a cousin of mine. Remember that dust storm in Illinois that killed seven people a spring ago? Two of them were my cousin and his wife. So, we went down for the funeral near Champlain, and while there, I located Rainbow Court. My mom always said we lived at 14 Rainbow Court. It's still a trailer court, and I'm pretty sure I found that tree because it's one big-ass oak now. That would make the tree sixty years old. We wandered around it, took some pictures. Back sixty-five years ago, it was all open prairie farmland—no trees, of course. Now Champlain has lots of trees."

I asked Bill whether he'd lived there very long, noting that his dad had been in school while raising a family there.

"We moved to Madison, Wisconsin, and my dad got a job as an architect, a small private firm that has since turned into a large, well-known, established firm in southern Wisconsin. He only stayed with that company for a few years, and then he took a job with the state because it was steadier work and had benefits. But we grew up in Madison back in the '60s, which might explain some things about me that you possibly have observed. The '60s were interesting years to grow up in places like Berkley, Madison, and Ann Arbor. I saw things as a teenage boy that nobody should ever see, maybe ever. But certainly not at that age. The block parties and the counterculture, flower power, and the Vietnam War—that whole era. Madison literally was an explosive atmosphere. Mom and Dad tried to keep us out of downtown, but whenever we went to the movies, we actually saw Mifflin Street block parties."

Bill then talked about other parts of his youth. He hung out with "misfits," as he called them, though he was in the Boy Scouts and became an eagle scout. His grades were so good that he could have graduated a year earlier as a junior, but he stayed for a portion of his senior year. And one of his classmates loaned him a book about hiking the Pacific Crest Trail. Bill found it so interesting that he hopped on a Greyhound bus from Madison to San Diego. At the time, he was seventeen and hiked the trail in before hitchhiking back to Madison. "We were free-range boys," he added.

As Bill spoke I thought, *I was also raised in a family of free-range boys, so I can relate to how Bill grew up.* I was only fourteen when my parents put me on a train headed for a camping adventure in New Mexico. It was no wonder I wanted to know what came next.

"At the time, I was still intent on becoming a medical doctor," Bill said. "A general practitioner in a small town somewhere, and I had this romantic notion of taking half a beef and a chicken for payment."

"You mean like Dr. Welby," I said.

"Exactly, so I went in for a physical and told the doctor I wanted to be a GP. He asked, 'What do you like to do?' because he knew I had just gotten off the trail. I told him I liked to hike and camp. He said, 'Then you don't want to be a doctor. You're going to spend the first twelve years working your butt off inside. You won't even see the outside, except on the commute, and that will be mostly at night. Then you're on call all the time, so you can't take trips.' I thought, *He's right, I don't want to do that.* He told me to do what I want to do. I said, 'What I like to do, I can't get paid for.' From Boy Scouts, I did know about forestry, wildlife management, and water resources. In high school, we had dirt science [earth science], but the teacher wasn't the most engaging instructor on the planet. Still, I was fascinated with the topic. Plate tectonics and different rocks could lead to a career in forestry. Plus, my dad, who was a project manager for the state of Wisconsin at the time, was working on University of Wisconsin campus projects and putting the finishing touches on a new building for the College of Natural Resources in Stevens Point. He said, 'I'm going to talk to the dean today about some last-minute things with the building project.' He asked me to come along. And that's when I met this fabulous character by the name of Dean Trainer, a tall, personable man with a straight shock of white hair who loved students. He actually took the time to talk to me. So, I decided I wanted to go to Stevens Point, and I loved the undergraduate work there. I came out with four majors: forestry, wildlife management, natural resources, and biology as part of my bachelor's degree. Plus, I spent two semesters abroad and did a summer camp in the Black Forest of Germany, which was great fun. I treated myself at the end of all that with a trip to Malaysia—which was where I met Betsy. In Singapore. We got married, and forty years later, we are still together."

"How did you get to Michigan State?" I asked. Circuitously, as I was about to find out.

"I had a series of jobs as a forester back in the late seventies and early eighties when forestry jobs were few and far between. Unlike today, now it's a graduate's choice to go almost anywhere they'd like to work. Back then, you took whatever you could get. So, I took a series of jobs and decided to go back to school."

At that point, Bill enrolled in the College of Environmental Science and Forestry at the SUNY-Syracuse campus, where he earned a degree in International Forestry in Third World Development.

"I did my graduate work on the big island of Hawaii, where I worked at bio energy plantations. They needed someone out there because they had five or six plantations that had formerly grown sugarcane. When Reagan pulled the subsidy from the sugar industry, the business collapsed, but the company had all this land, and they didn't know what to do with it. One idea they had was to use the leftover sugarcane for energy production—using wood chips instead of biogas. I was part of that research project. Actually, I was disappointed with that assignment because I had my heart set on a project in Samoa, but that fell through. At any rate, it all turned out quite marvelously, and I walked out of there with my sheepskin. But when I came back to Wisconsin, the only job I could find was in a Smucker's jelly and jam factory in Rippen. At the time, we were living with my brother, his wife, and their kids. Then I got a job on the Menominee Indian Reservation. Worked there eighteen months or so, then got a real job up in Bemidji, Minnesota, working for the Bureau of Indian Affairs on the Red Lake Nation. We moved to Bemidji in the middle of January when Betsy was seven months' pregnant. When we rolled into our driveway in our U-Haul, it was 25 below zero as we dragged stuff into the house. We lived there for over seven years."

Then Bill saw a job posting for a position with Michigan State University Extension Services. At that time, he had worked in the forestry field for ten years. Yet, all along his goal was to make an impact in forestry, and there was no better way than through education. Besides, he had always wanted to live in the U.P., and working out of the MSU research center in Escanaba seemed to be a good fit.

"I spent twenty-three years working with all sorts of people. I was given a laptop, a slide projector, and an overhead projector, and my supervisor said, 'I have no idea what forestry does or what you are supposed to do. You let me know in about a month or so what you think you want to do, and that's how I'm going to evaluate you.'"

Bill spent the next few months driving across the Upper Peninsula, stopping by all the extension offices, visiting the local newspapers, and introducing himself to farmers, foresters, and lumber producers. Then he asked people what they needed. He next put together a plan that involved speaking at conferences, meeting individually with people involved in forestry, and creating educational handouts and a support system that still existed twenty-three years later.

"Even though I've been retired for three years, I still do the fun parts of the job. I have a magazine I still write for, I answer emails with questions from private forest owners, and I meet with some of the consultants because I still have a lot of connections."

"What is the health of the forest like now?" I asked.

"We are in very good shape in the U.P. People often don't understand what a healthy forest is and want to leave it alone, which is a myth. Our forests are all second-growth forests. They were highly affected by the logging era. Now there are new pressures from climate change, from invasive species and many other

Bill Cook, forester, near Escanaba, Michigan

things. If we don't manage our forest resources, they are going to degrade. That's a fact of life. You might not like it, but it's true. You can't manage the forests unless you cut trees. You can't cut trees unless you have a place to sell the trees. Forests are ecological systems that depend on what ecologists call *catastrophic disturbances,* which is a fancy term for wildfires, windstorms, and insect disease. Aspen, Jack pine, red pine, paper birch all have adapted to having the crap beat out of them by nature and having to start all over from scratch. Here in the Ottawa National Forest especially, it's largely northern hardwood, which is a different animal all together. Its life strategy is to put a lot of energy into defense. An aspen tree's whole strategy is to grow as fast as it can and die a violent death. Sugar maple, on the other hand, is very conservative. It puts a lot of energy into defense, it grows slower and more cautiously, and its photo period windows are much tighter than that of aspen. Many people don't know that most trees do all their metabolic functions based on their photo period. It doesn't have much at all to do with weather. So, when the fall color change comes, it's all timed to a tree's photo period. But different species have different photoperiodic gaps. Sugar maple is pretty narrow every year; it's within a two-week period. Aspen is a little more opportunistic."

I asked about a hike in the Ottawa Forest I had taken with Bill on a different occasion when he said there was a battle going on. He had predicted which species would win, based on the undergrowth. The soil was largely sandy and would support the pine species better than the northern hardwood maples in that section of the forest.

Then Betsy interrupted to ask whether we wanted our grilled cheese sandwiches with or without ham. I said without, and Bill said with.

As I drove through Escanaba, I was reminded of the first time I'd heard the name of the city in grade school. We had a new principal whose son I got to know. One day I asked where he was from. At the time, my entire world consisted of the town just to our north, the one to our south, and the one where my cousins on my father's side lived, which to me was way far away—Grand Rapids, an hour's drive from our house. So, when the principal's son told me they were from Escanaba, I looked it up on a map and couldn't even begin to imagine how far away it was. And when I found out his former town was a trifle larger than mine, I began to dream about what it must be like. It was on the same lake, Lake Michigan, but it was as far away as it could get on what we called "the Big Lake."

I had my first chance to see Escanaba when traveling west. I had decided to cross the Straits of Mackinac and drive through the Upper Peninsula to get to my destination. That was a good forty years ago when I was a young skier, looking for adventure at ski resorts in high mountain country. Bear in mind, where I lived we had only seasonal ski hills that took more time to climb on a rope tow or a two-seat lift than it did to get down the hill. But in those days, gas was cheap, and avoiding big cities like Chicago while heading west was more desirable than taking interstates, which saved time but had nothing of interest along them.

Even back then, my road of choice was US-2, which, when I first took it, I realized passed through Escanaba. So, I was excited to see the town I'd heard so much about when I was young.

Escanaba was incorporated as a city in 1883 and remained the third-largest town in the Upper Peninsula. Yet, its roots ran much deeper. The remains of Native American villages were found by early white Europeans, including the French explorer Jean Nicolet in 1634. The first permanent white resident was the fur trader L. A. Roberts, who settled on the banks of the Escanaba River, a name derived from the Ojibwa words that sounded like Escanaba—meaning "land of the red buck and flat rock." The town's initial growth was driven by lumbering, commercial fishing, and freighters shipping iron ore to steel mills in Gary, Indiana, and Chicago, Illinois.

One idea that caught on was the name Yooper. It began in a 1979 contest in the *Escanaba Daily Press* that asked contestants to come up with a name for people who lived in the Upper Peninsula. Possibilities included Bastian and Skeeter-eater, but they settled on the name Yooper.

Escanaba was in a region known as the "banana belt," having a milder climate than other parts of the U.P. It offered protection from the cold winds off Lake Superior, had more moderate temperatures because of the relatively warm waters of Green Bay, and tended to receive less lake effect snow from Lake Michigan. All the land along US-2 from Escanaba to the Mackinac Bridge was near or within Hiawatha National Forest and Lake Superior State Forest.

13

Situated among the forests was Manistique, population roughly 2,800—often called the Emerald City because of the deep-green water of nearby Kitch-iti-kipi (the "Big Spring"), the largest natural spring in the state of Michigan.

In Manistique, I stayed at the Colonial Motel, where I met the owner, Michael Phelan, who lived there. I asked Michael how long he'd owned the motel and why he'd purchased it. Michael said he grew up in a Chicago suburb where "I grew tired of the busyness of living there, along with the corporate life of an engineer." For the next few years after leaving that life, Michael lived and worked in Texas and later in Nashville. But because he wanted to be an entrepreneur, he began to look into owning and operating a motel. That led him to the Internet, where he checked out opportunities to own a motel property that he could afford. He came across the Colonial Motel in Manistique, whose owners were retiring. "I wanted to buy a motel in a smaller town somewhere and then stumbled on the Upper Peninsula of Michigan. Someplace I'd never been to before. After talking with the owners, I decided to make the six-hour-and-forty-five-minute drive to see it."

"You counted the exact amount of time to get here," I said. "That's impressive."

"Well, I was an engineer, after all."

After Michael purchased the motel, he started renovating the aging rooms, fixed up the lobby, and even bought a new coffee machine. But what Michael mostly did was market his property and get guests to fill out questionnaires so he could get even more business. I asked how that had worked out.

"I've gotten good reviews online," he said.

I asked Michael what it was like to live in the motel and whether he got any time to himself. As he petted his two dachshunds, one on the belly, the other behind the ear, he said, "I joke that I have a ten-second commute to work. It's the best job in the world for me. . . . I like the mid-century modern feel."

We talked about the difference between Manistique and the large cities where he'd lived previously. "Being a small town of less than three thousand people, we don't have any big-box stores, which can be a challenge. If I need a pair of jeans, I'm either going to drive to Marquette, an hour and a half away, or to Escanaba, nearly an hour away. So, the challenges are that you have to plan things better. I don't get to leave here very much because as a motel operator without a staff, I'm the only one here."

Our conversation then drifted to young people living in a small town and what opportunities they had living in Manistique. "There's not as many opportunities here. Unfortunately for young people who grew up here, unless you're working at the paper mill, you need to move away to better yourself. Most of the regular jobs here are things like working in fast food, on the counter at a convenience store, or in grocery at the food market. But those jobs don't have benefits. They are mostly part time without pensions, 401(k)s, paid vacations, or healthcare."

I asked about his business, whether he had guests year round. "My motel is open April through November, though I do open up for deer-hunting season, but it's not that busy here during that time. The peak tourism season for this part of the U.P. is generally from the third week of June, after the kids are out of school, through the third week of October for the fall colors. Snowmobile season is not important here because we are in the warmer part of the U.P. where there is much less snow. So, our peak season is only four months long or a third of the year."

"What do you do in the off season?" I asked.

"I go south. I have a place down there where it is warm in the winter." He added something to the effect that he was no fool.

And I got it. My route was ten thousand miles of northern weather where winters could be harsh.

The next morning I drove through Blaney Park, twenty miles or so from Manistique. It brought back memories of when I had a place north of there and would ride my bike to Blaney Park, a 45-mile jaunt. When I was growing up, my parents traveled with friends to Blaney Park to stay in a cabin, which had since been torn down to make room for a cannabis shop. For many decades, those cabins had rotted away.

Up the road a bit, I saw what remained of Blaney Park: a water tank with the town name painted on it, a somewhat-abandoned air strip, the ruins of an old inn, and a couple of antique stores. It was once a tourist destination and, before that, a logging village.

East of Blaney, I drove past Gould City, Engadine, Naubinway, Epoufette, and Brevort—towns that started during the lumber boom but with the added bonus of getting income from fishing along Lake Michigan.

On the last leg of the highway, near the Mackinac Bridge, I drove past sandy beaches on the south side and thick forests to the north. The forested land was once logged out and came back only through the efforts of the Civilian Conservation Corp (CCC), a program during the 1930s Great Depression that put men to work planting trees.

As I crested the hill before entering St. Ignace, I could see the view of the Mackinac Bridge. Just past that was the Historic Totem Village. Its owner, Ron Daniels, told me that before the Mackinac Bridge was built, shops and restaurants in the area did better because people crossing the straits needed to wait for the ferry. That gave them plenty of extra time to explore area businesses. I had assumed that businesses in this area benefited from the bridge and the traffic that crossed it, but I was wrong. The term *tourist trap* had certainly been appropriate here because people waiting for the ferry to cross the straits surely were trapped.

Ron said I could investigate his family history and suggested that after I leave his store, I should drive nine miles to the west where a monument still stood. "Just before Brevort Lake Road," he said, "you'll see two cables and a chain running across the road. Stop there and look off into the distance, and you'll see a monument. Walk toward it to see the monument up close. That was the last homestead of Odawa tribal chief Amable Ance, who was my great-grandfather. He died in 1910. It's also where the Totem Village used to be."

Ron said that the Odawa had called northern Michigan home for hundreds of years and established their current presence in Saint Ignace in the late 1600s. They were known for their ability to negotiate with other tribes, along with the French and the British after they arrived. "Trading was a special skill of the Odawa."

It was a perfect place for the Odawa to live because the Straits of Mackinac had always been strategically important. Ron added, "That's why trading in Saint Ignace was so successful." It was also why so many travelers today relied on Ron at the Historic Totem Village because he offered a wide range of arts and crafts by indigenous artists and artisans native to his region and worldwide. As we walked through his store, I could see his dedication in the fine details of the goods he sold. He showed me authentic birch-bark canoes in miniature sizes, pipes made from polished Petoskey stones, dance rattles and medicine bags made from turtle shells, hand-painted dreamcatchers, miniature teepees with a bulb inside to imitate a lit fire, hand-stitched moccasins, wild rice from the waters of the Great Lakes, handmade jewelry, and traditional native drums.

Ron explained that the Anishinaabe, or "original people," consisted of the three fires tribes: the Ojibwe, commonly known as the Chippewa, who were the keepers of the ceremonies and song; the Odawa, or Ottawa, who were the keepers of the trade; and the Potawatomi, or Bodewadmi, who were the keepers of the fire. "Technically, we are all Mackinac up here," Ron said. "The individual names came from people such as Henry Schoolcraft, who was the superintendent of Indian affairs for Michigan from 1836 to 1841. He had studied the tribes and in the process assigned English names to them."

The first white person to visit what became St. Ignace was the French explorer Jean Nicolet, who traveled thorough the straits during his 1634 exploration of lakes Huron and Michigan. There was a monument to Nicolet on Mackinac Island and a street named for him in St. Ignace.

After Nicolet, the next arrival of a white European was Father Jacques Marquette, who in 1671 started a mission named for St. Ignatius of Loyola, the founder of the Jesuit order. Later, the name was shortened to St. Ignace. Ron told me, "If it weren't for the French and their homesteads here in St. Ignace, our tribe would never have settled here." There would not have been any trade.

But the Odawa weren't immune to the policies of the U.S. government. In 1830, during the Andrew Jackson administration, the "Indian Removal Policy" became law. Although the Odawa managed to negotiate a way to stay in place, they still lost much of their identity. The U.S. government set up a boarding school system that intentionally reprogrammed tribal members to fit in with white Americans through religion, language, and social training. This changed in 1994 when President Bill Clinton signed Senate Bill 1357 into law. It reaffirmed the federal status of the Little Traverse Bay Bands of Odawa Indians as a federally recognized tribe.

Ron, who was born in St. Ignace, moved with his family to the Lower Peninsula town of East Lansing, Michigan, in 1964, when he was five. Then, shortly afterward, they relocated to the small town of Perry, followed by a move to nearby Morris. He explained, "My dad was a Michigan State Police trooper, so we moved around a lot." Then, in a complete turn of events, his family purchased a farmhouse just outside of town where, on the first night after they moved in, it burned to the ground. Astonished, I asked Ron what did they do then?

"We moved back to Mount Morris to our former house." But that didn't last long, because a year later, in 1969, Ron's dad quit his job with the state police and took a job as an airport manager in Ashtabula, Ohio. At that time, they lived in Jefferson, Ohio. But they stayed there for only a year before they moved to Clearwater, Florida, where his dad's father lived.

As Ron remembered, "My grandfather on my father's side was originally from St. Ignace but left on an oxcart for Dunedin, Florida, which is now part of Clearwater. While he was living there, he started what became one of the largest dairy farms in the state of Florida. So, the connection between Florida and my dad's father and us up here meant we traveled back and forth to Florida for a while." A year later, their family finally decided to move to Florida.

What happened next changed the trajectory of Ron's life. Six months after the family moved south, his father was killed in an airplane crash. "So, I grew up without a father—four brothers living the American dream," Ron said in a cynical tone. After high school, in 1977, Ron tried college for about a year. "My dad had served in the Korean War, so I got veterans' benefits, one hundred and sixty dollars a month for my college education." But he was able to afford to take only one class on what the government paid, and he learned after the first semester that the government benefits depended on him being a full-time student. He had to drop out of college. To make matters worse, the government wanted his mother to pay the government back for a year's worth of benefits.

I asked what he did after that. "I went to work. Been a construction guy all my life. Worked my way up to becoming a general contractor." Then, after doing that for around twenty years, Ron moved back to St. Ignace in 1999. "I brought my kids," he said. "At the time I was still married. Got my first glimpse of tribal things, skirmishes, distrust between chiefs. Before moving back, I didn't identify as being native. Because of the way we were treated, being a native, my parents never talked about it. After 1978, when the Freedom of Religion Act was passed, my mother still didn't tell me until my youngest brother graduated from school. Then we found out and enrolled in the tribe right away. But I still didn't know anything and would ask my uncle, who lived here, about being native, and he wouldn't tell me. He spent his entire life on a spiritual journey, and in 1999, when we came up here, I said, 'I really want to know what's going on. I want to learn about my roots,' but he still wouldn't tell me. I asked, 'Why not?' and he said, 'It will take you from your family.'

"And it did.

"The journey, the spirituality, is a solo journey."

Then came the 2009 financial crash, and Ron lost everything. He had owned a business, and suddenly it was gone. At that point, even though he was experienced, nobody would give him a job. "Because I was too qualified for any jobs—it wasn't that there weren't any jobs. So, my wife had to support me, which she resented, despite me supporting her all those years while she got a college education. Now she was bringing home the bacon and had to support me."

Then Ron learned about the Sun Dance. He went to his first Sun Dance and was allowed to participate and help out. That was when he realized how powerful he felt to be involved in the dance. "They kinda threw me into the fire. And I danced, and it was amazing."

Ron told me he kept going back, every year since. For the next three years, over and over, he went back, and the more times he did, the more he enjoyed it. "By the third year of my involvement, I was beginning to question everything," Ron said. "Things like, what was I here for? Why was I alive? I started realizing

Ron Daniels, in front of his store in St. Ignace, Michigan

what I'd been missing." At the time Ron was a drinker, and it was becoming a problem. "I became sober in 2013. I couldn't live that life anymore. Everyone I knew, all they wanted to do was drink, make fun of people, use racist language, and tell jokes that just weren't funny anymore."

One by one, Ron's old drinking buddies started dropping dead from heart attacks, cancer, and other things. It got him wondering whether he would be next. His blood pressure was out of control, and he was diagnosed with an enlarged heart. Realizing all the partying and conflicts in his marriage were not doing him any good, he filed for divorce.

I asked Ron what he did after his divorce.

"I started praying. Giving thanks to the Creator. I hadn't realized that was all I had to do. Be a thankful person. I started forgiving everybody for everything and anything. I began to examine myself for all the stupid things I'd ever done."

He mostly learned to forgive himself. And once he did, he was in a beautiful place. That was when he met a wonderful woman who helped him run his store. "She helped me out. She's stuck with me. Then she went through cancer, and we prayed together, and that helped her get through it. She's doing fantastic now."

Ron took me around the store, pointing out things he'd like to do. One was to provide a venue for live music. "There are so many beautiful people who stop in. They come in and are so humble and so appreciative of the things that are here. Often, when people enter, they come in as strangers and leave as family. They are so thankful the totem museum is still here."

The area along the straits had always been strategic, both militarily and for trade. Driving east along US-2, I passed many businesses geared to travelers. Some, like the Historic Totem Village, carried on the long-established tradition of trade that defined the region for hundreds of years.

14

Once the Mackinac Bridge was thought to be a structure that could never happen. Yet people kept talking about it. After all, a state with two peninsulas that weren't connected had divided the state economically, politically, and socially. Yet, building a bridge over the treacherous five-mile Straits of Mackinac was thought to be more of a dream than a reality. It was first discussed in 1884 after a Traverse City, Michigan, newspaper reporter wrote an article about an experimental year-round ferry service that had failed. He recommended a bridge or a tunnel similar to New York City's Brooklyn Bridge or London's Thames Tunnel, which crossed the River Thames, to span the straits. The only question was the cost. Soon, the idea of a year-round way of crossing the straits started to pick up steam. Some suggestions were outright crazy, such as a floating tunnel or multiple bridges that would island hop as a way for people to cross. The breakthrough came in 1934 with the creation of the Mackinac Straits Bridge Authority, which studied the feasibility of constructing a bridge and a way to fund it.

Construction began in 1954, and the Mackinac Bridge was dedicated in 1957.

Before construction, when all travel across the straits was by car ferry, my parents vacationed in the U.P. and, while waiting to board the ferry, captured photos of it. Those photos were now in my collection.

My personal involvement with the Mackinac Bridge started when I was little and grew when I was an adult and owned a place in the U.P. One of my most memorable crossings happened one winter when icy conditions caused traffic to stop midspan. The bridge, which had a built-in sway to keep the structure from collapsing, was enough to nearly make me sick to my stomach.

On this part of my journey, I was heading east, which landed me in Mackinaw City, the gateway to the Lower Peninsula. Though it had a long history that stretched back to when Native Americans lived there, it was now a town where the primary income came from tourism.

My route took me through the Lower Peninsula of Michigan from Mackinaw City to the Port Huron Blue Water Bridge into Canada by hugging the shoreline of Lake Huron. The area had small towns, sandy beaches, high-bank vistas, seasonal lake cabins, and year-round homes and farmland.

The northern shoreline of Michigan's Lower Peninsula was littered with shipwrecks, now part of an underwater preserve that involved the towns of Cheboygan, Presque Isle, and Alpena.

Once in Alpena, I asked who I should talk to about the underwater preserve and was told to speak with Al Moe. He was retired and had served on the board of the Friends of Thunder Bay National Marine Sanctuary, the organization that helped raise money to fund the sanctuary.

On meeting Moe, I asked him to tell me his story. He said, "I was raised in Montevideo, Minnesota. My parents were both of Scandinavian descent and grew up in Minnesota and eastern South Dakota. I think my mother was well into her thirties before she got married. I also have a sister."

Al told me that early on, he learned the importance of volunteering from his parents, even though his family members were low-income earners. His mother worked in a JC Penny store, and his father had jobs in a couple of appliance stores. "But we were a rock-solid family, pretty active in our local church. When Dad died, at his funeral the church was full. He had made an impact on a lot of people."

When Al graduated from high school, he went to Concordia College in Morehead, Minnesota, which, he said, "is a good Lutheran college."

I asked how could he afford to go there?

"There was no grant money, other than what you could get at the time. National Defense Loans, so I borrowed enough money to attend," Al said.

"I started out as a biology zoology major and got married between my sophomore and junior year, which was a bit foolish. It was a time when everybody seemed to get married quite young." In Al's junior year, Concordia required a minor, so he took an economics class to see if a minor in business was possible. His logic was that the business route could be "a smoother way to go" because unlike the sciences, which required eight hours in a lab each week, for a minor in business he only needed to attend classes. "The first class I took was healthcare administration. After I had been in the class a week, I came home and told my wife, 'This is what I'm going to do.' So, I changed my major and finally chose a double major in business administration and healthcare administration, with biology as a minor."

And though Al ended up in Alpena, it took him a few earlier jobs to get there.

"My first job was five years as an administer at a small hospital in Perham, Minnesota, and its nearby long-term-care facility, where I worked with a bunch of Franciscan nuns. There, I was kinda a referee between the nuns, ages from about nineteen to ninety. It was a precursor to what I did my entire career in hospital administration."

I asked where he went next.

"A non-Catholic hospital in Crookston. There were two hospitals in town. The Franciscan order hospital had to close, which was political suicide because it really split the community. So, we built a brand-new hospital, which was a good experience for me. I was there about five years, RiverView Health. We had a 150-bed, long-term-care facility there. "

"How did you end up here in Alpena?"

"One night a recruiter who wanted to fill a position at a hospital in Michigan called. After that, I came to Alpena to interview for the position. The administrator here had been in Minnesota the same time I was. We both sat on the same hospital association board of directors, and we knew of each other. When I interviewed, he and I hit it off great. I worked with him for thirty years here in Alpena, which was rare—to stay in one facility for that many years."

I asked Al how things changed during the years he was in Alpena.

"Alpena didn't have many specialty services when I came," he said. "At that time, we had around twenty-seven physicians on our medical staff. When I retired, we had slightly under a hundred. We did a lot of work to keep most specialty services local so people didn't have to travel to the west side of the state for healthcare."

I asked Al about the administrator he worked for—a man named John McVeety.

"He was an interesting guy," Al said. "I think he sailed in thirty-six Port Huron to Mackinaw Island races. An ego beyond anyone you've ever met. John needed that stroke, and I was just the opposite. I don't need that kind of adulation. But we worked very well together, for so long that we knew who should do what and which of us should deal with certain people and groups."

John McVeety retired in 2007 and ten years later died suddenly. As for Al Moe, he retired in 2009. The Alpena Regional Medical Center became part of the MidMichigan Health system on April 1, 2016, and changed its name to MidMichigan Medical Center – Alpena.

After retirement, Al didn't sit on a couch, wasting away. Instead, he increased his involvement in the Alpena community by serving on the board of the Friends of Thunder Bay National Marine Sanctuary, the Thunder Bay National Marine Sanctuary advisory council, and the board of the Thunder Bay Community Health Services.

Al was especially interested in the work of the Thunder Bay National Marine Sanctuary and the support for the sanctuary through fundraising by the Friends of Thunder Bay National Marine Sanctuary.

The Thunder Bay National Marine Sanctuary was one of fifteen national marine sanctuaries that were part of the U.S. Department of Commerce's National Oceanic and Atmospheric Administration, better known as NOAA. The mission of NOAA was to be the country's trustee for a network of underwater parks encompassing more than 620,000 square miles of marine and Great Lakes waters. The National Marine Sanctuaries were responsible for everything under the water, in partnership with the state of Michigan and NOAA.

"When I first moved here," Al said, "there were three or four divers who were salvage guys or, more correctly, shipwreck pirates. That was how we got involved with those guys because they needed a hyperbaric chamber, and they wanted us to get one, which we leased for a while. It was for dive accidents. That's how we first got involved with the sanctuary, before it was officially a sanctuary."

In addition to assisting divers, the chamber was also instrumental in the hospital's wound-management program because it delivered 100 percent oxygen that not only helped divers recover but also helped heal patients' cancer burns from radiation treatments. Al said, "In the state of Michigan, ours is the only hospital whose hyperbaric chamber is available 24/7 during the dive season; others are available on call."

Al also backed educational programs that the Friends of the Sanctuary supported, raising a lot of money for them. He helped with economic development that brought the Viking Cruise Lines to make twenty-six stops that year in the area. More than 386 people on each ship came once a week on an educational expedition.

Al often took visitors on tours in order to show the opportunities that existed in Alpena. "Here, we are short of housing, yet we have all that property," he said. "When I first came to town, they did not want tourists. The attitude was that we were a working town." However, one by one, factories in Alpena were closing. DPI, which made hardboard like Masonite, closed its doors about a month ago, putting 150 people on the street. Then Panel Processing closed. It had been the largest manufacturer of pegboard in the world. "So, what happens now?" Al asked. "All the loggers here cutting trees down, chipping wood, and bringing logs in here. What happens to their businesses? Hundreds of trucks a day were hauling logs, where are they going now? We still have a lot of logging going on here, but the price will be impacted by fewer sources having a need for the timber."

I asked Al, who was recently named "Marine Sanctuary Volunteer of the Year," why he volunteered. For the first time during our talk, Al Moe became tongue-tied, searching for an answer. After a long pause, he said, "I wish I could express myself better than I can. Let me start by saying I'm disappointed that so few people do it anymore. I think unless you grow up with volunteering in your

Al Moe, in front of a sign near the Lake Huron waterfront in Alpena, Michigan

family, you don't understand it. I do it because I see a need and emptiness or something where just a little nudge will advance . . . it's hard to express it."

"What is inside of you that reacts to that need?" I asked. "Is it empathy, wanting to jump in and just be part of something?"

"I think there is a certain amount of it. You see a need, you feel a need. For me, it's the satisfaction I get out of it. And you get a lot of recognition, not that I'm seeking it, but it's amazing. I sit on all the sanctuary boards, so I see inside a lot of things. I'm so deeply involved in everything, people on the outside almost feel jealous, saying, 'How do I get involved?' We keep encouraging people to volunteer, and we do get some. Plus, I've always liked change and growth. When I was on my job at the hospital, it was about building things. I've been around construction and have loved every inch of it. I was a chief operating officer, but my heart was in the dirt—building stuff."

From Alpena, I followed the Lake Huron shoreline by taking a series of two-lane highways. My goal was to get to the Canadian border crossing at Port Huron as quickly as possible over rural roads. It meant passing through the towns of Harrisville, Oscoda, Au Sable, Tawas City, Au Gres, Standish, and Pinconning, then taking local roads through Bay City, and eventually jumping onto M-25, the road that would take me along the shoreline of Lake Huron around the Thumb of

Michigan. In most places along that route, lake cottages were on the left side of the road, and farms were on the right.

After passing through Sebewaing, Bay Port, and Caseville, I finally stopped to take a break in Port Austin because by then I was bored, and my legs needed to be stretched. As I walked through Port Austin, the weather turned from sunny skies to one heck of a storm. The wind suddenly kicked up, resulting in rough waves coming off Lake Huron. At the time, I thought, *I've been gone a long time, and though I've always enjoyed traveling, this particular journey has gone on long enough.*

During the next stretch of driving, I found a roadside park just south of Port Sanilac. It overlooked Lake Huron, where a historical marker told the story of the Great Storm of 1913. While there, I spotted an eagle swooping down over the lake, hunting for a fish dinner. I grabbed my camera and captured that image before hustling back to my car to make the 30-mile drive to Port Huron. There, I took the Blue Water Bridge to cross the St. Clair River and enter Canada.

As I approached customs, I wondered how it would go, given my history of having issues at border crossings. This time it was without incident.

The border agent asked whether I planned to visit any particular places. I said I was following the pathway of the Underground Railroad riders who, once they arrived in Canada, were declared free and deemed no longer enslaved. The border agent said he had recently taken his family on that route and how much of an impact the Underground Railroad pathway through Canada had made. He gave me advice on where to stop and what site impressed him most, saying, "Whatever you do, don't forget to stop in Buxton"—which, he assured me, was "worth it."

15

The rural roads from Sarnia to North Buxton ran through mostly flat, irrigated farmland known for its soybean and corn production, interspersed with small towns.

Once in North Buxton, I stopped at the Buxton National Historic Site & Museum, where I met Michelle Robbins, its newly appointed curator.

As we walked through rooms filled with historical exhibits, Michelle told me that the United States had passed the Fugitive Slave Act of 1850, which empowered local officials and citizens to seize runaway enslaved people and return them to bondage. Because it happened after slavery was abolished in

Canada and throughout the British Empire by the Slavery Abolition Act of 1834, the Canadians were emboldened to help enslaved people who escaped to Canada. Michelle said, "I am a seventh-generation descendent. My family settled here in 1852. She pointed at the land across from the museum. "That is the farm where I grew up."

Michelle told me that Buxton was originally called the Elgin Settlement and was one of four Black settlements that were founded in Ontario in the mid 1800s. She said the town had been established in 1849 by a Presbyterian minister named William King, and the settlement was one of the last stops on the Underground Railroad.

"Reverend William King was an abolitionist who inherited fifteen enslaved people by different circumstances," Michelle said. "He wanted to find an area where the formerly enslaved people could be freed. That was because in the U.S., the law prevented the formerly enslaved from living there. He was able to acquire the land in what became Buxton, which was crown land. At the time it was heavily forested and very swampy."

"What was meant by crown land?" I asked.

Michelle, realizing I was an American and didn't know Canada's long history, said, "Canada didn't become fully independent from Great Britain until 1982 when our constitution was ratified. We did become the Province of Canada in 1867, however, and were self-governing then, but when Reverend King acquired the land here, we were still governed by the British."

Continuing, Michelle said that Reverend King was able to acquire 9,000 acres, which he divided into 50-acre plots. "Each of the initial fifteen settlers he had earlier inherited received fifty acres, as did each of the first two thousand settlers who followed that first group."

I asked how a minister from a church could ever afford to purchase 9,000 acres.

"It was complicated," Michelle said and explained that when Reverend King lived in Louisiana, he got the passion for freeing enslaved people. He dreamed of establishing "a city of God" where the enslaved he'd acquired, along with other fugitives of slavery, could live in freedom. "He knew it couldn't happen in the United States, so in 1848 he emigrated to Canada West, which eventually became Ontario."

Michelle told me that the Presbyterian Church agreed to assist Reverend King, as did other Christians and the government of the newly formed Canada West. By this time, King had decided that the evils of slavery, and his intolerance of it, meant he no longer wanted to live in the United States. King had earlier accepted a position as a missionary to Canada, which gave him the right to purchase property. Then he leveraged the land to bring in more enslaved people.

"This was a very self-sustaining community," Michelle said, "and you had to be Black in order to purchase land here. However, the outlying communities didn't want Black people to live here. They thought this community couldn't take care of the land, the homesteads, or pay taxes because the earlier enslavement in Canada had fostered a mentality that Blacks were 'less than.'"

As we walked from exhibit to exhibit, Michelle told me that to quell the objections of people opposed to the settlement, Reverend King had put rules in place. Every home had to have four rooms, it had to be thirteen feet from the road, and it needed a fruit and vegetable garden and a three-foot-high picket fence in the front yard. She said, "Everyone who could pay $2.50 an acre for the fifty acres got land and had ten years to pay off those fifty acres and purchase more land if they chose."

Michelle told me the formerly enslaved residents eventually turned the land into highly desirable farmland, and their farms were still farming that same land today.

She said the formerly enslaved had "a lot of cash crop farms. And because it was such a self-sufficient community, we had everything here. We had a blacksmith, hotels, a sawmill, a train station, we had all those things people needed to be able to work and live here. It was pretty fascinating how people started their lives and their homes here because they didn't have that when they were enslaved." She emphasized, "This was, after all, their first taste of freedom."

I asked, "Where did the enslaved people who came to Buxton cross the border?"

"Many came by way of Detroit, but more came through upstate New York, where they crossed at Niagara Falls."

I asked Michelle where her family was originally from.

"My family came here from Tennessee, where they had been enslaved. So, I'm a generational descendent, which is why being part of this particular settlement is incredibly important." She went on to say her daughter helped out with tours and was able to talk about their family history.

Michelle added, "I knew my grandparents. They were farmers, and my grandmother was a homemaker and also worked at the local hospital. But they were mostly farmers. We had a tomato farm, and we had cattle, horses, and chickens."

Walking through the museum, I noticed the knotty pine walls and ceiling with glassed-in displays holding items of historical value. There was an antique bed from the era, along with a handmade quilt with a stitched-in "Buxton Settlers" and a scene of the settlement. Down the hall was a recreation of life aboard a slave ship with iron shackles, bunks barely large enough for the enslaved to turn around, and vivid signage telling the story of the passage from Africa where, in a period of 350 years of enslavement, millions had died, many thrown overboard

Michelle Robbins, curator, Buxton National Historic Site & Museum, North Buxton, Ontario

to lighten the load because the slave traders had forced too many enslaved people onto the slave ships.

In the lot next door was the original schoolhouse with desks and blackboards that looked as if it were ready for students and teachers. The Colbert-Henderson Cabin exhibit showed how life was for the newly freed, enslaved people who lived in Buxton. Nearby was a barn equipped with farm tools of the time: a hand-powered fanning mill, a wooden apple press, and a two-person rip saw.

Michelle described the proud history of North Buxton. "In 1861, four years before the Civil War broke out in the United States, three hundred Blacks—most of them former slaves from Southern plantations—walked proudly along the streets of nearby Chatham to vote in the local courthouse. The people had walked ten miles from Buxton, which had been settled six years earlier. When the votes were tallied at the end of the day, the incumbent provincial parliament member who had won his seat on an anti-Negro immigration platform had been defeated. I'm proud to say it was the first demonstration of political Black power on the North American continent."

Things were getting busier in the museum, and I could tell Michelle had other duties. As I left, she said, "If you're crossing the border at Niagara Falls, I suggest you stop by the Niagara Falls Underground Railroad Heritage Center. It is an interactive museum that visually tells the story of the Underground Railroad. It was a primary point of entry for those seeking freedom."

I asked where the museum was located.

"It's easy to find; it is a wing of the Amtrak station."

Not wanting to take the busy superhighway 405, I decided to find my way to Niagara Falls by following the northern shore of Lake Erie east along the more picturesque roads that sat on or near the lake.

While slowly wandering through Ontario on my way to Niagara Falls, I began to wonder when I'd return home. I was now in a mood to take things easy. My attitude had become one of thankfulness for my travel and my life beyond. Though I still wasn't ready to return to where I had started, I could feel myself beginning to get there. Mentally.

While I made the crossing back into the United States, my mind drifted to a time when I was young. I remembered carrying a Kodak Instamatic camera to take pictures of the falls from the Canadian side. On that trip, my family stayed at the Fallsway Motor Inn, within walking distance of the falls.

Though Niagara Falls was known for the American, Horseshoe, and Bridal Veil Falls, my primary objective was to visit the Niagara Falls Heritage Center.

Locating the museum was fairly simple because the Amtrak Station was within walking distance of downtown Niagara Falls, New York. The Heritage Center sat next to the Amtrak Station in the U.S. Customs House, ironically built in 1863 when slavery still existed in the United States. The center overlooked the former location of the Niagara Falls Railway Suspension Bridge, a point of crossing for many freedom seekers—including Harriet Tubman, who rode the train across the border.

Before entering the Heritage Center, I noticed a free EV-charging terminal. I plugged in my hybrid, which would net me thirty-five miles of free driving.

The Niagara Falls Underground Railroad Heritage Center building was a stone structure built into a railroad embankment. I proceeded along the brick walkway and entered the building through its double arched doors. On the stone wall just outside the doors, a sign read, "One more river to cross," in type arranged in a wave pattern to resemble the flow of the river.

As I walked into the center, behind the front counter sat Josh Poole, a specialist for the museum. We chitchatted a while, during which I learned that Josh was a graduate of SUNY Geneseo with a degree in history that focused on African American history and that he had lived in the area his entire life. He said, "Growing up here, I've always known that this area had a unique history, which I now enjoy sharing with our guests."

I asked Josh whether he had the time to grant me an interview so I could accurately record our conversation. He said he did because it would be an hour before the center opened. As for recording him, he said he was used to it.

What impressed me about Josh was his welcoming manner and contagious enthusiasm for local history. We talked a little about Harriet Tubman, though he soon reminded me, "Everyone knows about Harriet Tubman. But when you really look at the Underground Railroad, it was a massive movement that involved many more people."

Over the next few minutes, Josh told me about Niagara Falls and its significance in the history of indigenous people. We talked about its role during the War of 1812 and how it figured in presidential history. Josh went on to say, "The Underground Railroad was a massive movement of freedom-seeking people. Here, at the Heritage Center, we like to say it was the first Civil Rights movement. The extent to which people participated and helped other people escape to freedom is really unknown." We discussed the passage of the Fugitive Slave Act of 1850, requiring enslaved people to be returned to their owners even if they were found in a free state like New York. Josh said, "That act made the federal government responsible for finding, returning, and trying those who escaped. It gave the City of Niagara Falls, as a border town with Canada, much more importance."

I asked how many had escaped enslavement through Niagara Falls.

Josh said it was never determined because the Underground Railroad was secret. But he was sure more than 75,000 had escaped. "This area had a huge network of people who wanted to help."

We then walked over to the Cataract House exhibit, though Josh told me the actual Cataract House was located two miles from the Heritage Center across from Goat Island. The Cataract House was now a gazebo within Niagara Falls State Park because the original structure had been destroyed by fire in 1945.

Josh said the Cataract House was the place to meet. "You had people like Abraham Lincoln, who stayed there before he became president." He mentioned that the entire waitstaff was African American, and 80 percent of them had previously been enslaved and were living as free people. They were the ones who helped others escape. "We have these instances where enslavers from the South came to Niagara Falls on vacation and brought enslaved people with them to carry their luggage or take care of their young children. So, they came, they visited, they stayed at the hotel, and the waitstaff came in contact with these people, then helped them escape across the border to freedom."

I asked where on the river they had escaped because the Niagara River had strong rapids, especially close to the base of the falls. I remembered stories like that of Annie Taylor, the sixty-three-year-old school teacher from Michigan, who along with her cat survived the falls in a barrel in 1901, only to end up poor and destitute on the streets of Niagara Falls twenty years later. Or Jean Albert Lussier, who took the plunge over Niagara Falls on July 4, 1920, in a huge rubber ball, becoming the first daredevil to survive the falls in an inflated device. But, as I recalled, those were oddities because most of the people who entered the rapids drowned, the vast majority being suicides.

"The enslaved didn't go over the falls to escape," Josh said. "They took a boat at the bottom of the falls near where the *Maid of the Mist* takes tourists safely every day." He told me that once the International Suspension Bridge began carrying trains over the Niagara River in 1855, enslaved people crossed over in larger numbers. Though the cost was great if enslaved people were caught trying to cross into Canada, they would do anything to get to freedom. Josh emphasized that point, saying, "Everyone wants to be free."

He told me that after the Civil War ended in 1865 and slavery was abolished by the 13th Amendment, there was still work to be done. The 14th Amendment (passed by Congress on June 16, 1866, and ratified on July 28, 1868) granted formerly enslaved people citizenship; declared no state could deprive anyone of life, liberty, or property without due process of law, or couldn't deny any person within its jurisdiction the equal protection of the laws. The right to due process of law and equal protection of the law also applied to both the federal and the state government. Then came the 15th Amendment, which granted African American men the right to vote (passed by Congress on February 26, 1869, and ratified February 3, 1870). Women did not receive the right to vote until the 19th Amendment was passed by Congress on June 4, 1919, and was ratified on August 18, 1920.

"We like to point out that there was one exception to the Thirteenth Amendment," Josh said, "which is that slavery can still be used as a punishment for people who are imprisoned. So, if you look at the South after the Civil War, they passed a lot of laws called 'Black Codes,' which you can tell by the name targeted formerly enslaved people."

I learned that Black Codes were a bunch of petty laws, if taken in the context of today, but back then they were different. For example, vagrancy and loitering laws were selectively enforced against formerly enslaved people, who were arrested for being on the street in the middle of the day and not working. Other examples of Black Codes dealt with employment, where the formerly enslaved were required to sign annual labor contracts that gave them the lowest pay possible. The contracts also contained anti-enticement clauses to prevent prospective employers from paying Black workers more than they had received from previous employers, making it impossible for the formerly enslaved people to earn more, even when they learned what the pay was for normally better-paying jobs. For example, if they went from being a common laborer to learning a trade, such as plumbing or carpentry.

I asked Josh what the difference was between Black Codes and Jim Crow Laws.

He said Black Codes were passed by Southern states after the Civil War to limit the freedom of formerly enslaved people, to limit their choice of employment, and to prevent them from owning property. They were different from Jim Crow laws, which were passed later to enforce racial segregation—for example, where African Americans could live, where they could eat in terms of restaurants, where they could travel when it came to lodging, and to make African Americans work separately from whites. The term came from the racist "Jim Crow" character played by blackface actor Thomas Dartmouth "Daddy" Rice in minstrel shows in the early 1830s.

Josh took me over to an exhibit that showed the treatment that former slaves and their offspring suffered through in the days of Black Codes and during the Jim Crow era.

To understand how working at the center had affected its employees and volunteers, I asked Josh how his job at the center had changed him as a person.

"From my personal perspective, I grew up in a town just east of Niagara Falls, and I was ignorant about a lot of this history until I started working here and hearing the stories. Once I got this job, I started educating myself. I don't want to speak on others' behalf, but some people are just plain ignorant about this topic and haven't come here to learn about it, even though it is near where they live." Josh talked a bit about the school in the suburban town nearby where he grew up. "In my junior and senior high school, this history was completely ignored." He said he heard similar stories from visitors to the center. "They learned about the Underground Railroad to a minimal extent. They might have studied a little about Harriet Tubman but not to the extent of what the Underground Railroad was. Most important, you don't hear a lot about the problems that still are affecting this city."

While pointing toward the window that showed the area where the center was located, Josh said, "As you were driving up here, you probably saw rows of abandoned houses, buildings, and that the main street was neglected and deteriorating. You also probably saw a lot of our murals. That's because way back in the day, the city was redlined."

I remembered how dilapidated a lot of buildings were in the downtown area and how many empty storefronts there were. I also noticed that across the river on the Canadian side, things looked much different. Houses appeared to be better cared for, and the downtown seemed vibrant. I mentioned to Josh that there was redlining in many cities near where I lived, but that had happened years ago and seemed to be on its way out.

"Here," Josh said, "the city is still dealing with the ramifications of redlining. People who experienced it are aware of it. But a lot of people are still ignorant of it. The same thing was true twenty miles to the south in Buffalo, New York."

I told Josh about my own upbringing, that I was born, raised, and still resided in a nearly all-white town. Yet only a few miles to our north was a city mostly of color that had suffered for many decades. "Even our local newspaper won't cover stories from that town," I said.

Agreeing, Josh said, "Putting things into perspective, Niagara Falls has historically always been a Black community, yet to its east and north, the towns there are mostly white. Our newspaper here in Niagara Falls tries to highlight issues of poverty and race, yet you don't see that newspaper available in my town."

We discussed downtown Niagara Falls, New York, and how it contrasted with downtown Niagara Falls, Ontario. To me, because I had been exposed to the Ontario side, that downtown seemed fairly successful, while the downtown area within walking distance of the Heritage Center was blighted in spots. However, the parks on the New York side were more spectacular than those in Canada. The architecture on the American side was classic and, with funding, could lead to a renewal that would spread to the downtown.

Josh Poole, Visitor Experience Specialist / Operations Specialist, Niagara Falls Underground Railroad Heritage Center, Niagara Falls,, New York

Josh knew from living nearby that Niagara Falls, New York, saw things differently, that the deterioration was caused by white flight from the city to towns farther north and east. As for new investment, he was all in favor of it but worried that modern-day redlining would keep people from getting funding. He mentioned Detroit, which was across from me in the state of Michigan, as having similar problems as Niagara Falls.

Josh, in his twenties, seemed level-headed and certainly knew his history, so I asked whether he was similar to one of his parents. "My mom's a schoolteacher who teaches sixth-grade English, along with social studies. I've had great conversations with her where she talks about how social studies have not been funded recently or at least less than they once were. More funding goes to STEM programs. So, she's talked about the difficulties of educating students about history, which is important because we deal with it every day, whether we know it or not. My dad has worked for General Motors his entire life—like a lot of people in Michigan where you are from. And like you, we also have a manufacturing industry base. It's definitely union here. Our plants here make air conditioning systems for GM cars."

Just before leaving, I asked Josh where he saw himself in the next five years.

"I'm looking at master's programs, and I'm trying to decide what I'd enjoy doing the most, a decision I want to make before I pay a ton of money for another degree. I'd like to keep doing the sort of work we do here, whether it's a museum or a library."

16

To the solo traveler, there came a time to be alone and a time to test the patience of others. That was how I felt as I drove alone to the town of Bath, New York.

To get to Bath, I turned onto NY-53, a route that allowed me to see the wineries dotting the region.

Once in the Village of Bath, I met up with John Gould, who was originally from my hometown. John was an ordained Presbyterian minister with an interesting calling. Instead of serving particular churches, he served what was called a "specialized ministry."

I asked John whether his calling was similar to the specialized call of the Presbyterian minister Fred Rogers, who for decades hosted a children's television program on Public Broadcasting named *Mister Roger's Neighborhood.*

John Gould said he had a similar calling as Fred Rogers, but he'd received his in a different manner. Though John had been raised in the same church as me, I did not know him then. Instead, I knew his younger sister. So, when I arrived in a parking lot in Bath, New York, it was the first time John and I had ever met.

I was struck by his kindly manner, his deep beliefs, and his love of the area he now called home. John said, "After graduating from high school, I went to Alma College in Michigan because my brothers Jim and Rob were already there. One reason I went there was that my Grandpa and Grandma Lee had donated a scholarship fund to the college. A fund that is still in existence."

Knowing that Alma College was affiliated with the Presbyterian Church, I asked whether he had already decided to become a minister. But he hadn't—at least, not yet. "My roommate was going to be a minister; I was going to be a high school teacher." But John's roommate saw something special in John and suggested he also become a minister. Interestingly, John's roommate ended up becoming a teacher.

John got married in college to a woman in pre-law, but he gradually began to contemplate whether to become a minister. After his then-wife decided to go to law school in Chicago, he investigated seminaries in the area. He ended up going to McCormick Seminary.

I asked how he had ended up in Bath.

One day he had seen a note on the seminary bulletin board about a ministerial position at a small Presbyterian church in the town of Prattsburgh, fifteen miles from Bath. The note had been tacked on the bulletin board by the president of the seminary, who had served that same congregation thirty years earlier. When John saw the note, he knocked on the door of the seminary president and was told Prattsburgh was a small rural town in upstate New York that was very pleasant. So, John contacted the church, and they did the usual thing: interviewing him and having him guest preach. As John recalled, "We came out here in June 1974, and I became the Prattsburgh Presbyterian Church's full-time paster. I was there three years."

Because three years was a very short time for a minister to serve in a church, I asked him why he'd left when he did.

John said there was an incident after his wife became pregnant, and they needed a nursery. At the time, they were living in the church-owned manse, which had rented out an upstairs room to an elderly woman. John asked whether the woman could be relocated to make room for their baby. He was told the woman was beloved by the community, so they would have to make do with what they had. John said, "Apparently, I'd asked the wrong question. Soon after, I decided it was time to move on."

I asked what he did next.

"I got connected with a pastor friend who did part-time work in the Clifton Springs hospital alcohol rehab unit, thirty-five miles north of Prattsburgh. They asked whether I'd be interested in some part-time work as a clergy counselor at the twenty-two bed, thirty-day-intensive alcohol rehab unit." After working there for six months, John got a full-time job, setting up a drug treatment program, which he realized wasn't what they needed. Instead, John suggested a drug education program for youths, which he helped establish. At that point, Clifton Springs hospital asked him to come back to work full time, so he stayed there four years.

John said, "I was the first non-addiction counselor who wasn't a recovering addict they'd ever hired to work on the unit." While there, John was sent to the Hazelden Foundation in Minnesota to learn about the Alcoholic Anonymous twelve-step program because as the clergy counselor, his responsibility was to help people complete their four-step inventory. He asked me whether I knew about the program.

John explained that Step 4 of AA was a crucial component of the recovery process. The step allowed individuals to confront their past, identify character defects, and make amends where necessary. John was also the Step 5 person, in what was commonly known as the "confession step." It encouraged members to acknowledge their struggles and whatever harm they had caused to themselves and others in pursuit of alcohol. He explained that in AA, the alcoholic was one person, God or a higher power was ever present, and John was the other person. John estimated that he'd listened to around two hundred people give their personal inventories during his three years working there. At the time, he was the chairperson of the alcohol and substance abuse committee and was working with the community services director. One day the director told John that if he wanted to continue working in human services, his master's of divinity degree wouldn't get him very far in his career and suggested he get a master's of social work degree. On the director's recommendation, John applied for and was admitted to Syracuse University, where, during the next two years, he earned a master's of social work degree in family mental health.

"I commuted back and forth from Bath to Syracuse, a two-hour drive each way. The man who recommended I get the degree hired me to supervise the outpatient psychiatric intensive case management program. Then the county director hired me for the county alcohol substance abuse outpatient treatment program, where I worked for four years. Next, I got a job here in Bath at the Veterans Administration Medical Center for a job in the dormitories as a social worker, where I worked for twenty-one years."

During that time, John was placed in a ministerial category of the Presbyterian church that specialized in ministry counseling. "I did tons of supply preaching," he said, "filling in for ministers on vacation. I preached at a lot of churches near here.

Then my wife, whom I was still married to back then and who was an attorney, said, 'Why don't you advertise that you'll do adoption home studies for parents who want to adopt children? They need a home study done to qualify for becoming adoptees.' So, for the next twenty-some years I did adoption home studies. I would go into the house, interview the family, then write up a report, recommending them for adoption. I did that during the same time I was working at the VA."

When I asked John why he felt the VA was important, he said, "I can summarize my years of service as a mental health social worker at the Bath VAMC with the phrase "The price of freedom is visible here." My eternal gratitude is for the men and women who served during the Vietnam era. They were there for me so I could become a minister, and as a social worker I could be there for them, along with some amazing women and men of many different professions. I will always honor all veterans. My uncle was a copilot of a B-17 during World War II and was killed in combat. If you enjoy living in a free country, thank a veteran for their part and also support the Veterans Administration."

John retired from the VA in his early sixties, which allowed him to get more involved in his church. Rather than attend a Presbyterian church, he decided to instead join the local Methodist church where he then led a Bible study and filled in on occasion to preach. In the meantime, he had gotten divorced and remarried Debbie a couple of years later. They'd been married for nearly thirty years.

All the while as we talked, John took me on a tour of Bath and the surrounding areas. We went to Hammondsport on the southern tip of Keuka Lake, one of the Finger Lakes, where he told me about Glenn Curtiss, who had been born there. "He was as big in aviation as the Wright Brothers and is called the father of naval aviation. A museum here is dedicated to him."

John told me that the Finger Lakes region of New York, known for its vineyards, had a "Wine Trail." I learned about three different wine trails in the region: the Keuka Lake Wine Trail wineries date back to 1860.

We drove through downtown Bath, where he showed me historic churches and buildings and mentioned that many buildings were being rehabbed but that challenges still existed. Then we headed to the VA facility at the edge of town. John pointed out several buildings—some housing vets, others providing VA services, and the hospital—and finally, we went up the hill past the VA administration building. That was when it hit me, the heartbreak of seeing those perfectly arranged marble grave markers stretched out over acres of manicured lawns.

"They do an excellent job maintaining the cemetery," John said. "There are soldiers from the Revolutionary War on up to current times. I get chills from just driving through here."

Farther in, after passing the Preservation of the Union Monument dedicated to Civil War soldiers and sailors, we talked more about our earlier lives. It seemed appropriate, given we were in a place of remembrance. John spoke about his family.

"Dad died in 2004; he had Parkinson's disease. He and his wife had moved to Tuscan, Arizona, where they were living when he passed away. My mother died in 1981 from suicide. My mother's brother was killed in World War II. I don't think my grandpa or grandma or my mother or her sister ever recovered from his death. It traumatized the entire family. My mother had problems with manic depression for a good part of her life. The miracle was that despite being an alcoholic, through a treatment program in AA, she stayed sober for the last seventeen years of her life. I call them the angels of AA. While her moods and her depression and mania were all over the place, she never started drinking again. To me, that's a miracle. I owe a lot to AA, and I finally learned after she died that she was not the problem in my life. The problem in my life was her alcoholism and her manic depression. It was just as much a problem for her as it was for me. So, I was finally able to get to the point where I could forgive her for everything I thought she did or didn't do."

I told John I also had the same issue, of finding forgiveness in the midst of suicide. As did my father, who discovered my grandmother's body. My father had been the dutiful son, and we'd lived just up the road from my grandparents' house. Each evening, for as long as anyone could remember, whenever my grandmother called, my father had stopped by to check on her, but one night he'd decided not to visit her, on the advice of others. The next morning my grandmother's body was found. Some of my family members thought she had not meant to overdose, but later I had discovered paperwork signed by her doctor, asking the court to admit her into a mental care institution because she could not cope with life and would be safe only with round-the-clock care. It was something that had plagued me ever since it happened. That was when I said to John, "I know it was not her fault. It was her depression, and I now can finally forgive my grandmother."

After I finished my family's story, John asked whether I was up for dinner. We headed back downtown to a nice family restaurant where, over our meal, he said, "I'm of the age where I'm very concerned about the legacy I'm leaving for my children and grandchildren. Not money or property but the legacy of my life. So, I've written a lot of things down, and I've already told my son if anything happens to me, look for this envelope on my desk. In it are a lot of my writings, about my life, my role models, how I treated people. That is what I want to leave for them."

A while later, John wanted to talk about his father. He said, "One of the biggest role models for me was my dad. In his later years when he had Parkinson's, he had to live in a care home. He worked with a social worker there, probably someone like me. One day the social worker sent an email to all six of us kids, saying she just had to tell us something. When she'd arrived at the care home that

John Gould, retired social worker Veterans Administration, Bath, New York

morning, she went out in the back, and their dad was sitting on the deck. She went up to him and asked how he was doing. He said, 'Well, I've got a paper, and I'm reading the sports, and I just read the comics, and the birds are singing. What more could you ask for?'"

Thinking about his father on the day he retired from the factory he ran, John said, "This one guy comes up to me and says, 'John, I remember the first day your dad came to work. We were pushing brooms together.' Another guy came up to me and said, 'I remember when you were two years old, and you had to wear your toy six guns before you'd lie down on the table to go have your tonsils taken out.' Those are the kind of memories I have of the plant that my father headed."

We finished our dinner and walked to our cars. As John was about to pull away, he rolled down his window and said, "Why do people stare up at the sky for the kingdom of heaven? That's what Jesus' message was to us. That it's not someplace up in the sky with a gold-plated room. It's our job as followers of Jesus to establish the kingdom of heaven on earth in our own lives and in our communities and in our nations and in all of the relationships we have. I have made it a common theme for my basic spirituality. Something that makes sense to me. I boil it all down into a phrase that I use. Keep it simple: Love God and neighbor, and that is all you need to know. I tried to integrate it into my mental health work because spiritual health is just as necessary as mental health."

17

John's words were in my thoughts as I drove out of Bath early the next morning. He had given me permission to forgive those whom I felt had wronged me. My family and friends. It was not my mother's fault that she suffered from postpartum depression. Nor was it my older brother's fault that he had mimicked what he saw my mother do when he bullied me. Nor was it my grandfather's fault that my grandmother had committed suicide.

Finally, I found myself needing forgiveness as well. Forgiveness for what I had done earlier in my own life. For running away from home and my life in 1980 and leaving the family business behind. For turning to drugs and alcohol as a way to lessen my pain. And though it was a long haul getting off that stuff and needing to check myself into a psychiatric ward at a nearby hospital, where I was treated for a month for depression and panic disorder, I am thankful that during my time in the hospital, I became a new person in terms of how I lived my life.

After that, I began exploring the world beyond my small beach town. I also began to attend the church where I had been baptized as an infant, and for several years I became highly involved. It led me to approach the Presbyterian Church (USA) to research and write a book about the various ministries within a denomination that stretched across the United States. After four years of nearly nonstop travel, I returned to my hometown to restart the business I'd left behind.

Yet, after so many years of involvement in my local church and its denomination and serving on the board of a storied Mississippi HBCU (Historically Black Colleges and Universities), I had had enough and needed a break.

As if by rote, I repeated those words of forgiveness over and over again. I was still repeating them as I passed by the remaining Finger Lakes and made my way to Schenectady. And I was still saying them when I met up with Alan Schroeder, a photographer from my hometown, who lived near the Albany Pine Bush Preserve.

By this time, dare I say, I had new feelings—a need for familiarity. I had just spent part of a day with John Gould, who stirred my feelings of forgiveness for others, and now I wondered whether I was getting a bit homesick. I had been away for many weeks, going on four months.

When I drove into Alan's driveway, it became immediately apparent to me that he loved the outdoors. It reminded me of places I was familiar with: Duncan Woods, Water Tank Hill, Dewey Hill, the Lake Michigan beach, its piers, lighthouses, and "clean as a whistle," singing sand beaches.

The preserve was across the road from his house, and his backyard was filled with all manner of natural habitat for several species of birds, waterfowl, insects, and small animals. Once I met Alan, I could feel the warmth he exuded. At that moment, he was deep into research about something that dated back to the ice age, saying, "I wish we'd had the Internet when I was in school." I'd forgotten Alan was a few years ahead of me in school, and when I asked him about his experiences, he said, "Growing up, honestly, I didn't have a lot of friends in school because I'd rather go out and sit in the field and watch what was going on."

What Alan said about not having a lot of friends in school and enjoying being outside reminded me of my own growing-up days when I felt the need to get outdoors to be away from people. I would take my toy trucks to a place within feet of our house but hidden from view. A place that was just over a ridge separating our lot from nearby houses. Though it was in the city, it felt rural. There were rolling hills and forested woods across the road and behind our house. On each side of the house were steep hills where I could hide and feel safe. Safe from the bully who lived upstairs.

I asked Alan whether he liked to be outdoors to get away from people or because he had an interest in specific things outdoors? Or was he, like me, hiding?

"No, quite the opposite. I wanted someone to take an interest in me and the things I wanted to do. For example, when I was fourteen, I walked into a science class where the teacher had covered the walls with photos of birds. I believe his name was Mr. Kammeraad. He saw that I looked to be interested in birds and admitted to me that he was a bird watcher."

With that door open, the teacher started telling Alan everything about birds: their habitat, what they feed on, and information about birding organizations. Alan said it was the first time a schoolteacher had shown an interest in something near and dear to him. Because he was working in the library, Alan started doing research on birds.

Then Alan found a copy of a journal that listed a man who lived in a town a few miles to the north and banded birds. "I told my friends, 'Let's go up there.' They said, 'You don't know him.' So, we went up there. The guy was a dentist from a town to our south, and we became very close friends. He taught me how to band birds and helped me get a banding license when I turned eighteen."

Not knowing very much about birds, I asked Alan how birds were captured so they could be banded.

"You can use ground traps," he said. "What they do is take a very fine filament net that stretches out—it's so fine that the birds don't see it. The birds hit it, and they just fall down, and the net forms a little pocket around them. You pull them out, weigh and measure them, and then band them. Once you do that, you let them go."

I asked whether that was when he decided to go into photography.

"Not then. I had serious issues with teachers because I didn't like their attitudes, for the most part. There was a teacher couple, one taught gym and the other was the art instructor. They were 'Look at me' kinda people. I disliked the woman teacher with a passion. As luck would have it, I ended up in her art class. I got past her ego because I enjoyed art. My grandmother was an artist, and she could pick up anything and draw it perfectly. One of my aunts was also an artist. Two cousins were artists; one became a graphic designer. So, I was surrounded by artists. As for me, I was frustrated because I couldn't draw a stick figure. That's why I went into photography."

"What was your first camera?"

"A little Brownie. It had a plastic body. That's all I can remember."

Alan said his grandfather was in construction, a house builder, and his three sons, including Alan's father, had joined him in his business. Though Alan worked summers for them, it didn't pique his interest, so he decided to go to community college. He attended for a while, but, he said, "My issue with a college education was they wanted me to pay them for two years of classes that I absolutely had no interest in before I could even take something I had a real interest in. I thought, *This is not going to work.*"

At that time, the draft was underway, and the government used a lottery system to determine whom to draft into service. Reality set in when Alan drew a very low number, in the low double digits, as he recalled. Knowing he would be drafted into the army, he decided to take control of the situation.

"I have an instinct about things, and I woke up one morning and went down and signed up for the navy. I went in on December 26 to Great Lakes for training, and my assignment was in Memphis."

Because Alan enlisted, it allowed him to request the kind of service he wanted. In his case, he wanted to get into photography school but was instead sent to electronics school. That made Alan question their decision. "They must have known that I failed math, right?"

As he told his story, it reminded me of my father's service during World War II. His mother—my grandmother—speculated that our country would soon be at war. My father, who had graduated from high school in the spring of 1940, was attending college as the war in Europe began to ramp up. To keep my father from serving in active duty, my grandmother insisted he enroll in typing classes. As a result, when my father enlisted, he was assigned to desk duty, rather than to serve in combat.

Even though Alan was not proficient in math, he was very good at figuring things out when someone showed him how to do something. And though he failed to get passing grades in the tests, when they handed him a bunch of parts and asked him to build a radio, he did it successfully. As he remembered, "They were going to send me out to the fleet to one of these lousy jobs, but then they made a mistake and sent me to Quonset Point Naval Air Station in Quonset Point, Rhode Island."

The next winter, Alan was sent to Key West to avionics school to learn about planes. After that, he was sent to the North Atlantic to help trace Russian submarines. During his five months there, he had time to read the navy photography manual, which he remembered as being very thick. He took the photography test. As a result, when he returned to shore duty, his commanding officer said, "I've got good news for you. You passed the exam, and your application to photography school was approved." Alan said, "They sent me to Pensacola, Florida, where the school was located, and I spent the winter there."

After Alan completed photography school, he was assigned to Washington, D.C., where the main photographic center for the navy was located. As he recalled, "I started in the black-and-white department and got bored. It was like seven to four every day. Got off at four and walked over to another department, where I'd learn about that department, got bored with that, went up to another department, and eventually learned everything in the building." Then Alan was asked to apply for a position in the camera repair department, which got him an invitation to the naval repair school back in Pensacola, where he was able to spend another winter. After passing the test, he was sent back to D.C. and got bored again. Then one of the chiefs asked him if he would be interested in a part-time job processing color film. When Alan asked where the job was, he was told it was at NASA's Goddard Space Flight Center in Greenbelt, Maryland, the nation's largest organization of scientists, engineers, and technologists whose job was to build spacecraft and instruments to study the earth, the sun, the solar system, and the universe. While there, Alan processed color images sent in by earth resource satellites. "It turned out that the images were right in the middle of China and were secret," he said.

Now, when people asked Alan what the military did for him, he said, "The military will do anything you want if you show an interest and actually want to do the job—even at the height of the Vietnam War."

Near the end of his military service in 1974, Alan met his future wife at his best friend's wedding. In the meantime, he moved to the Albany area and took a job in a department store's camera department. While there, he learned about a job opening as a photographer for the New York State Senate. During the interview, Alan asked whether the job was political because he was not fond of politics. Despite his concern, he took the job and worked as a photographer for more than thirteen years.

I asked Alan about any specific instances that stood out while he worked for the state senate. "Among the more memorable meetings were with Governor Clinton of Arkansas and Governor Mario Cuomo." The latter happened during an event with Governor Cuomo when a longtime employee who was about to retire said she had only one regret. She had never met any of the governors she had worked for.

Alan said, "I walked up to Governor Cuomo and mentioned that he might want to pose with the woman who was retiring. I explained that she had worked twenty-five years for the state and had never met a governor. He said, 'Well, we can take care of that. Where is she?' So, I called her over, and Cuomo spoke with her for several minutes. While he was doing that, I took a picture of them. Cuomo called me over and asked me to get some enlargements made and bring them to his office so he could sign them for her. I didn't always agree with his politics, but I respected him. He was honorable and a gentleman."

Though the job had been a good experience, after thirteen years Alan had had enough. Times were changing. Video had become more important, and though the basic skills were similar to photography, a lot more equipment was necessary, and video required editing—something Alan wasn't keen on learning. Plus, it was getting hard to put up with all the hypocrisy in politics, so he decided to leave that job and open his own studio. He ran that for about eight years before moving the studio into his house and concentrating on commercial and public relations work, which was more lucrative than shooting portraits. One day his best friend called from his job with the state police at the airport, asking whether Alan would be interested in a job shooting aerial photography. "So, I went over there. They had just gotten an expensive aerial camera and bolted it onto a twin-engine plane. They wanted aerial photographs of state prisons and the surrounding areas. In case something happened, they wanted a map of what the terrain around the prison looked like."

All of a sudden, the pilot did some unexpected maneuvers to see whether they would frighten him. Alan told the pilot he used to hang out of helicopters while in the military, so it would take a lot to scare him. He mentioned he'd had an interest in getting a pilot's license. The pilot, who was also an instructor, told Alan to take the controls and warned him to watch out for other planes. Then one day, while they were heading back to the airport, the pilot said he had paperwork to do and told Alan to take them back to Albany. During that flight, the pilot had Alan do some point-to-point flying, then make a slow circle around the airport, and line the plane up to the runway. Only then did the pilot finally take the controls back for the landing. Later, on another flight, they heard a sudden bang. Alan looked out the side and saw that one of the tires was blown. The pilot kept the plane up just enough to land it on the median. As Alan remembered, "I had no thoughts of it crashing. I wanted to find out what was wrong and figure out how to fix it."

After the aerial job ended, due to budget cuts, Alan's mother-in-law told him that the post office was giving exams for some open positions. That was in the late 1990s, and Alan stayed with the post office until he retired in 2016. He was looking forward to spending time with his wife because she had only a year until she could retire.

Looking at a photo in the dining room, I asked, "How long has your wife, Lois, been gone?"

Silence followed. Then . . . "October 2019. She was having some problems. She was still working. Then she started using a cane, so I took her to the hospital to have her checked out. She was there at least three weeks, going through a series of tests. After a wait, the doctor came in and said she's got two months. Brain something. Something that attacked the brain. It would cause something to fold, and there was no cure for it. They don't know why it does that, but it is always lethal."

For the next two months, Alan cared for her. He turned the living room into a bedroom, which made it easier for hospice to help. Alan had been trying to get Lois to retire for a while but had always gotten blowback whenever he mentioned it. "She didn't always listen to me because I was more forceful about certain things. She worked for one of the banks and had less than a year to go before she was vested in their retirement system."

When the bank fired her for some unknown reason after she had worked there for so many years, Alan urged her to hire a lawyer. She wouldn't, even though she had a good case. But then out of the blue, "that" happened, and everything changed in an instant.

Alan Schroeder, photographer, Schenectady, New York

Alan said, "I firmly believe that I've been guided and watched over my whole life. I'm not a terribly religious person. I don't feel I need to sit in a building that they have dedicated to that person. That person is with me every walk I take. I don't have a problem talking when I'm out there."

As I left Alan's, I felt a bit of anxiety. More like dread, I suppose. Alan and I had talked for a few hours about all the amazing things he'd done in his life. But I hadn't thought to ask him about the death of his wife, Lois, until it was nearly time to leave. It had been only three or so years since she'd died. They had been married for forty-five years, which was a lifetime of emotion that Alan still carried. I knew he had friends and his daughter lived nearby, yet I got the feeling there still had to be a pit in his stomach when he remembered their time together.

I kept thinking about Alan's love of the outdoors, the feeders he had planted around his yard to photograph birds and animals, and his taking on new projects with the Pine Bush Preserve. It was good that he was staying busy. I couldn't imagine what it was like for him, losing his wife just before what they had hoped would be their retirement years. I dwelled on these thoughts while weaving my way through Albany and heading west toward New Salem, Massachusetts.

When I first began my journey, Leigh Cummings had told me about when Maine was part of the Commonwealth of Massachusetts and the land that was now Houlton, Maine, had been deeded to the New Salem Academy. I wanted to report to Leigh what I'd found when I visited New Salem. I still recalled exactly what Leigh had said, that "Maine learned a hard lesson—Massachusetts was not going to protect them. Even after Maine became a state, Massachusetts retained ownership of half of the unappropriated townships. Not only did they get money from stumpage from the huge white pines of Maine, but once the trees were cut, Massachusetts sold much of the land to land speculators. As a result, even after statehood, Maine remained a good source of revenue for the Commonwealth of Massachusetts. They didn't give up all the land when Maine became a state; they wanted that money. Money always talks."

What surprised me was that New Salem Academy had become the New Salem Museum and Academy of Fine Art, and it occupied the building where students of the New Salem Academy once resided. I stopped a woman who was out walking and asked her whether she knew anything about New Salem Academy's history and its being deeded half of what became Houlton. She didn't. She had lived in New Salem her entire life and had never heard about Houlton.

18

In the Village of Contoocook, I found Dustin Road and the Dustins, Dave and Kathi. He was a retired international contract negotiator and she, a well-known artist who found new ways of expressing her art with inventive new materials.

"We live on the old Dustin farm," Dave said, "which passed into my father's family back in the early 1800s, probably about 1810. In 1810, New Hampshire became prime sheep-farming country because the consul general to Portugal was a New Hamshireman."

He explained further, "Portugal is home of the Morino sheep, and the king of Portugal prohibited their export. But, of course, the consul—a diplomat from New Hampshire—found a way to spirit a whole bunch of Morino sheep out of Portugal and send them to New Hampshire where, all of a sudden, they propagated. So, this used to be a sheep farm. It's got rocks and boulders everywhere from the glacial activity back in the ice age, so you can't grow things like you can in the Midwest or New York State. Sheep were great livestock for this farm, and my ancestors raised them here. The wool went to mills that were powered by all the rivers and streams that coursed through northern New England states."

"When did they stop farming?" I asked.

"My father's father—my grandfather, Daniel Herbert Dustin—retired from farming in 1955. By that time, his sons, his family, his children were all leaving. His oldest son, Alvin, wound up in Connecticut, where he ultimately became the principal of a high school. His next-oldest son, who had joined the army in World War II, had gone on to MIT. He became involved in surface-to-air missile systems in the U.S. Army, which were a new thing in World War II. Ultimately, he became a director of this at MIT's Lincoln Laboratory on Hanscom Air Force Base outside Boston."

"How about your father? What did he end up doing?"

"My father, Eben H. 'Dusty' Dustin, joined the army in 1942, the year he graduated from high school right here in Contoocook, and went into the tank corps. But when he attended tank school in Fort Knox, they gave him a test, and Dad aced it. They said, 'Son, we want you to decide whether you'd like to be an army engineer or an army doctor.' Dad said, 'I'm not really great at math. I think I will become a doctor.' And with that, they sent Dad to Princeton. So, Dad spent the principle years of World War II wearing an army uniform with a whole bunch of other army guys, going to pre-med classes at Princeton. And they all graduated in three years with their pre-med degrees."

Kathi asked, "Can I just mention that his family was not wealthy? They were into learning, reading, and education. He was the youngest kid, but by the time he was around, there wasn't any money left to send him to college."

David said the army had discovered his dad's potential, which was why they sent him to Princeton for his degree. And when World War II ended in 1945, he still wore a uniform while working at a large army hospital in Massachusetts. At that point, they told him he was going to start medical school at Boston University. When the Korean War broke out, he was called back to active duty. The government told him to pay back what they'd invested in him when they'd financed his medical school education.

"They told him to pick his branch of service," David said, "because 'you're going to wind up in Korea.' Dad asked, 'Any branch? Okay, I pick the air force.' So, Dad was reactivated and taken into the air force, where he became a flight surgeon in Korea."

After serving in Korea and winning a bronze star for his service, David's father decided on discharge that he would go to northern New Hampshire and open a practice in Groveton. At the time, it was a thriving company town and the home of Groveton Papers, which employed upward of eight hundred workers—huge for a town with a population under two thousand.

David said, "I remember playing as a kid with my friends. We'd be up there on the railroad trestles, seeing all the effluent coming out of the paper mill, an ugly meringue curd about four to five feet thick above the water. It just floated out of the paper mill and went down into the Connecticut River. So, I have a real appreciation for the Federal Water Pollution Control Act of 1972 because it's since cleaned those rivers up."

After practicing medicine in Groveton for roughly ten years, David's father was leafing through the *Journal of the American Medical Association* and noticed an ad from the U.S. Department of State, looking for doctors to enlist in Foreign Service. He joined up, and because he had been a country doctor in rural New Hampshire setting bones, delivering babies, removing tonsils, and performing other minor surgeries, they loved him. His first assignment was to Kabul, Afghanistan, to be the regional medical officer. At the time, the United States Agency for International Development (USAID) was giving lots of money to Afghanistan to build highways and bridges and to fund its schools and university. As Dave recalled, "It was a real country then, and we loved it there."

"Oh," I asked, "the same USAID that the current president is trying to abolish?"

David said something to the effect that this was a huge mistake that would destroy our country's reputation as a caring nation.

He went on to say that in 1968, when he was a junior in high school, his father asked where he'd like to go to college. Because David knew so many kids his age from all over the world, his options were no longer confined to New Hampshire. He wanted to attend college someplace other than New England and decided to go to Hope College in Holland, Michigan.

For her part, Kathi also had an urge to see the world. "Don't get me wrong, I loved Grand Haven. It was a great place to grow up, but I had real wanderlust. I wanted to go to faraway exotic places—not just Paris or London. Hope College had a lot of junior-year, study-abroad programs, so I got into one for the American University in Beirut, Lebanon."

At the same time, David also wanted to travel abroad more. That's how the two of them met, at a gathering of students interested in the junior-year program overseas. They both ended up going on the program to Beirut.

"You could have any major," Kathi said. "I was majoring in math at the time, but I was also interested in art. I took Islamic art and architecture, which had a heavy emphasis on decoration and architecture."

Though Kathi had told her parents that she would major in math, her mom said she should be in art. She graduated with a degree in math and worked in that field for a number of years, but she eventually realized her mother was right, that her heart was in making things.

For his part, after graduating from Hope, David went on to grad school in Arizona to get a degree in international business. Kathi took art classes and earned a master's of fine arts degree in ceramics. As she recalled, "Earning that degree made me realize who I was."

Though David was the primary breadwinner, Kathi became a success in her own right by using her entrepreneurial skills to market her art. Then she discovered "a plastic-y colored material that you work with like clay, a craft-y kind of material that is essentially like clay but not in the brown or gray color but instead in colors that can be mixed together to make your own colors."

She described working with that material. "What you're doing is sculpting color in your hands. Not painting on the surface like with clay. It's only baked at a low temperature in an electric oven, not a kiln. It is a bit like PVC, the material plumbers use. I get it as a soft, malleable material in bricks of colors. The reason I started working in that material was because Dave got a job in Saudi Arabia, and I couldn't drag a ceramics studio with me. I loved living overseas. One of my mantras is the quote 'Travel is fatal to discrimination, prejudice, bigotry,' which Mark Twain said."

Hearing Kathi say that made me proud that she was from my hometown. Though I wasn't exactly homesick, being away made me more appreciative of where I was from.

As for David, he next went to journalism school at Northwestern University in Evanston, Illinois. His first job out of college was working for a printer in Grand

Haven as a typesetter, then as a journalist with the *Muskegon Chronicle*. Soon after accepting that job, he went back to school, to Thunderbird School of Global Management, and earned an M.I.M., International Management degree. That degree opened up other doors for him. For the next few years, he worked out of Washington, D.C.; Saudi Arabia; Virginia; Turkey; and back to D.C., finally ending up at the Johnson Space Center in Houston. There, he negotiated and administered contracts for the Space Shuttle program. In all the places he worked, David saved his employers large amounts of money and funding by negotiating and managing contracts that were favorable to the countries they served.

"Looking back now," Kathi said, "we had lived outside of the Washington, D.C., area in the suburbs, in Saudi Arabia, in Turkey, and then in Houston—always in cities or suburbs. But about twenty-two years ago, Dave had a midlife crisis. He said, 'I hate my job, I hate Houston, we're moving to New Hampshire.' And I said, 'Okay,' because I was not wedded to living in one place. I wanted four seasons. So, we moved up to New Hampshire in 2000. At the time, one of our daughters was in college at Hope; our second daughter was in a huge high school in Houston that wasn't good for her. When we came here, our high school was much smaller, yet was an excellent school. In this environment, our second daughter was really able to shine. She played in the steel drum band, was involved in the high school play. She became a star in this high school, so it turned out fine."

I asked Kathi, "What did each of your daughters do after college?"

"They're both stay-at-home mothers. Our oldest daughter is real involved in a foster parents program in Ann Arbor. They adopted two kids that they fostered. So, she's very involved but not in a paid way. The younger daughter lives in Boston, so they both moved to larger cities."

I asked David what he did once he returned to New Hampshire.

He said, "I came back here and did some consulting for a while but didn't have a fixed job. So, I worked on government proposals for a branch of the state government. Then I met an engineer with his own engineering firm. He was getting into environment remediation activity with the EPA, and he needed someone who understood government projects and government contracts. I helped him land hundreds of millions of dollars of EPA contracts. I also administered the contracts and defended the company in claims. That was what I did during my career: contract management as a federal contract negotiator and contract manager on the contractor's side."

David said the firm where he worked investigated and remediated projects all over New England, including a bunch of old mines in New Hampshire and Vermont that were highly contaminated and were superfund sites.

I asked Kathi, "As an artist, is it harder to sell your art here than it was when you lived in large cities?"

"I was pretty apprehensive about moving from the large cities to the woods. I really feel more like an urban person. It took me about a year to adjust, and now I love it. But part of it is because I do some big retail fine-craft shows, so I can go to the big city, stay in a nice hotel, eat in a nice restaurant, and get my big city fix but then not have to deal with all the traffic and the dirt and the noise when I get back here. And it turns out that this town has a lot of artists and craftspeople here as well. I have a better community of artists and craftsmen here than I ever did in a big city. Even though I was a member of art centers and still have friends in big cities, I do not feel starved for culture being out here. Plus, with the Internet I don't need to be in a city."

I asked Kathi about Nepal and her involvement in a nonprofit there.

"It is part of the wanderlust thing. I found out about an organization, a women's shelter, where they supported themselves by making jewelry out of the same material I use. I am one of the pioneers in the United States in using the material as a fine craft material and not just a hobby craft for making gnomes and dolls. At the time, I was getting ready to retire, but then I started looking at their website to see what they had been up to. I saw their beads, and I thought they could use an update, so I sent an email asking if they were interested in me working with them. They enthusiastically said yes. So, I started doing Zoom classes with them a couple years ago. Initially, I just wanted to help them make more money because they didn't have much of a market in our country. They had a market in Australia because of the two founders of the center: one is a woman lawyer in Nepal, and the other is an Australian woman."

Kathi said, "So, we did some new designs. But as time went on, I realized what they really needed was to be able to help with the design and work with someone who would recognize their own skills—not merely let another person push ideas on them. But they were raised in a culture where women were expected to act like servants and have babies, and they believed that their ideas didn't have value."

I asked how they were treated by their husbands.

"When their husbands beat them up or break their legs or worse," Kathi said, "the courageous ones leave. Many, however, stay in those relationships because it's in their culture. So, this Nepali woman started this center about fifteen years ago. What they really needed was to gain self-esteem. We started by having them be involved in the design, and now they are getting more and more involved, to the point where I have taught them some different shapes that they can use as they want. I've also taught them different techniques to use in various ways but only if they want to use them. So, now they've got a sort of vocabulary to express some of their own ideas. But they also still need to be shown what Western tastes are like because that's how they make their money: selling in the West. We've even thought about what would happen if they sold in Nepal to the local population. Yet, that

David and Kathi Dustin, Contoocook, New Hampshire

wouldn't be sustainable at this time because their work is so poorly valued. If they sell their art in Nepal, they'll make only seven dollars when they can get ninety-five dollars if they sell the same item in the West. They receive a salary for their work; it's not payment per piece. We don't want them at home at 2 a.m., stringing beads together to make a few extra cents. They get paid for coming in for the days they work. Three of the women are now on the board of directors."

I asked Kathi whether she had met the women. "Yes," she said, "I went there recently to meet them in person and see what their studio was like. I became very fond of them, and they became fond of me. Even though their life experience is fundamentally different from mine, we get along very well. I learned how smart they are. They are great problem solvers. And now they feel more enabled to present their problem-solving ideas because they've seen that I'm not this big white artist from America. I'm a person like them. That's pretty cool.

"Anyhow, these women don't feel like they are smart because most haven't gone to school. But now their children are getting high school educations. So, things are improving."

19

As I left Contoocook, I realized I had only one more stop before my journey ended: return to Houlton where I planned to spend some time with Leigh Cummings at the Farm Co-op.

I drove along rural roads to Houlton, which snaked along parallel to I-95. Though the trip took seven hours instead of the four hours on I-95, it was well worth it.

What finally made me realize I needed to go home was meeting a young man from India named Rome. He worked in a convenience store near a small town along the final stretch of my 10,000-mile journey. He said his family told him to go about his life in America in order to see where he belonged. Rome was from a high-ranking military family, which qualified him, by birth, in India to be in an upper caste. Though he worked very hard during his time in the store, he had gotten the job because of his connections. He was given a week off every month to travel and was paid generously by his boss, who wanted to stay in good favor with Rome's father. Rome had been to more than a dozen national parks, had visited several large cities, and was able to see both coasts in every season. I asked whether he missed any of his loved ones. He did, he dearly missed them. But by traveling so often, he felt he was outrunning his sad feelings, which bordered on depression.

I told him I could relate and had similarly outrun my own feelings. He asked what those feelings were. I got to thinking deeply and felt an answer as it bubbled up. It was about guilt. My own. The lost relationships and never getting to know my son before he died. We had words ten years ago that cut deeply. I knew he was an alcoholic, that he suffered from his own feelings of guilt. We stopped talking. No relationship whatsoever. Nothing. No communication. But when I received that short terse email, saying something to the effect that my son had died yesterday—or did it say today?—I felt shock and disappointment and still do. Whenever I've thought about the what-ifs, my sadness has been overwhelming.

This all happened fifty miles before I reached Houlton. I felt like a marathon runner who was losing steam within sight of the finish line. I stopped by Leigh and Sandy Cummings' place when I got back to Houlton. We had a nice, yet short, visit because something in me needed to head home.

John Steinbeck said something about houses and children and graves being home. That had begun to make sense. During this journey, I had imagined picking up stakes and driving them in elsewhere. Maine, the Upper Peninsula of Michigan, the plains of North Dakota, the mountains of Montana, the Tetons of Wyoming—all had gotten my interest. But then came that feeling, that realism: I could still visit those places and many more. I didn't have to live there to call them part of my world. They already were that. It was time to go home. Now.

I couldn't tell you exactly which route I took home, but they were not rural roads. They were a series of highways—wide, fast, congested. My journey was now completed. What had I learned? It had come to me over time and hit me quickly in that small convenience store in rural Maine. I was learning to live the best life I could from all whom I had met on my journey.

I had learned that it was people who knitted the lives of others together. Each of those I had met along the way had taught me lessons—some through their work, others with their beliefs, and still others with the way they lived their everyday lives. I had been so fortunate, having the chance to meet so many remarkable people, all in their own ways. I had left home feeling that at times in life, I wondered whether my own life's journey had been at all worth it. During this journey, the word *home* took on new meanings. Now, it was time to go home and get there soon.

So fly I did, over the Canadian superhighways to the Port Huron border crossing and onward along interstates as they crossed the Lower Peninsula of Michigan and toward West Michigan. Then, finally, home.

Was there a welcoming? No. It was subdued. Coffee with friends, stories to tell, catching up to do. I was home. Make that, I am home.

Afterword

Often, when I told the people I'd met that I lived in a beach town, they looked at me sideways. They'd say something to the effect that nobody lived in a beach town, people visited beach towns. I'd say, "My town is just like yours," mentioning that we had expensive houses in the hills, cottages overlooking the lake, houses in suburbs, and even a small number of unhoused individuals. People lived in condos over downtown stores; independent retailers, in the stores below the condos. We had an old-growth forest in the middle of town and a central park just off the downtown. Chain stores, strip malls, small independent restaurants, and fast food franchises. Coffeehouses and ice cream shops. In other words, places that were like all small towns. I had once run away from home, expecting to make my way in a new place. And when I felt unsafe due to circumstances beyond my control, I jumped in my car and came back to where I'd left.

Months after returning from my journey, something kept gnawing at me. Then came an email from the man who had been responsible for my opportunity to travel across the country for two years to research and write the book about the Presbyterian Church. Now retired, he wrote, "Isn't it about time you went back to church?"

I thought about what he had written, and I remembered my own family history within the Presbyterian Church (USA) denomination. My father had been an elder, my mother credited the church for her own recovery after suffering from postpartum depression, my grandparents on my mother's side had been members of a Presbyterian Church in Wyoming after their retirement, it was the church that held the funeral for my grandmother on my father's side after she committed suicide, and it had been the church that welcomed my grandfather after he was kicked out of the ministry. And for myself, like my father before me, I had been an elder in the Presbyterian Church before I left for what now seemed to be a silly reason.

As I sat in my place in Grand Haven on Christmas Eve, something new gnawed at me. Would it hurt for me to go to church on this particular occasion? I couldn't see any reason not to. So, there I sat, in a back-row pew, listening to a prelude and remembering I had more than once said I could not stand organ music. But this time, it was different. Was it the organist's talent or that I had grown older? But there I sat. Soon the choir marched up the center aisle, one wearing a Scottish kilt—a reminder of the Presbyterian's roots in Scotland. After a few meaningful choruses and prayers, the pastor got up and gave a message of inclusion, the need for diversity and equity. There were two pastors, one male and the other female. The so-called frozen chosen were no longer icy or uppity; they were regular people. A lot like those regular people I had interviewed while away. For a small beach town of around twelve thousand, it had a tall steepled church with stained glass, comfy cushions, and sink-to-the-knees carpeting.

I shook hands with the pastor as I left, and he said, "Please consider returning. We will not make you feel unwelcome." I asked whether once a month was okay. He said yes. And from then on, I've darkened the halls of the church exactly once a month. And each time I enter and exit the church, I think about Enright Bighorn, Sr., of the Fort Peck Reservation, who said, "When they say God, think about Creator." Although I realize the person doing the preaching doesn't know with any scientific certainty about what happens next, he does talk about hope, love, and forgiveness.

I will leave it at that.

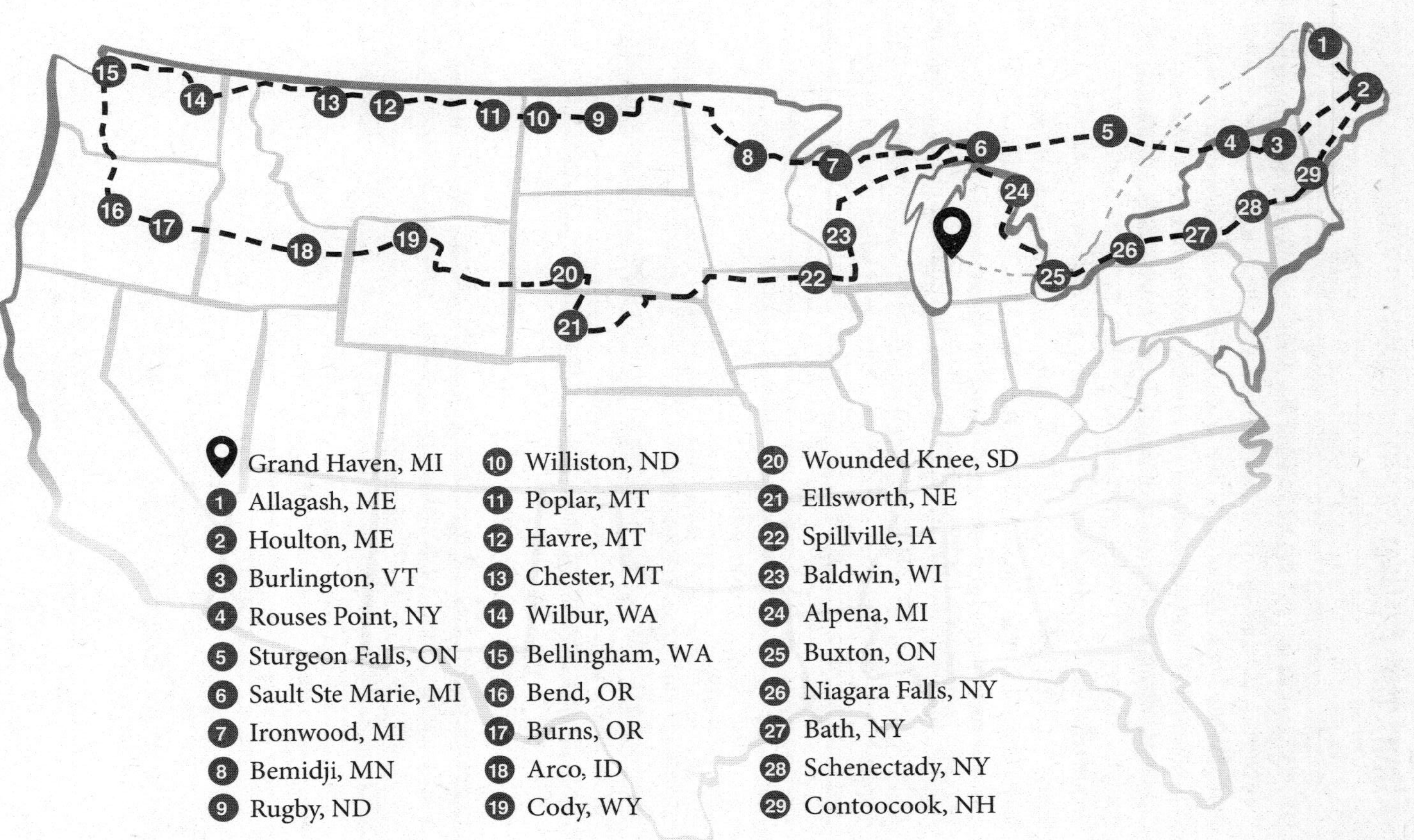

Grand Haven, MI
1 Allagash, ME
2 Houlton, ME
3 Burlington, VT
4 Rouses Point, NY
5 Sturgeon Falls, ON
6 Sault Ste Marie, MI
7 Ironwood, MI
8 Bemidji, MN
9 Rugby, ND
10 Williston, ND
11 Poplar, MT
12 Havre, MT
13 Chester, MT
14 Wilbur, WA
15 Bellingham, WA
16 Bend, OR
17 Burns, OR
18 Arco, ID
19 Cody, WY
20 Wounded Knee, SD
21 Ellsworth, NE
22 Spillville, IA
23 Baldwin, WI
24 Alpena, MI
25 Buxton, ON
26 Niagara Falls, NY
27 Bath, NY
28 Schenectady, NY
29 Contoocook, NH

About the Author

Dirk Wierenga is a self-described rural wanderer who always travels by car and has been to all of the lower 48 states and several Canadian provinces multiple times. When not on the road, he lives in Grand Haven, Michigan, where he was born, was raised, and still remains. He attended Eastern Michigan University in Ypsilanti, Michigan, where he majored in music. After a variety of jobs, he co-founded a successful design and marketing firm with large corporate accounts. In 1998, he was commissioned by the Presbyterian Church (USA) to travel the country to research and write the book *Presbyterians: A Spiritual Journey*. He later founded a small publishing house that was sold to a larger publisher. He is currently with Principia Media, where he is director of publishing and heads up the company's documentary filmmaking studio. In addition to being an author, he is also a documentary filmmaker, a professional photographer, and a podcast producer.

About the Publisher

Principia Media is a tenacious, small, scrappy, and fiercely independent publisher and documentary film studio. Founded at the kitchen table of Vern and Irene Jones, it has since grown to become the publisher of several books and multiple full-length documentaries. Yet Vern still signs many of his letters and other communications with "Love, Vern." That tells you a lot about the man behind the company. He is a special kind of person, a man who loves deeply, yet is himself very independent.

Principia Media publishes a broad range of books, though only a select few each year. To be published by Principia, its authors must also be special in a good way. The people who do all of the work in getting Principia's books in print and its documentaries produced are indeed talented and special. To be with Principia means to be both independent and deeply committed to each project. Notable long and involved projects include several books on solving the D.B. Cooper case and the four-part documentary series *D.B. Cooper: The Real Story*. Another long-term project is on rural Americans, which so far includes the full-length documentary *Route 2 Elsewhere* and the book *Route to Elsewhere: A Personal Journey*.

To learn more, go to **principiamedia.com**.